Acclaim for **Jonathan Harr's**

A CIVIL ACTION

"Gripping . . . a page-turner filled with greed, duplicity, heartache and bare-knuckle legal brinksmanship." —*Newsweek*

"Do not think about skipping this important work. . . . A fascinating work of literary reportage as deeply involving as *In Cold Blood.*" —*Boston Globe*

"ONE OF THE BEST BOOKS OF THE YEAR. . . . A suspenseful narrative full of intellectual surprises and bold-faced characters." —*Time*

"Both readable and riveting . . . it works brilliantly. . . . Harr captures detail, color and anecdote, sketching them in clear and unself-conscious prose. . . . Even minor characters come alive on every page." —*Los Angeles Times Book Review*

"Page-turning, stay-up-way-past-the-hour-reason-tells-you-to-turn-off-the-lights stuff. I cannot say enough wonderful things about it. . . . *A Civil Action* is easily one of the best books of the year." —Linnea Lannon, *Detroit Free Press*

"Important. . . . Mr. Harr grants the litigation masterly treatment. . . . *A Civil Action* is a consequential work, one deserving of attention." —*The New York Times Book Review*

"A compelling human drama told in exquisite detail. . . . As engrossing as it is unsettling." —*USA Today*

"The book is absolutely marvelous." —*Washington Monthly*

"Plan to spend a long weekend with *A Civil Action*. . . . Once you begin reading, you won't put it down." —*Houston Chronicle*

"A triumph . . . brutally accurate." —*Seattle Times & Post-Intelligencer*

"BEST BOOK OF THE YEAR. . . . A taut, gripping narrative—the best legal thriller we've ever read . . . a genuine feat of reporting and story-telling." —*Entertainment Weekly*

"Artfully written, suspenseful . . . immensely absorbing . . . rife with human drama. . . . *A Civil Action* is such an important story and so compellingly told that while you're submerged in it nothing else seems to matter." —*New York Newsday*

"So compelling a true story that a reader may well ask: Why bother to read fiction when the facts are this absorbing?" —*Philadelphia Inquirer*

"Be forewarned: Once you start *A Civil Action* you probably will not be able to put it down until you finish, and it will stay with you for a long time even then. As it should." —*Washington Post Book World*

"Beneath its sleepy title, *A Civil Action* has the racing heart of a thriller." —*Elle*

"*A Civil Action* is a rare find: a work of nonfiction that draws you in and compels you to keep turning pages. It is a masterful work of reporting and writing." —*Washington Legal Times*

"A compelling narrative." —*The New Yorker*

"A nonfiction David and Goliath face-off that reads like a thriller." —*People*

"A paranoid legal thriller as readable as Grisham, but important and illuminating. . . . As rich as any novel on the scene." —*Kirkus Reviews*

Jonathan Harr

A CIVIL ACTION

Jonathan Harr lives and works in Northampton, Massachusetts, where he has taught nonfiction writing at Smith College. He is a former staff writer at *New England Monthly* and has written for *The New Yorker* and *The New York Times Magazine*. *A Civil Action* was awarded the 1995 National Book Critics Circle Award.

A
CIVIL
ACTION

JONATHAN HARR

VINTAGE BOOKS

A Division of Random House, Inc.

New York

TO THE READER

This is a work of nonfiction. All the characters and events depicted in this book are real. Much of the material comes from my own observations over a period of eight years, beginning in the winter of 1986, and from repeated interviews with those persons directly involved. The voluminous official record, particularly some fifty thousand pages of deposition and trial transcripts, provided another vital source. The reader can find further information in A Note on Sources and Acknowledgments at the end of the narrative.

Jonathan Harr

For Diane Apollon Harr

FIRST VINTAGE BOOKS EDITION, SEPTEMBER 1996

Copyright © 1995, 1996 by Jonathan Harr
Maps copyright © 1995 by Anita Karl and Jim Kemp

All rights reserved under International and Pan-American Copyright Conventions. Published in the United States by Vintage Books, a division of Random House, Inc., New York, and simultaneously in Canada by Random House of Canada Limited, Toronto. Originally published in hardcover in slightly different form by Random House, Inc., New York, in 1995.

The Library of Congress has cataloged the Random House edition as follows:
Harr, Jonathan.
A civil action / by Jonathan Harr. —1st ed.
p. cm.
ISBN 0-394-56349-2
1. Anderson, Anne, 1936?– —Trials, litigation, etc.
2. W.R. Grace & Co.—Trials, litigation, etc. 3. Trials (Toxic torts)—Massachusetts—Boston. 4. Groundwater—Pollution—Law and legislation—Massachusetts—Woburn.
5. Drinking water—Contamination—Massachusetts—Woburn. 6. Liability for water pollution damages—Massachusetts—Woburn. 7. Schlichtmann, Jan. I. Title
KF228.A7H37 1995
346.7303'8—dc20
[347.30638] 95-2088
Vintage ISBN: 0-679-77267-7

Random House Web address: http://www.randomhouse.com/

Printed in the United States of America
9B8

Contents

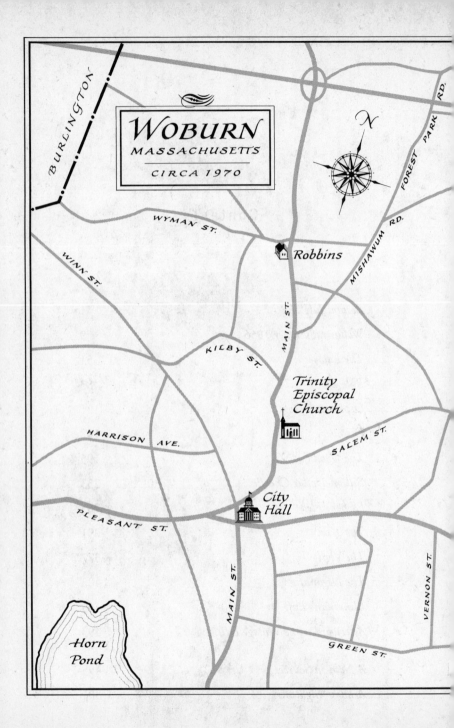

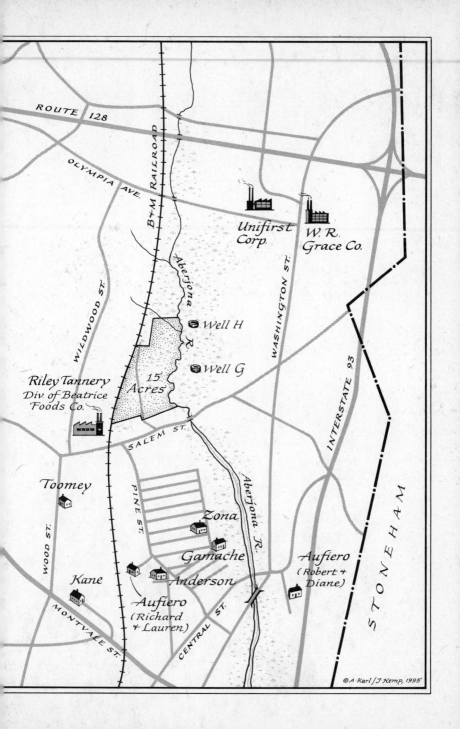

ROUTE 128

OLYMPIA AVE.

B&M RAILROAD

WILDWOOD ST.

Aberjona R.

Unifirst Corp.

W. R. Grace Co.

WASHINGTON ST.

Well H

Well G

Riley Tannery
Div. of Beatrice
Foods Co.

15 Acres

SALEM ST.

INTERSTATE 93

Toomey

PINE ST.

WOOD ST.

Zona

Aberjona R.

Gamache

Anderson

Aufiero
(Robert + Diane)

Kane

Aufiero
(Richard + Lauren)

MONTVALE ST.

CENTRAL ST.

STONEHAM

© A. Karl / J. Kemp, 1995

Boston: July 1986

The lawyer Jan Schlichtmann was awakened by the telephone at eight-thirty on a Saturday morning in mid-July. He had slept only a few hours, and fitfully at that. When the phone rang, he was dreaming about a young woman who worked in the accounting department of a Boston insurance firm. The woman had somber brown eyes, a clear complexion, and dark shoulder-length hair. Every working day for the past five months the woman had sat across from Schlichtmann in the courtroom, no more than ten feet away. In five months Schlichtmann had not uttered a single word directly to her, nor she to him. He had heard her voice once, the first time he'd seen her, but he could no longer remember what it sounded like. When their eyes had happened to meet, each had been careful to convey nothing of import, to make the gaze neutral, and to shift it away as quickly as possible without causing insult.

The woman was a juror. Schlichtmann hoped that she liked and trusted him. He wanted desperately to know what she was thinking. In his dream, he stood with her in a dense forest, overgrown with branches and roots and vines. Behind the woman were several people whose faces Schlichtmann recognized, the other jurors. The woman was trying to decide which path in the forest to take and Schlichtmann was attempting to point the direction. He beseeched her. She remained undecided. A dream of obvious significance, and unresolved when the phone rang and Schlichtmann awoke, enveloped by a sense of dread.

The man on the phone identified himself as an officer at Baybank South Shore, where Schlichtmann had an automobile loan that was several months in arrears. Unless Schlichtmann was prepared to pay the amount due—it came to $9,203—the bank intended to repossess the car, a black Porsche 928.

Schlichtmann had no idea whether or not Baybank South Shore had been paid in the last several months, but on reflection he felt pretty certain it had not. He told the banker to speak with a man named James Gordon. "He handles my financial affairs," said Schlichtmann, who gave the banker Gordon's telephone number and then hung up the phone.

Schlichtmann was still in bed twenty minutes later when the phone rang again. This time the voice on the other end identified himself as a Suffolk County sheriff. The sheriff said he was at a pay phone on Charles Street, two blocks from Schlichtmann's building. He had come to repossess the Porsche. "I want you to show me where the car is," said the sheriff.

Schlichtmann asked the sheriff to wait for ten minutes. Then he tried to call Gordon. There was no answer. He lay in bed and stared at the ceiling. Again the phone rang. "Are you going to show me where the car is?" asked the sheriff.

"I think I will," said Schlichtmann.

The sheriff, a large, heavyset man in a blue blazer, was waiting for Schlichtmann at the front door. It was a clear and brilliantly sunny morning in the summer of 1986. From the doorstep, Schlichtmann could see the sun glinting off the Charles River, where the white sails of small boats caught a brisk morning breeze. The sheriff handed him some documents dealing with the repossession. Schlichtmann glanced at the papers and told the sheriff he would get the car, which was parked in a garage three blocks away. Leaving the sheriff at his doorstep, he walked up Pinckney Street and then along the brick sidewalks of Charles Street, the main thoroughfare of Beacon Hill. He walked past several cafés, the aroma of coffee and freshly baked pastries coming from their doorways, past young mothers wheeling their children in strollers, past joggers heading for the Esplanade along the Charles River. He felt as if his future, perhaps even his life, hung in the balance while all around him the world followed a serene course.

In the garage bay the Porsche had acquired a fine patina of city grime. Schlichtmann had owned the car for almost two years, yet he'd driven it less than five thousand miles. Throughout the winter it had sat unused in the garage. When Schlichtmann's girlfriend had tried to start the car one weekend this spring, she'd discovered the battery was dead. She had the battery charged and took the Porsche out for a drive, but then James Gordon told her the insurance had lapsed and she shouldn't drive it anymore.

Schlichtmann drove the car back to Pinckney Street and handed the keys to the sheriff, who took out a screwdriver and began to remove the license plate. Schlichtmann stood on the sidewalk and watched, his arms folded. The sheriff shook open a green plastic garbage bag and collected audio cassettes and papers from the dashboard. In the cramped backseat of the Porsche, he found some law books and several transcripts of depositions in the civil action of *Anne Anderson, et al.*, v. *W. R. Grace & Co., et al.* The sheriff dumped these into the garbage bag, too. He worked methodically and did not say much—he'd long since learned that most people did not react warmly to his presence. But the transcripts made him curious. "You're a lawyer?" the sheriff asked.

Schlichtmann nodded.

"You involved in that case?"

Schlichtmann said he was. The jury had been out for a week, he added. He felt certain they would reach a verdict on Monday.

The sheriff said he'd seen the woman, Anne Anderson, on the television program *60 Minutes*. He handed Schlichtmann the garbage bag and asked him to sign a receipt. Then he squeezed his bulk into the driver's seat and turned on the ignition. "Nice car," he said. He looked up at Schlichtmann and shook his head. "It must be a tough case."

Schlichtmann laughed at this. The sheriff laughed, too, and said, "Well, good luck."

Schlichtmann stood on the curb and watched as the sheriff turned the Porsche onto Brimmer Street and disappeared. He thought to himself: Easy come, easy go.

. . .

Two days later, on Monday morning, Schlichtmann dressed in one of his favorite suits (hand-tailored by Dmitri of New York), his best pair of Bally shoes, and a burgundy Hermès tie that he considered lucky. Usually he took a taxi to the federal courthouse in downtown Boston, but since he had no money on this morning, he had to walk. On his way across the Boston Common a man in a grimy coat, his belongings gathered into a green plastic trash bag, approached Schlichtmann and asked for money. Schlichtmann told the man he had none.

Schlichtmann walked on, struck suddenly by the precariousness of one's position in life. In a technical sense he was close to being homeless himself. His condominium association had just filed a lawsuit against him for failing to make a single maintenance payment in the last six months. He was also in arrears on his first, second, and third mortgages. By the time the jury had started deliberating, after seventy-eight days of trial, all the money was gone. "You're living on vapor," James Gordon had told Schlichtmann and his partners. The few dollars that came into the firm of Schlichtmann, Conway & Crowley each week were the result of old business, fees on cases long since settled. It amounted to no more than fifteen hundred a week. Salaries for the secretaries and paralegals alone were four thousand. American Express had filed suit against the firm. There had been no payment for more than four months on twenty-five thousand dollars of credit-card debt. Heller Financial, a leasing company, had threatened to repossess the law firm's computer terminals by August 1. If he lost this case, Schlichtmann would be sunk so deeply into debt that it would take five years, Gordon estimated, for him to climb back to even.

But money was the least of Schlichtmann's worries. Oddly, for a man of lavish tastes, he didn't care that much about money. He was much more frightened of having staked too much of himself on this one case. He was afraid that if he lost it—if he'd been *that* wrong—he would lose something of far greater value than money. That in some mysterious way, all the confidence he had in himself, his ambition and his talent, would drain away. He had a vision of himself sitting on a park bench, his hand-tailored suits stuffed into his own green plastic trash bags.

In the courtroom corridor at a quarter to eight, perspiring slightly from his walk, Schlichtmann began waiting. He knew this corridor intimately. Usually he stood near a heavy wooden bench, somewhat like a church pew, which was located directly across from the closed door of Judge Walter J. Skinner's office. At the end of the corridor, next to a pay phone, a pair of heavy swinging doors opened into Judge Skinner's courtroom. Schlichtmann had spent hundreds of hours in there and he had no desire to go back in now. He preferred the corridor. The opposite end was a city block away, past a bank of elevators, past a dozen closed doors that led to jury rooms, conference rooms, and offices. There were no windows in the corridor. It looked the same at eight o'clock in the morning when Schlichtmann arrived as it did when he left at four in the afternoon. The lighting fixtures were old fluorescent models, recessed into the ceiling, and they cast a feeble light, like dusk on an overcast day. The corridor smelled of floor polish and disinfectant and stale cigarette smoke.

At around eight o'clock, the jurors began arriving for their day of work. They conducted their deliberations in a small room at the end of the corridor, up a narrow flight of stairs, a room that Schlichtmann had never seen. Some mornings two or three of the jurors arrived together, talking among themselves as they got off the elevator. They always fell silent as they neared Schlichtmann. They might smile, a tight, thin, constrained smile, or nod briskly to him. Schlichtmann looked studiously down at the floor as they walked past him, but from the corners of his eyes he watched every step they took. He studied their demeanor and their dress and tried to guess their moods.

The jurors' footsteps receded. In a moment, Schlichtmann was alone again.

Woburn: Summer 1966

1

When the Reverend Mr. Bruce Young arrived at Woburn Trinity Episcopal Church in the summer of 1966, he was twenty-eight years old
and ambitious. Trinity was his first church. It was a plain but sturdy-
looking building, with a steeply peaked roof, a white clapboard exte-
rior, and three small stained-glass windows along each side. The new
minister could see that the church had fallen on hard times. Weeds had
invaded the lawn, which was brown and scabrous in spots, with
patches of bare earth showing through. The bushes needed trimming,
the shingles on the roof had curled, and the Gothic-style front doors
needed paint. Even in the best of times, the church, which was built in
1902, had never been prosperous.

By the time Bruce Young arrived, only about fifty parishioners, most
of them nearly old enough to remember when the church was new, still
attended the Sunday service. Young often remarked that Trinity was
the only Episcopal church on the planet without a lawyer or a doctor
in its congregation. Young and his wife, who had a degree in social

work, agreed that Woburn was a good place to begin a career but not a place they intended to stay for long.

Woburn, a city of thirty-six thousand situated twelve miles north of Boston, needed paint, too. A few blocks south of Trinity Episcopal, past a Sunoco station, an Army-Navy recruiting center, and several pizzerias, lay the town square. It was a small island, surrounded by city traffic, dominated by a towering bronze statue of a Civil War veteran. On pleasant days a few workers from City Hall would eat lunch on the square's park benches. Each spring the city's public works department cultivated tulips, marigolds and petunias in the square, but the department could not afford a full-time gardener. The weeds competed for space, and each year by midsummer the weeds had gained a clear advantage.

The town square was surrounded by two- and three-story buildings, the heart of Woburn's once bustling commercial district. The buildings dated to the turn of the century, but many of the original brick and stone façades had been covered by plastic tiles, orange and lime green, a style fashionable in the 1950s, Woburn's last period of prosperity. Many of the storefronts were dusty, their windows streaked with dirt, the doorways filled with small piles of windblown debris. Marram's Shoes & Tuxedos and the pet supply shop had recently gone out of business. In the grimy window of Perillo's Sub Shop, a sign read CLOSED, under which someone (perhaps Perillo himself) had added FOR GOOD. Several pizzerias survived, along with the Woburn Bowladrome, the Tanner's Bank, and Mahoney's Barber Shop, established in 1899.

Woburn's first commercial enterprise had been a tannery, built by the Wyman brothers in 1648. Back then the land was densely wooded, hilly in the west and north, flatter in the east where the Aberjona River flowed through marsh and bog. The Wyman brothers prospered until King Phillip's War, when John Wyman's eldest son was killed by Indians in a swamp fight. That season the Wyman leathers spoiled in the tanning fats. Another tanner named Gershom Flagg cleared an acre of forest near the Town Meeting House and built his dwelling and tannery. By the Civil War, Woburn had twenty tanneries, matching Philadelphia in the production of leather. The city acquired the nickname Tan City. The most prosperous bank in town was the Tanner's Bank, and now the high school football team called itself the Tanners.

The leather trade supported other industries. In 1853 Robert Eaton founded a chemical factory in northern Woburn, along the banks of the Aberjona River, and supplied the tanneries with the chemicals—blue vitriol, Glauber's salt, sulfuric acid—necessary to produce leather. At the turn of the century, Eaton's factory was one of the largest chemical plants in the country. But the tanning industry began to wane after World War II. By the late 1960s it had been eclipsed by competition from abroad. A decade later, only the J. J. Riley Tannery in east Woburn, near the Aberjona River, still produced leather. That tannery's immense red-brick smokestack, two hundred feet tall with the name J. J. Riley inscribed vertically on it, could be seen from the town square, almost a mile distant.

To attract new businesses the city cleared and developed many acres of land in northeastern Woburn for industrial parks. Scandal arose when several city officials were discovered to have an undisclosed financial interest in the land, but development proceeded nonetheless. Up on Commerce Way, near Interstate 93, several small manufacturing and trucking firms moved in. Robert Eaton's old chemical factory on the banks of the Aberjona River was taken over by Monsanto. W. R. Grace, another chemical giant, built a small plant on land that had once been an orchard. Woburn didn't lack for industry, but somehow there was never enough money to fix all the cracked sidewalks or the potholes in the street.

Bruce Young had planned to stay in Woburn for only about five years. There was plenty of ministering to do in Woburn, but a poor parish like Trinity Episcopal could sap a young man's energy and ambition. After a few years Young had made some inquiries about moving on. But the sort of parish he was seeking didn't open up every day, and when it did, he faced stiff competition.

His Woburn parishioners liked him, but even the fondest had to admit that he was not a stirring public speaker. He read rather than declaimed his Sunday sermons, and his voice tended to trail on in a monotone. To his credit, he recognized this shortcoming and kept his sermons brief. He was always available for counseling, and his advice was usually sound. He had a manner that made him seem truly interested in the problems people brought to him. He had a particular talent for ministering to the sick and infirm, and beginning in January 1972, his sixth year at Trinity Episcopal, the sick became the heart and soul of his ministry.

2

Jimmy Anderson's parents thought he had a cold. It was January, a season for viruses, and his older brother and sister both had the classic symptoms, too—coughs, runny noses, slight temperatures. Even his mother, Anne, had not been feeling particularly well. By mid-week, however, everyone except Jimmy, who was three years old, seemed to be on the mend. He had a fever that waxed and waned, and his appetite had decreased considerably. He was pale, and Anne noticed several bruises on his limbs and torso, which struck her as odd because the child had been in bed most of the time. She and her husband, Charles, decided to take him to the family pediatrician the next morning.

The pediatrician, Dr. Donald McLean, was alarmed by Jimmy's appearance. The fever suggested an infection, and indeed the child had some upper respiratory congestion. But this did not look like an ordinary infection to McLean. At the very least, the child was seriously anemic, with a profound pallor and lethargy. McLean thought the bruises might indicate a deficiency of platelets, the blood component that acts as a clotting mechanism. He performed a quick physical examination and found slightly enlarged lymph nodes but nothing else remarkable. Pallor, bruises, and a persistent fever: the clinical signs pointed to a blood disorder.

McLean suspected that Jimmy Anderson had leukemia, but he did not mention this suspicion to the Andersons. Leukemia is a rare disease, occurring in fewer than four out of one hundred thousand children each year. McLean wanted to see the results of a blood test before he made a diagnosis. It was late Saturday morning, but McLean arranged for the lab to analyze the boy's blood sample that afternoon. He told the Andersons he should know more by then, and asked them to call him.

On the way home from the doctor's office, Anne said to Charles: "I think he has leukemia." The tone of her voice as much as what she'd said caused Charles to turn and look at his wife. She looked very frightened, and that in turn frightened Charles.

When Charles called Dr. McLean that afternoon, the doctor's voice was grave. "There appears to be a problem with your son's blood. We're going to have to do some more tests to find out exactly what's wrong." He told Charles he would set up an appointment for Jimmy on Monday morning at Massachusetts General Hospital. He made no mention of leukemia, and Charles did not press him for a diagnosis. "If he knew what Jimmy had, he would have told us," Charles said to Anne.

The Andersons had guests for dinner that Saturday night. In the kitchen, Anne wept. Nothing Charles said could dissuade her from the conviction that Jimmy had leukemia. The disease held a particular terror for Anne. In 1950, when she was fourteen years old and growing up in Somerville, a girl who lived in her neighborhood had gotten leukemia and died within a matter of weeks. Anne had never been close to the girl, but they'd known each other in passing. Word of the girl's death had spread in hushed, whispered conversations around Anne's junior high school. For the first time in her life, Anne understood mortality and death. The disease seemed especially frightening to her because it was such a mystery. It struck suddenly, it was invariably fatal, and no one knew what caused it.

On Monday morning, January 31, Anne and Charles drove to Boston with their son. Jimmy Anderson was examined by Dr. John Truman, the chief of pediatric hematology at Massachusetts General, Boston's biggest hospital. "Thin, sad-faced 3½ year old with history of pallor and easy bruisability," noted Truman. "Presents with moderate generalized lymphadenopathy and occasional bruises, but no petechiae. Spleen not palpable."

Truman performed a bone marrow aspiration ("difficult pull with scant return") which revealed 32 percent blast cells. Blasts are primitive white blood cells that multiply rapidly but are incapable of developing to maturity. Their numbers left no doubt in Truman's mind about the diagnosis: acute lymphocytic leukemia.

That afternoon, Truman brought Anne and Charles into his office and told them what he had found. Anne remembered that the winter day was cold and clear, and that the afternoon sun angled through the blinds. She felt oddly distant, as if she were hearing Truman from afar, her attention drawn to the motes of dust that floated in the sunlight.

The next few weeks were very important, said Truman. He would attempt to induce a remission in James by using a combination of powerful drugs and radiation. The chances of a successful remission were good. There was, however, a 10 percent chance that James might die during the next four weeks. The greatest danger was not from the leukemia itself but from an opportunistic infection. Chemotherapy would kill cancerous cells in the blood and bone marrow, but it would also suppress the body's ability to fight infection. A common childhood illness—the chicken pox, for example, or even a cold—could prove fatal.

When Truman began working with leukemic children in the early 1960s, there was no effective treatment for leukemia. Most children died within weeks of diagnosis. But in the last two years, great advances had been made by the St. Jude Children's Research Hospital in Memphis. Truman explained to the Andersons the nature of the new treatment program, which was known as the St. Jude protocol. After the initial dosage of chemotherapy and radiation, which would take about a month to complete, James would have to return to the hospital's outpatient clinic on a regular basis over the next three years. He would follow a maintenance program that included periodic doses of chemotherapy. The regimen, although aggressive and with many side effects, appeared promising. If James went into remission with the first round of chemotherapy, said Truman, his chances of surviving for the next five years were 50 percent or better.

Truman also talked about what caused childhood leukemia. Most parents, he had found, worried that they had done something wrong, or that they could perhaps have prevented the disease. Truman tried to allay the parents' fears. The cause of acute lymphocytic leukemia was not known, he would tell them. Because that answer seemed so barren, he usually continued with a small disquisition on what was known. Some types of leukemia can be caused by ionizing radiation, or by chemicals like benzene. But that type—acute myelocytic—was not what James had. Some scientists also suspected that viruses might cause leukemia in humans. Viruses were believed to cause leukemia in cats, cows, birds, and rodents, and scientists at Harvard were currently trying to isolate a leukemia virus in cats. But that disease, Truman explained, was a very different illness from the one that afflicted humans.

Jimmy Anderson began the St. Jude protocol on Tuesday, the day after his diagnosis. He received several blood transfusions in an attempt to increase his platelet count. Truman examined the boy each day, looking for signs of infection or new bruises and petechiae, the cluster of small, purplish skin hemorrhages characteristic of leukemia. Anne came to the hospital early every morning. At first she returned home to sleep at night, but soon she began spending the nights with her son in his hospital room. Anne's mother came to Woburn to look after the two older children.

By the end of the first week, James's platelet count was still low but holding steady; he had no new bruises or petechiae. He was losing hair and experiencing severe nausea because of the drugs, but Truman felt he was clinically stable. By the end of the month there was no evidence of leukemic cells in either his peripheral blood or bone marrow. He had entered remission precisely on schedule. Everything had gone according to plan, and Truman felt optimistic about the boy's recovery.

Anne Anderson was thirty-five years old the winter her son became ill. She was a handsome woman, tall and big-boned, from Norwegian ancestry, with high cheekbones, striking blue eyes, and blond hair. She had grown up in Somerville, across the Charles River from Boston, the youngest of four children, the only girl in a family of modest means. After high school, she went to work at the Somerville Public Library. When she was twenty-four years old, still living at home, she met Charles Anderson on a blind date. He was a year older than she, the son of a longshoreman. He had ideas about getting ahead in life. He'd gone to college and he wanted to work in computers. Charles and Anne courted for a year, and then, in 1961, they married.

They lived in a small apartment in the Boston area until, in 1965, they began looking for a house. They had often visited Woburn, where Anne's best friend from childhood, Carol Gray, had moved with her family several years earlier. Carol and her husband had told a real estate agent that they wanted a house in the country, something close to Boston but with plenty of trees and some open spaces, and the agent had taken them to eastern Woburn.

In the mid-1960s, east Woburn had a pleasing rural aspect. The Aberjona River, a narrow, placid stream, only a few feet wide and waist-deep, ran through a marshland of reeds, cattails, and grassy tussocks. Much of the land on either side of the river valley had been farmed, and several small farms, an orchard or two, and open fields still remained. Along the river itself, at the edge of the marshes, grew copses of maple, oak, and hickory.

To Anne and Charles, east Woburn seemed like a fine place to settle down. Anne particularly liked the Pine Street neighborhood, not far from where Carol lived. It was a small enclave of about a dozen streets, a mile and a half from the center of town. It occupied the ridge of a low bluff that sloped gently to the east, to the marshlands of the Aberjona. The streets were quiet and shaded by trees, the homes modest, many of them constructed before World War II. No one with money to burn would look for a house in the Pine Street neighborhood, yet once people settled there they seemed to stay for a long while. Charles found the house, a ranch-style built in the early 1950s. It had three small bedrooms and a large picture window in the living room. The shingle siding needed paint, the kitchen floor needed new linoleum, but the price was only $17,900.

Once the Andersons settled in, they began attending Trinity Episcopal Church. Reverend Young was delighted to have new members join his flock, youthful ones at that. Charles and the minister were about the same age and they quickly became friends. In a short while, Charles began serving on the church's board, and then, at Young's request, as treasurer of the church.

Jimmy Anderson returned home from the hospital in mid-February. Some of the Andersons' Pine Street neighbors came to visit, bearing casseroles and baked goods. One woman, Kay Bolster, who lived a block away on Gregg Street, mentioned to Anne that two families on either side of her each had a young boy with leukemia. Kay thought Anne might find some solace in talking to other parents who were going through the same experience. One of the mothers, Joan Zona, was a regular customer at the beauty parlor where Kay worked. Joan was a warm, outgoing woman, said Kay, although she had the impression that Joan was having a difficult time coping with her son's illness. The boy, whose name was Michael, was not doing well in treatment. The other family, the Nagles, Kay knew only in passing, although from what she had heard it appeared the Nagle boy was doing well.

Shortly after Kay's visit, Anne phoned Joan Zona. Joan seemed eager for company and invited Anne over for coffee. They spent two hours together that first day. When Anne left, she and Joan hugged each other. The visits and phone conversations with Joan soon became part of Anne's daily life. "Joan and I sort of hung on to each other," recalled Anne some years later.

Michael Zona, the youngest of Joan's four children, was being treated at the Children's Hospital in Boston on a protocol similar to Jimmy's. He had been diagnosed ten months before Jimmy, and Joan knew all about the hospital routines, the drugs and radiation, the side effects, knowledge that she readily shared with Anne.

One thing after another befell young Michael Zona, like toppling dominoes, and it seemed that nothing could intervene to save him. His problems had started with a mild cough that had gotten progressively worse. The family doctor had treated him with cough syrup and antibiotics, but he had failed to improve. One night when Michael complained that he couldn't breathe, Joan took him to the emergency room. At first, the doctors thought he was suffering from bronchial asthma. Then they discovered a tumor the size of an olive in the mediastinum, a lymphosarcoma, between his right and left lungs. He underwent radiation treatments. A bone marrow biopsy later revealed that he had acute lymphocytic leukemia, the same disease Jimmy Anderson had.

Anne thought it strange that three cases of leukemia should occur in the same neighborhood, within a few blocks of each other. She wondered if it was coincidence, or if a virus of some sort was circulating. Dr. Truman, she remembered, had mentioned that some cancer researchers suspected a virus might cause childhood leukemia. Although she knew that was an unproven hypothesis, she and Carol Gray spent hours speculating about it.

Anne mentioned her suspicions to Joan Zona, too. Joan agreed that three cases of leukemia in the same small neighborhood did seem unusual, but she did not dwell on the subject the way Anne did. She was too preoccupied with Michael's downward spiral to care about much else. In June 1972, while Jimmy was in remission and his prospects looked good, Michael Zona relapsed. His doctors attempted to induce a second remission with an experimental drug called Adriamycin, a highly toxic drug that causes deterioration of the heart muscles at levels near the therapeutic dose for leukemia. The therapy worked, and by July Michael was again in remission. It was short-lived, however. In late October, with his blood counts still alarmingly low, Michael's doctor performed a bone marrow aspiration and found that 25 percent of the cells were blasts. Michael had relapsed for a second time. The cycle began again: another protocol was attempted, and yet another remission was induced. But the chances for Michael's long-term survival were not good.

During a visit to the clinic at Massachusetts General that spring, Anne told Dr. Truman about the Zonas and the Nagles. Wasn't it unusual, she asked, that there were three cases in the same neighborhood?

Truman listened in his polite, attentive manner, tall frame slightly stooped, but he would admit later that he did not give Anne's question any serious consideration. He'd learned over the years that parents of children with leukemia tended to develop a heightened awareness of the illness. Everywhere they turned it seemed they encountered a reference to it, or someone else whose child had it. To Truman, this was not an uncommon psychological phenomenon. Many years later, in a deposition, Truman recalled his reaction to Anne's queries: "My response was that on the basis of the number of children with leukemia that I was aware of at the time, and considering the population of the city of Woburn, I did not think the incidence of leukemia appeared to be increased. In essence, I dismissed her suggestion."

Nor did it occur to Truman a year later, in June 1973, that there was anything unusual about the illness of a two-and-a-half-year-old boy from east Woburn named Kevin Kane, Jr. The boy had been referred to Truman from Winchester Hospital, where his mother, a nurse, had taken him because of a persistent fever, pallor, and irritability. Two weeks earlier he had been treated unsuccessfully for a respiratory infection that did not respond to penicillin. His history on presentation at Winchester Hospital included several respiratory infections as well as recurrent episodes of earaches. Winchester referred Kevin Kane to Dr. Truman at Massachusetts General with a "high suspicion" of acute lymphocytic leukemia. Truman confirmed the suspicion. He began treating Kevin Kane on a chemotherapy regimen similar to the St. Jude protocol. The child responded well. At four weeks, a bone marrow aspiration revealed that he was in remission.

Kevin Kane, Sr., and his wife, Patricia, lived with their four children on Henry Avenue in east Woburn. Henry Avenue curved around the perimeter of a low bluff overlooking the Aberjona marsh. From the back door of the Kanes' house, looking east across the expanse of marsh, you could see the houses of the Pine Street neighborhood a quarter of a mile away. If you looked closely, you could see Orange Street and, through the trees, the red-shingled ranch house of the Andersons.

Anne found out about the Kanes' child from Carol Gray, whose fourteen-year-old son delivered the *Woburn Daily Times* every afternoon along Henry Avenue. In the summer of 1973, as Carol's son made his rounds, he learned that one of the Kanes' children had leukemia. He reported the news to his mother, who went immediately to the phone and called Anne. "What the hell is going on here?" Carol said to Anne.

With the discovery of yet another leukemia case, Anne began writing down some of her thoughts. She made the first of many lists of the cases she knew about, writing in a spiral notebook the names of the children, their addresses, their ages and the dates when she figured they had been diagnosed.

The notion that each case shared some common cause began to obsess her. "The water and the air were the two things we all shared," she said in a deposition some years later. "And the water was bad. I thought there was a virus that might have been transmitted through the water, some kind of a leukemia virus. The water had never tasted right, it never looked right, and it never smelled right. There were times when it was worse than others, usually during the summer, and then it was almost impossible to drink. My mother would bring some water from Somerville to the house on weekends, probably about three quarts, which we used as drinking water. The rest of the time, when we could mask the flavor of it with Zarex or orange juice or coffee or whatever, then we used water from the tap. But you couldn't even mask it. It ruined the dishwasher. The door corroded to such a degree that it had to be replaced. The prongs that hold the dishes just gave way and broke off. On a regular basis, the pipes under the kitchen sink would leak, and under the bathroom sink. The faucets had to be replaced. The bathroom faucet dripped constantly. It seemed like no sooner would I get everything fixed and we'd have another problem."

3

Long before Jimmy's diagnosis, Anne's neighbors in east Woburn would talk among themselves about the water the way most other people would talk about the weather. Like the weather, it seemed there was nothing one could do about the water, although people kept trying.

When Carol Gray moved to Woburn in 1961, there had been nothing unusual about the water. But by the time Anne and Charles moved into their house on Orange Street, in 1965, people in east Woburn had started to notice a change. "Does the water taste funny to you?" Anne had asked Carol during her first summer in Woburn. "Or is it just me?"

In retrospect, it became clear that the moment of change began in November 1964, when a new city well started pumping water into the Woburn system. The well, known as Well G (Wells A through F had been drilled in central Woburn over the previous forty years), had been sunk in the marshland on the east bank of the Aberjona River, half a mile north of the Pine Street neighborhood. The well penetrated an ancient valley that had been formed twelve thousand years ago by the last glacier to cover New England. Over the millennia, the valley had filled with gravel, sand, and silt, and the roaring ancestral river had become the tame Aberjona. Under the river, the sediment-filled valley acted as a sponge, creating a subterranean reservoir.

Even with Well G on line, Woburn needed more water. City officials did not want to pay to get it from the state Metropolitan District Commission. The Aberjona aquifer had proved so plentiful and inexpensive that the city had another well dug, Well H, three hundred feet from Well G. In 1967, three years after Well G went on line, Well H also began pumping. Although both wells were connected to the city water mains, they served only the homes in the east and, to a much lesser extent, those in the north and central sections.

Whitman & Howard, the engineering firm hired to find a suitable site and then to dig the two wells, congratulated the mayor on having so bountiful an aquifer close at hand. "We feel the city is fortunate in finding an additional groundwater supply of good quality in east Woburn," wrote the engineer in charge, L. E. Pittendreigh, to the mayor. "The development of this supply will aid in overcoming the city's Water Problem."

As it turned out, Pittendreigh could not have been more wrong. The city's real water problem began with the drilling of Wells G and H.

In the summer of 1967 the Massachusetts Department of Health contemplated shutting down both wells because of "the poor bacterial quality of the water supplied therefrom." The city protested. The state health authorities relented, permitting the wells to remain open on the condition that the city subject the water to continuous chlorination.

Chlorination began in April 1968. That spring and summer, residents from east Woburn called the city's public works and health departments to complain about the taste, the odor, and the murky, rust-colored appearance of the water. "The odor is almost like clear bleach," wrote one angry resident. "Why can't we have water like the rest of Woburn?" A woman from east Woburn wrote the "Tell It to Joe Action Line," a daily column in the *Boston Herald Traveler,* and other residents complained to the *Daily Times* that "the water is very unpotable, very hard, and has a strong chemical taste."

The Woburn City Council appointed a special committee to investigate the problem. The city engineer told the committee that the chlorine, which was the source of complaints about taste and odor, was added to the water to kill bacteria. The rusty color came from the water's naturally high iron and manganese content, which the chlorine caused to precipitate out. The engineer assured the committee that the water was perfectly safe to drink.

Despite this assurance, a group of east Woburn residents formed their own committee in the spring of 1969 to force the mayor to close Wells G and H. They presented the mayor with a petition in August, and by October, after the peak demands of summer had eased, the mayor shut the wells. The following spring, the city engineer ordered the wells to start pumping again. The complaints about the odor and taste began "to pour again like so much water through a broken dam," in the words of Gerald Mahoney, an east Woburn councilman. That summer was hot and dry. The engineer at the Woburn pumping station declared the water "absolutely safe." The wells were closed again in January, when the risk of drought had passed. Four months later, in May 1971, the wells were reopened. Councilman Mahoney told the *Woburn Daily Times* that he had been "bombarded by calls of complaint" about the "putrid, ill-smelling, and foul water." This was, said Mahoney, "the fourth successive year that the residents would be compelled to use it for drinking and other household purposes." Nine days after the wells opened, Mahoney succeeded in getting them closed. But a month later, in July, the city engineer ordered them put back on line once again.

The cycle seemed unending. Anne Anderson called the city board of health and the public works department to complain. Carol Gray and Kay Bolster and other friends also complained. "Did you call today?" they would ask each other. "What did they say?"

"It was the same story all the time," recalled Anne. "There wasn't any problem with the water; the water had been tested and it was fine. I think toward the end, I felt like the answer was never going to be any different. Neighbors would talk, people would call, and everybody would give their own report of what they had heard."

During the summer of 1972, six months after Jimmy Anderson's diagnosis, the reservoir in central Woburn fell ominously low and the superintendent of public works told the citizens of Woburn that they had to conserve water. If they failed to observe a voluntary ban on certain activities—washing cars and watering lawns—the superintendent announced he would reopen Wells G and H, which had remained closed throughout the winter. The superintendent's threat worked. The wells were not used that summer. Anne was preoccupied with caring for Jimmy. Since the water flowing from her taps seemed relatively pure, she gave no thought to it. The following spring, in 1973, the superintendent once again warned Woburn residents to conserve, but a severe drought compelled him to open Well G in August.

Charles Anderson was doing well in his job as a computer analyst at GTE. His work required that he travel a great deal, but in some respects that was a relief. Everything in the Anderson household seemed oriented toward illness and caring for Jimmy. The boy was thin and undersized for his age and he clung to his mother. To Anne, he appeared pitifully vulnerable, and she felt compelled to protect him. Nearly two years after his diagnosis, he began school. Anne bought him a wig to hide his wispy hair and bald patches caused by maintenance doses of chemotherapy, but she still feared that the other children would ridicule him. He missed days at school because of visits to the clinic or because he didn't feel well. He missed more days because he disliked school and begged his mother to let him stay home. Usually she acceded. Charles argued against such special treatment. He wanted the boy to lead as normal a life as possible. As it was, Jimmy had no friends; Anne was his constant companion. She and Jimmy had developed a special, intimate way of relating to each other. He would kiss and hug his mother and constantly require her touch, even as he grew older. Every night he slept with Anne and Charles in their bed. That practice had begun with his diagnosis, but it did not end as he grew older.

Reverend Bruce Young often drove Anne and Jimmy in to Massachusetts General. He didn't mind the drive. He considered the task a part of his ministerial duties, and he enjoyed his chats with John Truman and the nurses at the hospital. He watched with curiosity the relationship between Anne and her son. "They seemed to draw from each other to the exclusion of others around them," Young recalled some years later. "Anne cut everybody else off. She did it in the name of Jimmy and the fact that he was so sick and dependent on her. It became absolutely necessary for her to find some reason for why the kid was so sick. She had to find an enemy, a reason, something to focus her rage on for afflicting her son."

Charles listened to his wife's speculation about the connection between leukemia and the water. At first he was dubious. And as Anne became more adamant, he became increasingly skeptical. The problem with the water was no secret, he'd say. Everyone knew about it—the public health department, the city council, the mayor. It wasn't as if people weren't alerted to the fact that the water didn't taste good and was discolored. When Anne talked about the water causing leukemia, he told her it was wild speculation. "If it's something as obvious as the water, don't you think somebody else would know about it?" Charles asked.

Long before Charles lost his patience, long before he stopped listening, Anne could see from the expression on his face how angry the subject made him. She couldn't help bringing it up anyhow.

"What else could it be?" she asked once as they set out in the car to Lowell, to visit friends.

"What makes you think you know something the public health people don't know?" he said. "If there's a reason, I'm sure Dr. Truman would know. He's treated dozens of cases."

They argued all the way to Lowell. When they arrived, they were terse and white-lipped and said barely a word to each other all evening.

Charles believed that Anne's phantom notion about the water causing leukemia had become a destructive obsession. It was, he told Bruce Young, contributing to the deterioration of their marriage. He asked the minister if he could use his influence with Anne. "Can you make her see reason?" he asked.

The minister had often heard Anne talk about her water theory during their trips into Boston. Usually he just let her talk. But now he felt obliged to try to intervene. When Anne brought up the water again, he told her about the experience he'd had after buying his car, a Volvo, that they were riding in. He had suddenly noticed Volvos everywhere he looked. But that had been an illusion, he said, a trick of the mind. There really weren't a lot of new Volvos around; he'd simply become more aware of them. He suggested to Anne that she was experiencing the same sort of phenomenon with leukemia.

"I tried not to talk about it all the time," Anne said in a deposition some years later. "I knew how I was being received by my husband. I stood for emotionalism; I was the hysterical mother. With Dr. Truman, I'd try to pick my moments. He was always very patient. I'd tell him: 'If I stand on my front porch, I can see all these houses where children with leukemia live.' His theory was that because more children were surviving, that's the reason I was seeing more leukemia."

Truman didn't discourage Anne's questions, but neither did he encourage her. He listened impassively. "From the outset, she, as indeed most mothers, asked what is known as to the cause of leukemia," Truman observed. "It's very tempting to look at the immediate environment, I suppose."

When Anne pressed Truman for a response, he'd tell her there was no scientific evidence linking childhood leukemia to external factors. "We had, I'm sure, over a dozen conversations about it. She commented on the taste of the water and the aroma of the air in Woburn on several occasions and asked if they could be related to the leukemia."

Anne realized that her search for an explanation had become an obsession. "I really wanted to believe that the water wasn't a problem. But it just nagged at me and it wouldn't go away. It *was* a fact—there really *was* this number of children with leukemia."

. . .

For three years, until February 1975, James Anderson received a program of maintenance chemotherapy as prescribed by the St. Jude protocol. On February 21, a bone marrow aspiration confirmed that he was free of blasts and the maintenance was discontinued. Everything had progressed according to schedule. The Andersons were optimistic. The boy was still small, underweight and pale, as fragile as a porcelain figurine. But he appeared headed for a cure, one of the 50 percent that make it.

On September 15, seven months after the maintenance chemotherapy had ended, during a routine visit to the outpatient hematology unit at Massachusetts General, Truman noticed a troubling decrease in platelets in Jimmy's blood. He ordered a bone marrow aspiration, but the results of that test were inconclusive. The boy continued to bruise easily and Truman suspected an early relapse. He ordered a second, and then a third bone marrow aspiration. By November, Jimmy began developing petechiae and suffering nosebleeds. A fourth bone marrow revealed 44 percent blasts. He had definitely relapsed. Truman was greatly discouraged. He believed he could induce another remission in Jimmy's leukemia. But even if he succeeded, he knew the remission would probably be only temporary. The prospect for an ultimate cure was remote indeed.

Jimmy Anderson commenced a different protocol. Anne felt certain her son was dying. She had difficulty containing her anger. Her tone in dealing with the nurses and doctors became sharp. On occasion, Truman was the target of her anger.

That November, Anne remained with Jimmy in the hospital each day and throughout most nights. Often she slept with her son in his hospital bed. On an unseasonably warm day, she stood alone at the end of the hospital corridor, by an open window, looking out over the rooftops of Boston. Another woman—she was older than Anne, her hair gray, her face lined with sadness—came into the corridor from a nearby room. She walked up to Anne and said, without preamble: "A child just died of leukemia." Anne felt exhausted. Her own child was dying and she had no energy for sympathy or even perfunctory condolence. She wished the woman would tell her story to someone whose child was in for a hernia operation, or a broken arm, something simple and curable. But the woman (a grandmother? wondered Anne later) was distraught, with such an urgent need to talk that she failed to notice Anne's coldness. She rambled on: the child had been a boy, just a baby still; he'd gotten sick so suddenly; the family lived in Woburn; their name was Lilley.

4

Back in the summer of 1966, when Bruce Young first arrived at Trinity Episcopal, Donna Carner was sixteen years old. She was the prettiest of the four Carner sisters, with a smile that dimpled her cheeks, and thick, dark hair. With boys, she adopted a languid and skeptical manner that implied she wouldn't be surprised by anything. That manner served, she thought, to hide her shyness.

She immediately developed a crush on the new minister. All the girls in the small congregation seemed to have a crush on him. Despite his white clerical collar, his black shirt and his worn, shiny black suit coat, Donna found nothing stiff or pretentious about him. She thought he had a worldly manner. He smoked cigarettes, and in private conversation he might swear occasionally, as if to demonstrate that although he was a man of the cloth, he was not sanctimonious.

The Carner family of north Woburn did not dwell much on the more philosophical questions of faith. But they did attend the Sunday service at Trinity Episcopal without fail. Donna Carner quelled her adolescent love for Reverend Young after the minister's wife gave birth to their first son. Donna found her first real romance one Saturday when she was a senior in high school. On a trip to Boston, she and her sister got involved in a bantering exchange with a good-looking boy who was in the Navy and stationed in Boston. His name was Carl Robbins and he was from Alabama. He fell in love with Donna the moment he saw her (or so he would tell her later). He came out to Woburn to meet her parents, and soon he became a regular weekend guest. By the time Donna was nineteen and two years out of high school, she and Carl had decided to marry. She worked as a book-keeper at the General Aluminum Corporation in Woburn and had saved some money. Carl completed his military service and found a job as a welder. Reverend Young performed the wedding ceremony at

Trinity Episcopal, and he attended the festive reception at the Carner home afterward.

Donna and Carl found a three-room apartment on the ground floor of an aging, slightly shabby tenement on Main Street, a mile northeast of downtown Woburn. Donna kept her job as a bookkeeper. The couple could afford to go out on occasion and they bought a few pieces of new furniture for the house they hoped they would own someday. Two years after the wedding, in March 1972, Bruce Young baptized Donna's first child. She named the boy Carl Robbins III, although from the first day everybody called him Robbie.

He was a big, fine-looking baby, chubby and good-natured. But from the beginning, he had a difficult time in life. Before he was a year old, Donna had taken him on seven different occasions to the doctor for earaches. The infections resulted in a perforated eardrum. The pain kept the child awake and crying on many nights. Along with the ear problems, Robbie suffered repeatedly from skin rashes—eczema and dermatitis of unknown origin. Donna applied creams, ointments, and salves prescribed by the doctor, but the skin problems kept recurring. The child's constant illness strained the marriage. Carl would help to care for Robbie, but he had to rise early for work and the boy's crying kept him up at night. Donna had quit her job when she had Robbie, and the many small costs associated with the child's illnesses grew into a dismaying debt. Their tempers grew short and the three-room apartment began to feel cramped.

In the midst of this, Donna got pregnant again. She talked to her gynecologist about her marital problems, and he recommended that she and Carl see a family counselor. Carl seemed to approach counseling with a good attitude. Donna came away from the first session feeling as if they could handle their problems after all. Their second son, Kevin, was born in 1975, the sixth year of their marriage. Carl still made an effort to help care for the boys, but the apartment felt smaller than ever now, and their debts mounted. "Things kept going downhill," recalled Donna at a deposition many years later. "It was always kind of shaky, but what really finished it off was the summer when Robbie got very sick. It happened in July 1976, when he was four years old. He complained of a pain in his groin, and then suddenly he just stopped walking. It happened overnight. He also had a fever of a hundred and one. I took him to the pediatrician, and he sent him to the hospital for X rays."

Robbie was tested for juvenile rheumatoid arthritis, but that test proved negative. An orthopedic surgeon at Choate Memorial Hospital in Woburn thought that Robbie's left hip joint might be septic and proposed aspirating some fluid to see if that was the case. That procedure yielded no signs of infection. Nonetheless, the surgeon recommended draining the boy's hip. Donna gave her consent, and Robbie was operated on that summer.

He recovered slowly. When he began to walk again, he had a peculiar lurching gait and dragged the toes of his left foot. He had to lift his knee high in order to bring forward the dangling foot. And he still complained of pain, now in the other hip. The pain became so severe that he could not turn over in bed. Doctors performed more tests. Robbie began complaining of pain in his knees, shoulders and neck. He could no longer walk, and in a short time he could barely move. In September he was referred to the New England Medical Center in Boston with a tentative diagnosis of juvenile rheumatoid arthritis. His lameness and the condition of his left leg and hip were a subject of inquiry and consternation, although the doctors agreed that this was clearly not his underlying problem. Many doctors examined him, but none could figure out what ailed him.

"I was scared to death," said Donna of that time. "I didn't know what was going on with Robbie. One weekend when I needed my husband at home the most with the two kids, he took off on his motorcycle. It was more important for him to go away for the weekend than to help me. I decided it wasn't worth dealing with both things—with my marriage and with Robbie being so sick—so I filed for a separation."

That was on October 12, 1976. The next day, during another visit to the New England Medical Center, three months after Robbie's first complaints of bone pain, doctors noted that his spleen was enlarged and that he had a decreased white-blood-cell count with a high percentage of immature cells—blasts—in the peripheral blood. A bone marrow aspiration was performed. The bone marrow confirmed what the doctors had begun to suspect: Robbie had acute lymphocytic leukemia.

Donna spent most of the following two weeks with Robbie at the hospital. She missed church services, but her mother told Reverend Young about Robbie's diagnosis. The minister drove to the New England

Medical Center to visit Donna and Robbie. He asked Donna if the doctors had mentioned anything about the cause of Robbie's leukemia. Donna said, no, they hadn't. All they'd said was that no one knew what caused leukemia. It was, so to speak, an act of God.

Reverend Young asked Donna if she thought the water could have played a role in Robbie's illness. The question surprised Donna, although she knew the water was bad. From the beginning her husband had complained about the taste of Woburn water. He used to put tap water in the refrigerator because he thought that chilling it muted the smell and the chemical taste. Donna had tried to disguise the taste by mixing it with frozen juice concentrates or iced tea. She and Carl never had much money, so she used to economize by purchasing big boxes of powdered milk and mixing that with tap water. Robbie, of course, drank that. When the water smelled really awful, she would boil it before she mixed in the powdered milk. Still, it had never entered her mind that the water could have something to do with Robbie's illness.

She gave Reverend Young a quizzical look and said, "Do you know something?"

The minister shrugged his shoulders and said, "Nothing, really. It was just a thought."

Donna had often seen Anne and Charles Anderson at church with their three children. She knew, of course, that Jimmy Anderson had leukemia. But in the three years since Jimmy's diagnosis she'd never spoken directly with Anne because she never knew quite what to say. She felt awkward expressing her sympathy. She feared it would come out wrong, as if she were merely being nosy. And then, as time passed, Donna felt that the opportunity to say something to Anne had passed, too.

It was Anne who approached Donna at Trinity Episcopal one Sunday morning, a month after Robbie's diagnosis. Anne offered her sympathy and told Donna that she understood what she was going through. Her son, Jimmy, she said, had almost died not long ago. If Donna ever needed someone to talk with, said Anne, she was available.

Standing there on the church steps, Donna began to cry. "I just want to know how you stand it," she said to Anne.

From that day on, Anne and Donna talked often on the telephone about the details of treatment, about the drugs, the radiation, the side effects, blood counts, and doctors. When Robbie lost his hair from chemotherapy, Donna took him to Boston to a wig shop recommended by the hospital. The chemotherapy made Robbie nauseated, and while they were in the store, he began to vomit. The clerk grew furious. The entire affair, meant to comfort Robbie, went badly and ended in humiliation. Donna called Anne. Often it wasn't even necessary for her to explain how she felt. Anne knew already.

In February, with Robbie's leukemia in remission, doctors at New England Medical Center addressed the problem of his left leg. A nerve conduction study revealed that his sciatic nerve had been injured during the operation at Choate Memorial. The flexor muscles in his leg and foot were paralyzed, resulting in a condition known as "foot drop." The muscles had already atrophied to the point that his left leg was an inch shorter than his right. The injury to the nerve, the doctors told Donna, was probably permanent. But to prevent further foreshortening of the tendons and muscles, Donna had to strap Robbie into a cast every night. During the day he wore a brace and required special shoes made of thick leather to withstand the unnatural wear. Donna had been forced to go on welfare. The shoes were expensive and Medicaid did not pay for them because they were not, strictly speaking, a medical expense. Donna lived frugally, saving what little she could to buy Robbie special treats—the television hookup when he was in the hospital, and restaurant meals when they went in to Boston each week for outpatient visits.

During one visit to the medical center, an orthopedist shook his head ruefully as he considered Robbie's leg. "This should never have happened," he told Donna.

"What do you mean?" she asked.

The orthopedist said he doubted there had ever been anything wrong with Robbie's hip. In all probability, there had been no reason to operate. And even if Robbie's hip had been septic, his sciatic nerve should not have been injured in a simple drainage procedure. "If I were you," advised the doctor, "I might consider going after the guy."

The more Donna thought about the botched operation, the angrier she became. Finally she called the only lawyer she knew, a Woburn attorney who'd done the legal work for her divorce. She felt he'd done a good job on the divorce, and he had not charged her much. He had a small office on Main Street, not far from Trinity Episcopal. The lawyer told her that he didn't do medical malpractice cases, but he knew a lawyer at the firm of Reed & Mulligan in Boston who specialized in them.

A week later, Donna drove into Boston with Robbie to meet Joseph Mulligan. Donna addressed him as Mr. Mulligan. He insisted that she call him Joe. He was an enormous man, over six and a half feet tall and about three hundred pounds. In his office, he kneeled down on the carpet to talk directly to Robbie, and within a moment he had the boy laughing. Donna liked Joe immediately. At the end of their first meeting he told Donna that he thought Robbie might have a promising case, but he would need to get the opinion of one or two other doctors. When Donna asked, with some hesitation, about paying Mulligan, the lawyer said, "Don't worry about that. It won't cost you anything." He explained that he would pay all the expenses and take a percentage of whatever recovery Donna got in the end. Usually, he said, his fee was one third, but given Donna's circumstances, he would make it one quarter.

Several weeks later Joe Mulligan arranged to have Robbie evaluated by two doctors, an orthopedist and a neurologist. Donna would call him periodically. She'd leave a message, and Mulligan would usually call back within a day or two. He would assure her that he had not forgotten about her. "These things take time," he'd tell her.

Two years passed. During that time, Robbie's leukemia remained in remission. Donna began keeping the books at Trinity Episcopal, a job that paid nothing but got her out of her apartment. Robbie and Kevin usually came with her to the church. Robbie was in the first grade by now, and he liked school. Despite his pronounced limp, he was gregarious and made friends easily. He joined the Cub Scouts. At the outpatient clinic, he was a favorite among the nurses and doctors. In his chart they often referred to him as "charming" and "happy," and noted his ebullience. Although he was plagued by headaches and nausea from the drugs, when a doctor asked how his stomach was feeling, he said, "It feels beautiful!"

Robbie's first relapse occurred in 1979, three years after his diagnosis. His doctors tried to induce another remission with a slightly different protocol, but that failed. He was still in relapse and declining quickly when they tried a third protocol, which was successful. The entire ordeal took two months.

He remained in remission for the next year. He was nine years old when his third and final relapse was discovered during a routine visit to the hematology clinic. His death was inevitable, although Donna would not admit that to herself.

Reverend Young spent many hours with her and Robbie at the hospital. "Bruce taught me about God," said Donna. "I couldn't believe in a God cruel enough to let Robbie suffer the way he did. But Bruce made me feel that there's a place we're all going where we'll be safe. I used to tell Robbie, when we went to a department store, that if we ever got separated he should meet me in the back left-hand corner. Toward the end, he used to say to me: 'We'll meet in the back left-hand corner of Heaven.' "

Robbie knew he was dying. On his twenty-sixth and last admission to the New England Medical Center he was treated with another course of chemotherapy in an effort to stem the production of blasts and relieve his pain. He suffered from intractable bone pain, a symptom not uncommon among leukemic children. The drugs no longer had any effect in controlling the leukemic cells, which multiplied in his bone marrow at a furious rate. He was in the final, fulminate stage of the disease. Morphine relieved his agony somewhat, but even the narcotic finally had no effect. He told Donna he wished he would die so the pain would stop.

For three weeks Donna lived at the hospital, sleeping on a cot in Robbie's room. Reverend Young visited often; her mother and sisters came. Robbie had waking dreams and hallucinations. Donna would stroke his arm and head and speak softly to him. She stayed by his side for thirty-six straight hours until she could no longer keep her eyes open. She was asleep in a hospital lounge when he died, at eight o'clock in the morning. She had wanted to be with him when he died. She'd thought he would live one more day.

A year after Robbie's death, on a hot afternoon in late June, Donna was standing in a line at the service desk at DeMoulas Supermarket, holding a half gallon of milk gone sour that she'd just bought that morning. In front of her was a blond-haired man in his early thirties. He looked tired. He was pale and had dark smudges under his eyes, and he stood in a weary slouch. He, too, held a carton of milk. He noticed Donna with her milk.

"Sour milk?" he asked with an exasperated laugh.

Donna nodded and smiled back. The man had a friendly face, and he seemed to have a need to talk.

"This is the last thing I need right now," said the man, gesturing with the carton. "I just spent a week at the hospital with my son."

"Gee, I'm sorry to hear that," said Donna. "What's wrong with him?"

"He has leukemia," said the man.

They stood inside the supermarket for half an hour and talked. The man's name was Richard Aufiero, and he was a long-haul truck driver for Mayflower Moving, although he'd done little driving that summer because of his two-year-old son, Jarrod. He and his wife, Lauren, rented an apartment on Carmen Terrace, a cul-de-sac in the Pine Street neighborhood of east Woburn. Donna told Richard about her son Robbie, and also about Anne, who lived no more than a three-minute walk from Carmen Terrace. As they parted, Donna said to Richard, "Give me a call if you need somebody to talk to."

Three months later, in September, Donna heard that Richard Aufiero's boy had just died. On a Sunday afternoon that September, Lauren Aufiero had called Children's Hospital in Boston, where her son was being treated for leukemia, and told the nurse who answered that she was worried about the boy. He seemed lethargic and unresponsive. "Does he have a temperature?" the nurse asked. Lauren said no, and the nurse told here not to worry unduly. "Bring him into the clinic on Monday morning," the nurse said.

On Monday morning Jarrod's breathing was shallow and Lauren could not wake him. Alarmed, the Aufieros got into their car and drove south on Route 93 toward Boston. Near the Somerville exit, Lauren, who was holding Jarrod, said, "Oh my God, I think he's stopped breathing." Richard pulled the car to the side of the highway and began giving his son mouth-to-mouth resuscitation. He tried for several minutes without success to revive him, and then he got back on the highway and raced for the Somerville exit, where he knew there was a fire station. The firemen tried to revive Jarrod, and they kept trying as they took him by ambulance to Massachusetts General, the nearest hospital. But by the time they arrived Jarrod was dead.

5

The Woburn police were summoned in the spring of 1979 to investigate the appearance of 184 barrels of industrial waste on a plot of vacant land in northeast Woburn. The person responsible for dumping the barrels in Woburn, the so-called midnight dumper, was never caught, and the barrels were taken away before their contents could cause any harm. The whole event would have been inconsequential had it not been for the vigilance of the state environmental inspector who handled the case. He thought it prudent to test samples of water from Wells G and H, which lay just a half mile to the south.

The results of those tests reached the desk of Gerald McCall, acting director for the northeast region of the state environmental department, on Tuesday afternoon, May 22. McCall took one look at the analysis and quickly telephoned the Woburn city engineer. He told the engineer to shut down Wells G and H immediately. Both of the wells were "heavily contaminated" with trichloroethylene, commonly known as TCE, an industrial solvent used to dissolve grease and oil. The lab found 267 parts per billion of TCE in Well G and 183 in Well H. The wells also contained lesser amounts of four other contaminants, among them tetrachloroethylene, known as perc, another industrial solvent. The Environmental Protection Agency listed both solvents as "probable" carcinogens.

McCall had gone to Woburn to see the 184 barrels for himself. He had agreed then with the state inspector that it was highly unlikely any of the contents had gotten to the city wells. Now he was certain of it. The substance in the barrels had been identified as a batch of polyurethane resin that had gone bad, and none its constituents matched the solvents found in the wells. But where, McCall wondered, had the TCE and perc come from? He had no idea, but he wanted to find out. In a letter to the mayor of Woburn, McCall wrote: "The Department will continue to aid you in an investigation of the cause of the contamination of the subject wells."

The *Woburn Daily Times* reported the closing of Wells G and H two days after the event. As it happened, Anne did not see the story. She'd gone with her family on vacation to New Hampshire. Bruce Young also missed the story. In an attempt to economize, he no longer subscribed to the Woburn newspaper.

But even if they had read it, the significance probably would have been lost on them. The article, written by the newspaper's City Hall reporter, stated only that "a contaminant" of an unspecified nature had resulted in closing "the long controversial G and H wells." The story focused on the mayor's concern about a "severe" water shortage and his announcement of yet another ban on lawn watering and car washing.

A short paragraph at the end of the article assured residents that the city's water was safe. The *Daily Times* quoted the Woburn city engineer as saying that "the water coming into their homes is potable and there is no fear in drinking it. The problem wells have been out of service since Tuesday afternoon, and will remain out until the problem is solved."

The city engineer, whose name was Thomas Mernin, lived on Wood Street in east Woburn, a quarter of a mile from Wells G and H. Over the years he had heard plenty of complaints about the water from neighbors and even his own wife, who was upset at the way clothes came out of the wash stained with rust-colored spots. "The water had a taste of chlorine," Mernin would say at his deposition. "But I never had any problem personally with the chlorine."

Next door to Mernin on Wood Street lived Richard and Mary Toomey, whose three children often played with Mernin's children. Richard Toomey was a sheet-metal worker, a large, good-natured man devoted to family life. He'd been brought up a Catholic in the Charlestown area of Boston, but he didn't come to understand the true value of religion until his first son, Michael, had been struck by a car and killed while picking flowers for his mother at the edge of Wood Street. His second son, Patrick, became an altar boy.

More than once, Richard had talked to his neighbor, the city engineer, about the quality of the water. Richard believed that the water was responsible for rotting out the pipes in his house, which seemed in constant need of repair. Mernin would bristle a little at the complaints. "We do all the tests that are necessary," the city engineer would tell Richard. "It's perfectly potable."

All three of the Toomey children suffered terribly from skin rashes. Mary had taken them to dermatologists many times over the years. She'd been told there were two general categories of eczema. One type was caused by external irritations—poison oak, parasites, and some chemicals—and the other type by either an inability to tolerate certain foods or nervous reactions, with no apparent external cause. The dermatologists first prescribed lotions for the Toomey children. When that didn't help, they performed allergy tests and recommended diets free of milk and eggs. The eczema abated at times but never really cleared up. Mary Toomey wondered if the water that rotted out the water pipes in their house was the cause of her children's skin afflictions.

In June of 1979, a month after the closing of wells G and H, Patrick Toomey fell ill. His illness began with an earache and fatigue and continued throughout the summer. In August a blood test revealed that Patrick had a high white-blood-cell count. His pediatrician suspected leukemia and referred Patrick to Dr. John Truman at Massachusetts General Hospital.

Truman performed a bone marrow biopsy and confirmed the suspicion. Patrick, who was ten years old at the time, had chronic myelocytic leukemia, a particularly lethal form of leukemia. His prognosis was not good. He would almost certainly die. Truman asked Richard and Mary Toomey if they knew of anyone else in their neighborhood with leukemia, and both parents said they did not.

6

Anne Anderson got a call from her friend Carol Gray on the afternoon of September 10, 1979. "Read the newspaper" was all that Carol would say. Anne went out to the front porch and picked up her copy of the *Woburn Daily Times*. On the front page was a five-column banner headline: LAGOON OF ARSENIC DISCOVERED IN N. WOBURN. It was a pleasant, sunny day in late summer but Anne was oblivious to the world around her. She read the newspaper as if in a trance. "Everything seemed to stop still for me," she recalled some years later.

The article, by a young reporter named Charles C. Ryan, told of the discovery in north Woburn that past July of a half-buried lagoon, nearly an acre in size and five feet deep, that was contaminated with arsenic, lead, chromium, and traces of other heavy metals. The lagoon had been uncovered by a construction crew working at the site of the old Merrimack Chemical Company, producer of arsenic-based insecticides and tanning chemicals. The crew had also unearthed several pits containing the rotting remains of animal hides, hair, and slaughterhouse wastes, the legacy of Woburn's tanneries. "Arsenic in small doses," the article stated, "is suspected as a cancer-causing agent," and chromium was a known carcinogen that caused tumors of the lungs and nasal passages when inhaled. It was unclear, stated the article, whether these toxic metals had contaminated Wells G and H, situated a mile to the south. But the article did note that the two wells, which had pumped as much as a million gallons of water a day during the fifteen years since their construction, had already been closed "because they were contaminated by trichloroethylene, an industrial solvent that has been found to be carcinogenic."

When Reverend Young heard about the *Daily Times* article, he went out at once to buy a copy of the paper. "Suddenly," he recalled, "everything Anne had been hammering away at seemed plausible, just from one day to the next." That evening, he decided it was time for him to act. The logical first step, he reasoned, was to find out exactly how many leukemia cases had occurred in the city during the last fifteen years. He had once tried to find this information, but neither the state nor the city kept a record of the incidence of leukemia. Anne had told him of eight cases that she knew of. That did not seem like an excessive amount in a city the size of Woburn. Were there more cases? the minister wondered. How many cases was too many?

The next day he called Anne and told her he had come up with a plan. He would write a letter for publication in the *Daily Times* asking parents who'd had a child diagnosed with leukemia in the last fifteen years to come to a meeting at Trinity Episcopal. Maybe they wouldn't discover anything they didn't already know, the minister told Anne. Maybe no one would show up at the meeting. But it was worth a try, he said, and Anne agreed.

On an evening three weeks later, Reverend Young propped open the door to the church meeting hall and arranged several rows of metal folding chairs on the scuffed linoleum floor. Donna Robbins arrived early to help him. The minister went to the door to greet people as they came in. He recognized several parents from the hospital clinics. By seven-thirty, he counted more than thirty people, mostly couples, standing in small groups, talking with one another. The minister waited a few moments longer, and then he stood and introduced himself. He explained why he'd called the meeting. "We want to find out if there is a problem in Woburn, or if there isn't," he said. He passed out copies of a questionnaire that a nurse at Massachusetts General had helped him to prepare, and asked that they be returned to him as quickly as possible.

Toward the end of the meeting, people began asking questions, voicing their worries and suspicions. Some people talked about their children, but not everyone who had come had a leukemic child. A few had family members with different sorts of cancers, one had a cat with leukemia, and others had come simply out of a concern about the local environment. The atmosphere felt loose and friendly. Many people joined in the talk. Anne was not one of them. Throughout the meeting she sat quietly with her husband. She had told Reverend Young that she didn't want her role in this affair mentioned, and he respected her wishes. She did not like speaking before groups of people, and she also feared that others might ridicule her intuition. "I did not make my opinions known," she explained some years later at her deposition, "because I was living with paranoia, because I saw myself as a housewife without training."

Reverend Young waited for the questionnaires to be sent back. Several weeks after the meeting he and Anne met in his office at the church. They had information on twelve cases. That still did not seem to Young like a particularly large number over a fifteen-year period, but he did not mention this thought to Anne. He had purchased a street map of the city. Anne read aloud the address of each case, and the minister marked it on the map. Of the twelve cases, eight were located in east Woburn, and six of those were clustered in the Pine Street neighborhood, where perhaps two hundred families lived. Young thought the distribution looked highly unusual, especially when plotted on the map. He told Anne he'd call Dr. Truman the next morning and make an appointment to show him the map. He asked Anne if she wanted to come with him, but she told the minister he should go alone.

When Reverend Young arrived at the hospital some days later, he found the doctor in his office, about to eat lunch. Truman offered to share his meal, but the minister declined. He began telling Truman about the October 4 meeting. Truman listened politely. Young unfolded the map and placed it on Truman's desk.

"Here," explained the minister, finger to the map, "is east Woburn, and here is Anne Anderson's house. And this is the Zonas', and right next door are the Nagles. Here are the Kanes, and the Toomeys. Over here are the Carlsons; Donna Robbins, and Barbas, Ryan, Veno . . ."

Truman abandoned his lunch and looked intently at the map. "This is very interesting," he murmured as if he were talking to himself.

"We've identified twelve cases altogether," continued the minister. "There may be more. The problem is, I don't know if twelve is unusual for a fifteen-year period."

"This is a very striking cluster," said Truman. "There's no doubt about that."

Truman told Young that he knew a doctor at the Centers for Disease Control in Atlanta who had investigated other leukemia clusters. "I think the next step is for me to call him," Truman said, and he reached for the telephone.

The man whom John Truman called at the Centers for Disease Control was Dr. Clark Heath. He was the world's foremost expert in leukemia clusters. It was a distinction that Heath himself might not have valued highly, since he was no longer sure that such a thing as a leukemia cluster existed.

Heath had first encountered what seemed to be a cluster in the spring of 1961, as a young doctor in his second year at the CDC. He'd been sent to the town of Niles, Illinois, a Chicago suburb, after a pediatrician there had reported the deaths of four young girls from leukemia within three months. In Niles, Heath methodically combed through death certificates and discovered four additional cases, three girls and one boy. The eight victims had lived within a single parish of Niles, an area slightly more than a square mile in size. All but one of the victims had attended the parish parochial school or had siblings who did, and the one who did not, a ten-year-old girl, had lived within a block of the school. Heath also discovered three adult leukemia cases in the parish. Two of those adults had children at the school. All the cases had been diagnosed within the last three years.

Heath was a young man then. He began to hope that he might discover in Niles the cause of childhood leukemia. He and a colleague from the University of Chicago studied each leukemia case in great detail, scrutinizing medical records, examining samples of bone marrow and blood, testing the blood of family members, monitoring the levels of background radiation in the homes of the victims and at the parish school and church. They found no evidence of any hereditary factor. Heath felt almost certain that some infectious agent, probably a virus, had caused the disease. Researchers had identified leukemia viruses in animals—in mice and birds—and it seemed reasonable to suspect that such a virus also existed in humans. Moreover, leukemia occurred most frequently in children under six years of age, a time when they were most prone to infectious diseases. In Niles, Heath discovered that a "rheumatic-like illness" had circulated among children at the same general time as the onset of leukemia, and this, he thought, suggested "some infectious process." But he could not link it with any certitude to the leukemias. After a year of work he was no closer to knowing what had caused the outbreak in Niles than on the day he'd arrived. Back then, he did not doubt that he'd seen a genuine leukemia cluster. In a report published in the *American Journal of Medicine* in 1963, Heath wrote: "The cluster of eight cases of leukemia among children in Niles cannot reasonably be attributed to the effects of random distribution. These cases constitute a clearly defined micro-epidemic."

Over the years, other leukemia clusters began to surface. Heath went to the small town of Orange, Texas, to investigate three cases that had occurred within nine months. From Douglas, Georgia, came a report of a "leukemia house," where three residents and a regular visitor had, within ten years, contracted the disease. In Rutherford, New Jersey, six children, four of whom had attended the same elementary school, were diagnosed with leukemia. From Almond, New York, a rural village with a population of two thousand, came reports of four leukemias in less than a year. In all of these places, as in Niles, investigators failed to find a cause, or even a significant lead.

Two decades had now passed since Heath had gone to Niles. He knew more, and was certain of less. "Results have suggested little if any tendency for cases to come in clusters beyond what chance would predict," he wrote in 1982 in the textbook *Cancer Epidemiology and Prevention*. Others in the field agreed with this position. Some epidemiologists at the CDC, for example, explained apparent leukemia clusters by analogy to the "Texas sharpshooter" effect: a man shoots at the side of a barn and then proceeds to draw targets around the holes. He makes every shot into a bull's-eye. If an epidemiologist were to draw a circle around, say, the greater Boston area, he would find an incidence of leukemia comparable with the rest of the United States. Draw a circle around Woburn and he'd find a worrisome elevation. Draw a circle around the Pine Street neighborhood and he'd find an alarming cluster. Was it a real cluster? Or was he just drawing bull's-eyes where he found bullet holes?

Despite Heath's doubts about clusters, he still felt it was "highly likely" that infectious agents played a role in the cause of childhood leukemia. But any such agent, he thought, would have to be a pathogen of low potency, one that was widespread but affected only a very few susceptible individuals. And he no longer had much faith that epidemiological investigations would yield any answers to childhood leukemia. The available techniques were too crude and the disease too rare to establish any firm connection between cause and effect.

Nevertheless, when John Truman called him, Heath was duty-bound to investigate. He arranged to send an epidemiologist to Boston to meet with Truman and to collect the records of leukemic children from other Boston area hospitals.

7

Reverend Young left John Truman's office more certain than ever that there was an epidemic of leukemia in east Woburn. And then events began to converge. Charles Ryan, the *Daily Times* reporter who had written about the arsenic lagoon, had just completed a story concerning a study of cancer mortality by the state's department of public health. In Woburn, deaths from all cancers had increased by 17 percent during a five-year period in the mid-1970s. The incidence of leukemia in particular, and to a lesser extent kidney cancers, was alarming. "Even though cancer seems to be on the increase in Woburn," wrote Ryan, "there is no way of knowing if that increase is due to the toxic wastes found in north Woburn."

After reading this story, Reverend Young immediately called Charles Ryan at the *Daily Times* and told him about the leukemia cluster he and Anne had discovered. Ryan's second story appeared on December 12, 1979, on the front page of the paper under the headline CHILD LEUKEMIA ANSWERS SOUGHT.

The mayor, unhappy with the publicity the city had received about the arsenic lagoon in north Woburn, was even less happy with Reverend Young's activities. "For anyone with little or no authority to give the impression that there is a major health crisis within the confines of the city, without factual evidence to back up their statements, is totally irresponsible," announced the mayor at a city council meeting. Reverend Young heard that the mayor, in private conversation, was furious about the "panic" and "hysteria" created by reports of high cancer rates. The chamber of commerce warned publicly about declining property values and other serious economic effects. "Businesses may decide not to expand, or even to move out of the area," one speaker told the chamber. "Industrial land may not be sold because of the problem. Property values may be down." The chamber's vice-president foresaw "an exodus of business" and said, "We've got to try to head that off."

That December the Centers for Disease Control formally requested permission from the city to launch an investigation into the possible leukemia cluster. With help from the Massachusetts Department of Health, an epidemiologist from Atlanta began designing a study for Woburn. Trained researchers from the department of health would be sent to the homes of the twelve families with leukemic children and conduct in-depth interviews on a wide range of subjects. The researchers would also interview twenty-four other Woburn families that had been selected as controls, matched by age and sex with the leukemic families. The study, said the experts, would take a year to complete.

Reverend Young worried that those in authority would try to minimize or even suppress the results of the investigation. On Sunday mornings, from the pulpit at Trinity Episcopal, he began to speak about environmental contamination in Woburn and the high incidence of leukemia. He seized every opportunity to speak in public on the issue, and granted interviews to any reporter who asked. To a *New York Times* reporter, he said, "I set out to prove [Anne] wrong, that cancer and leukemia don't run in neighborhoods, but she was right." When Senator Edward Kennedy's office invited both him and Anne to testify in Washington before the Senate Committee on Public Works and the Environment, he immediately accepted. Anne told the minister she would not go. She had to take care of Jimmy. Young insisted. "You must do this for Jimmy," he told her.

So Anne went. She spoke only briefly, but her words became the headline in *The Boston Globe*'s story the next day. "We fear for our children, and we fear for their children," she said. "The neighborhood lives in fear."

8

Donna Robbins got a visit from two researchers working on the CDC investigation one evening in July 1980, seven months after John Truman's call to Clark Heath. The researchers asked Donna about the medical histories of everyone in the family, how often they had been exposed to X rays, how many pregnancies and miscarriages she'd had. They asked about her and her ex-husband's jobs, their ethnic and religious backgrounds, their church and community activities, their eating habits, hobbies, and household pets. Did she keep a garden? Had she or her sons ever fished or waded in Woburn lakes and streams? Had she ever smoked cigarettes? Painted her apartment? Used hair spray or hair dye? Traveled outside Woburn? The entire process took nearly two hours. Donna answered as best she could. After the researchers left, she realized that they had never asked her about the tap water.

A few weeks later, Donna got a call from the Woburn lawyer who had handled her divorce, the same lawyer who'd referred her to Reed & Mulligan about Robbie's hip operation. The lawyer said he'd been following events in the newspaper. He asked Donna if she'd thought about a lawsuit, perhaps against the city. Donna said the idea had not occurred to her. "Well," said the lawyer, "you might call Joe Mulligan and see what he thinks."

Donna raised the subject with Reverend Young the next day. The idea intrigued the minister. He thought a lawyer might help them get some answers. He told Donna he'd be happy to meet with Mulligan and explain the circumstances in Woburn.

Donna called Joe Mulligan. The lawyer expressed interest in meeting with Young and seeing if there was indeed a case. Although nothing had yet come of the case concerning Robbie's hip, Donna still had faith in Mulligan. He had always treated her kindly. He still assured her periodically that Robbie's case was developing, and she believed him.

The following week Mulligan drove out to Woburn in his white Cadillac, and Donna greeted him at the back door of the church. She escorted him through the hallway cluttered with the Trinity Thrift Shop's wares, the piles of old clothes, the chipped dishware and battered toys. Bruce Young's small, dark office was almost as cluttered as the hallway, and Mulligan seemed to fill all the space.

Reverend Young unfolded the map with the leukemia cases and showed it to Mulligan. He explained how he and Anne had put the map together, told him about his visit to Truman's office, and described the way the city officials had reacted. "The odds of a cluster like this occurring by chance," the minister told Mulligan, "are on the order of a hundred to one."

Mulligan seemed impressed. Twelve children with leukemia—eight of them within a half-mile radius, six of them living almost next door to each other—and contaminated drinking water. It was, in legal terms, as Mulligan later said, "almost *res ipsa loquitur*"—the thing speaks for itself. There was, however, Mulligan pointed out, one significant problem: Who was to blame for the TCE in the wells? Reverend Young replied that the Environmental Protection Agency had just begun an investigation. Once the agency completed its report, they'd know the source. Mulligan suggested that he meet with the families. Reverend Young agreed to make the arrangements. And Mulligan departed, carrying a file of newspaper clippings that the minister had collected.

Since Anne knew most of the families, Reverend Young gave her the job of calling them to meet with the lawyer. The task made Anne uncomfortable. She wasn't certain how some of the people might react to the idea of hiring a lawyer. She wrote down what she wanted to say and rehearsed it a few times: "We thought it might be a good idea to meet with an attorney to see what the possibilities are."

One woman whose son had died recently said coldly, "That was never on my mind." The woman's tone seemed to accuse Anne of attempting to turn a child's terrible misfortune into profit. And a few families whose children were doing well in treatment declined the invitation. Anne thought perhaps they were superstitiously afraid, as if going to the law would cause their children to have relapses. But most of the families with leukemia in their households seemed interested.

The meeting with Mulligan took place late in August at the church. Mulligan introduced himself and talked a little about his firm and the sort of cases he had handled. For the most part he listened to the families tell their stories. The big question was whom to blame for the contamination of Wells G and H. Most people thought the old Woburn tanneries were probably responsible. One person suggested they could sue the city or the state. Certainly the city had been warned, time and again, about the water quality, yet the officials had paid no heed. Another man, the owner of a supermarket in town whose daughter had died two years earlier, vehemently opposed that idea. He feared his customers would disapprove of a lawsuit against the city, especially if it resulted in raising taxes to pay the cost of a judgment.

Someone asked Mulligan how much they would have to pay for his services. Mulligan explained that they would sign a standard contingency fee contract, which would entitle him to receive one third of any recovery, plus expenses he incurred in developing the case. The families had no obligation to pay him unless he settled the case or won a judgment in court.

Mulligan made a good impression on most of the families. They liked his confidence and assurance, and the way he listened to their comments and observations. He hadn't made any grand promises, but he had mentioned in passing some of the cases he had worked on, and he seemed like an able lawyer.

At a second meeting some weeks later, in September, Mulligan asked those families interested in signing on with him to call at his office and arrange for an appointment. Five of the families—Anderson, Robbins, Zona, Kane, and Toomey—decided to have Mulligan represent them.

That autumn, they drove into Boston to complete the paperwork and sign the standard personal injury contract forms.

9

Charles Anderson had been offered a promotion that required him to move to Toronto. He told Anne that he wanted to accept the offer, and he wanted her and the children to come with him.

Anne replied that moving now would be unfair to Jimmy.

"Toronto is not the end of the earth," said Charles. "They have good doctors there, too."

In the summer of 1980, after nineteen years together, Anne and Charles separated. Anne remained in Woburn with the children.

Jimmy was now eleven years old. He was small and frail, and he attended school fitfully, but since his relapse five years ago his blood counts had remained stable. Anne believed that he would, in time, be completely cured of the disease.

Late that summer, however, Dr. Truman noted that the boy's platelet count and white-blood-cell count were both falling. A bone marrow biopsy revealed immature cells with irregular nuclei. Although the cells were not typical of lymphoblastic leukemia, Dr. Truman feared the leukemia was recurring. He did two more bone marrow biopsies. The results were inconclusive. In November he discovered that the total number of cells in Jimmy's bone marrow was decreasing rapidly, a condition known as aplastic anemia. The boy did not have leukemia, but without a functioning bone marrow, he would die just as certainly as if he did.

Truman had never encountered this development before and it puzzled him. He stopped chemotherapy immediately. He tried to stimulate Jimmy's bone marrow into producing platelets and white blood cells by administering anabolic steroids. That had no effect. Jimmy's condition worsened. Truman tried a more experimental form of treatment with a compound known as ATG. "That, too, was unsuccessful," recalled Truman at his deposition. "Bleeding worsened. His normal protective white blood cells vanished. Infections worsened."

On December 22, 1980, Anne called the Woburn fire department and asked for an ambulance to take her son to Massachusetts General.

Jimmy was bleeding steadily and profusely from his nose and his mouth, and his urine was grossly bloody. As the ambulance crew loaded the boy onto a stretcher, one of the firemen asked Anne, "Is your son a patient of John Truman's?"

Anne, surprised, said, "How did you know?"

"My son had leukemia, too. Dr. Truman was his doctor."

Anne had not seen the man at any of the meetings. "What's your name?" she asked.

"John Lilley," said the fireman.

Anne knew the name. She remembered that day almost six years ago, during Jimmy's first relapse, when a distraught older woman had told her in the hospital corridor that a boy named Michael Lilley had just died.

Jimmy Anderson's bleeding was controlled, although never completely arrested, by massive transfusions of platelets. He was twelve years old, and he knew his fate. "I'm going to die," he told his mother angrily on the eighth day of his last hospitalization. "It's not fair. I'll never get out of here."

The pain, which had always been present in recent months, became unremitting. He shook with chills, bled from the nose and mouth, had ringing in his ears and blurred vision. He complained especially about the pain in his stomach. When pain medication was not immediately forthcoming, he demanded it. "Don't you understand?" he shouted at a nurse. "I really need it."

The following day he became despondent. The nurses tried to coax him out of bed, but all he said was "I'll never be able to go home." Anne rarely left the hospital. On occasion she went to the cafeteria to eat, but most of her time was spent on the children's cancer ward. Charles Anderson returned from Toronto to be with his son and to keep Anne company. By mid-January, the boy had reached a nadir. "Saga of intermittent fever goes on," noted one of the nurses. "Mother has been here constantly and they both appear exhausted. Jim asking: Why me?"

Jimmy died on Sunday morning, January 18, 1981. Five days later, the Centers for Disease Control and the Massachusetts Department of Public Health jointly released a report entitled *Woburn: Cancer Incidence and Environmental Hazards.* The report was based on the investigation that had started with Dr. Truman's phone call to Clark Heath at the CDC more than a year earlier.

The report confirmed that an unusual number of leukemia cases did indeed exist in east Woburn. It read, in part: "Analysis of residence at the time of diagnosis reveals a significant concentration of cases in the eastern part of Woburn, where the incidence of disease was at least seven times greater than expected. The incidence of childhood leukemia for the rest of Woburn was not significantly elevated compared to national rates."

The authors of the report said they could not establish a definite link between the contaminated drinking water and childhood leukemia. But they saw reason for suspicion: "Although the contaminants in wells G and H are not known to cause leukemia, the fact that organic contaminants were found in the water supply must be emphasized." The report pointed out that the wells had been "on line during the presumed critical exposure period of the childhood leukemia cases and they served primarily the eastern part of Woburn."

The authors noted that the source of the contamination of the wells was still unknown. The Environmental Protection Agency was attempting to trace the contaminants back to the point of origin, but that task, time-consuming and costly, would take at least another year, and probably longer.

The Lawyer

1

It was the Friday evening of Memorial Day weekend and the mood at Jason's, a fashionable bar in Boston's Back Bay, was festive. Teresa Padro, a young woman who worked as a clothing buyer for a chain of national discount stores, sat at the bar waiting for a friend to arrive. Teresa's job required that she travel a lot. She stayed in motels, worked late, and often had to fend off the advances of middle-aged male clients after business dinners. She was thirty-one years old. She had thick, dark brown hair that fell to her shoulders, almond-colored skin, and a body slim from regular exercise.

Two men at the bar were trying to strike up a conversation with her. On the road, this would have been an annoyance. At home, in Boston, she felt mildly flirtatious. One of the men was making his pitch when she happened to glance at the door and met the eyes of a man who had just walked in. He was tall and lanky, and he wore (her expert eye could tell even at a distance) an expensive suit. She thought he looked "interesting," as she later recalled, but just then one of the men beside her asked her to dance. She declined. Then his friend asked her, and she rejected him, too. A voice behind her said, "I'm the pinch hitter, since everyone else struck out."

She turned and saw the well-dressed man who had just walked in. He told her his name was Jan Schlichtmann, and then he asked if she'd ever heard of him.

She thought that was a most audacious question. "Why? Are you famous?" she asked in a droll voice.

He said he was a lawyer. He'd just settled the Copley Plaza Hotel fire case for $2.5 million. "The biggest wrongful death settlement in Massachusetts history!" he exclaimed. His picture had been in the *Boston Herald*. Hadn't she seen it?

"What kind of lawyer are you?" she asked.

"I represent people who've been injured."

"Oh. An ambulance chaser."

"No," he said firmly. "I represent victims."

"You probably sue doctors," she said. "You wouldn't fit into my life. My mother and my father and my brother are all doctors."

He asked her what she was doing that weekend.

"I'm going to the Cape," she said.

"Really? I'm going there, too."

"Are you driving?" she asked.

"No, I'm taking the plane."

"Don't you have a car?"

"Yes," he said. "I just bought a Porsche."

He was so unabashedly egotistical that she had to laugh. He was tall, six feet three inches, with a lean, narrow face and a prominent Semitic nose. He wore a thick but neatly trimmed mustache, perhaps to fill out his face. His suit was expensive—handmade, she could tell at a glance. But the tailoring could not hide the fact that he was as gangly as a boy. Even the collar of his hand-tailored shirt did not quite fit around a neck as spindly as his. The most attractive thing about him, she thought, were his brown eyes, which seemed warm and gentle. When she commented on his eyes some days later, he laughed and told her his father used to tease him by calling him Spaniel Eyes. That night, he did Irish and Italian accents for her and told jokes until finally, despite herself, she was laughing.

"Do you have a girlfriend?" she asked him.

No, he said, shaking his head, he didn't. She could tell by the smile just creasing his lips that he thought he was finally getting somewhere with her.

"Are you married?" she asked.

He said he wasn't.

She shrugged. "What's so great about you, then?"

When Teresa's friend Alma arrived, he danced with both of them. He was not, she had to admit, a very good dancer, too loose-limbed for grace, but he was enthusiastic and not self-conscious.

They spent most of that weekend together, in Boston. He lived on the top floor of an old and elegant nineteenth-century building on Beacon Hill. From his balcony he had a sweeping view of the Charles River and the Esplanade. He had more suits than any man she'd ever met, but she soon learned that he really knew very little about clothes. "He buys labels," she explained, after several years with him. "He's the type to buy Baccarat china because it's Baccarat. He doesn't have the self-assurance to believe it'll look good if it doesn't have a label." She began educating him about clothes. She bought him ties as gifts. After he won a big case wearing her ties, he became superstitious and would never appear in front of a jury without one she had selected.

He would take Teresa and her two best friends out on the town and entertain them the entire evening, laughing and dancing with each in turn. She thought he was astute about people. He could tell if she or one of her friends was having a problem of some kind. He'd ask about it and listen carefully to the answer. She became friends with the people who worked in his office, especially with his secretary, Kathy Boyer, who had worked for him since he started practicing law. When he won or settled a case, everyone in the office got a big bonus. He'd take the entire staff out for drinks and dinner whenever someone had a birthday. Sometimes he'd invite them all out for no reason at all. He always picked up the tab. When he prepared an opening or closing argument for a trial, he insisted that everyone in the office, even the receptionist and the filing clerks, listen and offer their opinions. During an actual trial, the entire office staff would come to the courthouse and sit in the gallery to watch him at work.

At first Teresa thought he was simply self-centered, a flaw he himself seemed to recognize in his character. "He's also very generous," said Teresa, "because he knows he's self-centered and he feels guilty about it."

. . .

Lawyers in America have never been well liked. One of the first lawyers to arrive in the New World was an Englishman named Thomas Morton, who landed at Plymouth Colony in 1625, four years after the Pilgrims. Two years later he was jailed for trading firearms to the Indians and then expelled from the colony. In Massachusetts, fifteen lawyers practiced the profession in 1740, collecting debts and litigating disputes among merchants. By the time of the Revolution, that number had grown to seventy. For some citizens, lawyers had become "cursed hungry Caterpillars" whose fees "eat out the very Bowels of our Commonwealth." Two hundred years later the basic complaint remains the same. "We may well be on our way to a society overrun by hordes of lawyers, hungry as locusts," said Chief Justice Warren Burger in 1977.

As a youth, Jan Schlichtmann had not thought highly of the legal profession. He was born in Framingham, a working-class city dominated by a General Motors auto plant. His father, a traveling salesman, had always told his three sons that they should work for themselves. At the dinner table, he saw in his second son, Jan, a gift for argument. The boy had a passionate desire to persuade others to his own point of view, and he was unrelenting in his efforts. Irksome as this was in an adolescent, his father thought he saw in it the makings of a successful lawyer, and he urged Jan to consider the profession.

At the University of Massachusetts, Schlichtmann studied philosophy. To him, the legal profession did not seem any more independent or exalted than the plumbing trade. That was the analogy that occurred to him when he thought about becoming a lawyer. People hired you to fix things in their lives—wills, divorces, collecting on bad debts—the same way they'd hire a plumber to fix clogged pipes and leaky faucets in their houses. Working in a big law firm would be even worse. You'd do the dirty work of the rich and powerful.

When he graduated from college, in 1972, he married a fellow student. They moved to Rhode Island, where his wife entered graduate school. Schlichtmann, with a degree in philosophy, could not find a job that suited him. For want of anything better, he started selling life insurance to graduate students. In six months, he sold nearly a million dollars of insurance, but he despised the work. His marriage was unhappy. One day in the spring of 1973, he stopped selling insurance and started watching the Watergate hearings on television. For three months he sat at home, engrossed in the drama. His wife accused him of indolence. When the hearings ended, he knew he could never go back to selling insurance. He told himself he wanted to do something useful, something to benefit society, but he could not figure out what. He combed through the newspapers looking for a job. Finally he found an ad that read: "National Social Service Organization opening Rhode Island Branch. Looking for young, dynamic person as Executive Director. $8,500 salary." He applied and discovered that the organization was the American Civil Liberties Union. One evening, he heard on the local television news that the ACLU had just opened its Rhode Island branch. Its new director, said the newscaster, was named Jan Schlichtmann.

His first case at the ACLU involved a group of nuns and welfare mothers who had gathered in the State House rotunda to protest the governor's cuts in welfare aid. The group convened at the State House once a week on Wednesday afternoons for half an hour. After a short prayer they'd sing, "Wake up, my people, wake up to the needs of all who suffer sorrow. . . . All across the nation, hungry people are starving." On the third Wednesday, the governor had them ejected, claiming they were disrupting State House business. When they returned the following week, the governor threatened to arrest them.

Schlichtmann looked for a lawyer among the ACLU's membership who would take on the case, and then, full of zeal and impatience, he began working on it himself. He discovered that after the governor had ejected the nuns and welfare mothers, a theatrical troupe, invited by the governor's wife, had performed in the rotunda for several hundred schoolchildren. Earlier that same week, the General Assembly had celebrated St. Joseph's Day in the rotunda with a feast of Italian food and music. No one had protested these activities or claimed that they had disrupted State House business.

Working on this case, Schlichtmann experienced a profound revelation. The concept of a system of justice—laws and courts that permitted *welfare mothers* to challenge *governors!*—seemed to unfold gloriously before him. He suddenly saw that lawyering wasn't just wills, divorces, and sordid criminal matters, the leaky faucets and clogged pipes of society. The law, he decided, was perhaps the highest calling a man could aspire to. On behalf of the nuns and welfare mothers, he drafted a complaint and held a press conference on the State House steps, surrounded by his clients. Camera crews and reporters came to interview him. He saw himself on television for the first time that night. He would have liked to argue the case himself in federal court, but he was not a member of the bar. He recruited a young lawyer just out of night law school and sat with him at the counsel table in Judge Raymond Pettine's courtroom, orchestrating the presentation of witnesses and evidence.

By then he'd already applied to law school. Cornell accepted him. His marriage ended. In his first year at Cornell, Judge Pettine's ruling, some thirty pages in ringing support of the nuns and welfare mothers, was reported in the Federal Supplement.

In law school, the big issues of law and society—civil liberties and the First Amendment—captivated him. Like every law student, he was required to study the law of torts, that broad field dealing with the compensation of people who had suffered loss or injury at the hands of another. He got a C in torts, a subject he found dull and unimportant.

He gave little thought to how he'd make a living as a lawyer. Most of his classmates were angling for big money jobs in big city firms, and Schlichtmann did the same. In his third year he had an interview with a senior partner from the New York law firm of Skadden, Arps, Slate, Meagher & Flom, one of the biggest and richest firms in the country. The interview got off to a bad start. The senior partner, who was cold and brisk throughout, asked Schlichtmann if he had any misgivings about working for the ACLU. He asked the question in a tone that suggested Schlichtmann *should* have misgivings. Schlichtmann said, "My only regret is coming to this interview," and he got up and left.

Schlichtmann flirted with the idea of becoming a country lawyer, but he finally decided on a job with a small Washington, D.C., law firm that specialized in dealing with the Federal Communications Commission. On the first day of his job one of the firm's lawyers took him to the FCC and introduced him to the government agency he would be dealing with. On the second day he was shown a towering stack of government forms he'd be filling out so that a television network could purchase new stations. On the third day Schlichtmann sat at his desk wondering how he would endure his job. That morning he got a call from his criminal law professor at Cornell, G. Robert Blakey, who had just been appointed chief counsel for the House Select Committee on Assassinations. There was an opening on the staff. Was Schlichtmann interested?

Schlichtmann went into the managing partner's office and asked for a year's leave of absence.

"Pro bono?" said the partner. "We don't do any goddamn pro bono work here."

"I thought it would look good for the firm," said Schlichtmann.

"The best thing for the firm," said the partner, "would be for you to get out now."

Schlichtmann spent nine months with the House select committee. He was one among many staff lawyers, and a low-ranking one at that. He felt stifled by the bureaucracy, by the need to report every action to superiors. He began to dream again about becoming a country lawyer, being his own boss, seeking fulfillment among the common folk.

He quit the committee and drove to Portsmouth, New Hampshire, with the idea of starting a practice. He discovered that Portsmouth already had plenty of lawyers. On the way back to Boston, he saw a sign for Newburyport, a coastal fishing village that was rapidly developing into a community of condominiums and boutiques. In Newburyport, a real estate agent told him it was just the sort of place that needed more lawyers, and he actually believed her.

Schlichtmann rented a second-floor apartment in a building in the center of town. He divided his living room into an office and reception area and hired a part-time secretary. He decided he would own the best law library in Essex County. He built his own bookshelves and started filling them with lawbooks, all bought on credit, no money down. In June he opened the office. Business was slow. He read his new lawbooks. By October he was broke and two months behind on the rent. He owed the landlord eight hundred dollars. One day that fall, a man walked into his office with an incredibly tangled real estate matter that he described at great length to Schlichtmann.

"Will you take the case?" the man asked finally.

"Yes," said Schlichtmann, with a sinking heart.

"How much will it cost to retain you?" asked the man.

"Eight hundred dollars," said Schlichtmann. He had begun to suspect that country lawyering was not for him.

During the next year and a half he worked on sundry legal matters. He recovered a security deposit in a landlord-tenant dispute. He handled a few workers' compensation claims, a drunk-driving case, a dispute between a customer and a local merchant, and a "slip 'n fall," as it was called in the trade—a young woman emerged from a bar, caught the heel of her shoe in a sidewalk grate and fell, shattering her elbow. Schlichtmann attempted to cultivate the local banks in order to get house closings, but he had no great success. He eked out a living. He fell behind on payments for his law library.

One morning, a shy, inarticulate young man named Lowell Eaton entered his office and asked, apologetically, if he might talk to Schlichtmann about a legal matter. Eaton explained that his only child, a three-year-old boy named Stuart, had drowned five years ago in a gravel pit next door to his house. It had happened on a Saturday afternoon, when Lowell and his wife were both working the morning shift at the shoe factory. The boy's grandmother was tending the child. She left him alone in the backyard for a few minutes while she went into the kitchen to get a basket of laundry. When she returned, Stuart was nowhere in sight. She went next door, where Stuart's aunt lived, but found no sign of the boy. After an increasingly frantic search, she found Stuart floating facedown among the reeds and overgrowth of the gravel pit. The very next day, Lowell Eaton told Schlichtmann, the construction company that owned the land had sent a convoy of dump trucks to fill the pit.

Lowell explained that he'd already gone to one lawyer. The lawyer had filed a suit against the construction company, but then nothing had happened. Lowell had called the lawyer every so often to ask about the case. Three years had passed. The last time Lowell had called, the lawyer had advised him to stop dwelling on the death of his son. By then, Stuart's grandmother had died and there were no witnesses to the boy's death. The case, the lawyer had said, was hopeless.

Lowell Eaton asked if Schlichtmann would take the case, and Schlichtmann agreed to look at the file. A wrongful death case was more complicated than anything he'd ever attempted. It required writing up lengthy interrogatories, taking the depositions of witnesses, and properly requesting documents. If the case went to trial, he'd have to choose a jury, give opening and closing arguments, cross-examine witnesses, and build foundations for evidence. He had never done those things before, but he had little else to occupy him. He told Lowell Eaton he'd take the case.

Schlichtmann filed an amended new complaint asserting that the construction company was negligent and reckless in allowing the pool of water to accumulate in the gravel pit, in not fencing the land, filling in the pit, or posting it as a hazard. The defense lawyer was named Clement McCarthy, a veteran of several hundred trials and a dour and gloomy man. He denied the accident had taken place on his client's land or that such a pit had ever existed. Certainly it did not exist today, said McCarthy. And even if it had once existed, Stuart Eaton had been a trespasser. Moreover, his parents had assumed the risk by choosing to live next to a gravel pit, if such a pit had indeed ever existed.

Schlichtmann began reading books on the fundamentals of discovery and trial practice. He hired a photographer to fly above the site of the old gravel pit and take aerial photographs. He collected photographs of Stuart in the week before his death, photographs of Stuart's parents proudly holding their son. In Rhode Island he located the newspaper photographer who had taken a picture of the pit and the pool of water on the afternoon of Stuart's death. He had all of those photographs enlarged to the size of movie posters and mounted for display in the courtroom. He hired a civil engineer and a doctor to testify as expert witnesses. Late one evening he realized that he had found his calling. "This," he said to himself, "is what I want to do with my life."

After four months of work, he felt prepared for trial. He struggled to get a trial date in the crowded state courts while Clem McCarthy requested and received one continuance after another. With each delay, Schlichtmann went back to the case and worked some more. By the end of seven months, he had spent fifteen thousand dollars on the case, most of it borrowed. He was deeply in debt. The lawbook company dunned him. His landlord threatened to evict him. Creditors called constantly. His part-time secretary, Kathy Boyer, was working full-time for no pay.

A week before the new trial date, the claims manager at Liberty Mutual, the insurance company that represented the construction company, called and offered to settle the case. "Let's get rid of this thing," said the claims manager. "Everybody in the case is dead—the owner of the construction company, the boy's grandmother, the boy. Without the grandmother, you don't have a witness to the boy's death. I'll give you five thousand dollars and you'll go on to the next case."

"I can't do that," said Schlichtmann.

"That's more money than this family has ever seen before. There's no way you can win this thing. With five thousand, you can get your expenses back."

"I've spent fifteen thousand," said Schlichtmann.

The claims manager laughed grandly. "You say this is your first trial? Maybe I'll come and watch this. I want to see the kid who blew the Eaton case."

The trial lasted eight days. Schlichtmann sat at the counsel table with Kathy Boyer. Clem McCarthy objected constantly on procedural grounds: "Lack of foundation, hearsay, leading question, irrelevant." Judge Peter Brady would summon Schlichtmann to the bench and explain the rudiments of trial technique. The judge was a patient man, and he was also impressed by the work Schlichtmann had put into the case. On the last day of trial the judge called both the lawyers to the bench. "I think somebody's going to get hurt here," he said. "My sense is that you should settle this case." He looked at Clem McCarthy, "I think seventy-five thousand dollars is fair."

"Judge, what are you doing to me?" said McCarthy with great indignation but also with an eye on Schlichtmann. "Jesus Christ, this case isn't worth that much!"

In the hall, Schlichtmann asked Kathy Boyer's advice. "Take it, Jan," she said, thinking about the many weeks she'd gone without a paycheck. The Superior Court clerk took Schlichtmann aside and offered his advice. "This is a tough county," he said. "A drunk driver ran down a kid playing on his own lawn and the parents only got twenty thousand. You should take the money."

But after nearly a year of work, Schlichtmann wanted to hear what the jury would say. He told the Eatons about the offer. "I think we'll win the case," he said, "and I think we'll get more money from the jury." Lowell Eaton told Schlichtmann to do what he thought best.

At the judge's bench, Clem McCarthy said, "I've talked to my client and they're willing to settle for seventy-five thousand."

Judge Brady looked at Schlichtmann.

"I can't accept it," said Schlichtmann.

"I was a trial lawyer for a long time," the judge said, looking soberly at Schlichtmann. "I think you ought to give this very serious thought."

Schlichtmann said he had given it serious thought. "My clients would rather take no from the jury than seventy-five thousand dollars from the insurance company."

Clem McCarthy shook his head in amusement. "You're not going to allow Mr. Schlichtmann any second thoughts after he's shed his tears, right, Judge?"

Schlichtmann gave his summation just before lunch. The jury began deliberating and Schlichtmann started pacing in the hallway, too nervous to eat. One hour and fifteen minutes later, the jury came back with a verdict of $250,000 for the Eatons, plus another fifty thousand dollars in interest accumulated since the time of Stuart's death. Clem McCarthy, a grim look on his face, demanded that the judge set aside the verdict on the grounds that it was excessive. The judge, amused, rejected McCarthy's motion. "You said there'd be no second thoughts after the tears were shed."

Schlichtmann's gamble had paid off, but it had been foolhardy, dignified only by his inexperience and the fact that he'd won. It was not necessarily the best sort of lesson for a fledgling lawyer.

2

Schlichtmann's fee from the Eaton case came to nearly a hundred thousand dollars. He paid his debts, gave Kathy Boyer a large bonus, and went to a tailor to get some suits made. He had decided to make his name as a trial lawyer, and the nearest place to do that, he knew, was in Boston. He wrote letters to the three most prominent personal injury firms in the city looking for a job. A month passed. He got no response. He sent out more letters. One of these he addressed to the firm of Reed & Mulligan.

He was waiting to hear from the Boston firms when, by a stroke of luck, he landed a major case. A Newburyport businessman, the proud owner of a new single-engine Piper Arrow, had flown to Atlantic City for a weekend of fun and gambling with three companions. On the return flight to Massachusetts, the plane had crashed into Long Island Sound, killing all of the occupants. The bodies had not been recovered, although some debris from the Piper Arrow had washed up on a beach. One of the passengers had been a young divorcée whose four-year-old son was now in the custody of her ex-husband. As it happened, one of Schlichtmann's part-time secretaries encountered the ex-husband one evening in a Newburyport bar. The man told her he was looking for a lawyer to represent his son's interests.

"I've got just the lawyer for you," Schlichtmann's secretary said.

Schlichtmann had just plunged into the case when he got a telephone call from the senior partner at the firm of Reed & Mulligan. Barry Reed said he'd received Schlichtmann's letter asking for a job and he wanted to meet with him. Would Schlichtmann come down to Boston for lunch?

Schlichtmann met Reed at an expensive Italian restaurant on Beacon Hill, a place frequented by the governor and the mayor and the state's other power brokers. Schlichtmann followed Reed across the restaurant, watching as Reed stopped at one table after another to exchange greetings, shake hands, and chat with acquaintances. Reed was at the height of his celebrity. He had written a novel, *The Verdict,* which was being filmed on location in Boston, starring Paul Newman. The Boston news media followed the filming closely, mentioning in nearly every story Barry Reed, author and lawyer. Often Reed's photograph accompanied the stories. He was himself as handsome as a movie star—in his mid-fifties, slim, a full head of wavy silvery hair, his features chiseled and rugged. He had a reputation as a raconteur, and at lunch with Schlichtmann he told one story after another about his cases, interrupting his tales only to wave or nod to passing acquaintances. Schlichtmann felt dazzled by Reed. He noticed, though, that Reed never once asked him about himself. By the second hour Schlichtmann began to wonder why Reed had invited him to lunch.

As Reed was signing the tab, he mentioned, as if the thought had just that moment occurred to him, that he represented the estates of two passengers in the crash of the Piper Arrow. The pilot had carried a million-dollar insurance policy, payable to the passengers if Reed could prove that the pilot had acted negligently. Reed said he had heard that Schlichtmann represented the third passenger. "I think you should let me handle that case," counseled Reed. Of course, he added, he would pay Schlichtmann a handsome referral fee when the case was settled, and Schlichtmann would not have to do any work.

"It's my only case," protested Schlichtmann, who had the distinct impression that Reed did not think him capable of handling it. "Why don't we work on it together?"

Reed didn't appear to like this idea. He tried again to talk Schlicht-mann out of the case, but Schlichtmann refused to give it up. In the end, Reed agreed to let Schlichtmann work with him, perhaps if only to keep a close eye on the young lawyer. "Okay," said Reed. "You can work out of the conference room at my office."

Schlichtmann began spending most of his time at Reed & Mulligan. Reed would stop by the conference room occasionally to see how the "kid" (as he began referring to Schlichtmann) was doing. Usually the kid was there when Reed left the office at night. Usually he was there when Reed arrived in the morning. These hours were something new at Reed & Mulligan. Sometimes the kid would disappear for a few days. Then he'd burst into the office brandishing a piece of the Piper Arrow or an article of clothing he'd found while combing a Long Island beach. The kid did not work quietly. Each new discovery brought shouts of jubilation from the conference room. The office settled back into tranquillity when the kid went to Atlantic City to trace the last days of gambling, drinking, and high living of the businessman and his three companions. It erupted when the kid returned with the business-man's credit-card receipts and affidavits from the bartenders and cashiers who'd seen the four revelers on their last day.

Schlichtmann believed the businessman had been drunk and there-fore negligent in operating the plane. Furthermore, he'd earned his pilot's license only four months before the accident and was not quali-fied to fly on instruments. Yet he'd left Atlantic City at six o'clock in the evening, taking off into overcast skies. He had entered the cloud cover near Long Island and encountered sleet and snow. Schlichtmann got a tape recording of the pilot's last conversation with an air-traffic con-troller at Kennedy Airport. The entire office of Reed & Mulligan gath-ered around to listen. They heard the businessman, his voice panicky as he lost his bearings in the clouds, request a lower altitude from the air-traffic controller. The controller instructed him to turn to the right during his descent. He turned to the left instead. He apologized, and then there was an unintelligible sound, high-pitched and keening. Per-haps it was a scream. Seconds later the Piper Arrow disappeared from the radar screen.

Schlichtmann filed suit in Massachusetts Superior Court three months after the accident. Within a matter of days he and Reed began negotiating with the insurance company that held the million-dollar policy on the pilot. The case would settle, Schlichtmann believed, for a sum close to the policy limit.

Never in the history of Reed & Mulligan had a case been put together so swiftly. Reed began to treat Schlichtmann like a son. He mentioned one morning that there were other cases in the office that needed work. "The kid is like a bulldog," Reed told his partner, Joe Mulligan. "Once he gets hold of something, he doesn't let go."

3

Donna Robbins had been calling the office of Reed & Mulligan off and on for nearly three years, ever since Joe Mulligan had taken the malpractice case concerning Robbie's hip. That case, a difficult one to begin with, had been rendered essentially worthless since Robbie's death by leukemia. Mulligan felt he'd be lucky to get Donna a few thousand dollars, a "nuisance-value" settlement.

Four months had passed since Mulligan had signed up the families in the Woburn case, and Anne Anderson had begun calling the office, too. Mulligan answered most of the calls at first. "These things take time," he'd explain to Anne, the very same words Donna used to hear when she called about Robbie's case. After a while Mulligan let his secretary handle most of the calls. She would tell Anne or Donna that Joe was out of the office or in a meeting. The secretary began feeling sorry for the women. After making yet another excuse, she'd walk into the office of one of the firm's associates and say, "What are we going to do with these poor people?" But the associate was a lowly member of the firm. He could only shrug. The case wasn't his.

Reed & Mulligan had many personal injury cases in its files. Mulligan was fond of calling especially promising cases "gold mines." A new case might look promising at first, but further investigation sometimes revealed a fatal flaw, and the case would die quietly in the files. Many cases in many firms across the nation expired in such a fashion.

Mulligan still regarded Woburn as a potential "gold mine," but he had done little work on the case. He had gone once to speak with the state environmental people, hoping they could tell him who had contaminated the wells. But they'd been "tight" (as he later put it) with information. He had also hired at minimum wage two students from

Suffolk Law School, where he himself had gotten his degree, night division. He had instructed the students to collect whatever pertinent information they could find in Woburn, and he'd left them to work on their own. One of them quit after a few weeks, and the other one did little more than clip newspaper articles from the *Woburn Daily Times*.

Mulligan had followed Schlichtmann's progress on the Piper Arrow case with interest. He was impressed with Schlichtmann's industry, and he decided to recruit the young lawyer for the Woburn case. One evening that winter, before leaving the office, he stopped at the library and invited Schlichtmann out for a drink. "I'll be at the Littlest," said Mulligan. "Meet me there."

The Littlest Bar on Province Street was Mulligan's favorite haunt. It was not only tiny but also subterranean, down six steps from the street. By dusk on a winter evening, the Littlest was crowded with men, most of them Irish, many of them lawyers, a tight nest smelling of whiskey and tobacco. Mulligan cut a huge swath in the Littlest. He towered over the bar and his stentorian voice rose above the babble. Among some patrons at the Littlest, word had it that Reed's hero in *The Verdict*, the dissolute but principled lawyer, was modeled after Mulligan. Mulligan never denied it.

When Schlichtmann arrived at the Littlest that evening, Mulligan bought him a drink and introduced him around. He put his arm around Schlichtmann's shoulder (he was taller by several inches than Schlichtmann, who himself stood well above an average crowd) and steered him to a stool in the corner of the bar. He began talking about the Piper Arrow case, telling Schlichtmann that he was impressed by how quickly he'd put it together. "There are other good cases in the office," Mulligan continued. "I've got one in particular I'd like you to look at, a mass-disaster case, best case in the office. This one could be a real gold mine. It'll require some hard work, but you're just the sort of guy to develop it." Mulligan began describing the Woburn case.

Schlichtmann had read in *The Boston Globe* about the leukemia cluster, but he hadn't known that Mulligan was involved, or that there was even a case. He felt flattered that Mulligan would ask him to work on a case of such importance and celebrity. "When can I see the file?" he asked.

Mulligan said he'd have his secretary get it for him tomorrow. "A lot of pieces are still missing from the puzzle," Mulligan confided. They

talked about Woburn for an hour over drinks. Mulligan told Schlichtmann several times he was "delighted" to have him working on the case.

On the conference room table the next morning Schlichtmann saw
a slender manila file labeled "Woburn Cases." The file, less than an
inch thick, looked very thin for a mass-disaster case. The Piper Arrow
file, by contrast, occupied almost an entire cabinet drawer. Schlichtmann opened the Woburn file and saw newspaper clippings and Mulligan's contingency fee agreements, standard forms in which the lawyer
had agreed "to do any and all necessary things in the prosecution of any
claims which the client may have against"—here Mulligan had filled in
the words—"any and all Defendants identified by the attorneys."

The only other item in the file was the report of the investigation by
the Centers for Disease Control and the state department of health.
Schlichtmann started reading the report. Some of it seemed promising—the fact, for instance, that it was very unlikely the cluster of childhood leukemias in east Woburn could have occurred merely by chance.
But other items in the report gave Schlichtmann pause. "With few
exceptions," said the report, "investigations of leukemia clusters have
failed to demonstrate significant associations or even promising leads
as to environmental causes. . . . None of the chemicals found in Wells
G and H are known to be leukemogenic, although trichloroethylene
and tetrachloroethylene have been found to cause tumors in laboratory
animals. The source of the present contaminants is unknown."

When he finished reading, Schlichtmann felt dismayed. A dozen
questions went through his head: Whose chemicals had polluted the
wells? Who had dumped these chemicals, and when had they gotten
into the water supply? Had they in fact caused leukemia? The file was
silent on almost every question. It was apparent that Mulligan had
spent little time on the case.

Schlichtmann took the file back to Newburyport and found himself
looking at it again. He could not even pronounce the names of the
chemicals in the Woburn wells, but he felt instinctively that they probably had caused the cluster of leukemias. He himself had always been
vigilant about what he ate and drank. His grandfather, owner of a phar-
macy and soda fountain, had once caught Schlichtmann's father eating
a handful of maraschino cherries. "Don't ever eat those," the grandfather had warned. "They're full of chemicals that'll make you sick."
Warnings of this sort had in turn been impressed on Schlichtmann at

an early age. His father had always done the family's grocery shopping. He'd read labels obsessively, long before most people gave labels any thought, and pointed out to his sons all the chemicals in canned foods. Dutiful in this respect at least, Schlichtmann never took any drug stronger than aspirin, nor had he ever smoked or drunk coffee. He rarely ate red meat and he avoided tap water, preferring instead bottled water, the more expensive the better.

At a glance, the Woburn case did look, as Mulligan had said, quite promising—polluted drinking water had apparently caused an epidemic of leukemia. But Schlichtmann knew that such a claim would be difficult to prove. He'd have to delve into the question of what causes leukemia, a question that medical science itself had not yet resolved. And it would be expensive. The Eaton case, by comparison, had been a simple affair, and yet he'd spent fifteen thousand dollars and seven months working on it. At this point in his career, Schlichtmann had been practicing law for only three years. He had taken only one case to trial. Woburn was too big, he told himself, too expensive, too complicated.

Mulligan's secretary began directing the phone calls from Anne and Donna to Schlichtmann. The message slips soon grew into a small pile. One evening that spring, Schlichtmann went out to Woburn to meet the families. It was dusk when he left the office. He drove through the Pine Street neighborhood, past the quiet orderly homes, the forsythia in full bloom. When he arrived at Anne's house, the families were gathered in the living room, awaiting him. He introduced himself and explained that Mulligan had asked him to work on the case.

He knew that these people wanted to hear what progress he and Mulligan had made. He explained that he had no basis yet for filing a lawsuit. That action would have to wait until the government agencies had identified the source of the contaminants in the wells. "Toxic waste dumps are surfacing all over the country," he told the families. "The EPA doesn't have the capacity or the leadership to investigate each one. You have to organize, you have to force them to do their job. This is a political battle now, not a legal one. We're not ready for the legal battle yet."

He stayed at Anne's house for nearly two hours, answering questions, getting a sense of his new clients. Anne's child had died four months earlier, and she looked pale, her eyes rimmed in red as if she had been

crying just moments ago. But Schlichtmann was struck by her forceful-
ness and the intelligence of her questions. He talked for a while with
Richard and Mary Toomey, whose son Patrick had also died earlier that
year. Richard, a sheet-metal worker for nearly thirty years, was a
reserved man, but he had a blunt, honest face, and Schlichtmann liked
him immediately. "We're not in this for money," Toomey told Schlichtmann. "We just want information. No one will tell us anything."

Schlichtmann left the meeting feeling sorry for these people. But he
also felt he could do little to help them.

4

In the files at Reed & Mulligan, Schlichtmann found dozens of other
cases, many of them gathering dust, waiting for someone to take interest. They were, he thought, like unpolished stones, like lumps of coal.
Many were of such small value—the one concerning Donna Robbins's
boy, for example—that they would barely justify his labor. A few were
completely worthless. But some looked as if they might contain a dia-
mond at the core. He kept searching for the most promising ones.
Soon the Woburn file was buried beneath the other cases.

Assisting Schlichtmann was a lawyer who occupied a small cubicle
next to Mulligan's office. The lawyer's name was Kevin Conway. He
was in his mid-thirties, several years older than Schlichtmann, short
and stoutly built, with a belly that was edging toward portliness. He
had a manner, unpracticed and unconscious, of conveying warmth and
concern. The office workers all seemed to come to Conway with their
troubles. When, for instance, Mulligan's secretary became upset by the
plight of the Woburn mothers, she went to Conway.

Conway had been at Reed & Mulligan for two years, doing piece-
work, getting paid by the case. The job was his third since graduating
in the top half of his class at Georgetown University Law School. He
had started his career working for a big company in New York, where
he'd had an office with a view and made a handsome salary. But after
six years there, he'd felt as if life were passing him by. He had no sense
of accomplishment. He'd looked at the people around him, people
who'd spent their lives working for the company, and he'd realized that
if he didn't leave soon, he might never get away.

Conway had decided to go into practice for himself. He descended from a position of relative prestige in the legal world—from an office on the fiftieth floor of a fancy building in New York—to the lowly status of a solo practitioner, close to the legal profession's bottommost rung. He moved into the basement of a century-old building in Belmont, a suburb of Boston. From the window of his office in Cushing Square, he had a pavement-level view of a working-class neighborhood of small shops. He knew this world well. He'd grown up near Belmont, not far from his new office, the second of nine children, the son of a schoolteacher. There had never been much money in the Conway family, but there had always been plenty of warmth and conviviality. Every Sunday afternoon the entire Conway clan would assemble in the living room with their musical instruments for a concert. The house was always a thick tangle of kids, crowded with Conways, but so inviting that many neighborhood kids gathered there, too.

For his new office in Belmont, Conway hired a secretary, a pretty woman in her early thirties named Peggy Vecchione who had once dated Conway's younger brother. By her own admission, Peggy could barely type and she knew nothing about legal work. But she needed a job badly. She had recently gotten divorced and had two children to support. Conway didn't think twice about hiring her.

Together they handled the legal problems of anyone who walked in Conway's door. Most of these problems were simple matters—wills, minor criminal infractions, house closings. Also some divorces, though Conway did not like divorces because they saddened him and he invariably spent too much time trying to reconcile the unhappy spouses. Peggy watched one couple walk out the door, irritated by Conway's counseling. "Don't you understand?" the man said, his voice raised. "We want a divorce!" Peggy told Conway he must have done a good job. "At least they're angry at you instead of each other," she said.

Conway came dutifully to work every day, even though there wasn't always much to do. He'd consult with Peggy about how much to charge a client. For a will of moderate complexity, she would advise one hundred fifty dollars. "They can't afford that," Conway would say of an elderly couple. He would charge fifty dollars. He'd ask Peggy how long it would take her to type the will, and she'd say, anticipating many errors and retyping, "Oh, about a week?" Conway would respond, "Hmm, that long?" But he wouldn't complain. When business was slow, he went to the arraignment courts and represented indigent defendants. For each case, he got paid seventy-five dollars by the state. He made only as much as he needed, and his needs weren't great.

After a few years in Belmont, Conway married a woman he'd courted since his New York days, and his needs grew slightly greater. He had known Joe Mulligan for several years, and when Mulligan invited him to come work at his firm, Conway accepted. He brought Peggy along with him. He didn't draw a salary. He got paid only from the proceeds of cases he helped to resolve.

He'd been at Reed & Mulligan two years, working out of a small cubicle, when Schlichtmann showed up. Peggy would never forget that day. "Kevin used to tell me, 'There's no passion in my life.' He was bored with what he was doing. Then Jan burst into the office. He represented somebody in an airplane crash, a client that Barry Reed wanted. Barry didn't have a chance against Jan. He was overpowering. Kevin was stunned by him. Kevin said, 'Jan's exactly like what you hope you're going to be when you get out of law school.' "

Conway had helped Schlichtmann draft the complaint in the Piper Arrow case. When Schlichtmann began digging through the files at Reed & Mulligan, Conway was his guide. Conway unearthed a case in which a three-year-old girl, vomiting and with a high fever, was examined by a doctor, treated with aspirin, and sent home. She developed fulminant meningitis and suffered brain damage as a result. Schlichtmann and Conway settled the case for $675,000. They worked together every day. In the evening they'd go downstairs to the Emperor of China restaurant on Tremont Street for dinner and then come back to the office and work some more. They took on a case in which a hospital incubator had overheated, causing brain damage in a newborn infant. They settled that case for $1.15 million. When an insurance company refused to settle a claim in which a surgical clamp had been left for nine years in the abdomen of a elderly man, Conway and Schlichtmann prepared for trial. It was an Essex County case, on the north shore of Massachusetts, not far from Schlichtmann's old office in Newburyport. They rented a room at a cheap motel near the Essex County courthouse. They lived there for two weeks, amid piles of law-books, medical texts, and legal pads. On the bureau was a portable typewriter, on which Schlichtmann typed last-minute motions. They ate their meals at a diner next to the motel, keeping company with long-haul truck drivers. They worked until two or three o'clock in the morning, and then got up to go to court. Conway felt punchy from lack of sleep, but he also felt exhilarated. "Working with Jan," Conway said of that time, "was the difference between being alive and being dead." The jury awarded their client $492,000.

Conway felt as close to Schlichtmann as a brother, although in most respects they appeared to be complete opposites. Schlichtmann was tall and slender, Conway short and stout. Schlichtmann's shoes were always polished to a high gloss, Conway's were always scuffed. Schlichtmann's tailored shirts were perfectly pressed, Conway's were taut over his substantial belly and billowed out of the back of his pants. Schlichtmann's tie, perfectly knotted, was held in place with a gold collarpin. The knot in Conway's tie had usually descended an inch or two by the time he arrived at work. Schlichtmann, fastidious about health and diet, watched Conway eat doughnuts for breakfast and drink "gallons" of coffee. "You treat your digestive tract like a sewer," Schlichtmann once told him. Conway had a kind word for everyone he encountered—the receptionist, the filing clerk, the office boy—while Schlichtmann, impatient and always hurrying, often failed to observe even common civilities. Conway tried never to judge anyone harshly. "You can never know enough about why someone acts the way they do," he would say.

They differed in their approach to money, too. Conway lived frugally, saving to buy a house and start a family. Schlichtmann spent every penny he earned. Conway noticed that Schlichtmann usually seemed depressed when he had money in the bank. He seemed driven by a need to get rid of money as quickly as possible, and when he had spent it all, he would burrow into another case and his spirits would rise.

Conway found the cases in the files of Reed & Mulligan and got Schlichtmann interested in them. But Conway didn't like the Woburn case. Whenever Schlichtmann mentioned it, Conway tried to steer him away. "It's a black hole," he'd warn Schlichtmann. Conway had never met the families, and he could view the case in a cold, unemotional light. He had learned by then that Schlichtmann never did anything in half measures, and the full measure of Woburn—the size, the complexity and the cost—scared Conway. "We don't want that one," he would say when he and Schlichtmann went downstairs after work to the Emperor of China restaurant and discussed new cases.

5

For a time after her son's death, Anne Anderson had rarely left the house, fearful she would break down and weep in public. She used to dream that Jimmy was still alive, and then she would awake, stunned by the fresh realization that he was gone. In the grocery store she'd see something he had liked and her tears would start to flow.

She recovered slowly. A few months after Jimmy's death, she began working at her brother's stonecutting business in Somerville, partly to pay the bills, but also to try to get her mind off Jimmy. She worked in the office, answering telephones and keeping accounts. But her thoughts kept returning to the contaminated wells. She wanted answers, and she wanted to bring to account whoever had caused her son's illness and suffering. As far as she could see, neither Mulligan nor Schlichtmann had done anything. Schlichtmann didn't even return her phone calls.

Driving home from work one afternoon in the fall of 1981, Anne turned on the radio and began listening to the Jerry Williams talk show on WRKO. The subject that day was lawyers. Listeners were invited to call in and ask questions of two lawyers who were guests on the show. Anne was listening with half an ear when she realized that one of the voices was familiar. It was Schlichtmann's voice. Here he was, on the radio, pontificating about the law, about serving clients, and she could never even get him on the phone. She drove home as fast as she dared. She ran into the house, picked up the kitchen phone and dialed the station without pausing to take her coat off.

"I've got a question for Mr. Schlichtmann."

"Go ahead, please," said the talk show host.

"What should you do when your lawyer never calls you back?"

"Wait a minute!" said Schlichtmann. "I know this voice. Is this Anne?"

"Jan, I call and call and never get to talk with you."

Over the air, Schlichtmann laughed painfully. "Your messages are right next to my mother's," he said. "I haven't called her back either." Then he added, "You can talk with Kathy, you know."

"Kathy doesn't have the answers," said Anne.

Schlichtmann didn't have any answers either, but he did not say so. He promised to call Anne the next morning.

Anne hung up the phone and then she picked it up again and called Donna Robbins. "Guess what I just did," Anne said.

Despite all its difficulties, the case tantalized Schlichtmann. He believed that it had merit. He kept thinking that if he was destined for something great in life, this case might be his opportunity. If he were to win it, he would set new legal precedents and gain a national reputation among his fellow plaintiffs' lawyers. He would no doubt make a lot of money. And he would have helped the families of east Woburn. Fame, fortune, and doing good—those were, in combination, goals worth striving for, he thought.

But by the winter of 1982 Schlichtmann still had not made a decision on the case. The statute of limitations—three years for a personal injury action in Massachusetts—had begun to run on the day the Woburn wells had closed, on May 22, 1979. If he was going to drop the case, he had to tell the families soon. If not, he had to start working quickly to prepare the complaint. As ambitious as he was, he also liked to think of himself as a businessman, a pragmatist. Conway had called this case a "black hole," and Conway was probably right. Schlichtmann decided there were other worthy cases he could devote himself to, cases he could win.

So in February he called Anne and asked her to arrange a meeting with the families at Trinity Episcopal. On the evening of the meeting, as Schlichtmann prepared to leave for Woburn, Conway came into his office. Conway made him promise that this time he would level with the families. He'd tell them that he didn't have sufficient basis to file a lawsuit. Conway followed Schlichtmann to the door. "When you come back, we won't have the Woburn case anymore. Right, Jan?"

"Right," said Schlichtmann.

. . .

At Trinity Episcopal, the small gathering of men and women sat in metal folding chairs around a long wooden banquet table that was usually used for church suppers. Reverend Young sat among them. The church hall was dimly lit and cold. Some of the women kept their coats on. Everyone but Anne thought that Schlichtmann had come to inform them of new developments in the case. She alone suspected that he had come to wash his hands of it, but she had not voiced her suspicion to the others, not even to Donna or Reverend Young.

Schlichtmann sat across from the families and recited the now familiar litany of difficulties—the absence of a defendant, the problem of proving that the chemicals had caused the leukemias, and the cost, especially the cost. "There are a lot of questions," said Schlichtmann, "and we don't have any of the answers yet. I'm afraid the resources to pursue this simply aren't there."

A sense of bleakness came over the group. Anne thought to herself, He's done everything but say good-bye.

For a moment, no one spoke. Schlichtmann, it seemed, couldn't bring himself to say good-bye, to get up and leave. Then Reverend Young cleared his throat and said, "What if I told you I know where we can get some money?"

Schlichtmann looked doubtfully at the minister. This was not a case that could be financed by church bake sales.

Reverend Young explained that he had spoken that very afternoon with a lawyer in Washington, D.C., the executive director of a new public-interest law firm called Trial Lawyers for Public Justice.

Schlichtmann grew suddenly alert. He knew about the firm! he exclaimed to Reverend Young. He was, in fact, one of its founding members! Six months ago, at a convention of trial lawyers in San Francisco, he had contributed a thousand dollars to help get the organization started. He had, of course, liked the name, and he was sympathetic to the goal of using the legal system to bring about social change.

The conversation with the Washington lawyer, continued Young, had come about by coincidence, the result of a call from a staff member in Senator Edward Kennedy's office. The staffer had read that Trial Lawyers for Public Justice was looking for a good environmental case. Woburn had come to her mind. She'd called Reverend Young, and then, at four o'clock that afternoon, she'd set up a conference call between him and the executive director, whose name was Anthony Roisman. Over the phone, Young had described the situation in Woburn, and Roisman had said the case sounded interesting. Moreover, Trial Lawyers for Public Justice had some funds already earmarked for an environmental case. But, Roisman had also said, he could not just step in and take the case away from another lawyer.

And that, Reverend Young told the gathering at Trinity Episcopal, was why he had not mentioned the conversation until this moment.

Schlichtmann, greatly animated now, questioned the minister closely about every detail of his conversation with Roisman. He remarked several times on the "amazing" coincidence of events. He told the families he would call Roisman the first thing tomorrow morning. He hoped that he and Roisman could work together on the case. When he left Trinity Episcopal that evening, the mood among the families was no longer somber.

The next morning Conway appeared at the door of Schlichtmann's office. "Well?" Conway said.

"We've still got the case," said Schlichtmann. "I couldn't say no."

6

Roisman flew up to Boston the following week. He and Schlichtmann spent two days together. Roisman was in his early forties, a Harvard Law School graduate who had been head of the U.S. Justice Department's Hazardous Waste Enforcement Section during the Carter administration. He knew how to assemble a complicated environmental case, and he thought that based on everything he had heard so far Woburn appeared most promising.

Schlichtmann invited Roisman to take over as lead counsel in the case. Roisman accepted, and asked Schlichtmann to remain on as local counsel. This arrangement suited Schlichtmann perfectly. He'd still be involved in an important case, and there was much he could learn working alongside a man of Roisman's experience. They agreed to split equally the costs of preparing the case. Roisman's organization would receive two thirds of any fee that might result from a settlement or a verdict, and Schlichtmann and Mulligan would split the other third.

After almost two years of little more than talk, events suddenly began to move swiftly. One of Roisman's assistants collected medical and scientific studies on TCE and the other chemicals in the city wells. Using the Freedom of Information Act, Roisman obtained from the Environmental Protection Agency a preliminary report of its east Woburn investigation. The agency had narrowed its focus to a single square mile of the Aberjona River valley, some 450 acres surrounding Wells G and H. Contractors for the EPA had drilled test wells along the periphery of that square mile. On the northeast side, chemical analysis of the groundwater revealed high concentrations of TCE migrating through the soil in a featherlike plume toward Wells G and H. Even higher concentrations of TCE were found in groundwater to the west of the two wells, under fifteen acres of wooded, undeveloped land alongside the Aberjona River. The EPA listed the names of several industries situated around the perimeter of the square mile, but it did not identify which of those were responsible for the contamination. "Further study is required," stated the report.

The EPA did, however, put the east Woburn aquifer on its National Priorities List, more commonly known as the Superfund. The agency ranked each site by a formula that involved the proximity of the polluted area to residential areas, the nature of the chemicals involved, and whether or not drinking water had been contaminated. By 1982 there were 418 sites on the EPA list. The east Woburn well field, the newest addition, was ranked thirty-ninth.

The EPA report was highly technical, filled with maps of bedrock and groundwater contours, well logs, and scientific jargon. To decipher it, Roisman hired a Princeton University professor, an expert in groundwater contamination and hazardous wastes. The professor told Roisman and Schlichtmann that the underground plume of TCE coming from the northeast appeared to originate at a manufacturing plant owned by W. R. Grace, the multinational chemical company. The other source of contamination, to the west of Wells G and H, came from the fifteen acres of wooded land that was owned by the John J. Riley Tannery. And the tannery, it turned out, was itself owned by the giant Chicago conglomerate Beatrice Foods, producer of dozens of consumer goods, from Samsonite luggage to Playtex bras, Peter Pan peanut butter and Tropicana orange juice.

Both companies ranked high in the Fortune 500. In the lexicon of personal injury lawyers, they had "deep pockets," and this fact had weight for Schlichtmann and Roisman. Personal injury law is not a charitable enterprise. To a lawyer working on a contingency fee and paying the expenses of a case himself, it is crucial that the defendant either have assets, preferably a lot of them, or a big insurance policy. To Schlichtmann, having Grace and Beatrice as defendants in the case was like learning that a woman his mother kept trying to set him up with had a huge trust fund.

On a sunny day in mid-April, Schlichtmann drove out to Woburn alone in his Porsche. On his visits to meet with the families, east Woburn had always seemed to him a familiar sort of place, dull and slightly depressing, a landscape of humble residential developments and suburban industrial parks, a place no different from thousands of others across the country, and hardly worth a second glance. But on this visit, everything he saw seemed to take on a sharper focus. Buildings and landmarks seemed more clearly etched, and their images remained in his mind.

He drove south down Washington Street, a busy two-lane thoroughfare near the junction of Interstate 93 and Route 128. Twenty years ago, the land to his left had all been farms. Some patches of woods and overgrown fields still remained between the new, low-roofed industrial complexes and office buildings. The right-hand side of the road was mostly hardwood trees, just now coming into bud. Beyond them and downhill lay the Aberjona marsh, but he couldn't see it from this part of the road.

He parked across the street from a large plain single-story building with a brick façade. It had a glassed-in entryway and, above that, the name W. R. GRACE in polished aluminum lettering. He studied the building from his car. In the midst of this scruffy landscape, the grounds of the Grace building stood out. A row of neatly pruned shrubs had been planted along the front of the building and the lawn was thick and well tended. On the lawn, beneath a young maple tree, there was a picnic table. Schlichtmann could see several employees in tan uniforms moving among the loading docks around the side of the building. From the EPA report, Schlichtmann knew only that this plant made stainless-steel equipment for the food-packaging industry. Trichloroethylene was a solvent used mainly for removing grease from machined metal parts. To Schlichtmann, it stood to reason that a plant such as this one would use TCE. He wondered if any of those men in uniforms were using TCE today. And just how did they dispose of it? He would have liked to speak to one of those men, or to walk into the plant and ask for a tour, but he couldn't, of course. For now, the building might as well be a fortress. Its façade told him little, and he soon grew tired of staring at it.

He pulled back out onto Washington Street and continued driving slowly to the south, in the direction of the Pine Street neighborhood. After a quarter of a mile, he turned west onto Salem Street, which crossed the northern border of the Pine Street neighborhood. He passed over a small concrete bridge that spanned the Aberjona River. Looking north, he could see the expanse of marsh surrounding the river. At the edge of the marsh, visible among a copse of still leafless trees, were the two brick pumping stations that housed Wells G and H. Their doors would be padlocked shut now. Ahead of him, as Salem Street began a gentle climb, loomed the immense brick smokestack of Beatrice's J. J. Riley tannery.

Schlichtmann parked near a chain-link fence that enclosed the tannery compound. The ripe odor of hides and animal waste hung thickly in the air. The tannery consisted of a large brick building, mottled with age, and several sheds and outbuildings. It looked as if later additions to the main building had been constructed of cement block and corrugated metal. A dozen or more large bales of raw cattle hide were piled behind the building.

On his way to the tannery, Schlichtmann had passed by the dirt road leading up to the fifteen acres of wooded land mentioned in the EPA report. This piece of land, also owned by Beatrice, was roughly triangular in shape, abutting the tannery to the west and the Aberjona River to the east. The tannery had a production well on the land, and the EPA had measured high levels of TCE in it, levels three times what they had found in the city wells.

At the tannery, Schlichtmann turned the Porsche around, and drove back down Salem Street. He turned left onto the dirt road. Twenty yards up the road a tall metal gate barred his way. To Schlichtmann's right, beyond a six-foot-high fence, was a sprawling junkyard owned by Aberjona Auto Parts. To his left was the Whitney Barrel Company, a refurbisher of used 55-gallon drums and underground oil tanks. Hundreds of drums were piled along a fence at the back of the Whitney property, and Schlichtmann could smell a strong chemical odor.

He got out of the car and walked up to the gate barring entry onto the Beatrice land. The dirt road on the other side looked well used, bordered by scrubby underbrush. Schlichtmann saw many more drums strewn beside the dirt road. He wondered if they had come from Whitney Barrel. Standing there, he found himself already framing arguments. Beatrice owned this land. It bore legal responsibility for its condition. And if Whitney Barrel had used this land as a dump site, the tannery had probably done so, too.

Roisman had started composing the lengthy complaint that would form the basis of a lawsuit against W. R. Grace and Beatrice Foods. Schlichtmann, who knew more than Roisman about Massachusetts personal injury and wrongful death law, assisted him. The complaint asserted that subsidiaries owned by Grace and Beatrice had poisoned the plaintiffs' drinking water with toxic chemicals. These chemicals included TCE, which the complaint described as "a potent central nervous system depressant that can cause severe neurological symptoms such as dizziness, loss of appetite, and loss of motor coordination. It can produce liver damage and cause cell mutations and cancer." The poisoned water, stated the complaint, had resulted in a cluster of leukemia, the deaths of five children, and injuries to all of the family members who were party to the lawsuit, including "an increased risk of leukemia and other cancers, liver disease, central nervous system disorders, and other unknown illnesses and disease." The plaintiffs sought compensation for these injuries, and punitive damages for the willful and grossly negligent acts of the two companies.

Roisman and Schlichtmann finished the complaint on May 14, 1982, eight days before the statute of limitations expired. Schlichtmann took the complaint by hand to Superior Court in Boston and filed it.

One week later a story about the lawsuit appeared in *The Boston Globe*. Alerted by that story, crews from two local television stations arrived at Reed & Mulligan to interview Schlichtmann. The camera crews set up their equipment in the firm's library. Conway watched from the door as first one television reporter and then another talked to Schlichtmann. Conway felt glad that he wasn't the one being interviewed. The cameras and lights would have made him nervous, but he could see that Schlichtmann basked in them.

That evening they went downstairs to the Emperor of China restaurant and ordered drinks at the bar. Schlichtmann asked the bartender to turn on the news so he could watch himself. He made the bartender flip the channel back and forth between the two stations so that he'd miss none of his performance.

While Schlichtmann watched himself on the news, Conway watched Schlichtmann. He knew that Schlichtmann would spend a good deal of time on this case, but he reminded himself that Roisman would be in charge. Roisman would do most of the work. They were just the local contact. Conway told himself he wasn't worried.

Rule 11

1

Every Wednesday afternoon, from February until May, Jerome Facher would leave his office in Boston shortly after three o'clock and take a subway to Harvard Square in Cambridge. The early winter dusk would be settling over the city by the time Facher disembarked from the subway and walked several long blocks up to the Harvard Law School. Facher was sixty years old. He had narrow shoulders, a small, spare frame, and neatly trimmed gray hair. He was the chairman of the litigation department at the Boston firm of Hale and Dorr, and for the past twenty years he had also taught a course in trial practice at Harvard. He still taught from the same textbook, now dog-eared and stained, that he had used in his first year of teaching. He carried it in a battered black litigation bag that was usually heavy with deposition transcripts, motions, and interrogatories from real trials. Some years ago the bag's leather handgrip had snapped under just such a load. Facher had twisted a coat hanger into a new grip and wrapped it with adhesive tape. When a seam burst, he repaired that with more tape, liberally applied. He owned several other litigation bags, each identified by decals of cartoon characters he'd once found in a cereal box. This particular bag, which might have been a hobo's suitcase, was his favorite. It was known as the pig bag because it had a Porky Pig decal on it. In the years he'd carried this bag in and out of courtrooms, to home and to work, Facher had not lost a trial. Some trials required the use of several bags, but Facher always brought along the pig bag. "You don't change your socks in the middle of the World Series," he would tell young associates at Hale and Dorr.

In his classroom at Harvard, Facher would sit at a plain wooden table in the well of a room that was shaped like a small amphitheater. Every year he faced fifteen new students, along with several first-year associates from Hale and Dorr who had come to learn from the master. Behind Facher's thick glasses, his eyes were heavily lidded, as if he were on the verge of dozing. During class and in the courtroom, he often pursed his lips in a skeptical and disapproving manner, like a candy-store proprietor guarding the goods against young hooligans.

Each week he assigned his class a case from the trial practice text-book and appointed students to conduct mock examinations. One Wednesday evening he told a young woman to represent the plaintiff. Until now, this student had not uttered a word in Facher's class. When Facher himself had been a law student at Harvard, in the late 1940s, he'd been reticent, too. He had felt intimidated by the brilliance of his fellow students, most of whom had graduated from Princeton, Yale, and Harvard. Facher had attended Bucknell Junior College. At Harvard he had lived each day in fear that a professor would call on him. When other students responded to a professor's query, Facher would say to himself, My God, I didn't think of that. During his three years of law school, he could recall speaking aloud in class fewer than a dozen times. But he'd gotten high grades and he'd made *Law Review*, the mark of academic distinction.

Now, as a teacher, Facher had changed his modus operandi. He maintained a steady stream of commentary. As the shy student struggled to build the plaintiff's case, Facher interrupted with a running critique of her methods. He did not feel much sympathy for her. Next year, she would probably have a job as an associate in a big firm in New York or Chicago, earning seventy thousand dollars a year. (Based on this performance, Facher thought he would not hire her at Hale and Dorr.) After thirty minutes the woman had made little progress. Her original strategy had been thwarted by objections from her adversary. Facher gave her some guidance, but his commentary became increasingly acerbic. In annoyance, he fiddled with his tie, tapped his fingers, straightened material on his desk. The woman attempted to enter a document into evidence and the opposing side objected on the grounds of authenticity.

"Now what are you going to do?" Facher asked her.

The young woman looked down and shuffled through her papers but said nothing. Her hair fell in front of her face, covering her eyes. Facher stared at her. The silence grew longer.

Finally another student suggested hiring a handwriting expert to testify to the authenticity of the document.

"What?" said Facher in irritation. "And pay five thousand dollars? Far too complicated." To the young woman, he said, "What are you going to do? Give up? Tell the senior partner you lost the case? Make a living selling cheeseburgers?"

The woman, head down, shoulders quivering, silently wiped a tear from her cheek.

Another student said, "Five-minute recess, Your Honor?"

Facher ignored the request. "This is an intellectual profession. You are not driving nails into a board." Although he realized suddenly that the student was crying (in twenty years of teaching, this was the first time it had happened), Facher decided a recess would only call attention to her plight and embarrass her more. "You ask the witness: 'Who prepared this document? Where did that happen? Who was present? Did your secretary type it?' "

The class was silent and uneasy.

"Little questions," continued Facher. "Little bricks build big walls. Too many of you are afraid to ask simple questions. The tools of the trade are the English language and the rules of evidence."

Facher's temper seemed to grow shorter as the day grew longer. The reason for this, he once speculated, was that he suffered from chronic insomnia. But by now he was feeling bad for the student. "Go slowly," he told her, not unkindly. "Ask one question at a time, and you'll find there is a rhythm to it."

And then, to turn attention from her, he said to the class, "Why wasn't there an objection to this document as hearsay?"

"Because it's original?" ventured one student.

Facher sighed. "*The Boston Globe* was original this morning and there's more hearsay in that than you'll find in your first five years as a lawyer. You're expected to make objections. Keep evidence out if you can. If you fall asleep at the counsel table, the first thing you say when you wake up is, 'I object!' "

After class, Facher would often return to his office and work until midnight before departing for home. He owned a condominium in Arlington, three miles from the law school. He lived there alone, his only companion an aged cat. He had been married once, for seventeen years, but that contract had been dissolved long ago. As a young lawyer, a skillful cross-examination would make his heart soar, and he rarely resisted opportunities to hone his skills. He used to practice on his wife. "I can't prove it," he once mused, "but I bet trial lawyers have more marital problems than any other type of lawyer. I wasn't the greatest husband in the world."

After his divorce, he began to work weekends and to experience sleepless nights. He'd lie awake, conducting cross-examinations in his head for hours. He found a soothing quality in the staccato rhythms of cross-examination, but he still couldn't fall asleep. Once, when his insomnia became intolerable, he sought relief at the Harvard Health Center. He was placed in a dimly lit room, recumbent on a comfortable chair, with electrodes monitoring his pulse, blood pressure, and respiration rate. A therapist gave him instructions in deep breathing and relaxation, and told him to conjure the most pleasing thought he could. He visualized an afternoon at Fenway Park, the Red Sox ahead by a run and their ace pitcher on the mound. In the laboratory he excelled at relaxation. In his own bed, where there was no one to marvel at his expertise, no one to compete against, he lay awake, furious at his inability to sleep.

Two hundred lawyers worked at Hale and Dorr, eighty of them in the litigation department. Some Boston lawyers thought that Hale and Dorr most resembled the big New York firms that specialized in what they called "bare-knuckle" litigation. In an era when many corporate lawyers never see the inside of a courtroom, Facher had tried more than sixty cases and won most of them. "I love to try cases," he once said. "That's the fun of being a lawyer. I've never had an unhappy day at Hale and Dorr."

The law firm occupied ten floors at 60 State Street, a glass and concrete skyscraper in downtown Boston, two blocks from the federal courthouse. Although the building was modern, the law firm's reception rooms, with thick Oriental carpets, Chinese vases, and dark oiled wood, gave the appearance of an old and venerable practice. Facher's office was on the twenty-fifth floor, across from the firm's law library. The office was small in relation to Facher's stature in the firm. He had been offered more spacious quarters on the twenty-seventh floor, but he had declined. He didn't spend much time in his office anyway. He would stop there in the morning to check the mail and phone messages and then he would vanish to one of his many hideouts, as he called them, where he could work without interruption.

He had hideouts on several different floors, but his current favorite was on the twenty-first, at the end of a windowless corridor, behind a heavy steel door. The door opened into a large, dimly lit storage room that served as a warehouse for the firm's moribund files. Dozens of gray metal filing cabinets, their drawers filled with legal papers, lined the walls. The overflow was stuffed into stout cardboard boxes that were stacked on top of the cabinets and on the floor, pyramids of paper reaching up to the ceiling. Some acoustical panels in the ceiling were missing, and electrical wires, wrapped in black tape, hung from the dark cavities. Near the center of the room, in a pool of lamplight, Facher had assembled three large tables to form a desk on which more paper—depositions, briefs, motions, affidavits—had accumulated. Piles of legal memoranda had taken root on a sagging, threadbare, mustard-yellow couch, a piece of furniture that would never be exposed to the soft lights and thick carpets of a Hale and Dorr reception room.

Facher would sit amid these files in his shirtsleeves, the breast pocket stained by a leaky pen, his collar and cuffs frayed. He looked like an aging clerk caught in the backwater of a large bureaucracy, yet one hour of his time would cost a client several hundred dollars and he earned more than he could ever spend.

He was a very frugal man. His partners had seen him bring a plastic bag to the firm's Friday lunch buffet and stuff it with leftovers to take home and freeze. He hated going out to restaurants, even if someone else was paying. He usually ate at his desk, from little napkin-wrapped bundles of celery and cauliflower or stale pieces of cake salvaged from buffets. "I hate waste," Facher liked to say. "I'm economical in my life. Some would say cheap."

Those who did not know him well tended to mistake his frugality for miserliness, but he cared little about accumulating money. When he bought his condominium in Arlington, his partners advised him to take out a mortgage so he would have at least one tax deduction. But Facher paid in cash. He viewed the interest on a mortgage as a waste.

Some senior partners had platoons of younger lawyers working on their cases. Facher, economical as ever, would assign only a junior partner and one associate to each of his cases. He did not readily trust the work of his subordinates. He was much harsher with them than with his students. In earlier years he would send what became known as "black hand" memos to those whose work especially disappointed him. "I think we made a mistake hiring you," he'd write. "Is English your first language?" On the draft of a brief, he would scrawl: "Bullshit! Who's going to believe this crap?" and "Why are you wasting my time?" Facher believed he had mellowed with age. Now he might write: "I think this is poorly written and poorly reasoned. Why don't you tear it up and start over?"

Most associates feared working with him. Yet those who survived his tutelage usually felt great affection for him. They were known around the firm as "Jerry's boys." They believed he was the best teacher in the firm, but even so, most would not choose to work with him again if they could avoid it.

The Woburn case arrived on Facher's desk in the last week of May 1982, sent to him by the assistant general counsel at Beatrice Foods in Chicago. Facher usually had thirty or forty cases in various stages of development, some of them several years old. He had lost a few trials in his career, and he had also settled many cases before trial, but he'd never seen a case that he thought he could not have won. "Every civil case can be won," he once told his Harvard class.

He had many important corporate clients, but none was larger or wealthier than Beatrice. One of Beatrice's lesser-known divisions, the John J. Riley Tannery in Woburn, was now alleged, read Facher, to have "contaminated with toxic chemicals . . . the groundwater used by plaintiffs and plaintiffs' decedents for drinking and household purposes" and to have caused the deaths of five children.

It was, on the face of it, a personal injury case, and most such cases tended to be simple matters compared with the commercial litigation that Facher was used to. Yet he saw right away that there was nothing simple about this complaint. There was a long list of plaintiffs, each purportedly suffering "an increased risk of leukemia and other cancers, liver disease, central nervous system disorders, and other unknown illnesses and disease." The burden of trying to prove such allegations—if they could be proven, which Facher seriously doubted—would be daunting, not to mention very costly.

Facher had heard about other big cases of this sort, environmental cases alleging all kinds of dreadful injury. They seemed to have come into vogue recently, but none of them had ever amounted to anything. This case didn't worry him. The complaint, however, had to be answered, and that required sending a lawyer out to Woburn to speak with John J. Riley, Beatrice's manager at the tannery. Facher gave the job to a junior partner, a former Harvard student of his named Neil Jacobs, who was known in the firm as one of Jerry's boys.

Neil Jacobs had met John J. Riley once before, while working with Facher on a minor matter, a breach of contract claim against the tannery, and he remembered the old tanner well. Riley was not the sort of man who faded easily from memory. He possessed an incendiary temper, and he was six feet tall, with an immense girth, limbs thick as tree boles, and a heavy, florid face. He had begun working at the tannery when he was seven years old, sweeping the beamhouse floor for his father, who had started the business in 1909, when twenty or more tanneries had operated in Woburn. The Riley operation was the last of them, and Riley himself was Woburn's last tanner.

In many ways that was a tribute to Riley's business acumen. He was in his mid-fifties now, a crafty, intelligent man, college-educated, and proud of what had once been the family business. He resented in particular the frequent complaints of east Woburn homeowners about odors from the tannery. He tended to regard such complaints as personal affronts. He himself had lived most his life in east Woburn, less than a mile from the tannery. He had once confronted a neighbor who had written an article about the tannery stench for the Civic Association Newsletter. Banging on the neighbor's door one evening, he had stomped uninvited into the living room, put his thick finger to his neighbor's chest and yelled that he, Riley, was a big taxpayer in the city, and by what right did the neighbor slander his business in such a manner? The neighbor, at first taken aback by the verbal tirade, finally told Riley to get out of his house.

New, more stringent environmental regulations also infuriated Riley. He made no secret of his belief that environmentalists were conspiring to drive him out of business, as all the other Woburn tanneries had been driven out. A few years back the state had ordered him to build a waste-treatment facility at a cost of a million dollars. Riley couldn't afford it. Around that time he heard from another tanner in the Midwest that Beatrice Foods was interested in acquiring a tannery because the company needed a steady supply of leather for its consumer products. Riley decided to sell the family business to Beatrice. He took no joy in this, but he stayed on as tannery manager, as Beatrice had required, at a handsome salary.

Jacobs drove out to Woburn to interview Riley. They met at the door of an old, dilapidated white frame house that served as the tannery's administrative offices. In a small, cluttered conference room, Riley told Jacobs that the lawsuit was nothing but lies. He had never dumped any chemicals on his property. He had never even used TCE. He admitted that the tannery had used tetrachloroethylene—"perc"—for a few years in the late 1960s when he had a contract to waterproof leather for U.S. Army combat boots. But Riley claimed there had been no waste solvent from that process.

Jacobs asked Riley about the fifteen acres cited in the complaint as the source of the TCE contamination. Riley explained that his father had purchased that land from the city some thirty years ago, in 1951, and had installed a production well there for the tannery. Aside from that, said Riley, the land was completely undeveloped, nothing but woods and underbrush. It was possible to walk from the tannery to the fifteen acres, but Riley preferred to drive. It took only two minutes. He and Jacobs got into a station wagon and Riley drove out of the tannery parking lot, turned left onto Salem Street, and then, fifty yards later, turned left again onto the dirt road.

Heading up the dirt road toward the fifteen acres, they passed Whitney Barrel, with its hundreds of 55-gallon drums, and the rusting hulks in the junkyard of Aberjona Auto Parts. Riley stopped to open the metal gate that had barred Schlichtmann's way, and drove onto the fifteen acres. Jacobs noticed more barrels along the side of the road, on the scrubby, hard-packed earth. These belonged to Whitney, Riley told Jacobs. The road was well traveled and clearly defined, although as Riley drove on the foliage grew more dense and tree branches slapped against the station wagon. After about a hundred yards, Riley stopped the car and Jacobs got out to take a look around. Twenty paces off the road, Jacobs noticed a large pile of debris. He walked closer, treading carefully—he was wearing a suit and a pair of good leather shoes. The pile, which later would be known as Debris Pile E, contained some rotting timber and several 55-gallon barrels in various stages of decay, one of them oozing a dark, thick material onto the ground. There were some corrugated cardboard containers with plastic linings used for packing chemicals, pieces of rusted sheet metal, several pesticide containers, and a pair of discarded gloves, a leather boot, a long-handled brush, and a collection of beer cans. The earth was darkly stained, and a sickly, nauseating chemical odor pervaded the air. A few yards further into the brush Jacobs could see another pile of debris and more barrels, overgrown with weeds and saplings.

Jacobs poked around the pile and asked Riley if he knew where the material had come from.

Once again Riley said he had never dumped anything on this land. Anyone could have driven up the dirt road and dumped debris there, he added. He knew that Jack Whitney, owner of the barrel company, used to store some large oil tanks on the land. He'd had a run-in with Whitney, told him to get his tanks off the land. Whitney did not run a clean shop, observed Riley.

When they returned to the tannery, Riley took Jacobs on a brief tour of the plant. They went through the beamhouse, where the hides were soaked in water, limed, and dehaired, and the tan house, where the skins were pickled in tanning liquors and fats and then dyed. Behind the tannery building, Jacobs saw a settling basin containing a thick, malodorous sludge, the waste product from the tanning process. Each day the tannery produced half a million gallons of wastewater that was pumped into the basin. When the solids had settled to the bottom, the liquid was flushed down the sewer and ultimately discharged into

Boston Harbor. The tannery had been identified by the state as the second largest polluter of the harbor, and the harbor was the most polluted in the nation. It was for this reason that the state had ordered Riley to build a million-dollar waste-treatment facility, and that, in turn, had led Riley to sell the tannery to Beatrice Foods.

The waste-treatment facility still had not been built, but that had nothing to do with this lawsuit or the TCE in wells G and H. As far as Jacobs was concerned, the fifteen acres had been contaminated by third parties—by Whitney, perhaps by Aberjona Auto, and by others unknown.

Back in Boston, Jacobs began working on the reply to the plaintiff's complaint. It was not hard labor, since most of the responses required only standard, time-tested language: "Defendant Beatrice Foods Co. lacks knowledge or information sufficient to form a belief as to the truth of the allegations contained in Paragraph 45 of the Complaint." Jacobs wrote that response sixty-five times, altering only the paragraph number.

Paragraph 53 of the complaint asserted that the fifteen acres "consists of wooded field and marshlands. There is a well defined dirt road located next to the marshland along which is [sic] deposited numerous tanks and drums. The drums are in various conditions: new and rusted, open and closed. Drums have also been deposited near the railroad tracks. There are some areas of distressed vegetation, indicating spills of hazardous materials."

In response, Jacobs wrote: "Defendant Beatrice Foods Co. admits that the land consists, in part, of wooded fields and marshlands and has a dirt road through a portion of it. Defendant Beatrice Foods Co. denies the remaining allegations contained in Paragraph 53 of the complaint."

Although Jacobs had seen the barrels with his own eyes, he was not about to make such an admission on behalf of his client. Among defense lawyers, this, too, was part of the time-tested tradition of the law. The burden of proving each and every allegation rested upon the plaintiff, upon Schlichtmann and Roisman.

When Jacobs finished a draft of the reply, he brought it to Facher, who read it quickly and gave his approval. Facher was preparing a big commercial case for trial and he had more pressing matters on his mind.

2

The other defendant in the case, W. R. Grace, was represented by a lawyer named William Cheeseman, a senior partner at the Boston firm of Foley, Hoag & Eliot. Unlike Facher, Cheeseman immediately regarded this lawsuit as a very serious matter. In part, that had to do with Cheeseman's client. On the day Cheeseman learned of the lawsuit, a Grace executive had told him, "This case will have the attention of the company from top to bottom." On the next day, W. R. Grace's corporate headquarters in New York issued a press release "strongly" denying the "irresponsible and unjustified" allegations in the complaint. The company's Woburn plant, said the release, did not make chemicals and therefore "could not have caused the water contamination problem."

This was not the first time W. R. Grace had been accused of polluting the environment. The corporate empire included chemical and manufacturing plants in two dozen states as well as in Europe, South America, New Zealand, and Japan. Cheeseman himself already represented Grace in another matter, one that bore a striking similarity to Woburn—a Grace chemical factory had been sued by the town of Acton, Massachusetts, for polluting its groundwater. But no one in Acton was claiming that Grace had killed five children and poisoned an entire neighborhood. It was those allegations, and the headlines they had created, that made the Woburn case an especially frightening specter to a company like Grace. Cheeseman understood that he should spare no effort to stop this case in its tracks.

He was well suited for that task. He specialized in pretrial maneuvering. He had a reputation at his firm for finding clever ways to kill lawsuits in their infancy, with motions of demurrer or summary judgment. He'd already filed a partial summary judgment in the Acton suit. Jury trials and personal injury cases almost never entered his life. Usually he represented one large company that was suing another, or was being sued by the government, in disputes that were complicated but dry and bloodless and almost invariably settled out of court. In his entire career, Cheeseman himself had tried only four small cases to a jury. He did not like jury trial work, and he recognized that he was not particularly good at it.

He had a vivid memory of watching a jury trial for the first time, fifteen years ago when he was a law student at Harvard. He had sat in the gallery of a Boston courtroom listening to a lawyer ask his client, a young woman, to describe the details of an accident in which a child had been killed. The woman had been holding the child, her sister, in her arms when a bus collided with the car in which she'd been riding. As the woman recalled the event on the witness stand, she broke into sobs. Her lawyer, an older man of obvious experience, stood next to the jury box, one eye on the jurors, while his client wept. When the woman recovered her composure, the lawyer gently asked another question. More weeping followed. Cheeseman saw one of the jurors take a Kleenex out of her pocketbook and dab her eyes. And Cheeseman, too, had felt moved.

When court recessed for the day, Cheeseman walked into the hallway and stood waiting for an elevator. A few minutes later the lawyer emerged from the courtroom with the young woman and her family. They were in high spirits, talking excitedly among themselves. The lawyer said something to the woman, and Cheeseman saw her laugh.

He was appalled. At that moment he believed that the entire courtroom performance had been a cynical charade. Later he realized that wasn't wholly true. The woman *had* suffered a terrible loss, and perhaps her laughter in the hallway had been simply a release of tension. But the experience had left Cheeseman disdainful of the tactics of personal injury lawyers and leery of juries. "Everyone understands that the deck is stacked," Cheeseman observed many years later. "Somebody who's been hurt has the sympathy of the jury. Big companies don't get that sympathy."

Jury trials are the rarest form of business at large corporate law firms, and they were especially rare at Foley, Hoag & Eliot, which employed a hundred lawyers but had only a few experienced trial lawyers. Cheeseman's firm took great pride in its reputation as an "intellectual" law firm. Most of its recruits came, as Cheeseman did, from Harvard, and most of them had been on the *Law Review.* "Scholarship has always been a hallmark of the firm's reputation," stated a Foley promotional brochure. "Scholarship" sometimes meant long and tediously researched briefs. Among the Boston bar, the firm was famous ("maybe infamous," Cheeseman admitted) for the length of its briefs.

Cheeseman had a rigorous, logical cast of mind. As an undergraduate at Harvard College, he'd studied mathematical physics. He knew he was smart, but in his most self-critical moments he saw himself as methodical and dull. His remedy for this perceived flaw was itself methodical. "I work hard to cultivate a little flakiness in myself," he once confessed. He cultivated various small eccentricities. Over time, he acquired a collection of hats—berets, tams, Greek fisherman caps, fedoras—which he wore to work, along with a bulky sheepskin coat instead of the cashmere overcoat that seemed part of the legal dress code. He wore his suits, bought off the rack, until the crease in the trousers disappeared and new creases laced the back of his suit coat. He let his hair grow so long and shaggy that even his eight-year-old daughter once told him he needed a haircut. He drove to work in a small English sports car, a Triumph, which he raced in Sunday-morning autocrosses in the empty parking lots of malls and supermarkets. He wanted to own a Porsche, and though he had a handsome income, he felt he could not afford one yet. He quelled his desire with a small toy model of a Porsche Carrera, which he kept on a bookshelf in his office. A psychiatrist friend once told him, "You're the loosest obsessive-compulsive I've ever met." Cheeseman remembered that remark as a compliment.

At the firm he was well liked. He was not snobbish to young lawyers who had not gone to Harvard, as some partners at the firm were. Office politics did not interest him. He tended to avoid the firm's parties and he did not hang around after hours to trade stories about clients and adversaries. In an occupation that could consume every waking hour, he set limits on what the firm could demand of him. Some young associates who toiled nights and weekends in the hope of making partner admired Cheeseman for this, although they did not often follow his example.

Cheeseman quickly learned the basic facts about Grace's Woburn plant from one of the company's in-house lawyers. The plant had been built in 1960. It employed about a hundred people in making machinery for the food-packaging industry, for vacuum-wrapping meats—turkeys, hams, hot dogs, and the like—in plastic film, which was also made by Grace at plants in Iowa, Indiana, and Texas. The Woburn plant had once used TCE in the early 1960s, but a search of the records revealed the purchase of only a single 55-gallon drum. Workers had used the solvent for hand-cleaning small metal parts. Some employees, it seemed, might have dumped small amounts of used solvent, no more than a few "teacups" at any one time, into a ditch behind the plant. But this small amount, Cheeseman was told, could not have contaminated the city wells, which were half a mile away from the plant.

A Grace executive showed Cheeseman a tape of Schlichtmann's press conference announcing the lawsuit. It began with a reporter standing in front of the Grace plant in Woburn. "Lawyers for the Woburn families," the reporter said, "allege that this W. R. Grace plant has dumped solvents and chemical wastes that have contaminated two city wells and caused the deaths of five children."

The picture faded to an interior shot of a law office. Cheeseman saw a tall, thin young man wearing a dark suit and vest, a red tie, and a gold collar pin. Behind him were shelves of leather-bound law books. "Jan Schlichtmann is one of the lawyers representing the families," said the voice of the reporter. "Mr. Schlichtmann, what do your clients hope to get out of this lawsuit?"

Schlichtmann, looking directly into the camera, said, "First of all, we want these companies to pay for the injuries they've caused these families. We want them to stop dumping their chemical wastes. And we want them to clean it up." The evidence, continued Schlichtmann, will show that W. R. Grace's plant had dumped chemical wastes on the ground for twenty years, ever since the plant had opened.

The tape ended with the reporter saying that some Woburn residents were already demanding that the city shut down the Grace plant.

Cheeseman found this fellow Schlichtmann's performance highly unprofessional. Public comment about a pending case, especially inflammatory comments about evidence, violated the Canons of Professional Ethics. A lawyer risked censure for such behavior. Schlichtmann looked young and untested, thought Cheeseman. Perhaps Schlichtmann believed he could intimidate Grace by inflaming public opinion. Perhaps he simply hoped to grab a quick settlement.

Back at his office, Cheeseman began making inquiries. None of his colleagues at Foley, Hoag & Eliot had heard of Schlichtmann. In itself, that was not surprising since Cheeseman's firm rarely descended to the level of personal injury law. In Martindale-Hubble, the national law directory, Cheeseman found that Schlichtmann was thirty-one years old, had gone to Cornell Law School, and had passed the bar exam barely four years ago. "He's as green as he looks," Cheeseman told one of his partners.

Cheeseman hoped to teach this young lawyer a painful lesson about dealing with companies like W. R. Grace. He decided first to remove the case from the state Superior Court to the federal court. W. R. Grace, with headquarters in New York and operations across the entire country, was entitled to federal jurisdiction. And the federal courts, Cheeseman believed, had a generally higher caliber of judges whose tolerance for personal injury cases of questionable merit was correspondingly lower.

Then Cheeseman wrote a letter advising Schlichtmann and Roisman to withdraw the lawsuit. "If you do not withdraw this action," Cheeseman warned, "please be informed that we will take appropriate steps to seek a prompt dismissal of the action, and we will seek an award of attorneys' fees and expenses against you and your associates."

Cheeseman never got a response to his letter. Throughout the summer and into the fall, he heard nothing more about the Woburn case. He was feeling circumspectly pleased. He began to think maybe Schlichtmann had abandoned the case. Cheeseman had known that to happen before—a plaintiff's lawyer hastily files a complaint in order to make the statute of limitations and only later begins to think better of his chances. Or perhaps the letter had scared Schlichtmann off.

It wasn't until one morning in October that Cheeseman learned the case hadn't gone away after all. He received from Schlichtmann a lengthy set of interrogatories, fifty-two pages of written questions to be answered under oath, concerning every aspect of the history and operations of the Woburn plant. Cheeseman was required, as all lawyers are, to answer the interrogatories within thirty days. But Cheeseman had no intention of doing that. Instead, he began preparing his next move, one he'd been thinking about since last spring.

It was a bold and creative stroke, exactly the sort of thing that had given Cheeseman his reputation for getting rid of difficult lawsuits. Among the many dozen rules of Civil Procedure was a little-known and rarely used provision—Rule 11—that had been conceived half a century ago, in 1938. The rule had been intended to curb frivolous and irresponsible lawsuits, but it was so weakly worded and easy to circumvent that few lawyers ever wasted their time invoking it. Cheeseman had heard, however, that the Senate Judicial Conference was revising the rule to make it much stronger. Among other things, the proposed revisions would lay out harsh punishments—large fines, public reprimands, and even suspension—for lawyers who filed "sham and false" claims. The new Rule 11 had not been enacted yet, but that didn't trouble Cheeseman. It had given him the idea, and as far as he was concerned, even the weak standard of the old Rule 11 applied to this case.

"It is certainly true that Rule 11 proceedings are, and should be, rare and serious matters," wrote Cheeseman in his motion to dismiss the case. And then he proceeded to enumerate his reasons for invoking the rule. Most compelling of all was an article he'd found in the *Providence Journal* two weeks after the case had been filed. The article quoted Roisman's research assistant as saying that there was "no firm proof of a connection between the families, the chemicals found in their wells, and the two companies. 'It's kind of a common-sense link,' " the assistant reportedly said. " 'It's a fairly safe assumption that there is some kind of link.' "

Cheeseman planned to use this statement—it was an admission, pure and simple, that the lawyers for the Woburn families had no grounds for the allegations—as the centerpiece of his Rule 11 motion. He would buttress it by showing that there was nothing in the medical or scientific literature to suggest that TCE or perc could cause leukemia. Furthermore, both the Environmental Protection Agency and the Centers for Disease Control had clearly stated in their reports that "the contaminants found in Wells G and H are not known to cause leukemia."

And finally, the EPA had never identified the Grace plant as a source of contamination. The agency had said that more research was necessary to find those responsible. If the EPA could not implicate Grace, then how could Schlichtmann and Roisman? To Cheeseman, it seemed obvious that his client had been selected because it was a six-billion-dollar corporation whose name was associated with the chemical industry.

As he worked on the Rule 11 motion, Cheeseman decided to call Neil Jacobs at Hale and Dorr to inform him of his plans. It made sense to Cheeseman that Grace and Beatrice, co-defendants in the case, should work together whenever possible. Last summer, Cheeseman had spoken with Jacobs about removing the lawsuit to federal court. Jacobs had readily agreed to that, and now Cheeseman hoped that Jacobs and Facher would also join the Rule 11 motion. Facher's name and stature, thought Cheeseman, would lend the motion even greater weight.

Over the phone, Jacobs sounded intrigued by Rule 11. He told Cheeseman he would discuss the idea with Facher and call him back.

3

Not all of the leukemia victims in Woburn were children. There was, for instance, Roland Gamache. He lived with his wife, Kathryn, and their two young children in the Pine Street neighborhood, one house away from the Zonas, a few blocks from Anne Anderson. In the summer of 1980, in his thirty-fifth year, Roland had gotten a small cut on his ankle while water-skiing at his summer home in New Hampshire. The wound bled for several hours. It was an annoyance, but it did not seem serious. A week later, back home in Woburn, he went to the dentist to have his teeth cleaned. The next morning he awoke and found blood in his mouth and on his pillow. After many tests at the New England Medical Center, doctors confirmed a diagnosis of chronic myelogenous leukemia.

The Gamaches, of course, had read in the newspapers about the east Woburn leukemia cluster. They knew that one of the Zona boys had died of leukemia. They also knew Patrick Toomey—he was an altar boy at their church. And their daughter, Amy, was in the same class at school as Kevin Kane. After Roland's diagnosis, Kathryn asked his doctor if he could have gotten leukemia from the Woburn water. The doctor said she didn't know. No one knew what caused leukemia.

In the two years since his diagnosis, Roland had felt fine. He was not on chemotherapy, and at times it was hard for him to believe that he had a fatal illness. His disease, however, was grave. In reply to Roland's blunt question, his doctor told him he could probably expect to live only five to eight more years. Roland buried himself in work at the family-owned business, Severance Trucking, which was prospering.

The firm now had fifty vehicles and eighty employees. He hoped to live long enough to see his two children graduate from high school and go on to college.

The early meetings at Trinity Episcopal Church had occurred before Roland's diagnosis. He knew nothing about the plans for a lawsuit until his neighbor, Joan Zona, knocked on his door one evening in April 1982, a month before Schlichtmann would file the complaint. She asked Roland if he would join the other families in the case. The lawyers, she told him, wanted to enlist as many Woburn leukemia victims as they could find. Roland said he would think about it. He and Kathryn talked it over, and they decided that if the lawsuit would stop big companies from polluting the environment, they should support it. Moreover, they had learned that TCE can cause skin rashes, and both their children had experienced chronic rashes during the years the wells had been opened. Roland didn't want his children exposed to any more toxic chemicals, and that seemed like the best reason to join the lawsuit.

Roland and Kathryn went in to Boston to meet with Schlichtmann. They spent an entire day answering questions about themselves, signed all the necessary papers, and after that they gave the lawsuit little thought.

Some months later, in the fall of 1982, Roland was making plans to take his eight-year-old son and two other boys to a Bruins hockey game. He had two season tickets to the Bruins, and he needed two additional tickets for the outing. As it happened, the Riley tannery had a pair of season tickets adjacent to his own. Roland decided to call on Jack Riley and propose a trade—two Celtics basketball tickets for the hockey tickets. He had never met Riley before, and he did not realize that he and Riley were now antagonists at law.   •

When Roland phoned the tannery that afternoon, a secretary told him that Riley was out but she expected him back shortly, and she offered to take a message.

Riley saw the message from Roland Gamache on his desk when he returned from lunch. He recognized the name immediately— Gamache was one of the plaintiffs in the lawsuit. He found it incredible that Gamache would call him about hockey tickets when he was suing him. "Tell him to come over," Riley said to his secretary. "I want to talk with him."

Gamache arrived at the tannery late that afternoon. He extended his hand to Riley and smiled pleasantly at him. He explained the trade he wanted to make.

"I'm not a basketball fan," said Riley coldly.

Gamache, taken aback by Riley's demeanor, began to rise from his chair. "Well," he began, "in that case . . ."

"I'm not a fan," continued Riley, "but I'm sure somebody here is. Tell me this: Why are you asking me to trade tickets when you're suing me?"

"Suing you?" said Gamache.

"Yeah." Riley looked intently at Gamache. "Don't you have leukemia?"

"Yes," said Gamache, surprised that Riley would know.

"Well, what are you suing me for?"

"I don't know what you're talking about."

"You're one of the plaintiffs who is suing the John J. Riley Company, division of Beatrice Foods."

Gamache was shocked. For a moment, he could think of nothing to say. He shifted uncomfortably in the chair. "Look," he said to Riley, "I'm sorry, but maybe I should leave. I didn't realize your tannery was part of the lawsuit. The lawyers were looking for people to join the case. All we want to do is stop the big chemical companies from dumping."

"Look, Roland, I was born and brought up in this town," said Riley. "I've been chairman of the school committee, on the planning board, on the board of a local bank. That goddamn land is my life, my blood, because that's where I get my water. If you think I'm dumping toxic chemicals there, you're crazy. You dump more when you change the oil in your car than I've dumped in a whole lifetime. I never dumped anything, and neither did Beatrice Foods. To accuse me and my company of giving people leukemia—I don't like it one goddamn bit."

Gamache was shaken by this outburst. Once again, he got up to leave, but Riley had not stopped talking. He was telling Gamache, his tone calmer now, that he had a case of leukemia in his own family, his sister's boy who lived in Rhode Island. "And I'm not being fresh, but he never drank a drop of Woburn water. I'm well aware of the emotional problems caused by this sort of thing."

"My biggest fear," replied Gamache, "is that the city is going to reopen those wells. I never want my children exposed to that water again. That's the reason I joined the lawsuit."

"Those goddamn wells should never have been used in the first place," said Riley. "That's what Denny Maher, the guy who drilled them for the city, told me. The water's only good for industrial purposes. I run a good clean operation, which is the reason I'm the only tannery left in the city."

Then Riley handed the hockey tickets to Gamache. "You take these tickets. Someday I'll call you for the Celtics tickets."

After Gamache departed, Riley called Neil Jacobs to tell him about the incident. "The guy didn't even know who he's suing," said Riley. "He said he did it because the lawyer got him into it."

To Jacobs, this sounded like evidence that Schlichtmann had actively solicited people to join the lawsuit. Jacobs wondered if a charge of barratry—"the groundless stirring up of lawsuits"—could be made against Schlichtmann. The crime of barratry had an archaic ring and it was rarely invoked nowadays, although early in the century it had been used frequently against personal injury lawyers, then a new breed widely despised by the established bar. All the same, Jacobs thought that Gamache's own words, as reported by Riley, seemed like an apt description of barratry.

Jacobs mentioned this to Facher, but Facher dismissed it with a wave of his hand. Jacobs also told Facher about Cheeseman's plan to file a Rule 11 motion. Facher dismissed that gambit, too. It had little chance of success, he told Jacobs. "I'm a great believer in doing things once," Facher liked to say. "If you're going to knock a guy down, do it so he can't get up again."

Jacobs called Cheeseman to tell him that Facher had decided not to participate in the Rule 11 motion. But there was another matter, continued Jacobs, that Cheeseman might find worth pursuing. Jacobs described the meeting between Riley and Roland Gamache. As long as Cheeseman was thinking about Rule 11, said Jacobs, he might also consider a charge of barratry.

Cheeseman liked the idea. He was disappointed that Facher would not join the Rule 11 motion, but he himself intended to use every weapon he could find against Schlichtmann. And barratry seemed to fit in perfectly with the Rule 11 charge of filing a groundless lawsuit.

Cheeseman added a new paragraph, under the heading "Barratry," to his Rule 11 motion. "We have highly specific and direct evidence to support this charge," he wrote, "but at this time, it is based on a privileged communication from counsel for W. R. Grace's co-defendant." Since the information was, in theory, protected by the attorney-client privilege between Jacobs and Riley, Cheeseman could not reveal it to Schlichtmann. To make the charge stick, however, he would have to reveal it to the District Court judge. "If the Court will entertain an *in camera* affidavit regarding the communication," wrote Cheeseman, "W. R. Grace will submit it for examination by the Court."

Along with the out-of-court statements to the press ("the opening day publicity effort," Cheeseman called it in his brief), Schlichtmann and Roisman had filed a groundless lawsuit and engaged in solicitation of clients, all violations of the Canons of Professional Ethics. Such behavior should anger any judge, thought Cheeseman. The Board of Bar Overseers might even decide to conduct disciplinary hearings. Schlichtmann could be publicly chastised and fined for his actions.

4

When Cheeseman removed the Woburn case from state court to the U.S. District Court, the file went to the office of the civil clerk on the fourteenth floor of the John W. McCormack federal building in downtown Boston. The Woburn case was one of 4,811 civil actions filed in the U.S. District Court in Boston that year. The in-take clerk assigned each new case to one of the court's nine trial judges by means of a lottery, a system devised to prevent lawyers from shopping for a judge they believed sympathetic to them or their case.

For the Woburn case, the clerk took a small sealed manila envelope containing the name of one of the nine judges from the top of the tort category. He ripped it open and shook out a slip of paper with the name "Skinner, W. J." typed on it.

At that time Judge Walter Jay Skinner had a backlog of more than five hundred cases. Each month, the lottery piled twenty to thirty new cases on top of that backlog. The vast majority of these cases would settle before trial, but they usually settled only after Judge Skinner had met with the lawyers in a pretrial conference and threatened an early trial date. The judge worked long hours to reduce his backlog. He was another graduate of Harvard Law School, fifty-six years old, his hair turning white, his blue eyes pale and watery behind horn-rimmed glasses. In his chambers he was a man of great rectitude and decorum. He referred to his wife as "Mrs. Skinner," and when a law clerk once called her "Sylvia," he gave the clerk a withering stare. Among the Boston trial bar, he was known as a hardworking and fair jurist, but one who could also be short-tempered and curt. "Pull up your socks and try the case," he'd warn lawyers. "I'm not going to hold up this trial while your minions labor in some library." He had once sentenced two lawyers to a seminar on trial practice for filing poorly researched and groundless motions. He would slap his hand with a resounding thwack on his bench and say in a menacing voice, "Now, that's the end of it! Life is short."

He was an avid tennis player, and when time permitted he liked to walk up the fifteen flights of stairs to his office for the cardiovascular benefit. He might have had a tall, imperious bearing were it not for a singular deformity—he had a humped back. The year he graduated from Harvard College, in 1948, he had his spine fused because of a painful disk abnormality. Ever since, he'd walked with his knees bent, his back bowed deeply forward at the waist, his head craned upward to see where he was going, like a man carrying a heavy but invisible load.

He was too busy to keep apprised of each new case assigned to him, but the Woburn case was a different matter altogether. He'd read the newspaper accounts of the Woburn leukemia cluster, he'd read about Schlichtmann filing the case, and he'd even seen Schlichtmann on the evening news. He thought Schlichtmann had skirted the bounds of legal ethics with his out-of-court statements, but that, the judge believed, was a matter for the Board of Bar Overseers to consider. He remembered Schlichtmann—tall, angular, earnest—from an encounter three years ago in his courtroom. He had rather liked Schlichtmann then. Certainly he had approved of Schlichtmann's case. Schlichtmann had represented the Clamshell Alliance, a group that wanted to protest the delivery of a nuclear reactor core to the Seabrook power plant. The protesters had planned to stage a march through the town of Salisbury; they'd gone to the board of selectmen to request a parade permit. Such permits had been routinely granted to other groups—veterans and

Columbus Day marchers—but the chief of police had denied the Clamshell's request. Skinner recalled that he had ruled swiftly in favor of Schlichtmann's clients and soundly reprimanded the police chief for violating the protesters' constitutional rights. Then Schlichtmann had demanded that the town of Salisbury pay his fee.

Judge Skinner had balked at this. "I think your clients ought to take this ruling and run," he'd told Schlichtmann.

"That's what I'm afraid of, Your Honor, and I'll be left holding the bag," Schlichtmann had replied.

Skinner had smiled. "What's your fee?"

"Sixty dollars an hour."

Skinner looked at the town counsel. "I have just one question for you. Is Mr. Schlichtmann worth sixty dollars an hour?"

"I guess so," the lawyer for the town had replied.

"Then pay him," Skinner had ordered.

Judge Skinner read Cheeseman's Rule 11 motion with great interest when it arrived in his chambers in mid-November. In his nine years on the federal bench, no lawyer had ever brought a Rule 11 motion in his courtroom, nor did he know of any other judge in the First Circuit who had heard such a motion. Skinner felt that there were a lot of worthless cases—"junk," he once called them—clogging the federal docket and contributing to his own immense caseload. He knew about the proposed revisions to the rule, and he thought them an excellent idea. In his opinion, lawyers should be encouraged to use Rule 11 much more often.

The rule was unusual in that it seemed to require the lawyer who had filed the complaint to take the witness stand and undergo cross-examination by his accuser. Such an occurrence was, like a Rule 11 hearing itself, exceedingly rare. A lawyer's job is to argue his client's cause, not to act as a witness whose very testimony could, perhaps, result in his client's case being stricken. But Skinner believed the rule called for Schlichtmann to take the witness stand and answer Cheeseman's questions. That, he decided, was how he intended to conduct this hearing.

Accompanying the Rule 11 motion was a lengthy memorandum from Cheeseman. In Skinner's experience, Foley, Hoag & Eliot always filed long briefs. It was a hallmark of the firm, and it had irked Skinner before. He was busy with other cases, and he did not read Cheeseman's memorandum thoroughly. He failed to notice on page nine the single paragraph entitled "Barratry."

The judge asked his clerk to schedule a hearing on the Rule 11 motion. The clerk found an opening in Skinner's busy trial calendar on Thursday, January 6, at two-fifteen in the afternoon. The clerk notified Cheeseman and Schlichtmann to appear in the judge's court at that time, prepared for an evidentiary hearing with oral argument and witnesses.

5

Schlichtmann telephoned Cheeseman the morning he received the Rule 11 motion. It was their first conversation. "These charges are ridiculous and you know it," he told Cheeseman. "This thing about barratry, it's outrageous for you to attack me personally."

"No more outrageous than the allegations you've made against my client," said Cheeseman.

"I want you to drop these charges so we can deal with the issues in this case," said Schlichtmann.

"Dismiss the lawsuit and I'll drop the charges."

"You know I can't do that," said Schlichtmann.

"Then my client intends to bring whatever charges it thinks are appropriate."

The cool, deliberate tone of Cheeseman's voice infuriated Schlichtmann. "Listen, you bastard, drop this thing now."

"No," said Cheeseman.

Schlichtmann slammed the phone down. He was breathing hard, his face flushed, so angry that his hands shook. Conway had never seen him in such a state. "This guy is an asshole," Schlichtmann shouted. "If the judge believes him, I could be charged with unprofessional conduct. I could be disbarred."

Roisman flew up from Washington to discuss strategy for the hearing. Judge Skinner had made it clear in his order that a Rule 11 hearing would require Roisman or Schlichtmann, or perhaps both, to take the witness stand and be cross-examined by Cheeseman. Roisman believed they had no choice but to comply with the judge. Schlichtmann said he would refuse.

"What if the judge makes you?" asked Conway.

"I won't go," said Schlichtmann. "It's wrong. I'm an advocate for my clients. He can't make me testify against them."

"He'll cite you for contempt," said Conway.

"I don't care. I won't go on the witness stand."

"Jan, he could throw you in jail," said Conway. "You know what the Charles Street jail is like?" Conway imagined Schlichtmann, in his polished Bally shoes, his red Hermès tie, his thousand-dollar suit, sitting in a Charles Street holding pen surrounded by drunks, thieves, and drug addicts. "You better bring your toothbrush on January sixth," Conway said.

It was Conway who came up with the idea of turning the barratry charge against Cheeseman. "It's based on an *in camera* affidavit, a secret charge. The judge isn't going to like it. I think he'll be outraged by it. What if you make that the issue? Maybe it'll get him angry at Cheeseman."

Schlichtmann thought the idea had possibilities. If he could get the judge angry at Cheeseman at the start of the hearing, perhaps Skinner would regard the Rule 11 motion more skeptically. Schlichtmann decided that the moment he entered the courtroom he'd start talking and he wouldn't sit until he had turned the judge's attention to the barratry charge and away from Rule 11. Whether he would succeed was another matter. Judge Skinner, he knew, liked to keep a tight control of proceedings in his court.

They decided to pack the entire case file—all the EPA reports, the leukemia study by the Centers for Disease Control, toxicology reports on the chemicals, newspaper clippings, every bit of data and piece of paper generated about the Wells G and H—and lug it all to court. They would pile it on the counsel table, in front of Judge Skinner's bench, as evidence of how much information they had to support the complaint. They loaded the files into three large cardboard boxes and placed those on a wheeled cart. Even in its infancy, the case had grown to an impressive size.

Conway looked at the baggage with a appraising eye. "Jan, don't forget your toothbrush," he said.

6

Thursday afternoon, January 6, 1983, was a gray, overcast day, the smell of snow heavy in the air. Out of the offices of Reed & Mulligan came a procession of lawyers—Schlichtmann in the lead, flanked by Roisman and Conway, followed by Reed and Mulligan and half a dozen others, friends who were coming to lend moral support. Word of the unusual hearing had traveled quickly among the Boston personal injury bar. The group marched up Tremont Street, past the black wrought-iron fence of the Old Granary Burying Ground, where the earthly remains of Paul Revere lie, and turned down Milk Street toward the federal courthouse.

The U.S. District Court for the District of Massachusetts is situated in the John W. McCormack federal building, twenty-two stories tall, built in the 1930s of granite and black marble. The building occupies an entire city block, a dark, massive structure of towering stone piers and tall, narrow windows. Heavy bronze grillework covers the lower windows and doors, and above the arched entryways carved stone spandrels depict battle-axes and eagles. In the crenellated battlements high above, peregrine falcons live and prey on the pigeons that feed in Post Office Square.

Under the cold winter sky the building looked foreboding to Schlichtmann. His brow was moist with sweat and his palms were damp. He had not slept well last night. He'd lain awake for a long time, thinking about disciplinary hearings, public censure, disbarment. He regretted ever getting involved in this case. When he arrived on the fifteenth floor, where courtroom No. 7, Judge Skinner's court, was located, he stopped first at the men's room. He washed his hands and splashed water on his face, stared for a moment out the window, trying to compose himself.

He entered the courtroom through a pair of tall leather-padded doors. The room was large, with high, vaulted ceilings, black polished marble wainscoting, and fluted columns along the walls. A pale winter light entered the room from a row of windows behind the jury box. Under the windows, old radiators hissed softly, emitting a stale, faintly steamy odor. From above the judge's black marble bench peered a large bronze eagle in bas-relief, its talons clutching arrows. The room was divided in half by a thick wooden railing, the long rows of the spectators' gallery on one side, the counsel tables, jury box, and judge's bench on the other. To the right of the judge's bench, directly across the room from the jury box, was the raised platform of the witness stand. It consisted of a narrow desk made of dark, polished wood, behind which was a heavy leather-upholstered chair.

Courtrooms were familiar places to Schlichtmann. He never entered one without feeling a sense of anticipation, a pleasing surge of energy and nervous excitement. But he'd never before seen a courtroom from the perspective of the accused. He might at this moment have been in handcuffs. The cavernous, stolid old courtroom looked gloomy, and the witness stand, where the judge would have him sit today, seemed menacing.

Schlichtmann went with Roisman and Conway to the long wooden table directly below the judge's bench, the counsel table usually reserved for the plaintiffs. The rest of his retinue, the friends lending moral support, sat in the front pew of the spectators' gallery. Two other groups of lawyers, seven or eight in all, entered the courtroom. Schlichtmann recognized none of them. A tall man, perhaps forty years old, in need of a haircut, wearing a sheepskin coat and a leather cap with a narrow brim, took a seat at one counsel table. Schlichtmann heard this man speak to a woman dressed in a dark suit who was seated next to him. He recognized the voice and knew that this was Cheeseman. To Cheeseman's left, at the third counsel table, sat two men, one who appeared to be about sixty, the other one younger, near Schlichtmann's age. The older man wore a cheap gray suit that looked as if it was made of polyester. The younger man was short and stocky with a mustache and glasses, and a round, moonlike face. Schlichtmann did not know their names, but he surmised that they must be counsel for Beatrice Foods.

The door to the right of the judge's bench opened and Judge Skinner appeared, black robe draped over his bent form.

"All rise," said the clerk. "This court is now in session. Civil Action 82-1672, Anderson et al. versus W. R. Grace, et al."

Judge Skinner studied the gathering of lawyers with a look of mild surprise. "This is the only case?" he said to his clerk. "There are a lot of lawyers." He saw Facher sitting at a counsel table. He'd known Facher for thirty years, since law school, and Facher had tried several cases in his court before. "Mr. Facher, do you have an interest in this case?"

"I am a co-defendant, so I guess I do have an interest," said Facher. "But it's not my motion," he added.

"All right," said the judge. "It's Foley, Hoag's motion, I guess. There's been a lot of publicity about this case. I consider that to be a disciplinary question that must be raised—if it is raised—with the Board of Bar Overseers and not in connection with the trial." The judge paused. "The remaining question is Rule 11."

Schlichtmann had remained standing. He did not know if Judge Skinner remembered him. "Your Honor, if I might, my name is Jan Schlichtmann."

"I know," said the judge.

"Your Honor," continued Schlichtmann, "this is a very unusual procedure for me."

"For me, too," replied the judge. "I'm taking quite an interest in Rule 11. I think it's been woefully ignored in the history of the federal rules, and that has probably caused the dockets of this and other federal courts to be clogged with a good deal of garbage over the years."

Schlichtmann took a deep breath. "I'd like to bring to Your Honor's attention an important matter. Under the heading of 'Barratry,' Mr. Cheeseman states that he has 'highly specific and direct evidence' to support the charge that we have engaged in the solicitation of clients, which is a violation of the disciplinary rules and could subject us to disbarment if proven. He says it's based on privileged communication from Hale and Dorr, counsel for the co-defendant in this case. They have information which they have supplied to Mr. Cheeseman concerning my improper conduct."

Judge Skinner looked mystified. He thought he was hearing the Rule 11 motion, not a charge of barratry. "Barratry?" the judge said. "It's a privileged communication from counsel for whom?"

"From Hale and Dorr, counsel for Beatrice Foods, which owns the John J. Riley Tannery," said Schlichtmann.

The judge looked at Cheeseman. "Where's the privilege supposed to be?"

Cheeseman stood to explain. "There was a communication from Beatrice Foods' client to their attorney, which was then communicated to me."

"Well, then," said the judge, "the confidentiality of that is destroyed, isn't it?"

"I think not," said Cheeseman.

"Why not?"

"Because we're engaged jointly in the defense of an action. My understanding of the rules—"

Judge Skinner waved his hand impatiently. "If you think you are going to give me secret stuff against this attorney"—Skinner pointed to Schlichtmann—"without giving him a chance to respond in open court, you are not. I'm going to send your motion packing. If you have a basis for this charge, you better reveal it. If you don't, forever hold your peace."

Schlichtmann started to speak. "Your Honor—"

"Wait a minute," interrupted the judge. "There's going to be enough spitting back and forth without you starting so soon." He glared at Cheeseman, awaiting his response.

"If Your Honor doesn't wish to see the affidavit," said Cheeseman, "I have no interest or desire in showing it to you at this time."

"I am not going to take an *in camera* motion on a matter that involves this attorney and his professional reputation. We'll proceed with the Rule 11 motion."

But Schlichtmann was not ready to proceed with the Rule 11 motion. "Your Honor, may I?" he said again.

Judge Skinner nodded.

"I hope you appreciate that this accusation of barratry compromises my relationship with my clients as well as with you, Your Honor, because I now appear before you under a cloud of impropriety."

"The cloud has not materialized," said the judge.

"But a lie is halfway around the world before the truth gets its boots on," replied Schlichtmann.

The judge looked amused by this piece of rehearsed wisdom.

"I ask that Hale and Dorr reveal what information it has so we can dismiss this charge and get on with the business of this lawsuit," continued Schlichtmann. "Otherwise I'll appear before Your Honor with these grave accusations of impropriety, and Your Honor has no idea whether they are true or not."

The judge sighed. "Mr. Facher, do you wish to reveal this material to Mr. Schlichtmann at this time?"

"I don't want to prolong this," said Facher, standing to address the judge. "The characterization that it's 'highly specific and direct evidence' is his characterization"—Facher indicated Cheeseman"—and not mine. We received certain communications, we said this is the information we received, here it is. We did nothing about it. I don't have any particular problem if Mr. Cheeseman wants to tell Mr. Schlichtmann, although technically, I guess, it still is privileged because it came from a client and we're engaged in a joint defense."

"I don't know about that," said Judge Skinner.

"I want the Court to know that this is not *my* characterization of the information," repeated Facher.

Schlichtmann, still standing, glanced at Cheeseman, who in turn was looking curiously at Facher.

"I make a motion to strike this material as being scandalous and immaterial," said Schlichtmann. "An allegation made by Mr. Cheeseman in an attempt to discredit me in front of this Court."

"I will not strike it," replied the judge, "but I will impound it. Who knows? Maybe it'll turn out to be correct."

"That's precisely the point, Your Honor," said Schlichtmann. "I'm in an impossible position."

"No you're not. You can consider yourself perfectly innocent until some proof has been raised. As a matter of fact, I think the whole notion of solicitation is undergoing some change, and quite properly so. Once you start talking about lawyers representing classes of disadvantaged people who, practically by definition, are not in a position to go seeking counsel, you have some element of solicitation. I'm inclined to think it's a good thing."

"Hale and Dorr said they would not characterize it—"

"Look, Mr. Schlichtmann," interrupted the judge, "I understand you're in a terrible state of concern. There's nothing I can do about it this afternoon but impound this document."

"I think Mr. Flasher"—Schlichtmann had not heard Facher's name correctly, and now he mispronounced it—"has an obligation to me. I ask that he give this information to the Court." Schlichtmann knew by the judge's reaction—a barely perceptible widening of the eyes, a slight compression of the lips—that he had gotten Facher's name wrong. From the counsel table behind him, he heard a muffled snort. He felt as if he had committed an indiscretion, a social gaffe; his ignorance of Facher's name and stature marked him as an outsider.

"I can't put the thumbscrews to Mr. Facher, can I?" said Judge Skinner. He seemed to articulate Facher's name with elaborate clarity.

"I'll be glad to inquire of my client," offered Facher.

"Do you want to go out and get on the phone right now?" asked the judge.

Facher had not meant to make the inquiry at this very moment, but he shrugged his assent and slowly departed the courtroom. There was a pay telephone in the corridor, right outside the courtroom door.

"Meanwhile," said the judge, "let's get back to the Rule 11 motion." Schlichtmann slowly sat.

"The matter before us seems to be a very simple one. The question is: What did you have before you when you drew up this complaint? And the best way to find that out is for Mr. Cheeseman to ask you. If you had a basis to file a lawsuit, that's the end of it. If you filed the thing without making some kind of investigation, then I'll strike the complaint."

Schlichtmann was on his feet again. "It would be, I believe, unseemly for a plaintiff's attorney to take the witness stand and answer questions by the defendant's attorney," he said. "I almost feel it would be necessary for us to have our own attorneys. I'm willing to provide the Court with detailed affidavits."

"No. I'm not going to decide the case on affidavits. Let there be cross-examination. The allegation, as I understand it, is that you charged W. R. Grace with running a chemical operation in Woburn, and what they actually have out there is a machine shop."

The judge had gotten this wrong, no doubt from reading Cheeseman's motion, which had made exactly that assertion. "It is not a chemical operation," agreed Schlichtmann. "It is a machine shop, but they do use various chemicals and solvents."

"Don't try the case here," said the judge, annoyed. "The motion is Mr. Cheeseman's and the floor, properly at this point, is his. I'm going to permit him to inquire of you."

"Your Honor," continued Schlichtmann, "we've provided affidavits about our investigation, the hours spent, the public documents we used, the experts we consulted. We came to the conclusion that we had good faith and good reason to believe that W. R. Grace used these chemicals and that these chemicals entered the groundwater and contaminated it, resulting in injury to the plaintiffs."

"Okay," said Judge Skinner. "Now Mr. Cheeseman is entitled to cross-examine you."

Cheeseman stood, legal pad in hand, ready to call Schlichtmann to the witness stand.

But Schlichtmann would not stop talking. "When I take the witness stand, I cease being an attorney for my clients. I become a witness in this case subject to all the rules of examination. I can no longer be a professional, objective advocate for my clients."

"The inquiry is going to be limited, Mr. Schlichtmann. I have no doubt that this is the way to proceed."

"Your Honor, I cannot take the stand without withdrawing as counsel in this case."

"No," said the judge, "I don't think that is right."

"I'm under ethical considerations not to be a witness in a case against my client, Your Honor. What I say on the witness stand will determine whether my client's complaint is stricken and the case thrown out of court."

"That's right," said Skinner.

"Is it not unseemly for an attorney—"

"Look," said Judge Skinner, visibly angry now. "I've decided how I'm going to do it, and that's how I'm going to do it. I will not listen to much more of this."

"Your Honor, forcing me into the humiliation and disgrace—"

"You will survive it," said Skinner curtly. "Being a lawyer is no bed of roses. Now you sit down, and Mr. Cheeseman can call a witness."

Schlichtmann complied, a grimace on his face.

The judge looked at Cheeseman. "Who do you want first?"

"Mr. Schlichtmann," said Cheeseman.

"I respectfully refuse to take the stand," said Schlichtmann, on his feet again. "I ask the Court's forbearance in allowing me to argue why it is unnecessary."

Judge Skinner had run out of forbearance. He could hold Schlichtmann in contempt, impose a fine, even jail him until he agreed to take the witness stand. Or he could dismiss the case outright. He seemed to consider the possibilities for a moment. Finally he said, "I'm not going to hold you in contempt if you are acting under what you think is your professional conscience. But I may dismiss the complaint."

"That's precisely the predicament I'm in," said Schlichtmann, hands outstretched. "I have an obligation to myself and to my client. It may result in my client having his case thrown out of court."

The judge sighed deeply. "I don't think there are six questions that Mr. Cheeseman can ask you, actually."

Schlichtmann could see that he was wearing the judge down. "Could we try it this way—have you ask those six questions?"

"You want Mr. Cheeseman to submit the questions to me?"

"Yes, Your Honor."

"Mr. Cheeseman, are you willing to do it that way?"

"I have a few more than six questions," Cheeseman said, who was obviously reluctant to do it that way.

"Well, whatever you have, do you want to give it to me?"

"I'm sure you can't follow my handwritten notes."

"Give me a chance." The judge beckoned Cheeseman to come forward. "Come over here to the side bar."

Cheeseman walked reluctantly to the side of the judge's bench, carrying his yellow pad of notes.

Schlichtmann watched in astonishment. All Cheeseman had to say was, No, he wanted to conduct the examination himself, it was his right to do so, and thereby affirm the judge's first instinct. But he had given in without a fight. Schlichtmann glanced at Roisman, raised his eyebrow, and smiled a small, quick smile.

Cheeseman and the judge conferred in whispers for several moments. The courtroom, with fifteen or so lawyers watching, was silent except for the murmured exchange at the bench.

Finally the judge cleared his throat and said, "There are a couple of questions Mr. Cheeseman wants answered, and the first one is addressed to Mr. Roisman: When were you first retained with respect to this case?"

At the counsel table, Roisman stood. "Mr. Schlichtmann asked us to get involved around February of 1982."

Judge Skinner conferred again with Cheeseman, who remained at the judge's elbow, looking unhappy. The judge asked when Roisman and Schlichtmann had first seen the EPA documents reporting the contamination near the W. R. Grace plant, and Roisman said in June 1982. There was another whispered conference between the judge and Cheeseman.

"The next question . . ." began the judge, and then he grunted. "I think that's a rhetorical question, Mr. Cheeseman."

"I think not, Your Honor," said Cheeseman.

"You better clarify it for me again."

Schlichtmann watched the two of them with interest. He thought the judge had lost all enthusiasm for this hearing. Skinner seemed uncomfortable, almost embarrassed, with a proceeding in which he and a lawyer conferred alone, off the record, *ex parte*, about another lawyer. Schlichtmann felt certain he had won.

After a few more desultory questions, Judge Skinner finally said, "All right. I think that is the end of the catechism, is it not, Mr. Cheeseman? Anything else before we bring this hearing to a close?"

"There is one other matter," said Schlichtmann. "I believe Mr. Facher has made his phone call to his client."

Facher had in fact returned after only a few moments outside the courtroom. He had seen everything that had gone on between the judge and Cheeseman. To Schlichtmann, Facher said, "I have no information. They are all out to lunch in Chicago. I have no personal problem with showing you the affidavit. It doesn't cast any great aspersions on you."

"Based on that statement," Schlichtmann said to the judge, "I ask the Court to make a finding that there is no evidence of any impropriety."

Judge Skinner seemed to consider this for a moment. "Mr. Facher has made a judgment, but I can't let his judgment be substituted for mine." Then he added, mostly to himself, "Ordinarily, I would give it great respect."

Schlichtmann started to speak again, but the judge cut him off abruptly. "Look, you've got an issue that's quietly dying on the vine here. Why do you run the risk of reviving it?"

"I don't want to be the one dying on the vine, Your Honor."

"As far as I'm concerned, it will remain a non-issue," said Skinner, rising to indicate the hearing was over.

After the judge departed, Schlichtmann turned and walked toward Facher, who was putting on his coat. Schlichtmann ignored Cheeseman, who stood a few feet away, busying himself with papers on the counsel table, and extended his hand to Facher. "I want to thank you," Schlichtmann said. "It was very statesmanlike of you not to join in this ridiculous attack."

Facher smiled at Schlichtmann in a soft, sleepy manner and accepted the handshake. Schlichtmann had gotten the best of both Cheeseman and the judge, and Facher had found that most entertaining. Schlichtmann's comment about statesmanship amused him further. Statesmanship had nothing to do with being a trial lawyer. To Schlichtmann he said, "You did a good job. I don't know if you're right about this case, but you certainly did a good job."

Judge Skinner issued his ruling two weeks later. "Rule 11 is a useful tool to restrain frivolous and abusive litigation," the judge wrote. "Rule 11 may not be used, however, to harass the serious litigant whose claim may depend upon circumstantial evidence and may not be fully developed at the time the complaint is filed." The EPA reports and the study of the Woburn leukemia cluster by the Centers for Disease Control constituted sufficient grounds for filing a complaint. "Accordingly, defendant's Rule 11 motion is DENIED."

Schlichtmann had already celebrated. He knew he'd won the moment the hearing had ended. At Reed & Mulligan that evening, he opened bottles of champagne. He laughed and did parodies of Cheeseman, of the way Cheeseman had walked stiffly up to the judge's bench, of the wounded look on Cheeseman's face when the judge said his question was rhetorical. Everyone joined in the celebration, which went on until late that night.

The next morning, Schlichtmann awoke without a thought of the Woburn case. It seemed to lie in a distant future. He still believed that he was merely Roisman's local counsel. He didn't realize then how large an investment Cheeseman's motion had given him in Woburn.

Orphans & Dogs

1

For most of the next year and a half, Schlichtmann let the Woburn case languish in the files. His life was busy, his career on the rise. He and Conway stayed on at Reed & Mulligan for a while. Barry Reed landed a big case—a hotel fire in which a businessman had died—and Schlichtmann jumped on it. He hired the nation's leading expert on hotel fires and spent twenty-two thousand dollars preparing courtroom exhibits. Then he invited the hotel's lawyers and insurance agents to a meeting. Reasoning that this case should be worth a lot of money, he spared no cost in arranging the setting for the meeting. He reserved the Grand Ballroom at the Ritz-Carlton and a private dining room for lunch and dinner breaks. At the end of the first day the parties retired to the dining room and continued their discussion over lobster bisque, tomatoes Provençale, grilled rack of lamb, and a grand cru Bordeaux, all paid for by Schlichtmann.

The negotiation went on for three days. Schlichtmann laid out his entire case, assisted by Conway and a young lawyer from Reed & Mulligan named Bill Crowley. Schlichtmann let the hotel's insurance agents and lawyers look at his exhibits and cross-examine his fire expert. The hotel brought in its own fire expert. The two experts discussed the evidence, agreeing far more often than not. On the third day Schlichtmann walked out of the Ritz with a settlement of two and a quarter million dollars.

He had invented a new way of doing business. The Ritz negotiation had been almost like a trial, but in an atmosphere that was congenial instead of adversarial. True, it had been expensive, but not nearly as expensive as a two-week trial, and much less risky. Schlichtmann felt proud of his newfound method. He saw no reason why the same approach shouldn't work in every case.

Barry Reed took a large portion of the hotel fire fee, even though he had never appeared at the Ritz negotiation. Schlichtmann split his share, with Conway and Crowley. And when a reporter from *The Boston Globe* called to ask about the settlement, Reed took the call and all the credit, too.

"You could have at least mentioned my name," said Schlichtmann.

Soon afterward, Schlichtmann left Reed & Mulligan to start his own firm. Bill Crowley came along with him. And so, of course, did Conway. There had never been any doubt in Conway's mind that he would go wherever Schlichtmann went. Life would have been unbearably dull without Schlichtmann.

The name of the new firm was Schlichtmann, Conway & Crowley. There was nothing modest about its beginnings. Schlichtmann saw to that. The Ritz negotiation had convinced him that the appearance of success often begets success. The three partners found an office on the second floor of an old three-story brick building, a historic landmark near the waterfront, at the corner of Milk and India streets, two blocks from the federal courthouse. Schlichtmann hired one of Boston's most fashionable interior decorators. The partners put all their earnings from the hotel fire case into renovating and furnishing the office, uncovering the massive oak beams and rebuilding the ancient brick archways. Schlichtmann ordered a large conference room table, made of bird's-eye maple and stainless steel, from the man who had designed a similar table for the Blue Room of the White House. Surrounding the table were eight chairs of soft, buttery leather, each like a sofa unto itself. Oak filing cabinets were specially built for the office, along with a library to hold Schlichtmann's substantial collection. He had the decorator install a kitchenette and bathrooms equipped with telephones and a spacious tiled shower. The firm leased the most advanced office computer system available. In keeping with the opulence of the new office, Kathy Boyer arranged for fresh flowers to be delivered daily.

The firm celebrated its opening with a huge party. A crane pulled up outside, stopping traffic on India Street for several hours, in order to hoist a grand piano through the second-floor windows. The first floor of the building was occupied by a venerable old Irish pub named Patten's Bar & Grill. Schlichtmann rented the pub for the evening and hired the best caterer in town to prepare the food. Waiters in black tie served champagne. One jazz combo played downstairs at the bar while another played upstairs in the office. Reed and Mulligan came to the party, along with a hundred other lawyers and their spouses, among them many insurance company lawyers and agents, Schlichtmann's past adversaries. Teresa was there, of course, and so was Schlichtmann's mother and most of the Conway clan. Late that evening, the party still in full swing, Conway ran into Schlichtmann coming out of the men's room. They smiled at each other. They had a wonderful future before them. "There's only one thing, Jan," said Conway.

Schlichtmann looked at his partner.

"Woburn," said Conway. "Get rid of it. Please."

Schlichtmann simply laughed.

Some types of personal injury cases are riskier than others. Medical malpractice claims, for instance, are usually much more complicated to prepare than most accident claims. They also tend to require large investments of time and money, and the results are far from certain. Among those malpractice claims that go to trial, the plaintiff can expect to lose, on average, two times out of three. Like most people, plaintiffs' lawyers don't like to take chances with their own money. They either settle or drop the vast majority of cases before trial. Furthermore, most successful personal injury firms try to carry large inventories of cases, many of which are small and uncomplicated. Small claims yield small rewards, but they also provide a regular stream of revenue for a firm.

That way of doing business didn't appeal to Schlichtmann. He didn't want to spend his career churning through small cases. He had grander visions. He wanted his firm to deal only in those cases that promised big rewards and required big investments. Conway went along with this strategy. He and Schlichtmann agreed that they would accept only ten new cases a year. It would be Conway, cautious Conway, who would serve as the firm's gatekeeper. He would weigh the questions of liability and damages and decide what cases were worth investing in.

Some of the claims that came to the new firm in its first year were patently frivolous and Conway quickly rejected them. (One prospective client wanted to sue "for bodily damages I have sustained as a result of drinking beer for a period of twenty-five years.") Conway called such cases "dogs." "Orphans," on the other hand, were cases that looked as if they might have some merit but that for one reason or another had circulated among several law firms, rejected by one and passed on to another. Most of these were medical malpractice cases. In time, Conway's reject file would contain many orphans, instances of disability and death from cancers, ruptured aneurysms, kidney failures, high fevers, and cardiac events. In most of those instances, Conway judged that doctors had not been responsible for the sad outcomes. They were, so to speak, "acts of God." Conway was easily given to compassion but not to recklessness. "You measure your success by the cases you don't take," he liked to say.

The grand piano had scarcely been lowered from the second-floor window when a classic orphan crossed Conway's desk and arrested his attention. Two Boston firms and the biggest plaintiff's firm in New York, Kriendler and Kriendler, had already rejected it. It was, on the face of it, a most puzzling case. A young man had been in an auto accident, had suffered whiplash, and had gone to the hospital for what everyone had believed would be a short stay. Five months later, he left the hospital in a wheelchair, completely crippled, the victim of a massive infection that had eaten away the bones of his hips. More hospitalizations and many operations had ensued. The young man's medical record had become a Manhattan phone book, a history of 622 days in various hospitals.

To Conway, it seemed amazing that a minor automobile accident could have resulted in such a medical nightmare. He wanted to adopt this orphan. He gave the file to Schlichtmann, who took it home one weekend to read. For the next six months Schlichtmann thought about nothing else. And the Woburn case, ignored by Conway and forgotten by Schlichtmann, became an orphan in its own right.

Schlichtmann began trying to unravel what had happened to the young man. By the time he had his answer, he'd spent two hundred thousand dollars on the case, far more than he'd spent on any other, more than anyone, including even Conway, thought prudent. He found that the young man, whose name was Paul Carney, had been treated with steroids immediately after the accident. This was the accepted treatment for reducing dangerous swelling in injuries such as whiplash. But Carney had received high doses of steroids for three weeks, much longer than recommended. Schlichtmann learned that steroids in massive amounts can destroy bone matrix, particularly in the hips. In Carney's case, this process was further abetted by an infection that had entered through a catheter. The infection had spread throughout Carney's entire body, its symptoms—swelling and fever—masked by the steroids.

Schlichtmann left nothing to chance in preparing the case. Twice he organized mock trials, presenting the case to panels of ordinary people who had been hired off the street to act as jurors. In both instances, the mock juries came in with similar verdicts: three million dollars.

Schlichtmann invited the defense lawyers and insurance agents to the Grand Ballroom at the Ritz-Carlton. As it had in the hotel fire case, the negotiation went on for several days. And it worked, after a fashion. The insurance company, which had earlier refused to offer a dime, now offered a million dollars, the limit of its policy. Schlichtmann turned it down.

On the street, rumors about the Carney case spread quickly. Million-dollar settlement offers, like million-dollar verdicts, were not all that common. Lawyers stopped Schlichtmann and asked if he had really rejected a million dollars. Some admired his audacity. Others thought him irresponsible. Almost no one believed the rumor that he had actually risked two hundred thousand dollars on one malpractice case.

The Carney case was a big story among only part of the Boston bar. Corporate lawyers don't travel in the same circles as personal injury lawyers. William Cheeseman hadn't heard about the Carney case. He hadn't laid eyes on Schlichtmann since the Rule 11 hearing, more than a year ago. He was strolling up the sidewalk on Milk Street toward his office one spring afternoon when Schlichtmann, walking as fast as a man can walk without running, nearly ran him down.

Schlichtmann shook hands with Cheeseman. The Rule 11 motion still rankled him, but even so he felt—it seemed odd to him then—a desire for Cheeseman's respect. They stood for a moment on the side-walk and talked, a few paces from the door leading up to Schlichtmann's office.

"I'm going to trial next week," said Schlichtmann. He told Cheese-man about the Carney case and the million-dollar offer by the insur-ance company. Cheeseman seemed interested, so Schlichtmann began describing the courtroom exhibits he intended to use.

"I'd like to see these exhibits sometime," said Cheeseman.

"You want to?" said Schlichtmann. "My office is right here. Come on up."

The office was in an uproar. It looked like the backstage of a major theatrical production just before curtain time. The exhibits occupied the entire conference room and spilled out into the hallway and the reception room. There were a dozen large, hand-colored illustrations showing the progress of Carney's disease from normal bone tissue to advanced necrosis. There were poster-sized blowups of the doctors' entries into Carney's hospital chart, and graphs documenting Carney's decline during the three weeks of steroid treatment. Schlichtmann had even produced a movie—*A Day in the Life of Paul Carney.* On the con-ference room table Cheeseman saw anatomical models of hips and prosthetic joints.

Schlichtmann gave Cheeseman a tour, explaining his theory of the case and how he intended to prove it. He noticed that Cheeseman's interest seemed more than just casual. Schlichtmann thought to him-self, He's thinking about what the Woburn exhibits might look like.

Cheeseman asked how much he had spent on the Carney case. Schlichtmann smiled. "A lot. A couple hundred thousand dollars."

Cheeseman raised his eyebrows. "The entire office is working on this one case?"

"That's the way we like to work," said Schlichtmann.

Cheeseman spent twenty minutes in the office. Neither he nor Schlichtmann mentioned the Woburn case. As he was leaving, Cheese-man said, "I'd like to see this trial. Will you give me a call when it starts?"

"Sure," said Schlichtmann.

Memories of this tour lingered with Cheeseman. He was amazed that Schlichtmann would risk so much on one case. If he were in Schlichtmann's shoes, he thought, he wouldn't be able to sleep at night. He really did want to see the Carney trial. He hoped that Schlichtmann would lose.

Being in trial, Schlichtmann once said, is like being submerged in deep water for weeks at a time. The world above becomes a faint echo. War, scandal, and natural disaster may occur, but none of it seems to matter. The details of the case occupy every waking hour and usually intrude into dreams as well. Existence becomes spartan. When you finally come to the surface to breathe normally again, the world seems altered in fundamental ways. Win or lose, you set about rediscovering pleasures only dimly remembered. Colors seem brighter, food tastes better, the weather is of compelling interest.

The Carney trial, six months in preparation, lasted fifteen days. Conway and Kathy Boyer bought sandwiches for Schlichtmann and begged him to eat, but he rarely did. By the end of the trial he had lost fifteen pounds.

On the Monday afternoon when Schlichtmann delivered his summation, the courtroom gallery was full. Everyone who worked at the office had come to watch. Schlichtmann's banker had also come. The banker had lent the firm money for the Carney case and he was there, as he put it, "to keep an eye on the collateral." There were many lawyers in the gallery, curious observers, but Cheeseman was not among them. Schlichtmann had forgotten—perhaps on purpose—to call him.

One of the lawyers in the gallery, a slender woman with fine, sculpted features and chestnut-colored hair, had flown back to Boston from Atlanta, where she was representing a drug smuggler, just to hear Schlichtmann's summation. Her name was Rikki Klieman. At the moment, her career was ascendant. *Time* magazine, in an article entitled "The New Women in the Court: Five of the Best and Brightest," had called her a "superstar." She'd spent a year as Judge Skinner's law clerk. She'd also worked briefly in the litigation department at Hale and Dorr, where Facher ruled. Some years ago Barry Reed had introduced her to Schlichtmann, and she'd found herself quite taken with him. Given the chance, she believed she could fall in love with him. She imagined they might marry someday and have children. "Somehow, in my fantasy life," she once mused, "Jan and I will work hard and then we'll end up together." As it was, she and Schlichtmann were just good friends. They'd gone out to dinner several times, but to her dismay they had always talked about the law.

Rikki Klieman thought Schlichtmann looked thin, even gaunt. His suit jacket seemed to billow on him. Before court had convened, she'd gone up to him in the corridor and wished him luck. His eyes had appeared glazed and distant. He'd nodded his head but he'd seemed barely to notice her.

She knew the architecture of a summation well; she had given many final arguments herself. Schlichtmann was working toward the emotional climax, describing the young man's helplessness, how his father aided him out of bed every morning and dressed him for the day. The summation was quite moving, the best Schlichtmann had ever given. In the gallery, some people brushed tears from their eyes. Although Rikki was practiced in the trial lawyer's art, she felt, to her astonishment, on the verge of tears herself.

Schlichtmann waited in the courthouse corridor for the verdict. On the afternoon of the second day, the jury foreman sent a message to the judge, who summoned the lawyers up to his bench. The jurors wanted the judge to explain the legal concept of negligence again. It was not a good sign for the plaintiff. The judge knew that Schlichtmann had rejected a million-dollar offer. He looked directly at Schlichtmann. "I advise you to talk to one another and see if you can reach some sort of settlement."

This was, word for word, almost exactly what the judge in the Eaton case had said. Schlichtmann had the eerie sense of history repeating itself, except that this time he felt a wingbeat of fear. This time the stakes were much higher.

That evening Schlichtmann went to the Parker House with Conway and Crowley and a group of friends, among them Rikki Klieman. Everyone was solemn and worried. Someone suggested that Schlichtmann go back to the insurance company and see if the million dollars was still on the table. Schlichtmann kept insisting there was no cause for alarm, as if saying so would make it true. It was merely a question that one juror wanted cleared up. "Don't you think so?" he kept asking everyone in turn.

That night, Schlichtmann went home and lay in bed trying to sleep, but he could feel his heart thudding and he imagined he could feel his adrenal gland squeezing adrenaline into his system with each beat. He thought about his reputation and career, about the lawyers who'd said he was foolish to reject a million-dollar offer, about Paul Carney in his wheelchair awaiting the verdict.

He arose at dawn and went to his office. At six o'clock, as he watched the sun rise over Boston harbor, he called Rikki Klieman. The phone rang several times before she answered, her voice thick with sleep.

Should he take the million dollars? Schlichtmann asked her. Or should he wait for the jury's verdict?

"You've made your choice," Rikki said. "You've turned down the money." She got out of bed and put on a robe, still cradling the phone to her ear. She brushed her teeth while she listened to him talk. She gave him no sympathy.

"What do you think the jury's going to do?" he asked.

"Jan, I don't read tea leaves," she said. "The jury's question is not good. But the only reason to be as crazy as you are is if you haven't made up your mind. Have you made up your mind?"

"Yes," he said.

"Then you've got to live with it."

The jurors returned their verdict that afternoon. They found the doctor and hospital negligent and they awarded Paul Carney $4.7 million.

Outside the courthouse in Pemberton Square, Schlichtmann danced. He jumped onto a park bench and did a soft-shoe, long arms akimbo, pirouetting with joy in his dark blue suit. Conway, looking rumpled, his shirttails emergent, his tie coming undone, stood and watched his partner. People stopped to stare. "He's just won a big case," Conway explained. The *Boston Herald*, a tabloid given to sensationalism, put the story on the front page with a headline that looked as if war had been declared. "The award is the largest in Bay State history," asserted the *Herald*, which had rounded the verdict to an even five million dollars.

Schlichtmann had taken five cases to trial, each one bigger than the last, and he had not lost once. The Carney case had given him plenty of money. And it had also given him a new measure of confidence. Any other malpractice case would now look pitifully small compared with Carney. He felt he was ready for something bigger. He felt he was ready for Woburn.

2

As it happened, events had conspired to bring Woburn back into the news without any help from Schlichtmann. He had been immersed in frantic preparations for the Carney trial when two professors at the Harvard School of Public Health announced that they had completed a three-year study of leukemia in Woburn. Schlichtmann had known that the study was going on, but he had played no role it. On the evening of February 8, 1984, he was just one of three hundred people who gathered at Trinity Episcopal Church to hear the findings of what would come to be called the Harvard Health Study.

The project had started back in the spring of 1981, when Reverend Young and Anne Anderson were invited to speak at a seminar at the School of Public Health. A professor at the school, a statistician in his mid-fifties named Marvin Zelen, had been intrigued by their talk. Woburn seemed to him like an interesting riddle. Was there or was there not a link between the well water and the cluster of leukemias? By the end of the seminar, Zelen thought he knew a way to solve this riddle.

Statistical studies of the sort Zelen specialized in had proved, for example, an irrefutable link between cigarette smoking and lung cancer, but those studies had been based on an analysis of tens of thousands of cases of lung cancer. Statistical studies rely upon large numbers, and Zelen had only twelve cases of leukemia to work with in Woburn. But Zelen thought he saw a way to get larger numbers. He reasoned that if the well water had, in fact, caused leukemia, it might also have caused a variety of other childhood health problems. If an unusual pattern of birth defects and reproductive disorders emerged among families that had gotten their water from wells G and H, that would tend to support the theory that the cluster of leukemia cases was not simply a coincidence, a statistical fluke.

Zelen and a colleague undertook an ambitious study. They began collecting information on the outcome of every pregnancy and child-birth in Woburn between 1960 and 1982. Although the most reliable health data came from house-to-house interviews, that method was expensive and time-consuming. Zelen and his team at Harvard settled on a telephone survey, a task that volunteers in Woburn could be trained to do. By the end of the survey, the volunteers (they numbered several hundred, among them Anne Anderson and Donna Robbins) had made seven thousand phone calls and collected health data on more than five thousand children.

"The combined weight of evidence," wrote Zelen and his colleagues in the completed 153-page study, "strongly suggests that water from wells G and H is linked to a variety of adverse health effects." The Harvard scientists found an increased rate of fetal and newborn deaths among pregnant women whose homes had gotten the largest quantities of the water. Among children in the Pine Street neighborhood, an area of high exposure, they found increased rates of allergies, skin afflictions such as eczema, and respiratory disorders—chronic bronchitis, asthma, and pneumonia. They also found a "significant excess" of congenital defects to the eye and ear, of kidney and urinary tract disorders, and of "environmental" birth defects, a grouping that included cleft palate, spina bifida, Down's syndrome, and other chromosomal aberrations.

And finally, the study determined that there was indeed a positive link between exposure to the well water and the high rate of childhood leukemia. On average, children with leukemia received 21.2 percent of their annual water supply from the wells, compared with 9.5 percent for children without leukemia.

When Zelen announced these findings at Trinity Episcopal on that night in February, a hush fell over the crowd. Then someone said, in a voice audible to all, "Thank God for Marvin Zelen," and the crowd broke into applause.

Some experts said that the Harvard Health Study was a good study. Dr. John Truman, who was in the audience at Trinity Episcopal, stated at his deposition a year later: "It's a very well-done study. It clearly shows that ingestion—drinking of that water—is associated with a higher incidence of leukemia. Prior to it, I didn't think childhood leukemia was caused by external factors, but now I think we have to consider external factors as a real possibility."

Others, however, maintained that the study was seriously flawed. "This report is characterized by . . . an ignorance of epidemiological issues," wrote one reviewer at the federal Centers for Disease Control. The American Industrial Health Council, an industry research group, denounced the study as biased, and even one of Zelen's colleagues at Harvard stated, "It was an incredible mistake to use as interviewers people who have a self-interest in the outcome. To my mind, that just destroys the credibility of it right there."

Whatever its true merits or failings, the study created an immediate public sensation. The headline on the front page of *The Boston Globe*— WOBURN LEUKEMIA LINKED TO TAINTED WATER—delighted Schlichtmann. As he saw it, the study confirmed to the world at large the legitimacy of the Woburn case, and it came with the imprimatur of Harvard upon it.

He wasn't disturbed by the critics, but he also understood that as a piece of evidence the study had limitations. It had not addressed the biological causes of leukemia. It did not prove that the contaminated well water had caused the leukemias. It showed only that those children who drank water from Wells G and H were more likely to get leukemia than those who did not. Schlichtmann knew that he and Roisman would need more than this study to prove that TCE had caused leukemia in Jimmy Anderson and the other children.

3

The Harvard Health Study also provoked response from another quarter—from Cheeseman. He had planned, in his methodical way, a long-range strategy for the Woburn case. After his disappointment with Rule 11, his strategy called for him to wait until Schlichtmann made the next move. Months had passed, and then a year, and Schlichtmann had done nothing. By then, Cheeseman felt he might have reason to hope that Woburn had become an orphan.

But the Harvard study dashed that hope. The day after its release Cheeseman started to prepare his next move, a motion for summary judgment. It took him several months. He had been working on it— had almost finished it, in fact—when he had that chance encounter on Milk Street with Schlichtmann. He was glad he'd gotten the tour of

Schlichtmann's office and seen the Carney exhibits. If Woburn ever went to trial, Cheeseman told himself, at least he'd know what to expect.

Cheeseman's summary judgment motion asked Judge Skinner to dismiss the Woburn case on the grounds that Schlichtmann would be unable to present any competent scientific evidence showing that TCE caused leukemia. Without such evidence, Cheeseman argued in his brief, the case, as a matter of law, could not go to a jury.

At first Cheeseman had figured his motion didn't stand much of a chance. He'd regarded it mostly as a means of educating Judge Skinner to the real scientific issues in the case. But he'd found himself growing more optimistic as he worked on the motion. At the Harvard Medical School he visited the labs of two doctors, both world-renowned experts in the study of blood disorders. Between them, they had treated more than two thousand leukemia patients. One of the doctors, Dr. James Jandl, had just written a chapter on leukemic diseases for his latest book, *Blood: Textbook of Hematology.* Jandl had reviewed all of the medical and scientific literature on leukemogenesis and had found nothing at all to suggest that TCE played a role in the disease. He regarded the Woburn lawsuit with thinly veiled contempt.

The Environmental Protection Agency, it was true, had listed TCE as a "probable" carcinogen. But it had done so on the basis of animal tests—lab experiments in which mice, rats, and hamsters were fed enormous quantities of TCE over long periods. In one experiment, white mice had developed cancers of the lymph system, which manufactures white blood cells. But that particular strain of laboratory mouse, Jandl pointed out, was known to have a high incidence of "spontaneous" lymphosarcoma, and even the authors of the study had discounted the results. Furthermore, both Harvard doctors told Cheeseman they had little faith in extrapolating the results of animal studies to human beings. The life spans of animals, their chromosomal structures, and their metabolism were just too different.

Cheeseman called Facher to tell him of his work on summary judgment. He would have liked Facher to join the motion, but once again, as with Rule 11, Facher expressed no interest.

Cheeseman went on by himself. He asked the two doctors to sign lengthy affidavits stating that there existed no medically accepted evidence to support the opinion that TCE could cause leukemia in humans. In the absence of such evidence, Cheeseman wrote in his brief to Judge Skinner, Schlichtmann could not make out a *prima facie* case on causation. "Summary judgment should therefore be entered, dismissing the claims."

Cheeseman felt confident the judge would schedule a hearing for oral argument in a motion of this importance, but he wanted to make certain of that. He ended his motion by saying, "Grace believes that oral argument with respect to this matter may be of assistance to the Court and therefore requests such argument, and estimates one hour will be necessary for both sides to be heard."

The arrival of Cheeseman's summary judgment motion—only a week after the Carney verdict—dampened Schlichtmann's spirits considerably. It was an excellent motion, well argued and supported by two illustrious doctors. Schlichtmann had hoped to take a vacation after the Carney trial, but now he and Roisman had only ten days in which to respond. They could ask Cheeseman for a thirty-day extension, but even so, that still wouldn't allow much time to reply to a motion of this caliber. Because of the shortness of time, they agreed that Schlichtmann would handle the reply largely by himself.

Schlichtmann called Cheeseman to ask for an extension. "It's a very good motion," he added. "I think you've got a chance of winning."

By now, Cheeseman thought so too, although it surprised him to hear Schlichtmann admit it. He didn't object to a thirty-day extension.

Schlichtmann went to work. He met with an immunologist from California who had been recommended by Roisman. The immunologist, Dr. Alan Levin, was experienced in legal matters. He had served as an expert witness many times before in cases involving toxic substances. He told Schlichtmann that he regarded lawsuits as a useful vehicle for social change. Schlichtmann found this attitude most unusual in a doctor. The medical community, Levin explained, was far too slow in recognizing the perils of environmental toxins. "Twenty years ago we were using X rays to see if our shoes fit, and zapping our gonads in the process," Levin said. "If you talk to any intelligent twenty-year-old today, he'd say nobody could be that stupid. Your children are going to ask you, 'Did they really spray insecticides from airplanes?' "

Levin had a theory about the Woburn case. He believed that constant low-level exposure to TCE had damaged the immune systems of all the members of the Woburn families. "These chemicals always do something," he told Schlichtmann. "Most of the time they don't do enough damage for us to notice. You might lose a few cells, but you won't notice it because we've got a lot of extra cells." A healthy, vigilant immune system will attack and kill aberrant cells. But if the immune system has been damaged, as Levin speculated, a malignant cell stands a far greater chance of surviving and proliferating.

All this made sense to Schlichtmann. But was there an objective way of testing for this damage? Levin said he knew of an immunopathologist at Harvard whose lab specialized in monitoring the immune systems of patients after organ transplant surgery. But the tests would be expensive, warned Levin, and he could not be certain what they would show.

Schlichtmann decided to go ahead anyway. Levin called the pathologist, whose name was Dr. Robert Colvin, and explained his interest in a series of blood tests. The working hypothesis, Levin told Colvin, was that exposure to chemicals in the drinking water had caused abnormalities in the immune systems of all the family members, not just those who had gotten leukemia.

Colvin had heard about the Harvard Health Study and the Woburn cluster. An interesting subject, he said to Levin. He asked what tests Levin wanted. A lymphocyte count, replied Levin, And a series of T cell assays.

The lymphocyte count—a simple count of white blood cells—was easy enough. Any lab could do that. The T cell assays were somewhat more difficult. All T cells look alike, but they perform different functions, and distinguishing one from another was a tricky business. The helper T cell, for instance, identifies foreign organisms—viruses, bacteria, cancerous cells—and summons killer T cells, which are equipped with cytotoxic enzymes. Another type of T cell, the suppressor, stops the attack of the killer T cells when the invading organism has been conquered.

Colvin used a technique for marking T cells with reagents to differentiate them, and then he counted them with a laser. But he had never heard of using T cell assays to document exposure to chemicals. Even if the tests did show something unusual, there would be no way of telling what had caused the abnormality. The assays would serve no diagnostic purpose, he told Levin.

Levin thought that Colvin might find an abnormality in the ratios of one set of T cells to another. He could not predict what sort of abnormality, however. The assays would be somewhat of a fishing expedition, Levin allowed.

Colvin did not like fishing expeditions. His lab was in great demand. It was hard enough for him to find time to fulfill all his colleagues' requests. Yet the idea intrigued him, and in the end he agreed to do the tests. "But," he added, "I don't think you're going to find anything."

Colvin suggested they start by testing just one family. The protocol was rigid: the blood could not be refrigerated, and it had to arrive in Colvin's lab on the morning it was drawn. It would take a full day to do one run of blood in the machine, to agglutinate out the red cells, to fix and stain the white cells, and to perform the cell counts. Schlichtmann would have to make the arrangements to have the blood drawn and transported to the lab. It would cost about ten thousand dollars to have all the families tested. Schlichtmann readily agreed to the price. After all, he had spent more than that for a conference room table in his new office.

The Zonas were the first to have their blood drawn. When the tubes arrived at Colvin's lab, a technician prepared the blood, marked the T cells with reagents, and ran the assays on the Spectrum 3 cytometer, the machine that counted cells by laser.

As Colvin began plotting the results on a graph, he knew immediately something was awry. To begin with, he saw far more white cells than he expected, a condition known as lymphocytosis, a sign of an immune system in a heightened state of alert. As he calculated the ratio of helper T cells to killer T cells, it became apparent there was another abnormality. The killer cells peaked sharply in all of the family members, particularly in two of the adolescent children. Colvin rarely saw such distinct peaks. He was not certain precisely what this meant. Perhaps their systems were reacting to a carcinogen, as Levin suspected. Whatever its significance, Colvin found it very unusual.

Colvin called Levin and described what he'd found. As a scientist, Colvin trusted results only if they could be replicated. "I think we ought to do the Zonas again, to make sure that this is something that persists," Colvin said.

Before performing a second assay on the Zonas, Colvin tested the accuracy of the Spectrum 3 cytometer. He regularly sampled his own blood and that of people who worked in his lab, and compared those results with the normal values reported by other labs. If the normals corresponded, Colvin felt confident that the machine was functioning accurately.

But when Colvin tested the new control group this time, he inadvertently included a lab employee who'd had skin cancer—a melanoma—several years earlier. Colvin saw at once that the killer T cell values for this employee were far outside the normal range, and he eliminated that individual from the control population. But those readings had looked, he thought, strikingly like the results for the Zonas.

Schlichtmann meanwhile got Cheeseman to agree to yet another thirty-day extension. In the weeks that followed, all twenty-eight living members of the Woburn families had blood drawn. Colvin tested the blood of each individual twice. By the time he finished he saw a distinct pattern. "The data are intriguing," he wrote in a note to Levin on June 15, "because they suggest that there is an increased number of cells in these patients that have a phenotype compatible with killer cells. The implication is that this might be a compensatory response to resist the effects of a carcinogen."

Levin flew in from California to meet with Schlichtmann. "Basically," explained Levin, "Colvin thinks that these people might have a carcinogen on board and they're constantly fighting it. The kids who developed leukemia have lost the fight."

By now, Colvin felt he was onto something interesting and he wanted to keep pursuing it. He suggested to Levin that he run another series of tests—functional assays, more complicated and more expensive than the first. He and Levin came up with the idea of testing a control group of fifty Woburn residents who had not been exposed to the well water and comparing those results with the eight families. A study of that scope would cost at least fifty thousand dollars.

Schlichtmann was excited by the initial results. He was eager to do the big study, and he wasn't daunted by the cost, but it would take months to set up, and he had no time for that now. The deadline for his reply to the summary judgment motion was only days away.

Levin had also been searching the scientific literature for studies of TCE. He'd found an epidemiological study of three hundred and thirty dry-cleaning workers, an occupation in which both TCE and perc, the other chemical in the Woburn wells, were commonly used.

The study reported significant increases of several different cancers, among them kidney, bladder, and cervix, and also found five leukemia victims where, statistically, only two had been expected. The author of the study considered the leukemia finding only marginally significant, however. And since the workers had been exposed to several chemicals—TCE, perc, and carbon tetrachloride—the study was unable to draw conclusions about the carcinogenic capacity of any single chemical.

Schlichtmann was beginning to feel slightly more confident. He still did not have any definitive medical evidence to show that TCE could cause leukemia in humans. But he did have the Harvard study; he had Colvin's blood tests; and Levin had found two more animal studies, overlooked by Cheeseman's Harvard doctors, suggesting that TCE had damaged blood-forming cells in the bone marrow. He and Levin worked on an affidavit in which Levin stated his belief, "to a reasonable medical certainty," that the TCE in the wells had "caused or substantially contributed to serious illnesses, including immune dysfunction and leukemia" among the families.

Schlichtmann sent copies of his brief by messenger to Judge Skinner and to Cheeseman. It was a Friday afternoon in late July. The judge always spent the month of August at his summer house on the Maine coast. Schlichtmann felt certain the judge would not schedule oral argument until September.

Cheeseman was unimpressed by Schlichtmann's brief. He began outlining what he would say at oral argument. His hopes were still high when, four days after Schlichtmann filed his brief, he got a call from Judge Skinner's clerk. "The judge has ruled on summary judgment," said the clerk. "You can pick up the order this afternoon."

Cheeseman thought he hadn't heard the clerk correctly. "The judge has ruled? What about oral argument?"

"There's no hearing scheduled," replied the clerk.

Cheeseman knew he'd lost again. The judge had flatly ignored his request for a hearing. Cheeseman went across the street to the courthouse. The judge's ruling was terse and it stung. "Since the complex factual issue of causation is a subject of heated dispute in this case, summary judgment is clearly inappropriate. Defendant's motion is DENIED."

Cheeseman felt convinced that the specter of Rule 11 had come back to haunt him. "Skinner thinks I jerked him around on that one," he would remember thinking. "He's got a bit of a temper."

These thoughts worried Cheeseman. He'd have to live with this judge for a long time yet.

4

Twice Schlichtmann had gone up against Cheeseman, one of Boston's best practitioners in pretrial maneuvers, and he had come out a winner both times. The case was two and a half years old now, and so far he had done nothing but respond to Cheeseman's attacks. Many years later Schlichtmann would say that if it had not been for Cheeseman, especially the Rule 11 motion, he might have followed Conway's advice and let Woburn slip away. But at the time, it seemed to Schlichtmann as if somebody were trying to tell him that Woburn really was his destiny.

He was summoned to Judge Skinner's chambers, along with Cheeseman and Facher, when the judge returned from his vacation in Maine. "I'm putting this case on a tight leash," the judge told the lawyers in a stern voice. He gave them nine months, until May, to complete discovery. He expected the lawyers to be prepared to select a jury shortly after that.

Conway reminded Schlichtmann that they were still just local counsel. The case really belonged to Roisman and Trial Lawyers for Public Justice, even though Schlichtmann had paid all the bills so far and done most of the work on summary judgment. That one motion, Conway calculated, had cost the firm twenty-five thousand dollars. If nothing else, it was by now perfectly clear that Woburn would require a true fortune to prepare. Levin recommended bringing in experts in half a dozen disciplines—neurology, cardiology, toxicology, internal medicine, among others—to perform complete medical workups on all twenty-eight plaintiffs. And then there was Colvin's big blood study with fifty controls. Where was Trial Lawyers for Public Justice? wondered Conway. Since Roisman and his organization stood to collect two thirds of any fee that resulted from the case, they should at least be risking some of their own money.

That fall, Schlichtmann flew out to Milwaukee, where Trial Lawyers for Public Justice was having its annual board meeting. He laid out for the directors his plan for preparing the case, and he estimated that it would cost at least three hundred thousand dollars, maybe as much half a million if it went to trial.

All of the board members were seasoned trial lawyers, older than Schlichtmann, and with many million-dollar verdicts to their credit. At the head of the table sat Ted Warshafsky, a Milwaukee lawyer who'd made his name suing drug companies. He was an excitable man in his late fifties, given to occasional explosive and profane outbursts. On the theory that a pet would have a calming effect, he had acquired a large boxer. The dog accompanied him everywhere. It took an instant dislike to Schlichtmann. When Warshafsky heard half a million dollars, he flew into an apoplectic rage, his face crimson as he shouted at Schlicht-mann. Immediately the boxer's ears went up. It leaped to its feet and put its paws on the table, a menacing eye on Schlichtmann, who half rose from his chair, prepared to bolt from the room.

Warshafsky got the dog under control. Still muttering at the far end of the table, he let Sal Liccardo, a California lawyer famous for his law-suits against car manufacturers, take up where he'd left off. "When I had the Ford case," Liccardo said angrily, "I only spent fifty thousand dollars on it, and that was a huge case. I never heard of anybody spend-ing three hundred thousand on a case. It's insane."

Schlichtmann, of course, had spent nearly that much on the Car-ney case, but this didn't seem like the time to bring that up. "It's the only way I know how to do this case," he told the directors, keeping a wary eye on the boxer. "But I'm happy to have you take it over. It's all yours."

That evening, Schlichtmann and Roisman went out for a drink. "The board's made a decision," Roisman said. "There can only be one captain of the ship. Since you've put so much time into the case already, we'll let you run with it."

Schlichtmann returned to Boston and told Conway the news. Trial Lawyers for Public Justice would still take 12 percent of any settlement or judgment as a fee for its early work, but all the strategy, and also all the risks, belonged to them now, and them alone.

5

Schlichtmann ran into Cheeseman again that fall, after returning from Milwaukee. He had just traded in his Porsche 911 for a new one, the top-of-the-line model 928. It was low-slung and it gleamed like a jewel. He was getting out of the car when he saw Cheeseman.

"Yours?" asked Cheeseman.

Schlichtmann nodded. "I just bought it."

"Business must be good."

Schlichtmann smiled and shrugged. "The Carney case," he said simply.

Cheeseman stroked the flank of the car, peered in the cockpit, and then asked if he could sit in it. The car had only a few hundred miles on the odometer. Taking the driver's seat, Cheeseman examined the controls. He dreamed about owning one of these. He asked about engine displacement, gear ratios, and torque.

Schlichtmann confessed he knew nothing about those things.

"This car is wasted on you," said Cheeseman, laughing.

By now, Cheeseman had found out some sobering news about Grace's Woburn operation. A search of the plant's records revealed that it had used at least four 55-gallon drums of TCE, considerably more than the single drum that Grace had reported to the Environmental Protection Agency. Cheeseman also learned that the plant manager had ordered workers to bury six drums that had contained toxic waste solvents, including TCE, in a trench behind the plant more than a decade ago. The EPA had ordered Grace to dig those drums up. A photographer from the *Woburn Daily Times* had attended the exhumation. The paper had published a huge front-page photograph of a crane lifting a rusted, partially crushed drum from the trench.

Cheeseman realized now that almost any jury would probably find his client guilty of contaminating the city wells, although he emphatically did not believe that such low levels of TCE had caused any harm. Yet he could imagine Schlichtmann calling the Woburn mothers to the witness stand. He could see them weeping, just as he'd seen that young woman weep on the witness stand fifteen years ago, when he'd been a law student. More than ever, it looked as if this case was becoming the sort of public relations nightmare that every big company feared. Cheeseman had no trouble imagining a huge verdict—tens of millions of dollars—against his client.

He had already lost two motions, but he wasn't out of motions yet. The EPA's preliminary report had implicated a third company north of the city wells. This company, a thriving family-run business named Unifirst, supplied work clothes to industries from Florida to Maine, and it used large quantities of tetrachloroethylene to clean those clothes. The company had admitted to an accidental spill of the solvent, but it claimed that the spill had been contained. Cheeseman didn't believe this, and he suspected there had been other spills, too. One way of shielding his own client from a huge verdict would be to drag Unifirst into the case and make it a defendant, a joint "tortfeasor," along with Grace and Beatrice.

Cheeseman prepared a motion to implead Unifirst. It was, on the face of it, a purely defensive maneuver, but Cheeseman also foresaw one other benefit—it would make life more difficult for Schlichtmann. He would have to deal with three separate defendants, each with its own big corporate law firm, and that would surely tax his resources.

As Cheeseman drew up the motion, he considered calling Facher to inform him, but Facher had refused to help with the earlier motions. So Cheeseman didn't bother to call the old lawyer, and that would turn out to be a costly mistake.

Judge Skinner approved Cheeseman's Unifirst motion, the first by Cheeseman the judge had approved. For his part, Schlichtmann had no objection to Unifirst's presence in the case. He might have sued the company himself had he not considered it to be a minor player. The city wells had contained only small quantities of tetrachloroethylene, and Unifirst had never used TCE, the main culprit in the case. As for making his task more complicated, Schlichtmann laughed in delight when he received Cheeseman's motion. "Listen to this," he said to Conway, reading aloud: " 'Unifirst breached its duty to plaintiffs by carrying out the manufacture, use, control and disposal of the chemicals in reckless disregard for the health, safety and economic interests of plaintiffs.' "

Schlichtmann laughed again. "My God, look at what Cheeseman's saying! It's exactly what we said about Grace!"

The next morning, Schlichtmann called the lawyer at Goodwin, Proctor & Hoar who represented Unifirst. "I see you got an invitation to the party," Schlichtmann said.

"It's very odd that you should call," replied the lawyer. "I was just thinking about calling you."

"When can we get together?" said Schlichtmann.

"How about right now?"

At their first meeting the Unifirst lawyer told Schlichtmann that he hoped they could work out an amicable settlement that would result in his client being dismissed from the case. Money would change hands, of course, but as he saw it, his client's real adversary was Cheeseman and W. R. Grace. Schlichtmann, after all, had not been the one to sue Unifirst.

Facher wasn't laughing. Up until this motion, Facher had rather liked Cheeseman, although he thought Cheeseman had shown bad judgment with the Rule 11 motion, and poor execution when he'd let Schlichtmann outmaneuver him at that hearing. Rule 11 had been bad enough, thought Facher, but this impleader of Unifirst was a more serious blunder. Unifirst would create havoc in the courtroom. The company would never cooperate in a joint defense, not after being dragged into the case by Cheeseman. They'd start pointing fingers. In no time, all three companies would be fighting among themselves about who had contaminated the wells. Facher had spoken briefly with Cheeseman about this before, and he thought they had agreed that such tactics would only help Schlichtmann.

Facher called up Cheeseman. The conversation, as Facher later remembered it, began with his saying, "What the hell is the point of this? You're claiming Unifirst dumped this crap and poisoned these people. It's the same thing Schlichtmann's saying. You can always blame Unifirst, even if they're not there. In fact, it's better that way because they can't respond."

Cheeseman said Unifirst would come to its senses. The company might be angry now, but it would soon realize that it was in its best interest to cooperate.

"Bullshit," said Facher. "They're not going to cooperate. You'll have to dismiss against them."

Facher was right. In the months that followed, Unifirst's lawyers filed countersuits against both Grace and Beatrice. Cheeseman still wanted to keep Unifirst in the case, but Grace's in-house corporate counsel finally overruled him. Unifirst was causing too much trouble and it did not look as if the company would ever cooperate in a joint defense. Against his will, Cheeseman was forced to dismiss all claims against the company.

Schlichtmann, meanwhile, had been negotiating with Unifirst. At the first meeting the company's lawyer offered a hundred thousand dollars. Schlichtmann set up a meeting at the Ritz-Carlton, just as he had done in the hotel fire case, and he brought in a groundwater expert from Princeton University. Unifirst's lawyer increased his offer to six hundred thousand. Schlichtmann wanted more. The negotiation stalled for a while, and then Schlichtmann organized another meeting at the Ritz. In the end, Unifirst offered to settle all claims for one million and fifty thousand dollars. The company would pay four hundred thousand in cash immediately, and the balance in five years.

Schlichtmann called the families together. On a Saturday morning at his office, they readily approved the Unifirst settlement, and they further agreed, at Schlichtmann's suggestion, to use the first cash payment to finance the Woburn case. This money was important. Schlichtmann and his partners had made a million dollars from the Carney case, but they'd already spent most of that. Everyone in the office, from Kathy Boyer down to the cleaning lady, had gotten a big bonus. Schlichtmann had renovated his apartment and bought the new Porsche, and Conway and Crowley had each bought large houses in the suburbs. But all of that was petty cash compared with the real expense facing the firm. The Woburn case, Schlichtmann knew, had begun in earnest.

Discovery

1

Everything Richard Aufiero knew about lawyers he'd learned from television and the movies. He was scheduled to go into Boston on the morning of January 7, 1985, a Monday, to have his deposition taken by the lawyers for W. R. Grace and Beatrice Foods. He awoke early that morning, feeling nervous. He imagined that the lawyers for the big companies would badger him, try to trick him into saying damaging things, or make him look stupid. "Like a moron," he told his wife, Lauren, whose deposition was scheduled for that afternoon, right after his.

Richard was the first of the Woburn plaintiffs—the first person in the entire case, in fact—to be deposed in that period before trial known to lawyers as discovery. Richard would have preferred coming later, so that he could talk to the other family members and find out what kind of questions he would be asked, but he had been given no choice in the matter. For whatever reason, the lawyers for Beatrice and Grace had selected him to go first. Schlichtmann had explained the deposition process to him and told him not to worry, but Richard couldn't help feeling nervous. He put on his best pair of pants and a clean shirt. He considered wearing his green nylon Celtics jacket, his favorite piece of apparel, but he decided he should probably wear a sports coat. He had only one, it was about eight years old and a tight fit now, but it was the dressiest item he owned.

Lauren was even more jittery than he. Ever since Jarrod's death she'd been having anxiety attacks, her heart pounding rapidly, feeling, she used to say, as if she was going to die or go crazy. She'd been hospitalized for a week after Jarrod died, and she'd been seeing a therapist since then. Richard didn't think it had helped her much. She'd started drinking more. For Richard, Jarrod's death had created the opposite reaction. It was a rare event now when he took so much as a sip of alcohol.

They were running late by the time they left the house, on a cul-de-sac in the Pine Street neighborhood, and heavy traffic caused them to make slow progress on I-93 to Boston. Richard made a living driving a truck, and he had traveled this route hundreds of times since the day when Jarrod, who'd been three years old, had died on the way to the hospital. Richard thought about that day every time he passed the Somerville exit, where he had raced off the interstate to the fire station for help. When Lauren had yelled that Jarrod had stopped breathing, Richard had pulled over into the breakdown lane and given the boy CPR, holding him in his lap. That moment was still vivid in his memory, Lauren screaming and carrying on, the cars and big semi-rigs roaring by them on the interstate, Jarrod lifeless in his arms. He thought about it often, but he and Lauren had not talked about it for a long time. And today, as they drove past the Somerville exit on their way to Boston, they kept their silence, even though Richard figured Lauren was probably thinking about it, just as he was.

Lauren had often said that she didn't want any part of the lawsuit. She didn't want to keep reliving the event. "Money won't bring Jarrod back," she would say. "I hate them, those people who put the stuff into the ground. Why can't they lose a son or daughter? Taking their money is not going to hurt them."

"We're not in it for the money," Richard would say. "We're in it to show that we've been harmed by what they did."

By the time they found a parking space and got up to Schlichtmann's office, it was fifteen minutes after ten. The deposition had been scheduled for ten o'clock at the law offices of Hale and Dorr, but

Schlichtmann seemed unconcerned about the time. He had them take their coats off and relax for a few minutes while he went over the ground rules of depositions again. "Listen carefully to the questions and don't volunteer anything," he told Richard and Lauren. "Answer only what they ask, and don't say, 'I don't know' all the time. It'll make you look evasive. Think each question through carefully, because whatever you say, we're stuck with it."

Richard wanted to know if he had to answer all their questions, even ones about issues unrelated to the case and Jarrod's death. He was thinking about some troubles he'd had as a teenager, and about his relationship with Lauren.

Schlichtmann knew all about Richard's past. He knew, for example, that Richard had abused drugs fifteen years ago, when he was seventeen, and that Lauren had once sought medical treatment for a cut she'd gotten when Richard had pushed her in the heat of an argument. And Schlichtmann knew that Facher and Cheeseman were also aware of these incidents. As part of discovery, Schlichtmann had been obliged to produce the medical records of each family member. He suspected that Facher had chosen Richard as the first deponent precisely because of these episodes.

"They can ask any question they want and you've got to answer," Schlichtmann told Richard and Lauren. "By the time they're done, they'll know more about you than you know about yourself. Tell them the truth, because if you lie and they find out, it'll be a lot worse when they get you on the witness stand."

Lauren waited at the office while Richard walked with Schlichtmann and Conway the three blocks to Hale and Dorr. By now, they were half an hour late. On the twenty-seventh floor, a secretary escorted them into a large, well-lit conference room, thickly carpeted, the walls paneled in wood. Picture windows framed a panoramic view of Boston's North End and the harbor. To Richard, the room seemed crowded with lawyers. He counted eight of them, all wearing dark suits and sitting around a long rectangular table. Their conversation stopped as he entered the room, and he felt their gazes turn on him—cool, appraising stares. He tried to smile and began to say something—a simple greeting—but it emerged as a guttural sound and he ended by looking down and clearing his throat. He felt Conway behind him touch his arm and whisper, "Don't worry, you'll be fine."

Schlichtmann steered Richard to a chair near the middle of the table, and then sat beside him. Conway took an empty chair directly across from Richard. The court stenographer, a heavyset woman, sat at one corner of the table, her small machine mounted on a tripod in front of her.

Facher presided over the gathering, sitting at the head of the table, with Neil Jacobs on his right and another young Hale and Dorr associate, unknown to Schlichtmann, next to Jacobs. On Facher's left was Cheeseman, along with three of his colleagues from Foley, Hoag & Eliot. The two firms had agreed to work together as much as practicable throughout the discovery process. Many later depositions would be held in conference rooms at Cheeseman's firm, but at this first deposition it was clear that Facher intended to run the show.

"Let's get started," said Facher. He asked the stenographer to swear in the witness, and he began by asking a series of questions about Richard's medical history, wasting no time in getting to the drug-abuse episode. Richard answered straightforwardly and Facher moved briskly on. "I take it the water began to taste funny to you from the moment you arrived in Woburn?" he asked Richard.

"From when I first started going out with my wife," replied Richard.

"So you were aware when you moved to Woburn that its water didn't taste so good?"

"Yeah," said Richard. "But a lot of places the water doesn't taste so good."

"I agree with that," said Facher.

"We were drinking bottled water off and on."

"From the beginning you resorted to bottled water?"

"Off and on. We split, half and half. Like we cooked with regular water and did other things. To make orange juice, we used the tap water, but to drink just straight water, I drank bottled water."

"Has any doctor ever told you that you had any dysfunction of your immune system?"

"No," said Richard, "but when my son died, they told us that was why he died. His immunity system was tore down to nothing."

Facher looked through the file of medical records in front of him. "There's been some reference to salmonella as the cause of his death. Do you know anything about that?"

The immediate cause of Jarrod's death had indeed been attributed to salmonella, although his doctors had said that he would not have died from the bacterial infection if his immune system had not been suppressed by chemotherapy. "That's what the autopsy read, something like that," replied Richard. "I'm not sure. I'm not a doctor."

"What caused you to have an autopsy?"

"Because he was doing good. He looked great. He only lived three months with leukemia and he looked fine."

"Did you have some personal talk with the doctor about this?" asked Facher.

"More of a violent talk with him," admitted Richard. "Because my son died like, like . . . nothing, all of a sudden, and they weren't taking any tests."

"By violent, you mean you were angry?"

"Yelling at him," nodded Richard. "He reassured us the tests that they didn't do are going to be done from now on, which is small compensation for my son's life."

"Let me see if I understand," said Facher. "Your son seemed to be doing all right, was in remission, you were optimistic about his future, and suddenly he became ill and died?"

"They said that was expected. Anybody with a disease like leukemia could die any minute."

"But you were angry and upset and maybe even accusatory when—"

"Anybody would be," interrupted Richard, sounding a little angry just now. "My son just died."

"I understand that," said Facher softly. "I was just trying to re-create the event."

"One day he's fine, he's playing, next day he's dead. That was the gist of the whole thing. You can tell when your child isn't feeling well. You try to explain it to them on the phone and they say: 'Has he got a temperature?' You say, no. 'He's all right, then,' they say. 'Don't worry. Bring him into the clinic Monday morning.' " Richard paused. "He died Monday morning."

"He was in the clinic when he died?" asked Facher.

"No. He was in the car on the way down I-93."

Facher had not known this. "He died in the car on the way to the clinic?" Facher asked.

"He died on I-93, up by the Somerville exit. We cut off and went to the fire station—" Richard was going to say more but he could not. He was on the verge of tears. He picked up a glass of water and drank deeply.

For a moment no one in the room moved. The only sound came from Richard, whose breath was raspy and labored. Conway, who felt very moved by Richard's anguish, put a hand up to his eyes. The motion must have caught Facher's attention, for Conway saw the old lawyer glance sourly at him.

Finally Facher said to Richard, "You had called, wanting to bring him in, and they said—"

"Called Sunday, Sunday morning, and they said bring him in Monday."

Facher asked a few more questions about the boy's treatment and then decided that he'd learned enough. He turned the deposition over to the lawyers for W. R. Grace. One of Cheeseman's partners asked several quick questions, taking only a minute or so, and then Facher said, "I have nothing further at this time, Mr. Schlichtmann." He looked at Richard. "Thank you very much, sir."

Richard pushed his chair back and stood. Schlichtmann stood, too, and gently patted Richard on his back. The defense lawyers remained seated and the room was very quiet.

Schlichtmann put on his coat and walked with Richard to the door. They had reached the door when Schlichtmann heard Facher speak.

"Good-bye and good luck," said Facher.

To Schlichtmann's ears, these words came out sounding contemptuous, almost like a sneer, as if Facher had said, "Good-bye and good riddance." Schlichtmann turned quickly on his heel and glared at Facher. "You're the one who's going to need the luck," he said.

Facher had not meant to sound contemptuous, but he had been greatly disturbed by Richard Aufiero's testimony. This first deposition had not gone at all the way he had planned. "Some cases a lawyer can't lose," Facher often told his Harvard students. "Some, maybe, he can't win. You play the hand you're dealt."

After Aufiero's deposition, Facher believed that this case was one he probably could not win, not in front of a jury. He could imagine

Aufiero on the witness stand with Schlichtmann slowly drawing out the details of Jarrod's death. The entire courtroom, maybe even the judge, would be in tears by the time Schlichtmann was done. And it wasn't just Aufiero. There were seven other families, each with its own tragic story to tell.

At that moment, Facher calculated the odds against him at about ten to one. He realized then that he might have to settle this case before trial, and that thought was distasteful to him. He was proud of saying that he had never yet paid more than a million dollars to settle a case, but in this instance, he suspected that settlement would not come so cheaply.

He told himself that he had to find a way to keep the plaintiffs off the witness stand. He did not know how he could do that, short of settlement. But it was early yet. Discovery had just begun. A lot would happen between now and the time a jury was impaneled.

2

The depositions of the thirteen Woburn adults took up the entire month of January. Schlichtmann attended every one of them, but he could not afford to take much satisfaction in the drama of his clients' stories. His thoughts were occupied with the job of building a convincing case against W. R. Grace and Beatrice Foods. To do that, he had to discover a great deal. Some human hands were responsible for the contamination of the Aberjona aquifer. Schlichtmann had to find out whose hands, and how much they had dumped, and on whose authority.

He began his own series of depositions, which were held in his office around the $12,000 bird's-eye-maple table. He turned his attention first to Grace. The company had admitted to the EPA that its employees had dug a pit behind the plant and placed several drums into it. The company had described this material as "generally innocuous," and had stated that no actual drums had been buried. But Schlichtmann knew that this admission had been incomplete at best, and perhaps even a deliberate lie. The EPA, after all, had subsequently unearthed from the plant's backyard six corroded drums, lying end to end, which had once contained TCE and other toxic solvents.

Schlichtmann wanted to bring before a jury the employees who had committed those acts and the supervisors who had overseen them. He asked Cheeseman to produce for deposition the Woburn plant's "most knowledgable person" concerning chemical use and waste-disposal practices. Cheeseman arrived at the appointed time, a Wednesday morning in the first week of March, with a man named Paul Shalline, head of safety and maintenance at the Woburn plant.

Schlichtmann learned from Shalline that he had worked at Grace for thirty years. He had only a trade school education but had risen, briefly, to the position of plant superintendent at Woburn. Then he'd been demoted. He was sixty years old and unprepossessing in manner and appearance. He replied to Schlichtmann's questions in a slow and deliberate manner, often giving vague answers or claiming not to remember. He said he had been appointed "pollution control officer" at the Woburn plant, but when Schlichtmann asked when this appointment had occurred, Shalline replied, "I don't remember."

"What were your duties?" asked Schlichtmann.

"I would oversee disposal and discharge to the drains, be sure we weren't polluting the air, and anything related to that field."

"Do you know if chemicals were disposed in back of the building, on the land?"

"I don't know that," replied Shalline.

This puzzled Schlichtmann. Cheeseman had admitted in his response to interrogatories that "small amounts" of chemical waste had been poured "from time to time" on the ground behind the plant. Cheeseman had produced Shalline as the person most knowledgable about waste disposal, but now Shalline denied knowing anything.

Schlichtmann tried again, quoting almost verbatim from Cheeseman's reply to the interrogatories. "From time to time, were waste materials disposed of by spilling them on the ground in the back of the plant?"

"If you know," interrupted Cheeseman.

"I don't know," said Shalline.

"Was material from the degreaser in the machine shop disposed of by spreading it on the ground in back of the plant?"

"I'm not aware of that."

"Was it the practice of the Woburn plant in the 1960s to dispose of waste material by spreading it on the ground in the rear of the plant?"

"If you know," interjected Cheeseman again.

"I don't know," said Shalline. "I don't know if it was an authorized procedure."

"Could it have been an unauthorized procedure?"

"It could have been. Somebody could have done it without my seeing it."

The deposition of Paul Shalline lasted two working days. By its end, after twelve hours of interrogation, Schlichtmann had gotten only denials and professions of ignorance from Shalline. The man claimed to know nothing about the six barrels of toxic waste that had been buried behind the plant and exhumed by order of the EPA. Schlichtmann believed that Shalline was lying to protect himself, or perhaps the company. He thought it would be just a matter of time until he exposed those lies.

In reply to Schlichtmann's interrogatories, Cheeseman stated that TCE had been kept in the plant's paint shop, where it was used to clean metal parts prior to painting. So Schlichtmann summoned the Grace painter for deposition.

The painter's name was Thomas Barbas. Schlichtmann studied him from across the conference table. He was in his early forties, heavyset, his round face plump and smooth, his straight brown hair receding high on his brow. He wore an ill-fitting blue sports coat, tight around his shoulders and under his arms, on which he had buttoned all three buttons. He looked ill at ease in these clothes, much as Richard Aufiero had in his, as if they were the sort worn only on rare occasions, to church or to court. He sat erect and stolid in the chair next to Cheeseman, saying nothing and barely moving. Schlichtmann had the impression of a man who was not just nervous but frightened.

The stenographer swore Thomas Barbas in and Schlichtmann began by asking him his occupation.

"Buyer," replied Barbas.

"You're a buyer?" said Schlichtmann in surprise. He had asked Cheeseman to produce the painter. "How long have you been a buyer?"

"Since the beginning of the year."

"Prior to that, what was your occupation?"

"Painter."

"And how long had you been a painter?"

"Approximately twenty-two years," said Barbas.

"Was there a reason why you changed your occupation from painter to buyer?" asked Schlichtmann.

"There was a job opening. I put in for it and I got it," said Barbas.

Schlichtmann questioned Barbas about the details of his job as a painter. Barbas answered in monosyllables, in a soft, sometimes barely audible voice. He admitted that when he first started working at Grace in 1961, he had dumped used cleaning solvents into a drainage ditch behind the plant. "At the end of the work day, take the solvent out and dump it on the ground," said Barbas. "We did like what we were supposed to do."

So this was where Cheeseman had gotten his information. "How long did you do that?" asked Schlichtmann.

"I'd say maybe a couple of months."

Barbas went on to say that he had stopped the practice after only two months. "It was my idea originally to put the used solvent and paint sludge in barrels and have them taken out legally. That was my recommendation to the boss."

"Who was the boss?" asked Schlichtmann.

"Paul Shalline."

"You told Mr. Shalline you didn't think it was a good idea to dump it on the ground?"

"Right."

"Why did you think it was a bad idea?"

Cheeseman objected to this question for the record. Under the rules governing depositions, all objections are preserved until the time of trial, when a judge is present to rule on the objection. Until then, a deponent is compelled to answer despite the objection, and Cheeseman indicated to Barbas that he should do so.

"I didn't think it was a bad idea," said Barbas. "I didn't think it was hazardous."

"Then why did you recommend having it hauled away?"

"After a while I thought it was a bad idea."

"Why?"

Again Cheeseman objected for the record, but Barbas had to answer.

"That would be similar to taking gasoline and throwing it on the ground," Barbas said. "It is not a good idea."

Barbas claimed that Shalline had agreed with his recommendation, and thereafter the painter had emptied waste solvents into 55-gallon drums that were kept by the back door of the plant. Barbas said he did not know what had happened to the drums after they'd been filled with waste.

"Mr. Barbas," said Schlichtmann, "did you at any time participate in disposing those drums of material into a pit in the rear of the plant?"

"No," said Barbas.

"Never did?"

"No," repeated Barbas.

"Did you witness it?"

"No."

"Do you have any information or knowledge that such an incident took place?" asked Schlichtmann.

"Yeah, they dug those drums up, didn't they?"

"Is that the only information you have?"

"I might have heard about something before, but I'm not sure," said Barbas.

"Who did you hear about it from?"

"I don't remember," said Barbas.

"What's your understanding as to what happened during that incident?"

"Well, now, I object," interrupted Cheeseman. "He has indicated he didn't see it, didn't hear about it, and you're asking him to describe it?"

"Uh-huh," said Schlichtmann, who kept staring at Barbas and asked: "What do you know about the incident?"

Schlichtmann's style—the intent stare, the rapid-fire questions, repeated again and again—annoyed Cheeseman. "Ignore the tone of voice and the way he's leaning across the table and staring at you," Cheeseman advised Barbas.

"I *am* leaning forward and staring at him," said Schlichtmann without taking his eyes off Barbas. "I'll lean backwards if it will make you more comfortable. I'll stand on my head."

Barbas seemed prepared for a battering, his head hunkered deep into his broad shoulders.

"What do you know?" Schlichtmann repeated.

"Just the things that we've heard about and read about in the paper—some barrels were buried," Barbas said.

Schlichtmann asked Barbas if he'd ever talked to Paul Shalline about the pit.

"I told him I didn't know anything about it," replied Barbas. "I told him that my job was to put the waste in the barrels and it was the company's responsibility to get rid of them legally, and that was it. That's all I said to him."

Schlichtmann could get nothing more out of Barbas, but he felt sure that Barbas knew much more. After the deposition, in the office that evening, Schlichtmann reflected on how very odd it was that Barbas should have gotten his first and only promotion just now, just before his deposition, after twenty-two years in the paint shop.

3

Three weeks later, on a Thursday morning in early April, the receiving clerk at the Grace plant, a man named Al Love, drove into Boston to have his deposition taken.

Love had already spent some time with Cheeseman, who had asked him a lot of questions about his job at the plant and told him what to expect at the deposition. Now, on their way down Milk Street to Schlichtmann's office, Cheeseman had a few more words of advice to offer. "Schlichtmann is a flamboyant sort of guy," Cheeseman said. "He can be very zealous and excitable. Just relax and don't get angry with him. Try to stick to yes or no answers."

In the conference room at Schlichtmann, Conway & Crowley, a short, stout man in a rumpled suit smiled pleasantly at Love and introduced himself as Kevin Conway. A few moments later, a man whom Love understood to be Schlichtmann, tall and angular, came into the room. He nodded brusquely to Love, and Love nodded back.

Love tried to follow Cheeseman's instructions, answering Schlichtmann's questions tersely, rarely speaking more than a few syllables. He told Schlichtmann he lived on Pine Street in east Woburn. He'd started working in the sheet metal department in 1961, six months after the plant had opened. Back then, before his promotion to receiving clerk, he had cleaned metal parts with a solvent he obtained from a drum in the paint shop.

"Did you ever see a name on the side of the drum?" asked Schlicht-mann.

"Yes," replied Love.

"What was the name?"

"I couldn't tell you."

"Did the drum indicate that it had trichloroethylene in it?"

"I don't remember," said Love.

Schlichtmann asked Love what he would do with the leftover sol-vent, and Love said he would take it back to the paint shop and pour it into a smaller container of waste. Had Love ever seen anyone dumping out these containers of waste solvent?

"Yes," said Love.

"Where would they take it?"

"Backyard," said Love in a low voice.

"What would they do in the backyard?"

"Dump it."

"Where?" asked Schlichtmann quickly. "On the ground?"

"Yes."

"And you saw that happen? You saw it happen on more than one occasion?"

"Yes," said Love, who could see that Schlichtmann was leaning for-ward, looking intently at him. It was plain to Love that his answers excited Schlichtmann.

"How did you happen to see this?" Schlichtmann asked.

"On coffee break."

"Who were those people you saw do it?"

"The names?" asked Love reluctantly.

"Yes, the names," said Schlichtmann.

Love named Tom Barbas and Joe Meola, the plant's maintenance man. Those two, he said, were the only ones he had seen.

"Where was it, the place where you have your coffee break?"

"In the field in the backyard," replied Love. "I used to go out there and hit nine iron shots, golf balls."

"Is that right? Enlightened employee policy at Grace." Schlicht-mann smiled broadly at Cheeseman. "Tell me exactly what you'd see them do. How did they empty this container?"

"Just tipped it over into a ditch."

"What kind of ditch?"

"Just an open trench that led down to the back of the property, to a natural waterway, a brook, I think."

Schlichtmann had Love draw a diagram of the Grace plant and mark the areas along the drainage ditch where he'd seen Barbas and Meola dumping material. Then he asked Love to mark the pit into which several drums of waste had been emptied. Love drew a square directly behind the plant.

"Was there more than one pit?"

Love said he recalled only one. It had been dug in 1974, during the construction of an addition to the main building. He and Tom Barbas had made jokes about it. "We referred to it as the 'recreation area.' That was supposed to be the 'swimming pool.' " He said he had never seen anyone dump drums of waste into it, although after the lawsuit had been filed he'd heard employees joking about such things.

By then, it was nearly one o'clock. The deposition had gone on without a break for almost three hours. "Let's take a two-minute break," Schlichtmann said to Love, "and we may get you out of here for lunch."

Schlichtmann stood and motioned for Conway to follow him out of the conference room.

Conway shut the door behind him. In the hallway they conferred in whispers. The deposition was about to end, but Schlichtmann had the feeling that he had left something undone. Love had been nervous at first, like the others before him, but Schlichtmann detected something else about the man—a poise, a sense of quiet self-confidence. Love had a rawboned, rangy build and he seemed like a man who could take care of himself. Barbas and Shalline might have difficulty lying effectively, but Schlichtmann thought that Love might have difficulty abandoning his self-respect enough to lie.

"What do you think?" Schlichtmann asked Conway.

Conway reflected for a moment. "He lives on Pine Street in east Woburn, just a couple of houses away from Anne Anderson. Why don't you ask him about the water? Ask him about his family's health."

Back in the conference room, Schlichtmann said to Love: "You've lived in east Woburn for how many years, Mr. Love?"

"Nineteen."

"And you have how many children?"

"Eight."

Schlichtmann asked for their names and ages, and Love complied. "That's quite a family," Schlichtmann remarked. "You know what the water was like in east Woburn?"

"When? Now?" replied Love.

"How would you describe the water during the 1960s?"

"Fine."

"How about the seventies?"

"Odor."

"What did it smell like?"

"Chlorine, or something," said Love. "Very pungent smell."

"And how about the color? What did it look like?"

"Sometimes very dark."

"Seem to have things in it? A residue?"

"Yes."

"Did you drink it or did you—"

"Yeah, I drank it," said Love abruptly.

"Were you concerned when you found out the wells were contaminated?"

Cheeseman objected. Donald Frederico, one of Facher's young associates, had been listening to the deposition with only half an ear. He had no particular interest in Love's testimony because it did not involve Beatrice, but Facher wanted a Hale and Dorr lawyer present at every deposition. Frederico had already sat through Shalline and Barbas, and on this morning he'd spent most of his time reading the *Boston Herald*. He had a low regard for personal injury law in general and a growing dislike for Schlichtmann in particular. "Plaintiffs' lawyers feed on death," Frederico once remarked. "They see a dead person as an opportunity to make a bundle." Now, when Cheeseman objected, Frederico looked up from the *Herald* and added his objection, too.

"Were you concerned for your own health?" asked Schlichtmann. Cheeseman objected again and Frederico joined him. Love answered yes.

"Were you concerned for the health of your family?"

More objections.

Love said yes again.

"Has any of your family experienced serious illness?"

The objections came with every question now, and they disturbed Love. He could not understand why Cheeseman and Frederico were objecting to questions about his family's health. Cheeseman was supposed to be on his side, but it seemed as if Schlichtmann was his ally, not Cheeseman.

Love said, "Yes, I'm concerned about their health. My youngest son has a seizure disorder. One of my daughters had a miscarriage and my granddaughter had a birth defect."

"Have any of your children experienced rashes?" asked Schlichtmann.

Frederico had put down his newspaper. "Are we going to sit here and go through his entire family's medical history?" he asked with a disbelieving laugh.

"You can leave," said Schlichtmann.

"Such irrelevant matter," snorted Frederico.

Love glanced darkly at Frederico. When he looked back at Schlichtmann, their eyes met for a brief moment. He thought he saw Schlichtmann give him a slight, almost imperceptible nod of understanding.

Then Schlichtmann's gaze shifted to Frederico. "You can leave," he said again.

"I'm not going to leave if you're conducting a deposition," snapped Frederico.

"Then sit and listen," said Schlichtmann in the tone one would use on a troublesome child. He looked back to Love. "Have you or your wife had problems with burning eyes?"

"Objection!" said Frederico.

Love nodded. "In the shower, during the time the water was bad in east Woburn."

"And your wife complained of it?"

"Objection!" said Frederico.

"Yes," said Love at the same moment that Cheeseman added his objection.

"Slow down a bit," said Cheeseman. "Give me a chance."

"Are you aware," asked Schlichtmann, "of any of your neighbors who have had leukemia in their families?"

"Several."

"Have you read reports about the contamination found in the wells?"

"Yes," said Love.

"Are you concerned about the health effect of what was found in the wells?"

"Yes."

"You're concerned for your family, is that right?"

"Yes."

Schlichtmann looked straight at Love and smiled. "All right, we're all set. Thank you very much, Mr. Love."

Love nodded and smiled back at Schlichtmann.

As Love remembered it later, he felt confused and angry after the deposition. His head throbbed and he could feel a headache coming on as he and Cheeseman walked up the street.

"You did very well," said Cheeseman in a kindly way. "I thought you'd be upset when he started asking personal questions about your family."

"That didn't bother me at all," said Love.

Cheeseman changed the subject and asked Love about the Woburn plant manager. Cheeseman said that he'd heard that the manager, whose name was Vincent Forte, had a quick temper. "What kind of guy is he?" Cheeseman asked.

Love thought this question was singularly odd coming from Cheeseman. He knew that Cheeseman had spent quite a lot of time with the plant manager, and he felt the lawyer was probing him, trying to see if he had a grudge against the manager or the company. His headache felt worse. "I never had any problems with Vin," Love replied. "I always got along with him pretty good."

On the sidewalk outside Cheeseman's office building, they paused for a moment. Love was anxious to leave Boston and get home, but Cheeseman was still talking. "If you've got any questions, or want to talk, I'm only a phone call away," Cheeseman said. Then, in a friendly voice, he asked, "Are you going back to work?"

Love looked at the April sky. It was overcast and a little chilly, but shafts of sunlight pierced the clouds. "No," he said with a touch of defiance. "I think I'm going to play some golf."

The more Al Love thought about it, the angrier he got at the way Cheeseman and especially Frederico had acted when Schlichtmann had asked about the health of his family. On a morning a week after his deposition he sat at his desk contemplating the telephone. Finally he dialed Cheeseman's number. He felt nervous and his words came awkwardly. "I've been thinking about this situation," he told Cheeseman. "I feel like I'm betwixt and between. I don't know which side I should be on, but I don't think everything that went on around here is getting told."

Cheeseman said he was planning to come out to the plant the next day. "Why don't we talk?"

The following afternoon Cheeseman appeared at the door of the receiving office. He suggested to Love that they go to the conference room, where they could talk in private. "Tell me what's bothering you, Al," said Cheeseman as he closed the door.

Love said that he was concerned about the health of his family. "I'm wondering if I should get a lawyer for my children's sake," he said.

"I can't advise you one way or the other about getting a lawyer," replied Cheeseman. "That's something you've got to decide for yourself." Cheeseman paused, and then he added: "As a practical matter, I don't believe those chemicals in the water made anyone sick."

"What about the leukemia cluster? That's been documented."

"No one knows what causes leukemia," explained Cheeseman. "And no one knows what caused this cluster. I personally think it's just a matter of chance. If you took a hundred pennies and threw them in the air, half would land heads and the other half would land tails. If you looked around carefully, you'd probably be able to find some heads grouped together in a cluster. But it's purely a matter of chance. No one can explain it."

Love thought about that for a moment. He shook his head slowly and said, "I can't buy it. I know that water was contaminated. And I know from people around here that barrels have been buried and things have been dumped. I wasn't the one who did it, but I know it happened."

"Al, this is very important," said Cheeseman. "I want you to tell me the names of those people."

Love did not want to become an informer. He had already named Barbas and Meola at his deposition, but he'd been under oath then. He and Tommy Barbas had known each other almost their entire lives. When Barbas had started work at the plant, fresh out of high school, Love had taken it upon himself to look after the younger man. At the company Christmas parties, Love and his wife, Evelyn, always sat at the same table with Tommy and his wife. They'd had the Barbases over to dinner at their house. Love wasn't about to cause any more trouble for Barbas. If Tommy had anything to tell the lawyers, he himself should be the one to do it. "I can't do that," Love told Cheeseman, shaking his head.

"Can you speak to these people and ask them to come to me?"

Love said, "Let me think about that."

"It's very important that we learn about everything that went on around here," said Cheeseman.

Listening to Cheeseman speak, it suddenly dawned on Love that perhaps the lawyer really did not know what had happened at the plant. Certainly Vin Forte, the plant manager, knew everything. If Cheeseman was in the dark, then Forte must have lied to the lawyers to protect himself. And Tommy Barbas must have lied, too.

"We need the information so we can disclose it to the appropriate officials," continued Cheeseman. "We need it so we can get the Environmental Protection Agency in, so we can clean up everything that might be in the ground."

Love shook his head.

Word spread quickly around the plant that day that Cheeseman had come to see Love. Some people whispered that Al had gotten himself into a predicament of some sort with the lawyers. Love had not risen far in the plant hierarchy, but he had a quiet authority that had led others to respect him and his word. When one of Love's friends, Cy Witmer, who worked in the sheet metal shop, heard the rumors, he took a break and came to see Love. "What's going on, Al?" Witmer asked.

"I do believe I'm on the wrong side of this whole thing," Love said.

During the next week, Love slept poorly. He could barely eat. His wife, Evelyn, worried about him. At night, after dinner, while Evelyn cleaned the dishes, they talked about whether he should go over to see Anne Anderson. She lived just around the corner, on Orange Street, a two-minute walk. Although they had been neighbors for fifteen years, the Loves did not know Anne well. Al had seen an ambulance come to her house on more than one occasion when her son had been ill, and he knew that she and her husband had separated. When the Woburn leukemias began to attract media attention, Al had thought Anne was "a fruitcake," as he put it, a sad case who'd broken under the strain of the tragedies that had befallen her. But lately he'd begun to reconsider. He wondered how Anne would receive him if he went over and knocked on her door. It occurred to him that since he worked for Grace she might blame him for what had happened to her son.

Evelyn had always told Al that someone in Grace management would surely come forward with the truth, somebody whose responsibility it was. But now, witnessing the turmoil that Al was in, she told him he should go speak to Anne and tell her what he knew. They tried to weigh the consequences of such an act, whether Al would lose his job if it came out. But to Evelyn, losing a job now seemed less important than doing what Al thought was right, and what would set his mind at rest.

On Wednesday evening, the first of May, three weeks after his deposition, Al Love walked over to Anne's house and knocked on the door. Anne invited him in, offered him coffee, and they sat at her kitchen table. He told her that he'd thought about coming to see her for some time, but he'd been afraid she might not want to talk to him because he worked for W. R. Grace. He said he cared about what had happened in the city and to her son, and he was angry about the way the company was handling itself.

Anne put her hand on his arm and said, "You have no idea how much this means to me." She had tears in her eyes, and she apologized for crying. Love said he was worried about the health of his own family. He'd heard rumors at the plant about many drums being buried. "Fifty or more drums," he said. "There's a lot that's not coming out."

He and Anne talked for almost two hours. Love remembered feeling clearheaded and calm for the first time in weeks. As he was about to leave, Anne asked if he would be willing to speak to Schlichtmann, to tell him what he had told her.

Yes, Love said, he would talk to Schlichtmann.

Schlichtmann arrived by invitation at the Loves' house the next evening. He and Al sat in the living room, talking for two hours about the Grace plant. Al told him about the rumors of fifty or more drums being buried under an addition that had been added onto the plant in the early 1970s. Schlichtmann had brought along the deposition transcripts of Tom Barbas and Paul Shalline, and he asked Love to read them as soon as he could.

A few days later, after Love finished reading the lengthy transcripts, he and Schlichtmann met again. Love, shaking his head ruefully, said that Tommy Barbas had not told the truth at his deposition. Love recalled how he'd sat in the cafeteria at work three years ago with Barbas and a supervisor named Frank Kelly, listening to the two men talk about the drums of toxic waste buried out back behind the plant. He remembered how Kelly, laughing, had pointed at Barbas. "Tommy knows all about it," Kelly had said. The other workers at the table had laughed, too, and even Barbas had smiled. Everyone had treated it like a big joke, Love told Schlichtmann.

Nearly every day for the next two weeks, Schlichtmann or Conway or someone else from the office called or stopped by Love's house. One night Schlichtmann arrived with a thick stack of aerial photographs of the Grace plant dating back to 1960. Schlichtmann spread these on the dining room table and had Love study them with a magnifying glass, trying to identify the areas where he'd seen the pits and where Barbas and Meola had emptied their buckets of solvent and the degreasing machine. Schlichtmann went over every detail four, five, six times, probing for more, and Love answered patiently. They worked until late in the evening, the lights in the house blazing, the windows open in the soft spring air, people from Schlichtmann's firm arriving and departing as if Love's house had become its Woburn office.

Schlichtmann wanted the names of former Grace workers who might know more about the buried drums. Love mentioned Robert Pasqueriella, an electrician who used to work at the plant. Schlichtmann asked if he would call Pasqueriella right then, and Love did so.

Pasqueriella had not worked at Grace for six years, and he had to think a minute before it came back to him. Then he remembered a conversation he'd had with Frank Kelly. "Sure," Pasqueriella said to Love. "Frank told me about those barrels."

Half an hour later, Pasqueriella was in Love's living room. Schlichtmann liked the man immediately. He was short and rotund, in his late forties, and he spoke in a rapid, staccato manner, often repeating a phrase several times. "I threw stuff back there myself," he told Schlichtmann. "Yep, threw it there myself. Eddie Orazine, the assembly foreman, he told me to throw stuff out in the gully there. Nothing will grow there. I didn't know at the time the stuff was toxic. My hands used to get white from it. I used to wash down the belts with the stuff, I don't know what it's called, I'm no chemist."

"Trichloroethylene?" asked Schlichtmann.

"Yeah, that's it. I'd work on the machine, drain out the old motor oil in the gearbox, put new oil in, let it run for a while to make sure it worked okay. If it was real dirty, I'd turn the gearbox on the side and put the solvent into it and swish it around. Then I'd dump it out back. In the machine shop, there used to be cutting oil, white like milk. Every once in a while Joe Meola used to drain the stuff out and go back and dump it in the gully. No one took it upon themselves to do anything on their own. None of the stuff was ever done without the permission of Paul Shalline and Eddie Orazine."

"What about Tom Barbas?"

"Tommy, he would dump his paint thinner and other stuff in the ditch."

"Barbas said he never did that."

Pasqueriella snorted. He waved his hand in a dismissive gesture. "I seen Tommy with my own eyes throw his stuff into that ditch. I stood right beside him while he did it. It was just routine. He was doing it for many years that I know of."

Schlichtmann asked Pasqueriella if he'd call Barbas and talk to him.

"Right now?" said Pasqueriella. "Why not? Sure."

Schlichtmann hoped that Barbas might even come over to Love's house, as Pasqueriella had. He knew he'd get much more out of Barbas sitting with him in Love's living room than he would at a deposition with Cheeseman present.

Pasqueriella dialed Barbas's number and spoke for several minutes. In the living room, Schlichtmann listened to Pasqueriella's end of the conversation. "Tommy, you handled that stuff," he heard Pasqueriella say. "So did I. Remember, I used to dump out in the back, too. I stood there talking to you while you did it." Pasqueriella listened for a minute. "You know exactly what's going on. If you're smart, you'll tell the truth. Everything you know, you better tell. You don't want to take the rap for Vin Forte."

Pasqueriella paused for a moment, and then he said: "Listen, Tommy, if they ask me, I'm going to tell the truth. I ain't lying for no one."

Pasqueriella hung up the phone. "He says he doesn't know anything about it. He was hemming and hawing. I know Tommy, and I can tell when he's nervous."

These revelations—especially the rumors of fifty or more drums being buried behind the plant—delighted Schlichtmann. It was clear to him that Barbas had lied under oath at his deposition. It was also clear that W. R. Grace had not told the EPA the whole truth about how much TCE the plant had really used, and what it had buried in the backyard.

But Schlichtmann wanted hard evidence. He had to squeeze information out of Grace and its employees. One way of doing that would be to get the assistant U.S. attorney for environmental affairs interested in the case. A criminal investigation by the Justice Department, carrying with it the threat of heavy fines, perhaps even jail sentences for some Grace employees and executives, could break the case wide open. Months earlier, Schlichtmann had gone to see the assistant U.S. attorney and urged him to investigate Grace. "They lied to the EPA, I'm sure of it," Schlichtmann had said. "Why aren't you investigating?"

"Give me facts, give me evidence, give me witnesses," the government lawyer had replied. "I can't do anything without evidence, and I'm not going to start an investigation just to help your case."

Now, with information from Love and Pasqueriella, Schlichtmann felt he had enough to interest the U.S. attorney. He persuaded Love to speak with the government authorities, and he arranged a meeting on a day that Love had already planned to take off work. Love's youngest son, who was sixteen years old and had experienced seizures since he was seven, had an appointment with a specialist at Children's Hospital in Boston.

After their son's appointment, Al and Evelyn Love went with Schlichtmann and Conway up to the seventh floor of the federal courthouse. The assistant U.S. attorney and two senior EPA officials interviewed Al for nearly three hours that afternoon. Evelyn sat next to her husband through it all. The demeanor of the assistant U.S.

attorney unnerved her. He stared intently at Al, eyes narrowed, the entire time. But Al appeared to handle it well. He spoke forthrightly and never seemed intimidated. He drew maps and told the government lawyers exactly what he'd told Schlichtmann about the pits and the rumors of fifty drums being buried under the addition to the plant.

Afterward, the assistant U.S. attorney took Schlichtmann aside and said that he would begin an investigation. He planned to issue subpoenas to Grace employees, commanding them to testify before a grand jury.

Schlichtmann had not managed to get Barbas over to Love's house, but he got the next best thing. One week after Love's visit to the assistant U.S. attorney, Barbas called Cheeseman to say that he had suddenly remembered something. He remembered now that he had been involved in dumping the drums into the pit.

Cheeseman, seated at his desk, had the sensation of "going suddenly cold," he recalled later. He stood and looked out the window to the courthouse as he listened to Barbas. He felt himself getting angry.

Barbas, his words coming in a rush, told him in detail about everything he had suddenly "remembered." The painter spoke about a red flatbed truck carrying barrels to the edge of a pit, opening the bung caps, Joe Meola helping him empty the barrels. To Cheeseman, it seemed as if Barbas believed that the more quickly he spoke, the less damaging his previous testimony would become. Cheeseman listened for a while, and then he started asking questions.

Cheeseman thought he understood. For twenty-four years Barbas had done what he'd been told. Barbas probably thought he'd go to jail for dumping toxic wastes on the ground, and this fear, perhaps, had led him to perjure himself.

That afternoon Cheeseman called Schlichtmann and said, "I won't object if you want to depose Barbas again."

"Tell me what's going on, Bill," said Schlichtmann, just as if he didn't know.

Cheeseman explained that Barbas had called him that morning. "He says he remembers emptying the drums into the pit."

. . .

"Mr. Barbas, you've had time to think about things since your first deposition?"

"Yes."

They were back in Schlichtmann's office. There were more lawyers in the conference room now. Cheeseman was there, of course, and one of Facher's associates, and also two criminal lawyers, hired and paid by Grace to represent Barbas in the federal investigation.

"Mr. Barbas," said Schlichtmann, "would you please tell me what you remember about your participation in the pouring of drums into a pit on W. R. Grace's property?"

"That I was a participant," said Barbas.

"Do you remember anything else?"

"Helping at the time was Joe Meola. And Frank Kelly."

"You've had time to think about who ordered you to dump those barrels, is that right?"

"Yes. Paul Shalline asked me if I would mind pouring the contents of the barrels into the pit."

"And what did you say?"

"Well, I asked him—all this time we were saving the material to have it sent out to a legal disposing firm. He said it was not hazardous, we could pour it."

"Now, Mr. Barbas, you poured waste solvents into the trench throughout the 1960s, didn't you?"

"I think I stated I only did it during 1961."

"I know what you stated. I want you to think about the question very carefully. You understand you're under oath?"

"Yes."

"You understand that the statement you're giving is under the pains and penalties of perjury?"

Barbas nodded.

"You know that Mr. Meola would on occasion pour waste material into the trench?"

"Yes, I do."

"You saw him do that."

"Yes."

"For what period of time did you see Mr. Meola do that?"

"He was always doing it."

Cheeseman interrupted and said to Barbas: "He's now asking for your direct observation."

Schlichtmann turned angrily at Cheeseman. "I'm speaking English, Bill. He's not Portuguese. He doesn't need an interpreter." Schlichtmann turned back to Barbas: "Did you ever assist Mr. Meola?"

"No," said Barbas.

Schlichtmann stared at Barbas. "Did you ever assist Joe Meola in pouring waste solvent onto the ground?"

This time Barbas nodded his head yes.

"You can't just nod your head," said Cheeseman.

"I used to bring it out on some occasions, if it was wet, and pour it on the ground."

"How often would you do that?"

"Whenever it needed to be done."

"Which is, approximately, a weekly basis?"

"Yeah, weekly. I'd say weekly."

Schlichtmann did need an interpreter for Joe Meola. Although Meola, now in his seventies and retired, had worked for twenty years as the maintenance man at the Woburn plant, he claimed at his deposition that he did not understand English. Schlichtmann hired an Italian translator and the deposition went forward in Schlichtmann's office. Meola denied emptying barrels into a pit. Nor had he ever dumped the contents of the degreasing tank—or anything else, for that matter—on the ground.

"Tom Barbas testified you would empty the degreasing tank on the ground," said Schlichtmann.

"He is a liar," replied Meola through the translator.

"Mr. Barbas testified that he would dump waste solvents on the ground behind the plant."

"Good for him." Meola clasped his head. "My head is already gone," he said.

"We don't want your head to go yet," said Schlichtmann.

"I am seventy-three years old," said Meola.

"You look wonderful," said Schlichtmann.

"I look wonderful? If I come here another time I will have to go to the cemetery where the cypresses grow."

4

Schlichtmann remembered the spring day, three years ago, when he drove out to Woburn and parked across from the Grace plant. He remembered how he'd wished he could go inside and look around, how its brick façade had looked to him like the wall of a small fortress then. But the door was opened now, and he was getting guided tours by deposition.

He learned that the Grace plant was, by most accounts, a fine place to work, providing you got along with Vincent Forte, the plant manager. Forte had ruled the plant like his own fiefdom for more than twenty years. Most employees were willing to live by Forte's rules (which sometimes included doing outside work for Forte on company time) because the company paid good wages and offered generous benefits. Every Christmas the employees were treated to a party at a local restaurant. Behind the plant, on the five acres of overgrown fields that had once been farmland, the company had cleared away brush and built a sandpit for playing horseshoes. When Barbas developed an interest in archery, he and another employee had set up a target out back for practice, not far from where Al Love would sometimes chip golf balls. The company had installed a basketball hoop, as well as picnic tables so that employees could eat lunch outside on pleasant days. Joe Meola had started a vegetable garden, which he tended during his breaks and after hours, and soon several other employees began their own small gardens. But it was now clear to Schlichtmann that even while the company and the workers had transformed the area around the plant into a park and playground, they had also turned it into a toxic waste dump.

From current and former Grace employees, Schlichtmann heard that Tom Barbas was a neat and meticulous man and a conscientious worker. His high school yearbook recorded his pet peeve as "unshined shoes." At the Woburn plant, management had commended him several times over the years for the orderly way he kept the paint shop. His job was a lowly one, but he was good at it and he did not seem much interested in advancement. Every day he would receive metal parts used in the construction of commercial food-packaging machines. These parts arrived at his shop covered with a film of oil, a residue from the machining process. Before painting the parts, Barbas would wipe off the oily film using TCE, which he obtained from a 55-gallon drum that stood in the paint shop. He would pump some TCE into a small can, into which he would dip a rag. He was supposed to wear rubber gloves, but some of the parts were small and difficult to handle with gloves on. After cleaning a part, he'd hang it in the paint booth, a device about the size of a closet, constructed of rubber walls. Against the back wall of the booth, a curtain of water flowed in a constant, recirculating stream. Barbas used a spray gun and enamel paints, which he would sometimes thin with TCE. The circulating water captured overspray from the paint gun and carried it to a trough at the bottom of the booth.

At the end of each day Barbas would scoop the congealed paint out of the trough and into a plastic tray. Then he would clean the spray gun with TCE in a five-gallon bucket. On a normal day he might accumulate a gallon or two of waste. During his first week on the job, Paul Shalline had shown him the gully near the back door of the plant where he was to dump the waste.

Other workers told Schlichtmann how they would routinely come to the paint shop to obtain small amounts of TCE from the 55-gallon drum. They used the solvent to wipe grease and smudges off the neoprene conveyor belts or to clean stains from the metal tunnels where the plastic film was shrunk around food products. One employee said that when he started work in the assembly shop in 1970, he asked his foreman what to do with the leftover solvent and motor oil that he'd collected in a five-gallon pail. The foreman told him, "Dump it out back." Almost every day during the five years this employee worked at the Grace plant he had dumped waste into the gully.

Shalline, his memory now "refreshed," as the lawyers would say, recalled Barbas's suggestion about pouring waste solvent into an empty 55-gallon drum. Shalline had agreed to that suggestion, but not because of any special environmental concerns. "It was more practical," Shalline explained in reply to Schlichtmann. "Winter was coming on and it would be more convenient to have it right adjacent to the paint shop, where Tommy worked. He wouldn't spend all the time having to go outside."

And yet Barbas had continued going out to the gully to empty his bucket of waste. This puzzled Schlichtmann at first, until he discovered that Barbas made a narrow distinction between paint sludge and the small containers of pure TCE, which he would use to clean metal parts. By Barbas's lights, there was no harm in putting the paint sludge on the ground, even though it contained TCE. A meticulous man, he would shovel up the paint remnants after a few days, when it had dried, and dump it into an ordinary trash bin.

Another matter also puzzled Schlichtmann. If Barbas was, in fact, reluctant to pour solvent on the ground, why did he often help Joe Meola empty the contents of the fifteen-gallon degreasing tank, which contained pure solvent, into the gully? This act was on its face inconsistent, and yet Schlichtmann could never get Barbas to explain his reasoning. That puzzle remained unsolved.

Schlichtmann formed an image of Barbas growing into middle age as he worked at the Woburn plant. In 1967 Barbas was drafted into the army and sent to Vietnam, where he spent an uneventful year in the military police. When he returned to Woburn, he resumed his old job in the paint shop. He married and had children, and moved into a modest ranch house in north Woburn. His hair thinned and receded, and he grew stout. Al Love told Schlichtmann that Barbas would occasionally take over for him in the receiving department. But new routines seemed to make Barbas anxious, and when Love returned to work, he usually found the painter flustered and worried about having made a mistake.

Exactly how much TCE had the Woburn plant actually used? Schlichtmann could never get a straight answer to this. Grace corporate executives initially told the EPA that the plant had purchased just one drum of TCE. "Total amount used up by 1975," Grace had reported. "Use discontinued after a single initial order." This, of course, was false. Cheeseman himself had later amended the reply to four drums. Schlichtmann didn't believe that, either. But apart from anecdotal accounts by workers, he had no proof. According to Cheeseman, the plant's records of chemical use prior to 1975 had been "routinely" destroyed.

And then Schlichtmann discovered in the documents produced by Cheeseman a note dated October 30, 1973. It was written in a large, almost childish script, the letters awkwardly formed, with the initials "PS" at the bottom. Paul Shalline admitted that the handwriting was his. The note had been written in response to a telephone inquiry by a state inspector. It said: "Up 'til September; Used trichloro, 150 gallons." To Schlichtmann, this could only mean that the Grace plant had used 150 gallons—slightly less than three 55-gallon drums—in the first nine months of 1973. If that inference was true, it meant the plant had consumed four drums of TCE a *year* up until 1973, not merely four drums throughout its entire history. And that translated into fifty or more drums of TCE.

It was in the summer of 1973, Schlichtmann learned, that Grace's policy concerning the use of TCE changed. And that change led to the pouring of a drum of TCE into a pit in the backyard of the Woburn plant. Schlichtmann pieced together the story as best he could from deposition testimony and documents produced by Cheeseman. It had begun when a Grace executive named Richard Stewart received a warning about TCE from the National Institute of Occupational Safety and Health. The warning had stated that TCE "is especially hazardous in 'open bucket use,' in which parts are brushed and dipped in the bucket of solvent." Inhaling vapor from the solvent could cause eye irritation, cardiovascular and nervous ailments, and damage to liver and other body organs, said the warning. The institute planned to adopt a more rigorous standard for plants where TCE was used, one requiring formal inspections, emergency showers, and periodic medical examinations of employees.

In light of the proposed new standard, Richard Stewart decided that the safest and most economical course for Grace would be to eliminate the use of TCE wherever possible. Stewart sent a memo to all Grace plants recommending that they stop using the solvent. He asked the plant managers to report back to him on their actions.

In Woburn, Stewart's memo ended up on the desk of the production manager, who in turn notified Stewart that the plant would cease using TCE by November. The production manager gave the task of phasing out the solvent to Paul Shalline, then head of the safety committee.

Months passed, but Shalline apparently did nothing, despite frequent reminders from the production manager. Then the manager noticed that a 55-gallon drum of TCE remained in the paint shop. Finally he lost patience. In a memo to Shalline, he wrote: "I assigned this project to you ten months and twenty-six reminders ago. Why couldn't you handle it?"

Reading this ten-year-old memo, Schlichtmann almost felt sorry for Shalline. The Woburn plant had never had any policy or method for the disposal of such material, beyond dumping it onto the ground.

Shalline, left to his own devices, had gone to consult with Barbas, who told him there were companies that would haul waste solvents away. Barbas testified that he had even given Shalline the name of a firm he'd heard about in Burlington. Shalline had said he would call the firm, but meanwhile he asked Barbas to move the drum of TCE outside, where a dozen or more drums of accumulated waste were lined up near the back wall of the plant.

Shalline admitted under oath that he never did call the waste disposal firm suggested by Barbas. The drums had remained outside until a year later, when a new addition was built onto the rear of the plant. In the course of construction, Vincent Forte asked the contractor to dig a pit for the disposal of construction debris and other waste. This pit became the "swimming pool" of Al Love's recollection. According to Barbas, Paul Shalline had come up to him and said, "I want you to empty those barrels into the pit."

"What have we been saving them for?" Barbas remembered asking. "I thought we were going to have somebody take them away."

Shalline allegedly had replied: "The stuff is not hazardous. You can pour it. I'll get somebody to help you." Perhaps Barbas had looked dubious—he knew that the drums contained TCE mixed in with cutting oils and paint sludge—because Shalline had added, "After this, we'll have them taken away."

Barbas told Schlichtmann that he had watched from the back door of the plant as the drums were loaded onto the hydraulic tailgate of a red truck and lifted to the truck bed. The next morning, he saw the drums lined up at the edge of the pit, which Barbas estimated to be twenty feet wide and forty feet long. He and Joe Meola began emptying the drums into the pit by turning them on their sides, opening the bung holes, and watching as the contents drained out. They had emptied a few drums in this manner when Frank Kelly, the foreman of the shipping department, came to tell Barbas he had a paint job to do. Barbas departed. Later that day, he had walked back to the pit and stood at the edge, looking in. There was a pool of liquid at the bottom and some bung caps were strewn on the sloping sides, but he'd seen no drums at the bottom. Someone had rolled all the drums back to the plant—Barbas could see the marks in the grass and dirt—and stood them near the building. Several days later, the drums were gone. Barbas heard they had been sold to a salvage company. He did not think about the pit again until five years later, when Wells G and H were found contaminated with TCE.

And then there was the interring of the six drums later unearthed by the EPA, about which Barbas steadfastly claimed to have no personal knowledge. Schlichtmann deposed a Grace employee named Paul Kelly, the twenty-one-year-old son of Frank Kelly, who recalled seeing a backhoe dig a long trench behind the plant. According to Kelly, his foreman had told him to fill in the trench at the end of the day. Kelly had done so, working with another Grace employee. He'd seen seven drums—one more than was later dug up—lying end to end in the trench, which he estimated had been thirty or forty feet long and four feet deep.

By his own tally, Schlichtmann counted at least two pits, and possibly even more if the recollection of Bob Pasqueriella could be trusted. Pasqueriella recalled a conversation he'd had with Frank Kelly, shortly after the EPA began its investigation. "If they ever find out what is buried back there, we're all in trouble," Kelly had told Pasqueriella.

Pasqueriella asked Kelly what he meant. Kelly had said, "There's twenty-one barrels buried back there, under the warehouse. They better not dig there." But Schlichtmann would never find out what Kelly knew. Kelly had died of a heart attack not long after speaking to Pasqueriella. And Vincent Forte, who was reputed to have known everything that went on at the plant, had also died of a heart attack, on the eve of his second deposition.

Discovering the whole truth of what had happened at the Grace plant, Schlichtmann realized, was impossible. In the beginning, the truth had been obscured by a web of lies, evasions, and self-serving accounts from both workers and Grace executives. In the end, it still remained hidden by death and the vagaries of memory. But for Schlichtmann's purposes, it really made little difference whether there had been two pits or three or four. He had uncovered more than enough to make his case.

5

While Schlichtmann was busy building his case against Grace, the federal investigation that he had set in motion with the help of Al Love was causing chaos at the Woburn plant. Barbas, Shalline, and four other employees, including a Grace corporate executive, received subpoenas to testify before a grand jury. On the plant floor, rumors traveled swiftly among the workers, who gathered in small groups and talked in low voices among themselves. Lawyers from Boston and the W. R. Grace office in Cambridge seemed to arrive every day. One after another, workers were summoned to the conference room for interviews. An air of gloom and secrecy hung over the plant. In the front office, lawyers searched through the files. Barbas and Shalline were often gone from work, called to Boston for more interviews. Word spread that they were now represented by criminal lawyers. Their fellow workers speculated in whispers about whether anybody would go to jail for dumping or for perjury.

Cheeseman, of course, found out that Al Love had been secretly talking to Schlichtmann and the U.S. attorney. Cheeseman appeared at the door of the receiving department one morning and told Love he wanted to see him in the plant manager's office.

Love thought he had prepared himself for this moment, but he had a sick feeling in the pit of his stomach walking into the manager's office. Cheeseman was seated there, along with the new plant manager, a man named Ulf Nordin, and a W. R. Grace in-house lawyer from the Cambridge office. There was also a stenographer present to take Love's statement.

"Mr. Love," said Cheeseman in a cold and formal manner, "the company has asked that you be present today to answer some questions. I want you to understand that you're free to leave anytime you want to. If you want to take a break, to go to the men's room, to get a drink, or for any purpose, you're free to do that. The company has asked you, however, to answer the questions that I have." Cheeseman looked at the plant manager. "Just to be sure that it's understood, Mr. Nordin, would you now ask Mr. Love to answer my questions?"

Nordin instructed Love to answer the questions. "You are aware what that means as an employee of Grace?"

Love was aware only that he was about to lose his job, but he nodded at Nordin and said, "Sure."

Cheeseman asked Love when he first met with Schlichtmann.

"It was after May first," said Love. "On the evening of May first, I went across the street to Anne Anderson's house and told her of the dilemma my wife and I were in. She asked me if I would talk with her attorney."

"What did you talk about with Mr. Schlichtmann?"

"I told him that during the deposition everything was going fine up to the point he started asking me questions about my family, and that was the only time you people were concerned about what I said. So many objections were raised."

"I see," said Cheeseman.

"My life has changed in such a fashion," continued Love. "I told Mr. Schlichtmann the stories I'd heard. I felt as though no one at the plant was coming forward with information. I felt there might be some sort of punishment to me if I didn't see someone and iron this out. He advised me to see the U.S. attorney."

"The next meeting with Mr. Schlichtmann, was that scheduled by telephone?"

"I think he just appeared."

"Was he driving that nice, new, shiny black Porsche?" asked Cheeseman.

"I think he was. He went over everything he'd asked me before. It was pretty much repetition."

"He has that habit," murmured Cheeseman, more to himself than to Love. Cheeseman knew that if Grace fired Love now, Schlichtmann would turn him into a martyr. Cheeseman could imagine the headlines in the *Woburn Daily Times* and *The Boston Globe*.

"There's no plan to impose any discipline on you for what you've told us, or for having talked with the U.S. attorney," Cheeseman told Love. "It's your right to find out what happened around here that might affect the environment." But Cheeseman made it clear that Love could not speak with Schlichtmann again, or the company would have no choice but to fire him. And then Cheeseman said, "Thank you for coming in and being honest with us."

Love felt an enormous sense of relief and a genuine gratitude to Cheeseman. "My pleasure," he said.

Schlichtmann drove the shiny black Porsche out to the Grace plant one week in July. He had applied for a court order to inspect the land. He had cracked the Grace case, but he still had to prove that the TCE dumped by Barbas and the other workers had actually gotten to the city wells, half a mile away. He had hired a team of geologists and engineers to inspect the Grace land, take soil samples, and drill monitoring wells to determine the direction of the groundwater flow.

Cheeseman was at the plant, too, with his own team of experts to watch over Schlichtmann's experts. The work went on for four days. It started to rain one afternoon, fat drops splashing on the asphalt parking lot, and everyone took cover inside the plant. Cheeseman ran out to raise the top of his Triumph sports car. He saw Schlichtmann's Porsche, its windows down, the sun roof opened. For a moment, he considered rolling up the windows and closing the sun roof, but he decided against it. The rain came down in sheets, a tropical cloudburst. Later, when Schlichtmann walked out to his car, Cheeseman watched him open the door. Water trickled out of the Porsche and Schlichtmann swore. Cheeseman laughed heartily, loud enough for Schlichtmann to hear.

6

The first deadline set by Judge Skinner for the completion of discovery had come and gone. The judge himself had extended the deadline once, after allowing Unifirst into the case, and then in July he granted another six-month extension, until the end of January, at the request of all parties.

Schlichtmann needed this extra time. He had a lot to do. The case against Grace had occupied him throughout the spring and into the summer, and he had done almost no work on Beatrice. He had taken only one deposition, that of John J. Riley, manager of the Beatrice tannery, and it had not gone well. The tanner had answered his questions with open contempt. Schlichtmann, patient at first, soon began responding in kind. An hour into the deposition, Neil Jacobs, sent along by Facher to represent Riley, felt compelled to interrupt Schlichtmann and say, "Hold on! Hold on a minute! There really isn't any reason to make this unpleasant or to be rude."

Schlichtmann ignored Jacobs. He asked Riley again to describe just how he had used a mixture of silicone and tetrachloroethylene to waterproof leather for the U.S. Army. "In what contraption was it used?" Schlichtmann asked.

Riley looked down at the glass of water in front of him. He had a massive, bejowled face and a darkly florid complexion with blue eyes that looked small, almost porcine. He picked up the water glass, holding it between thick sausage-like fingers, and then, looking directly at Schlichtmann, he emptied the glass onto the bird's-eye-maple conference table.

Schlichtmann stared at the pool of water on his $12,000 table, at the water dripping onto his carpet. "Let the record show that the witness has emptied a glass of water on the conference table."

"Just a few drops," said Neil Jacobs, attempting to minimize the act in the pages of the record.

"What do you intend to indicate by pouring the water on my conference table, Mr. Riley?" asked Schlichtmann.

"This is how the silicone was put on the leather," replied Riley.

"Poured right on like you poured this glass of water on my table?"

"A pump was pumping it," replied Riley.

"Some of the mixture would spill off the leather, like it spilled on my table, wouldn't it?"

"No."

Perc had been found in large amounts in the soil on the fifteen-acre parcel of wooded, overgrown land owned by Beatrice. But when Schlichtmann asked Riley how much perc he had used over the years, Riley said, "Very little."

"Do you know how many drums you purchased?" asked Schlichtmann.

"I couldn't answer you specifically."

"Do you have any idea?"

"Would have been very small."

"How much leather did you make for the government?"

"I don't remember."

And so it went for the entire day. Riley denied, repeatedly and emphatically, that the tannery had used TCE. "Never," said the tanner, shaking his massive head, "never." When Schlichtmann asked Riley if he kept records—purchase orders, invoices, formulas, records of any type—concerning the chemicals used by the tannery, Riley said that none existed.

"The records were destroyed?" asked Schlichtmann.

"We don't have the space to keep records for very long."

"How far back do the records go?"

"Three years," said Riley.

Riley's three-year-old records were all but useless to Schlichtmann. The city wells had been closed six years ago. "Is it company policy to destroy records after three years?" he asked the tanner.

"Yes."

"How long has that been company policy?"

"Forever," said Riley.

Schlichtmann didn't believe any of this. He pressed Riley on it, but the tanner stuck to his story, admitting only that personnel files were kept longer than three years. He angrily denied dumping tannery waste, toxic chemicals, or waste of any sort on the fifteen acres that bordered the Aberjona River. That land, owned by the tannery since the early 1950s, was used only for the tannery's production well, insisted Riley. But it was also strewn with dozens of rusting 55-gallon drums. Schlichtmann had walked through there. He'd seen the drums and smelled the characteristic sickly-sweet odor of chlorinated solvents rising from patches of bare, dark earth among the oak and maple trees. The land was so grossly contaminated with TCE and other solvents that the EPA had ordered Riley to erect a chain-link fence around it for the sake of public safety.

But when Schlichtmann asked Riley if he'd ever seen drums or other debris on that land, the tanner said, "No, sir."

Had Riley ever seen areas where toxic waste had killed the surrounding vegetation?

"No, sir."

How would Riley describe the land?

"Just plain wildlife, that's all."

"So, as far as you're concerned, Mr. Riley, up until today, that land has been essentially in a wild state and has not been used for waste disposal?"

"Yes," replied the tanner.

Schlichtmann felt certain that Riley had dumped tannery waste and drums containing perc and TCE on the fifteen acres, just as the Grace employees had dumped solvents behind their plant. He felt certain that Riley had records of chemicals used by the tannery. But he had no proof of that. This deposition reminded him of the first time he'd deposed Barbas and Shalline. He'd gotten nothing from them either, but he had persisted and then he'd gotten lucky. He needed the same sort of luck with Beatrice. He needed to find another Al Love.

. . .

Schlichtmann put in a call to a private investigator, a former police detective he had once hired to locate a vanished witness in a malpractice case. He asked the investigator to go out to Woburn and find former tannery employees.

The investigator quickly located an ailing but voluble sixty-six-year-old man who had worked at the tannery for thirty-eight years, his entire adult life. This worker had undergone four operations for skin cancer and had a degenerative muscle disease, which he believed had been caused by the tanning chemicals. He did not wish Riley well, but he could not recall the tannery's ever using TCE or tannery workers dumping waste on the fifteen acres. He did, however, know plenty of former tannery employees. "Jack Knowlty, he worked in the tan room, but he died two years ago of stomach cancer, and he was only in his forties. Maurice O'Connor, color room, he died of cancer, too, and he was a young guy. Nick Murray and Jim Feeney, they both had heart attacks. Frank Valente worked in the wringing room, he died of lung cancer."

This sad litany led Schlichtmann to conclude that working at the Beatrice tannery could cost a man his life. The old worker did name one colleague he believed was still alive, just barely. "Joe Palino, he was a color mixer, he worked with the chemist. He's got lung cancer, too."

Schlichtmann sent his investigator to visit Joe Palino, who, as it happened, had just returned from a long hospital stay. Palino sat on his living-room sofa, a pale green tube attached to his nose, a bottle of oxygen on a small wheeled cart beside him. He said he did not remember seeing anyone at the tannery dispose of drums or tannery waste on the fifteen acres. But he did remember trichloroethylene. He thought perhaps the tannery had used TCE for cleaning embossing plates.

To Schlichtmann, this sounded like the break he was hoping for. Fearing that Palino might die before trial, he arranged for a bedside deposition at Palino's home. But at the deposition, Palino flatly denied that the tannery had used TCE, and he accused Schlichtmann's investigator of falsely representing himself as someone "for Riley."

One after another, interviews with a dozen former tannery employees led Schlichtmann nowhere. None could recall using TCE, or dumping tannery waste and 55-gallon drums on the fifteen acres.

Schlichtmann began searching the files of local and state agencies that might have had dealings with the tannery. At the state public health department, he finally got his first true break. He found a report—he called it "the killer document"—that proved Riley had not told the truth at his deposition. It was two pages long, dated July 12, 1956, the typewritten notes of a sanitary engineer named A. C. Bolde who had gone to the tannery in response to repeated complaints by east Woburn residents about "terrible" and "foul" odors. According to Bolde's notes, he and Riley had walked up the dirt road leading onto the fifteen acres. "It was observed," wrote Bolde, "that large quantities of old sludge containing hair and some fleshings were deposited between the Access Road and the Aberjona River for a length of 500 to 600 feet. Some of those deposits were within a few inches of the water. . . ." Bolde told Riley that he'd have to remove the tannery waste. Riley objected, stating that he owned the land and could there-fore use it as he wished. "[I] pointed out to him," wrote Bolde, "that regardless of ownership, the placing of such materials which may result in polluting the river is in violation of existing state laws." Riley had finally agreed ("reluctantly," noted Bolde) to remove the tannery waste.

This document was thirty years old and it dealt only with tannery waste, which might or might not have contained TCE. But even so, Schlichtmann thought it had great value. Riley had sworn at his depo-sition that he had never dumped anything on the fifteen acres. Riley had lied then, and Schlichtmann—who didn't need much convinc-ing—believed that Riley was also lying about using TCE.

The report provided Schlichtmann with another lead. He began looking for the residents who had complained to the health depart-ment about the tannery odor. Some of them, he hoped, might have seen Riley's trucks dumping waste and drums of chemicals on the fif-teen acres.

Schlichtmann's private investigator began knocking on doors. He found an elderly woman named Ruth Turner* who had lived all her life in a shabby old frame house on Salem Street, less than a hundred yards from the tannery. The house, said Ruth Turner, had been in her family for more than a century. She recalled that when she was a young girl the Aberjona River had run clear and was full of fish. To the west of the house, where the tannery was now located, there had been an apple orchard, to the east a cornfield. But the character of that land had

---

*This name and the names of the other Turner family members are pseudonyms.

started to change in the 1950s. Her husband, Paul, would often walk down behind the house, in the forest by the Aberjona River, on the land owned by Riley. He would return from his walks and tell her about the barrels and piles of debris he'd seen there, and how sludge waste from the tannery would flow down the hill and onto the land. In the years before Paul's death in 1981, recalled Ruth, he often awoke in the middle of the night. On several occasions, he'd told Ruth about hearing the sounds of trucks at two or three o'clock in the morning. He had said that he could see the headlights of flatbed trucks full of barrels driving up the access dirt road onto the fifteen acres. "They're dumping stuff in the middle of the night," Ruth recalled his saying.

Ruth Turner informed Schlichtmann that her eldest son, Bernard, now a medical doctor in the Chicago area, knew a great deal about what had happened on the fifteen acres. He had often complained to the health authorities about the tannery.

Schlichtmann located Dr. Bernard Turner in Chicago. Over the phone, the doctor told Schlichtmann that he had a vivid memory of the fifteen acres in the 1950s and 1960s. "I'd go down there four or five times a week. It was a play zone. In the early days, it was quite wooded, farmland." Dr. Turner said that later, when he was older, he had complained to the board of health about the tannery and the condition of the land at least twenty times. His father and grandfather had both complained, too. "The odor would be unbelievable," Turner told Schlichtmann. "There were massive quantities of barrels, literally hundreds. There were drums corroding, leaking into the ground. The barrels were rotting because of the corrosive compounds. What interested me as a kid was the red hazard label on the barrels. They were solvents—xylene, toluene, butyl alcohol, trichloroethylene. One never forgets the smell of butyl alcohol or of trichloroethylene."

Schlichtmann could barely contain his excitement. He'd found a medical doctor who could testify that TCE had been dumped on the fifteen acres since the 1950s. He asked Turner how, as a boy, he'd been able to remember all those complicated names. The doctor explained that he'd been interested in chemistry. His grandfather had given him the *Handbook of Chemistry and Physics,* published by the Chemical Rubber Publishing Company, and he used to look up the names. "In fact, I've still got the book," he told Schlichtmann.

But twenty minutes into the conversation Schlichtmann began to worry. The doctor said he'd gotten his medical degree from a school in the Dominican Republic. Over the phone, Schlichtmann could detect a pompous, self-important manner in Turner's voice. Then Dr. Turner began offering a résumé that made Schlichtmann's heart sink. He informed Schlichtmann that he was currently a consultant to the government of Kuwait on environmental problems. He said he was also a consultant to a clinic in electromyography, and to a coal-oil gasification project, and to an investment firm that was building a blood fractionation plant in Costa Rica. As if all this were not enough, Turner went on to say that he was about to enter a consulting arrangement with the Environmental Protection Agency. In fact, he told Schlichtmann, he was currently under consideration by the EPA for the post of assistant director of Region Five.

Schlichtmann listened to this fantastic story with growing dismay. In a matter of minutes, the perfect witness had turned into a trial lawyer's nightmare. Yet Turner's childhood recollections did have the ring of truth to Schlichtmann. He believed that Turner really had seen those drums, even if he was not about to become an assistant director at the EPA.

Schlichtmann knew he could not risk putting Turner on the witness stand. He could imagine the delight Facher would take in cross-examining this doctor. But he listed Turner as a witness anyway, one who would testify about the presence and contents, including TCE, of hundreds of drums on the Beatrice property from the 1950s to the 1970s. If nothing else, Schlichtmann figured, this would probably give Facher cause for alarm.

The appearance of Dr. Bernard Turner's name on the witness list, and the description of Turner's testimony, did worry Facher. He had already made plans to fly out to Chicago to meet with Beatrice's assistant corporate counsel, and he decided that he would depose Turner while he was there.

Schlichtmann did not attend this deposition. He was too busy to go to Chicago. But he did read the transcript of Facher's interrogation of the doctor.

MR. FACHER: You were eleven years old when you saw these barrels?

DR. TURNER: That's correct. I saw the red hazard labels.

Q: What labels did you see?

A: I saw xylene, toluene, butanol. I saw trichloroethylene—

Q: This is as an eleven-year-old kid?

A: You are raising a little heat with me.

Q: As an eleven-year-old kid, you remember seeing labels with these long chemical names on them? More than thirty years ago?

A: That's correct.

Q: You're not taking names that you know today and putting them on sights and sounds that you saw thirty years ago?

A: I remember it today. Do you forget what your mother looks like?

Q: Do I forget what my mother looks like? My mother doesn't look like a chemical drum with a label on it.

Stenographic transcripts do not record the demeanors of the participants or the tones of their voices, but Schlichtmann did not need such descriptions to imagine the sound of angry voices and shouting.

Near the end of the deposition, Facher had asked the doctor if he was married, and Turner had said he was divorced.

Q: What's your former wife's name?

A: Sharon Turner.

Q: Do you know where she's located?

A: No.

Q: She remarried?

A: I don't think so.

To Schlichtmann, these last few questions seemed aimless, just the routine toil of a lawyer attempting to dig up whatever information he could.

Four days after Turner's deposition, a private investigator employed by Facher's firm located Turner's ex-wife at her home in Stark, New Hampshire, a tiny hamlet near the Canadian border. Over the phone, the investigator told Sharon Turner that he was calling about a case in which her ex-husband was to be a witness. He said that he'd come across a three-year-old *capias* for Bernard's arrest, signed by Sharon. "You took Bernard to court for not paying child support?" the investigator asked.

Sharon Turner admitted that was true.

The investigator said he knew where Bernard was living, and he also knew that Bernard owned some real estate and could afford to pay child support. He offered to have Bernard arrested when he appeared in Massachusetts.

Sharon Turner declined this offer, but the investigator persisted. Again Sharon declined, more firmly this time, and finally the investigator thanked her and left his telephone number in the event she reconsidered.

Schlichtmann learned about this incident from Bernard Turner himself, who was understandably incensed and vowed he would have nothing more to do with this case. To Schlichtmann, that made little difference. Turner's testimony had been stillborn from the moment of its arrival, and Schlichtmann couldn't find it within himself to muster much sympathy for Dr. Turner.

Schlichtmann had meanwhile found several other, more credible, witnesses who had lived near the tannery. One man, the owner of a small electrical-repair business, told Schlichtmann that he had often played on the fifteen acres as a boy. He and his friends used to call one area near the tannery Death Valley because of the white, powdery dust coming from the tannery that had coated the hillside and killed everything in its path. This witness recalled the time he'd found an old railroad flare on the fifteen acres. He'd lit the flare and stuck it into a block of Styrofoam. The Styrofoam began to burn and he'd thrown the block into a small pond. The pond had erupted in flames, a burning pool that gave off a heavy black smoke. The conflagration had brought the neighbors running, and then the Woburn fire department, led by the chief.

Schlichtmann heard from the fire chief of his mortification upon seeing hundreds of leaking drums strewn all about the property. The day after the fire, said the chief, he had called Riley to complain about the condition of the property, and he had also urged the health department to inspect the area. A year later another small fire brought the chief back to the Beatrice land. "Nothing had changed," the chief said.

It seemed that everyone but Riley recognized the fifteen acres as a toxic waste dump. Riley *must* have known about the condition of the property. Perhaps, thought Schlichtmann, the tanner really had been running an unauthorized waste dump. Perhaps he had charged his neighbor, Whitney Barrel, a fee for the use of the land. Jack Whitney had been in the business of refurbishing used 55-gallon drums, and the back of his property abutted the fifteen acres.

Schlichtmann began looking into Whitney Barrel. The more he looked, the more apparent it became that Whitney had run a dirty business in the dirtiest possible way. Schlichtmann learned from a man who had worked at the barrel company in the late 1960s that Whitney would empty the residue of 55-gallon drums that had contained pesticides directly into the sewer line, which ran untreated to Boston Harbor. This former employee also said that Whitney had instructed him on a few occasions—"maybe half a dozen"—to empty the residue of drums containing an unidentified "poison" along the dirt road that led onto the fifteen acres. Furthermore, this worker recalled using TCE to wipe clean the heads of 55-gallon drums before he painted them.

All of this suggested that Whitney had played an important role in the contamination of the fifteen acres. But Schlichtmann found it hard to believe that a man of Riley's temperament would allow anyone to use his property without getting paid for the privilege. Schlichtmann would have liked to question Whitney about the nature of his business relationship with Riley—if indeed there had been one—but Jack Whitney's testimony was forever out of reach. He had died a year ago, and the barrel company had gone out of business.

This information changed the complexion of the case. Even so, in the eyes of the law, Beatrice Foods still bore responsibility for what had happened on its land, for keeping an "open and notorious" toxic waste dump. Legally, it did not matter who had contaminated the land, but Schlichtmann knew very well that it would matter to a jury. He still had a case, but it was a far weaker one if he could not prove that Riley had done the dumping himself.

He had not given up on that yet. His team of engineers and geologists had shifted their attention from the Grace plant to Beatrice's fifteen acres. They were taking soil samples, mapping the location of each barrel, and probing into the piles of debris. Schlichtmann went out to visit them when he had time. They had found several small clumps of a greasy material that contained TCE. Lab analyses revealed that this material also contained high levels of hexavalent chromium, which the tannery used in curing leather. The stuff even smelled like leather. And furthermore, it was composed largely of fats and oils. Schlichtmann believed that these clumps had to be tannery sludge, offal, and pieces of flesh that came from scraping the raw cow hides clean prior to tanning.

If this material was indeed tannery waste, then how had it become contaminated with TCE, which Riley claimed he had never used? It was, of course, possible that someone else—Whitney, perhaps—had dumped TCE on top of it. That was possible, but to Schlichtmann the most logical explanation was that it had all come from the same place. And if that was true, it meant that Riley had lied about TCE.

There was no obvious way for Schlichtmann to prove that. He hadn't been able to find any tannery witnesses who could testify to using TCE. And Riley had testified under oath that there were no records of the chemicals the tannery had used before 1979. Those records had been routinely destroyed, if one could believe Riley's sworn testimony. The paper trail did not seem to exist.

The Woodshed

Discovery had transformed the offices of Schlichtmann, Conway & Crowley. Crowley's desk, books, chairs, and framed diploma had been moved into Conway's office, now so crammed with furniture that Conway had to shuffle sideways, crablike, to get to his own desk. Crowley's office had become what Schlichtmann called the War Room. Carpenters had built shelves along the length of one wall to hold the bound volumes of deposition transcripts. Eight gray metal filing cabinets occupied another wall. Overhead, jammed between the stout oak beams of the ceiling, were cardboard tubes containing dozens of rolled maps and charts from the EPA and the U.S. Geological Survey. Schlichtmann had aerial photographs of east Woburn, some dating back to the 1950s and 1960s, enlarged and pinned like the targets of a bombing mission on another wall. Beneath the windows that overlooked India Street, three computer workstations held the medical records for each of the thirty-three plaintiffs, along with hundreds of other documents in the case. Conway had recruited two new associates, both recent law school graduates, and a paralegal. From a temporary personnel agency, Kathy Boyer had hired a receptionist, three secretaries, a messenger, and a part-time bookkeeper. The office had once worked efficiently with nine people. Now, the staff was doubled in size. Some days, Conway felt as if he'd walked into the wrong office.

Schlichtmann arrived at work at six-thirty every morning and usually did not leave for home until around midnight. If he was not in Woburn interviewing witnesses or checking up on his team of geologists, he was at the conference room table, amid piles of medical texts, documents from Grace and Beatrice, government reports, and depositions. From these protruded tattered strips of yellow paper, like entrails, marking vital information. They bore Schlichtmann's nearly illegible scrawl. He, and he alone, seemed able to recall the precise location, volume and page number, of every piece of arcana related to the case. When, on occasion, a particular fact eluded him, he'd sit motionless, peering into space, a picture of industrious cogitation, until he summoned forth its location.

He held staff meetings every morning at eight o'clock for all office personnel. Attendance was mandatory, tardiness was punished by his wrath. He wanted the office to operate, he explained once, with the precision of a Swiss watch. Every pleading, every affidavit, every letter to a client or expert witness had to be flawless. A mistake, he used to tell them, even the most innocent one, could result in disaster—a motion lost, a witness unprepared, an opportunity overlooked.

The case had become Schlichtmann's entire universe. He no longer took the time even for common courtesies. Encountering someone he had not seen in days or weeks, he'd start, as it were, in mid-sentence, describing the testimony of a new witness or the import of a newly uncovered document. More than once the secretaries had seen him come rushing out of the office shower with only a towel wrapped around him, shouting in excitement about some new revelation.

Kathy Boyer had hired a tall, willowy young woman of twenty-two, fresh from college, to answer the telephones. The woman, Patti D'Addieco, was alert and capable, and Schlichtmann soon put her in charge of collecting the complete medical records of all the Woburn family members. This was a formidable task. It involved thirty-three individuals, and Schlichtmann insisted on absolute thoroughness. He wanted her to find the report of every visit to a doctor, of every scraped knee, sore throat, and common cold. For those children with leukemia, the records consisted of thousands of pages—lab tests, chemotherapy protocols, the notes of nurses, doctors, social workers, and psychiatrists. And for the adults, some records dated back to the 1930s.

Patti D'Addieco held Schlichtmann in awe. In truth, she later confided, she had a crush on him. She tried her best to please him, but she ran into difficulty finding many of the oldest records. One morning, as she hurried into work, she encountered Schlichtmann by the reception desk.

"You got all the medical records yet?" he asked.

"I can't get complete records for Anne Anderson because the doctor—"

"I don't care," interrupted Schlichtmann. "Just get them."

"Jan, I can't. The doctor's dead."

"I don't care!" shouted Schlichtmann, loud enough for everyone in the office to hear. "Dig the man out of his fucking grave! Go to his widow's house and get them out of the fucking basement! Do you think Facher cares why you can't get the medical records?"

Patti D'Addieco turned abruptly, tears in her eyes, and fled to the library. She heard Schlichtmann coming and she quickly picked up the telephone.

"Patti, put down the phone," he said.

"I'm upset now. I don't want to talk."

"Why are you upset?"

"I've been working really hard." She wiped tears from her eyes. "I just can't talk now."

"Okay," said Schlichtmann gently. "I'll talk, you listen." He spoke softly; he said he knew she'd been working hard and he appreciated her efforts; she was a valued employee. He continued in this vein for several minutes, but never actually apologized. Patti felt the tug of a gentle seduction and, against her will, she began to smile. Then Schlichtmann said, "Okay, now go get the medical records."

Some months later Patti D'Addieco got her revenge. For Schlichtmann's birthday, she wrote a song—the "Schlichtmann Rap"—and sang it to him at the office party.

> Now let me tell you a story 'bout a man named Jan
> Gonna rock you into justice like no other mother can
> You can see it in his smile as he's walkin' into trial
> His hands'll be washed and his clothes'll have style

Now I want medical records and I want 'em done right
I don't care if you gotta stay here all night
I want 'em perfect and I want 'em neat
And if you fuck 'em up, you be walking on the street.

What, no juice? I made it perfectly clear
That there's always gotta be some juice in here
And it's gotta be natural and it's gotta cost more
Than any other juice in any other store

Now before we end this Schlichtmann rap
Lemme tell ya one more thing 'bout this Schlichtmann chap
He's got a quick tongue and he's got a keen wit
And the best thing about him is he can take this shit.

Collecting all of the medical records had been the idea of a Chicago doctor, a specialist in occupational and environmental medicine named Shirley Conibear. Schlichtmann had gone to Chicago to recruit her almost a year ago. He had drawn up a list of doctors—cancer specialists, pathologists, immunologists, and toxicologists—who had testified in other cases involving toxic substances, such as Agent Orange and asbestos. Some of those doctors had told him they were too busy to get involved in Woburn. Some had rejected him outright, saying they didn't believe Schlichtmann had a case. To those who had seemed interested, Schlichtmann sent a thick file of material along with a check for twenty-five hundred dollars, his standard payment for his first consultation with an expert witness.

Dr. Shirley Conibear had published many articles about the health problems of industrial workers exposed to toxic chemicals. The Woburn case, particularly Colvin's T cell tests and the Harvard Health study, had intrigued her. She and Schlichtmann had spent several hours in her Chicago office discussing the medical aspects of the case. She had suggested then that Schlichtmann start collecting the medical records. If these people had indeed been injured by exposure to TCE, Conibear had said, a pattern of health problems should emerge in the records. Furthermore, Conibear could use the records to compare the state of the families' health before October 1964, the date Well G had gone on line, to the record of their complaints after they'd been exposed to the water.

For a handsome fee, Conibear had agreed to come to Boston and perform thorough physical examinations of all twenty-eight living family members. Schlichtmann had his staff prepare for Conibear's arrival by leasing a suite of rooms in a doctor's office building near the Boston University Medical Center and furnishing it with rented equipment. He also arranged accommodations for a week at the Ritz-Carlton for Conibear and her staff, which included two other physicians and a lab technician.

Conibear's first round of reports, more than nine hundred pages long, cost Schlichtmann $88,729. He felt they were worth every penny. He read that in 1964, the year Well G came on line, Richard Toomey had suffered an episode of gastric and abdominal pain so severe that he'd gone to see a doctor. By 1971, when the wells were operating full-time, Toomey's stomach problems had become chronic. He had also complained repeatedly of sore throats, headaches, nausea, severe sweats, and various rashes. Toomey's daughter, Mary Eileen, born in 1965, had suffered repeated rashes on her face and legs, sinus problems, vomiting, chills, and abdominal pains. To Schlichtmann, the record of her complaints looked remarkably similar to her father's.

The records of Anne Anderson told of a history of chronic abdominal pain, intestinal cramps, irritable colon, nausea, vomiting, and fatigue. Anne's oldest son, Chuck: rashes during the first three years of his life and upper respiratory tract infections. Kathryn Gamache: sore throats, epigastric pain, nausea, abdominal cramps, light-headedness, vertigo. Kathryn's daughter, Amy: rashes on the head, abdomen, and legs, nausea, diarrhea, irritable colon. Diane Aufiero: sore throats, nausea, light-headedness, skin eruptions. And each of the five children who had died of leukemia had experienced rashes, sore throats, and chronic earaches before their diagnoses.

One after another, the case histories of the plaintiffs looked astonishingly alike. Conibear told Schlichtmann that the pattern of chronic solvent poisoning was unmistakable. She had conducted a computer search of scientific journals and found more than a hundred articles on the toxic effects of TCE. Most of those articles dealt with workers who'd been exposed to the solvent, and they cited the same constellation of symptoms—dizziness, nausea, vomiting, fatigue, skin rashes. Among the Woburn families, any one person might have the misfortune to suffer repeated rashes, chronic abdominal pains and nausea, and sinus and upper-respiratory-tract infections. But for a group of families, related to each other only by geography and the water they used, to suffer so many common ailments and to have a leukemic child in the family—to Schlichtmann, that could not be coincidence.

Conibear had also made another important finding—nine of the fourteen Woburn adults showed signs of cardiac arrhythmia, or irregular heartbeats. This, too, seemed to fit the pattern of exposure to TCE. The scientific literature contained a dozen case studies documenting what one study called the solvent's "significant effects on the cardiovascular system." Autopsies of workers overcome by TCE fumes confirmed that several had died of "ventricular fibrillation"—a fatal arrhythmia—and "primary cardiac failure."

Conibear had given the Woburn adults standard twelve-lead electrocardiograms, but she told Schlichtmann that there were a battery of more extensive tests that could be administered by a trained heart specialist. Schlichtmann decided to send the families to a first-rate cardiologist. He found one in Boston, not far from his own office. This cardiologist, Saul Cohen, taught at the Boston University School of Medicine and also maintained a private practice. Schlichtmann called him up and explained that he wanted thorough cardiac workups, examinations of the sort the nation's president would receive.

Cohen was familiar with TCE and its pathological effects on the heart. But he was openly skeptical about the danger of such low-level exposures, especially in drinking water. All of the case studies he had read involved workers who had inhaled TCE vapor in much higher concentrations than the levels found in the Woburn water. "Are you going to want me to testify?" Cohen asked Schlichtmann.

Schlichtmann said yes, he hoped Cohen would testify.

"I'll testify to what I find, but I may not find anything," warned Cohen.

Schlichtmann didn't mention the fact that Conibear had already found nine cases of arrhythmia. It would be best, he thought, to have Cohen discover the arrhythmias on his own.

It took Cohen six weeks to complete his examinations of all the Woburn adults and the three oldest teenage children. He began with routine physicals followed by blood tests, resting electrocardiograms, treadmill cardiograms, and twenty-four-hour-long ambulatory heart recordings by Holter monitor. When he finished, he delivered to

Schlichtmann's office a summary of his findings, along with a three-foot stack of reports that contained hundreds of pages of rhythm strips from the electrocardiograms. And, of course, a bill for services rendered: $55,762.

Schlichtmann read that not just some but all of the seventeen individuals tested by Cohen experienced irregular heartbeats. The results, Cohen told Schlichtmann, had surprised him—"quite striking" were his exact words. Schlichtmann asked Cohen to review Conibear's physical exams and the index of past medical complaints that she had assembled. "That, in addition to my own findings, really stunned me," Cohen would testify later at his deposition. "I was very impressed with the consistency of these findings and the similarity of complaints in this particular cohort of patients."

Compared with the arrhythmias and the leukemias, and even with the rashes, many of the recurring health problems that the Woburn families had reported to their family doctors over the years were vague and hard to quantify. Headaches, fatigue, and depression, for example, could be caused by any number of things. They might simply be manifestations of stress or of psychological problems, without any underlying biological cause. But the scientific literature on TCE showed that the solvent had a potent effect on the central nervous system. It acted as a depressant, and it could have caused those sorts of symptoms. Conibear believed that the frequency of those symptoms pointed to neurological damage.

So Schlichtmann called a prominent Boston neurologist—Dr. Robert G. Feldman, the chairman of the Department of Neurology at the Boston University School of Medicine. Schlichtmann had met Feldman during the Carney case. He had asked Feldman to review Carney's file, and the neurologist had gone on to become Schlichtmann's star expert witness in that case.

Feldman was skeptical. He told Schlichtmann that he could give the families the same battery of neurological tests that he gave to workers who had been exposed to TCE. Cohen's results, Feldman admitted, were impressive. But even so, Feldman thought that the concentrations of TCE in the Woburn water were very small. The neurological tests were time-consuming and expensive—a thousand dollars for each person—and they might not show any nerve damage.

To Schlichtmann it seemed that everything was falling neatly into place, including Feldman's skepticism. Cohen had been skeptical, too, and then he'd discovered even more arrhythmias than Conibear. Schlichtmann wasn't worried. He had come to believe, at this point, that he had already discovered the truth of this case. Now it was just a matter of everyone else catching up with him, bringing along the details of proof that he would need in a courtroom. He arranged for the neurological examinations of the Woburn families.

Feldman had written several articles on the neurological effects of TCE, including a landmark case study published in 1970 in the journal *Neurology*. Alone in the conference room one night, Schlichtmann read all of Feldman's papers. The 1970 case study told the story of a twenty-six-year-old worker who had attempted to fix a leak in a large industrial degreasing machine filled with TCE. The worker had worn a faulty gas mask. After an hour and a half of exposure to the fumes, the man had emerged feeling slightly giddy. Twelve hours later he was suffering waves of nausea and vomiting, blurred vision, numbness of his face, mouth, and pharynx. On presentation, Feldman saw a lethargic, confused individual who had difficulty speaking and could not follow even the simplest commands.

Feldman's article cited two dozen other studies of exposure to TCE. Schlichtmann read one early account that told of a British shipworker who had swabbed the boilers of a frigate with TCE. This worker had emerged after four hours with a severe headache and complaining of dizziness. The next day, he was overwhelmed by nausea, unable to cough, swallow, or speak. The area around his mouth and nose was completely numb. His heart rate was greatly elevated. Until his death from a respiratory infection several weeks after his exposure, he was unable to retain any food. An autopsy revealed extensive damage to the fifth cranial nerve, also known as the trigeminal nerve. The myelin sheath, the fatty layer of tissue that insulates nerve fibers, had dissolved into "irregular globules." The TCE had literally *degreased* the man's nerve fibers.

As for his own patient, Feldman could do little to treat the symptoms, but he could measure the severity of the damage. He began with a series of nerve conduction studies, computing the speed and amplitude with which the worker's nerve fibers conducted electrical impulses. Feldman found that the young man's nerves functioned at the same rate as someone suffering from early-stage multiple sclerosis. Feldman also gave the man a wide range of psychological tests designed to measure memory and motor control. Over the next sixteen years, he followed his patient's progress closely. The numbness of the worker's face abated slowly during the first year, and nerve-conduction velocities gradually increased, but they never returned to normal. And the worker had lingering neuropsychological problems. Although he scored in the "bright-normal" range when tested for verbal intelligence, his short-term memory, his attention span, and his ability to think sequentially were all impaired. Psychological tests indicated a lingering depression, which Feldman attributed to the physical damage of his patient's central nervous system. "The affective disorder observed in this patient after 16 years is particularly disturbing," wrote Feldman in March 1985, in his second report on the worker. "[M]easurements indicate the likelihood of permanent neurological deficit following a single acute exposure to trichloroethylene."

Over a period of weeks, the Woburn families came to University Hospital to be tested by Feldman and his team of doctors. They sniffed vials of a dark liquid—it was coffee—and were asked to identify it, a test of olfaction, of the first cranial nerve. They stuck out their tongues on command and wagged them back and forth, a test of the twelfth cranial nerve. They listened to tuning forks. They had lights shined in their eyes. They had their skins pricked with a pin and then stroked with wool. They interpreted inkblots and tried to memorize long sequences of numbers. They took the Milner Facial Recognition test, the Wisconsin Card Sorting test, the Santa Anna Form Board test, the Albert Famous Faces test, the Benton Visual Retention test. In the electromyography lab, a darkened room where they reclined on a contoured chair, electrodes were attached to their faces, legs, ankles, and wrists. One of Feldman's assistants administered mild electrical stimuli and measured the amplitude, latency, and speed of their reactions.

The results of this entire battery of tests were not as dramatic as Feldman had seen in cases of industrial exposure. But in his judgment, they were not normal. Most of the Woburn people had problems with

short-term memory and motor control. Many showed particular difficulty in tasks involving visual and spatial organization. And all but four
ranked high on the scale for depression. Feldman deemed several of
them to be "severely" depressed.

The most telling results came from the "blink reflex" tests, which
measure in milliseconds how quickly a subject's eyelids react to an electrical stimulus. This test measures the functioning of the trigeminal
nerve, the nerve that TCE seems to affect most directly. Feldman found
that the blink reflex of every family member, of both children and
adults, was either slower than normal or fell barely within the normal
range. Feldman was impressed not so much by the degree of individual
impairment but by the uniformity of the group. He told Schlichtmann
that the results were "highly significant," that the odds of a group of
twenty or more people all testing out at the slow end of normal were "a
million to one."

The doctor who had actually administered the blink reflex tests, an
expert in electromyography, had known nothing about the history of
the Woburn families. This doctor had been concerned about the number of slow blink reflexes she was seeing among this group. She had
wondered about the accuracy of her TECA-4 machine. To test the
machine, she'd rounded up seven technicians from the hospital corridors. Their blink reflexes had all been textbook-normal.

Schlichtmann heard this story for the first time during that doctor's
deposition. Feldman had not thought it important enough to mention,
but it delighted Schlichtmann. He planned to use it during trial, to let
a jury know that these tests had truly been impartial.

Almost every medical expert Schlichtmann talked to knew another
expert that Schlichtmann might want to talk to. In this way, he heard
of a biochemist named Beverly Paigen who had investigated the health
problems of people living near Love Canal. Paigen worked out of a lab
at Children's Hospital in Oakland, California, and Schlichtmann flew
out to see her on one of his medical reconnaissance trips. She told him
the history of a case she'd investigated in the small town of Gray,
Maine: twenty-three households, their tap water contaminated for five
years by small amounts of TCE and perc—it sounded a lot like east
Woburn. In the first year, said Paigen, the residents had complained of

rashes and burning eyes after showering. In the second year, rashes again and also headaches. By the third year, dizziness, fainting, nausea, and abdominal pains. Among the twenty-three households, five women had become pregnant during the years the wells were contaminated. Two of those women had miscarriages and two others had lost their babies within four months of birth. Only one child had survived.

"Any leukemias?" asked Schlichtmann.

"No," said Paigen. "You can't expect to find cancer in small populations. Leukemia is too rare a disease. You need large populations—thousands of people—to look for cancer."

Like Schlichtmann's Woburn experts, Paigen had initially thought the concentration of solvents in the Gray well water too small to cause dramatic health problems. But the problems were undeniably there. Paigen and another scientist, Robert Harris of Princeton University, developed a hypothesis. They proposed testing the air in a bathroom while the shower was running. They reasoned that TCE, which was highly volatile, would turn into a cloud of vapor in the hot, running water.

And indeed, the test showed that as water flowed out of the shower head at the rate of six gallons a minute, TCE did vaporize, accumulating in the confined space of a bathroom at concentrations two to three times higher than in the tap water.

This seemed to explain why Richard Toomey and several other Woburn people had complained of a burning sensation in their eyes while bathing. Schlichtmann had always assumed that the primary route of exposure had come from drinking the water. That would have meant that the families had consumed only the TCE contained in a quart or so of water each day. But every ten-minute shower they had taken would release to the air most of the TCE contained in sixty gallons of water, which would have found its way inside their bodies through inhalation.

Another expert, a toxicologist at the University of California at Berkeley, confirmed this finding. The toxicologist also told Schlichtmann about another important route of exposure—absorption through the skin. A new study in the *American Journal of Public Health*, explained the toxicologist, demonstrated that the amount of TCE absorbed during bathing, when warm water dilated the pores of the skin, equaled or surpassed the dose one would get from drinking contaminated water. Absorption occurred most readily where the skin was sensitive—the inner thighs, the underarms—and was further increased if one had a sunburn, a cut, or a rash. And rashes had been common among the children of east Woburn.

The families would have gotten dosed with TCE in all three ways— by drinking the water, by breathing the vapor, and by absorbing the molecules. All this, it seemed, might account for the apparent discrepancy between the severity of their symptoms and the low levels of exposure. Those levels of exposure, it turned out, were not so low after all.

Schlichtmann learned around this time that the problem of TCE in drinking water was not limited to Woburn and Gray, Maine. In a document published by the U.S. Public Health Service, he read that "between 9 and 34 percent of the water supply sources in the United States may be contaminated with trichloroethylene." Even more astounding, the same document estimated that if a population of ten million people were to breathe air containing one part per million of TCE over a lifetime, as many as 93,000 would be "at risk of developing cancer." Schlichtmann vowed never again to take a drink of regular tap water.

He had come a long way. The case, he told himself, did not depend on the leukemia claim alone. He now had compelling evidence of chronic solvent poisoning. And even if the scientific evidence that TCE caused leukemia was weak, there could be no doubt now that exposure to the contaminated water had exacerbated the leukemias. The disease would not have run the same course. He could argue that more of the children would have survived if Grace and Beatrice had not contaminated the wells.

2

Schlichtmann's medical experts now numbered twelve, enough doctors to staff a small but elite hospital. But most of these men and women did not know each other or the work each had done on the Woburn case. Schlichtmann decided to bring them all together for a conference, a round-table discussion. He rented the Grand Ballroom at the Ritz-Carlton and paid the plane fare for the experts from California, Chicago, and Washington, D.C. He paid for their hotel rooms at the

Ritz, their meals and, of course, their time. Most of them billed around two hundred dollars an hour. The conference began with dinner and drinks on a Friday evening and continued throughout Saturday. It went so well that Schlichtmann arranged for a second one, out in Chicago.

Not long after that meeting, Conway discovered that Saul Cohen, the cardiologist, had charged a hundred dollars an hour for the night he'd spent sleeping at the Chicago Hilton. This was only half of Cohen's regular hourly rate, his sleeping rate, as it were. It infuriated Conway, but Schlichtmann said calmly, "No, he's worth it."

The steadily mounting bills alarmed Conway, but they didn't surprise him. He had known that Schlichtmann would spend every cent the firm had on Woburn, and then borrow more. Three years ago, Conway had predicted that the case would become a "black hole." Now, eight months into discovery, that prediction seemed on the verge of coming true. The nerve-conduction studies, the cardiology tests, physical exams, lab reports, and toxicology data jammed the filing cabinets. The large copying machine outside the war room ran from dawn until dusk, churning out copies of the experts' reports and the families' medical records. Deposition transcripts and files and reports seemed to multiply overnight and spread like a living organism, like a fungus, covering the conference-room table and spilling onto the floor and into the reception area.

From Woburn, where Schlichtmann had a team of engineers, geologists, and hydrogeologists digging holes and taking soil samples, came more reports. This fieldwork was crucial to the case—Schlichtmann had to prove that the chemicals from Grace and Beatrice had actually gotten to the wells—and it was very expensive. The engineers had drilled thirty new monitoring wells around the Aberjona marsh to plot the underground flow of contaminants. They had set off small explosives—seismic refraction devices—to map the bedrock contours of the area. They were combing every square foot of the Grace and Beatrice properties, followed by a video crew and a photographer whom Schlichtmann had hired to record every detail of their search. The videos alone would cost $19,021, a pittance compared with the estimated cost—more than a quarter of a million dollars—of the geological investigation.

Even the small items, such as the aerial photographs of east Woburn, along with an expert to interpret them, added up to almost fifteen thousand dollars. And as the piles of deposition transcripts mounted, so, of course, did the costs. The stenographers charged $3.50 a page for "expedited" overnight delivery, which meant that Schlichtmann had to pay, for instance, $1,256 just for his daylong interrogation of Tom Barbas. And there were many lengthy depositions of expert witnesses yet to come.

By the fall of 1985 Schlichtmann, Conway & Crowley had spent almost a million dollars on the Woburn case. The costs could only increase as the trial date, now scheduled for February, five months away, drew closer. The firm needed more money. Schlichtmann would have to visit their banker. He never went to see the banker alone. He always took Conway and James Gordon, their financial adviser, along with him.

Gordon was a wizard with figures. The fingers of his right hand would fly over the keys of his calculator like a maestro playing a piano, ending in a delicate looping flourish as he tapped the "Total" key. Gordon had a special talent for calculating the future value of a sum of money, as if he'd been born with compound-interest tables in his head.

Schlichtmann had met Gordon soon after he had moved down to Boston from Newburyport. He had just won the Eaton case and he was about to settle the Piper Arrow case for almost a million dollars. But his financial affairs were in terrible disarray. Gordon and his partner, Mark Phillips, had recently started their own business, called the Economic Planning Group. They had opened an office on Newbury Street, next to the Ritz-Carlton, in the fashionable Back Bay section of Boston. They had sat in their new office, waiting for wealthy Bostonians in need of estate planning to arrive. They found that they had a lot of time on their hands. Then Schlichtmann showed up, asking them to straighten out his finances. He'd just bought his first Porsche. He took Gordon to the window and pointed down to Newbury Street at his new car. Gordon saw that it was double-parked. A meter maid stood next to it, writing out a ticket.

Two months later, Schlichtmann called on Gordon and Phillips again. An insurance company had offered him a complicated settlement, to be paid out over forty years, which they said was worth $1.5 million. It sounded like a lot, but Schlichtmann was wary. He didn't have a good head for figures. He showed the offer to Gordon, who told him that the insurance company was actually putting up only $330,000; the rest was interest earned on an annuity.

"He *understands* money," Schlichtmann often said of Gordon. "It's just something he was born with."

From that moment on, Gordon and Phillips, who was himself a lawyer but no longer practiced, were involved in every one of Schlichtmann's cases. They soon gave up the idea of estate planning and began specializing in settlement negotiations and case management. They helped Schlichtmann and Conway settle the Copley Hotel fire case. In the Carney case, Gordon arranged the financing and Phillips organized the two mock trials. They saw Schlichtmann and Conway almost every day and dined out with them three or four times a week. Conway rarely accepted a new case until he'd discussed it with Gordon and Phillips, and Schlichtmann never negotiated another settlement without them. The four men worked well together. They became a team, and they also became the best of friends. Gordon and Phillips kept their small office on Newbury Street, but they installed a direct telephone line to Schlichtmann's office. And so, for all practical purposes, the Economic Planning Group now functioned as a part of Schlichtmann's firm.

Phillips, who came from an old and wealthy line of Boston Brahmins, called Gordon and Schlichtmann "the two Russian Jews, the *machers*," the ones who got things done. Gordon was three years younger than Schlichtmann, just as tall but soft and plump, without Schlichtmann's lean face and lanky build. As a short, fat boy, he'd worked bagging groceries and carrying them out to customers' cars at the Purity Supreme market in Brookline. He used to put his jacket over the sign that discouraged tipping, and then he'd spray his T-shirt with water to make it look as if he were sweating from his labors. He found that his ruse worked best on old ladies. He'd grown tall in adolescence, but his face was still round and boyish and he had a head of dark, unruly hair. He greatly admired Schlichtmann, and he often seemed to adopt Schlichtmann's mannerisms, especially the cadences and rhythms of Schlichtmann's speech. He tried to emulate what he saw as Schlichtmann's charm, but to Gordon, all interactions in life required devious manipulation of one sort or another. He liked to think of himself as subtle, but most people readily saw through his blandishments. When he wanted something from Kathy Boyer, he'd start by saying,

"Gee, that's a beautiful dress. You really look great this morning." At first Kathy had felt complimented, but she quickly learned to be wary. All of Gordon's compliments came at a cost. With the secretaries Gordon would use terms of endearment—"Honey" and "Sweetheart" and "Be a darling . . ."—that raised their hackles. Behind his back they'd roll their eyes.

Gordon even admired Schlichtmann's strange attitude toward money. But in that respect, at least, Gordon couldn't bring himself to emulate Schlichtmann. The specter of penury and financial disaster terrified Gordon. He had tucked several one-hundred-dollar bills in the underwear drawer of his bureau and had stashed ten gold Krugerrands in the filing cabinet in his office, small hedges against whatever the future might bring. When he happened to come across these small treasures, he'd count the bills and heft the Krugerrands, and feel reassured.

Gordon managed the Woburn case expenses, printing out computerized lists of the bills and making certain they got paid. He also organized and oversaw the geologists' fieldwork on the Aberjona marsh. He had been the one who tracked down the old aerial photographs of Woburn, and he'd made the arrangements for those expensive conferences of experts. When Schlichtmann needed something done immediately, or when something went wrong, he usually called on Gordon, his all-purpose troubleshooter.

It was Gordon who told Schlichtmann that they'd have to see the firm's banker. By Gordon's calculations, they would need another half million dollars to get through the rest of discovery and a trial that could last six weeks or more. And that, Gordon told Schlichtmann one evening that fall, was a conservative estimate.

"We've got to see Uncle Pete," Gordon said to Schlichtmann.

Uncle Pete was George Kennedy Briggs II, vice president of the Private Banking Group at the Bank of Boston. Although he had the perfect name for a Yankee banker, all of his friends, colleagues, and clients called him Pete. He did not often wear banker's pinstripes, preferring instead tweedy sports coats and bow ties. He had an elfin physique and thick, knobby features. When he smiled, which was often, his entire face seemed to light up.

Schlichtmann called him Uncle Pete, but he dreaded seeing him. He'd gotten it into his head that the banker, who was old enough to be his father, disapproved of the state of his finances, although Pete had never once chastised him. Still, in Pete's presence, Schlichtmann's demeanor underwent a drastic change. He always spoke softly, in a meek and timorous voice, and he would quickly defer to Pete's judgment in all matters. Alone, he could never bring himself to ask the banker for money. Quite the reverse, he always felt an unaccountable urge to give money to Uncle Pete. More than once, in need of a loan, he had offered to pledge the deed to his Beacon Hill condominium, the title to his car, or any other worldly asset he possessed. Pete had always smiled and turned him down. "I don't need it now," Pete had always said.

Pete Briggs had overseen the ebb and flow of Schlichtmann's account for four years, ever since Schlichtmann arrived in Boston. Large sums of money would come in and then quickly disappear, replaced by equally large debts. In thirty years of banking, Pete had rarely seen a personal account like Schlichtmann's. He handled the accounts of three hundred lawyers in the Private Banking Group, but he spent far more time on Schlichtmann's account than on any other. Even so, he referred to Schlichtmann and his partners as "the boys," and he seemed genuinely fond of them. When the bank's money was at stake, he liked to go to the courtroom to see Schlichtmann at work—"keeping an eye on the collateral," Pete called it. In the Carney trial, he'd heard Schlichtmann's opening and closing arguments, and he'd waited in the hallway, watching Schlichtmann grow increasingly nervous as the jury deliberated. "That," recalled Pete, "was nearly a disaster for the boys."

Pete had noticed the difference between Schlichtmann the trial lawyer and Schlichtmann the penitent debtor. "You get Jan offstage," said Pete once, "he's one of the nicest and most sincere guys in the world. He's very self-effacing about what he doesn't know about money and banking."

To prepare for the audience with Uncle Pete, Gordon drew up a business plan. He mapped out a complete budget for Woburn and took an inventory of all the other cases in the files. There were thirteen in addition to Woburn, and these comprised the firm's only real assets. Schlichtmann had already borrowed two hundred thousand dollars from Pete, and to get another half million Gordon knew he'd have to tell the banker how much Woburn might be worth.

Estimating the value of a case is somewhat like fortune-telling. One can never predict what a jury might do, but verdicts in other personal injury cases provide some guidance. In the calculus of personal injury lawsuits, a dead plaintiff is rarely worth as much as a living but severely maimed plaintiff. Severe injuries, like those suffered by Carney, usually mean a lifetime as a cripple, often with great pain, big medical bills, and loss of income, items a jury can consider in rendering its award. By this same cold calculus, a dead child is always worth less than a dead adult, especially if that adult had been the family breadwinner or mother to several children.

Past verdicts in Massachusetts suggested to Schlichtmann that a dead child was generally worth less than a million dollars. But he believed that once a jury took into account the long, agonizing illnesses and deaths of the Woburn children—their pain and suffering—the value would rise substantially. When he added to that equation the family members who had also been poisoned by the contaminated water, and the risk they faced of future illness, possibly even cancer, the value increased once again.

From the beginning, Schlichtmann had always thought of Woburn as a twenty-million-dollar case, and nothing had happened to change his mind. He and Gordon drew up a chart of verdict probabilities that ranged from zero—a complete loss—to forty million. Schlichtmann calculated that if the case went to a jury, he would stand a 5 percent chance of losing everything, and an equally small chance of winning forty million or more. The highest probability, according to the chart, was a judgment for the plaintiffs of twenty-four million, or three million for each family.

Schlichtmann hoped to conduct at least one mock trial before the real trial, using ordinary people rounded up from the street, and handsomely paid for their time, as jurors. Mock trials are best at identifying the strengths and weaknesses of a case rather than predicting the size of jury awards, but Schlichtmann had found mock juries to be pretty accurate in the past. For now, though, the chart for Uncle Pete would have to suffice. It looked scientific, even fancy, like a sales brochure for a shiny new product, and Schlichtmann believed in it. His common sense told him it was right. But in truth, it was based on little more than intuition and a hope that everything would go according to plan.

. . .

The meeting with Uncle Pete, however, did not go quite according to plan. Schlichtmann, Conway, and Gordon met with the banker in his office at the Bank of Boston, a modern glass and concrete skyscraper three blocks from the federal courthouse. Gordon gave Pete Briggs the Woburn budget, the inventory of other cases, and the chart, but Pete first wanted to settle the matter of the outstanding unsecured loan of two hundred thousand dollars. Gordon had promised Pete that he would use the first installment of the Unifirst settlement to retire that loan.

"You've got the Unifirst settlement to pay that off, of course," said Pete.

"We spent it!" said Gordon, his voice unnaturally high.

Uncle Pete seemed to have trouble catching his breath. Schlichtmann had never seen Pete angry before, and Pete was indeed angry. "I almost died," Pete would recall some months later.

Schlichtmann began to offer the banker the deed to his Beacon Hill condominium, but Pete interrupted him.

"Wait a minute," said Pete. "What did you spend it on?"

It had been spent on Woburn, of course. Gordon was prepared for this question. He opened the neatly bound business plan containing all the Woburn expenses, broken down into categories, and his estimate of future expenses.

After Pete calmed down, he agreed that the Woburn case had great potential. And he knew that Schlichtmann had an excellent track record. With Pete, at least, Schlichtmann had always been modest in his estimates of case values.

In the end, Pete agreed to increase the line of credit by half a million dollars. But he needed collateral to show the senior committee upstairs, if that should ever become necessary. Schlichtmann again offered to pledge his condominium, but Pete turned him down. He didn't like to take the deeds to his clients' homes. Instead, he had the boys sign over the rest of the Unifirst settlement, a six-hundred-thousand-dollar annuity due in five years, as well as another annuity, this one for a hundred thousand, the last of the money from the Carney case.

Pete wished the boys luck. With uncharacteristic sternness, he told Gordon to keep him up to date on developments in the Woburn case. He had not liked being misled about the Unifirst money.

"Bankers don't like surprises," Uncle Pete warned Gordon.

3

Everything about discovery was contentious. Each side filed motions asking Judge Skinner to compel the other side to produce documents, witnesses, and answers to interrogatories. And then each side filed counter-motions asking for protection against the other's demands. These motions, hand-delivered by messengers who crossed each other's paths, arrived daily, sometimes hourly, at each firm. They seemed to fall like leaves from a tree and settle in a thick pile on Judge Skinner's desk.

"So you're at it again," the judge said wearily to the lawyers. "I've been here a fair amount of time," the judge added, "and I've never had a case where there's been this kind of rancorous dispute over discovery. I hope it's the last one I have."

When Judge Skinner did not have time to hear their squabbles, he sent the lawyers down to the third floor, to his favorite magistrate, a judicial officer of lower rank who dealt with routine discovery disputes. The magistrate, a man in late middle age with bony, sunken cheeks and hollow temples, had taken a dislike to Schlichtmann at their first encounter. He had asked Schlichtmann how he intended to prove his case, and Schlichtmann, in reply, had given the magistrate two thick volumes of documents. "You can read that," Schlichtmann had said. This had infuriated the magistrate, and he was not one to forget a slight. "Every time you come here, you keep saying, 'You look at those two big volumes and maybe you'll find something,' " the magistrate complained at one hearing. "That certainly doesn't help me, Mr. Schlichtmann. That doesn't assist any court."

Schlichtmann tried to make amends for his unintended insult by flattering the magistrate. "You raised certain questions in your opinion two months ago, and I think you did an excellent job," he told the magistrate on one occasion.

But the magistrate would have none of it. "That's not going to get you to first base, Mr. Schlichtmann."

Facher and Cheeseman benefited from the magistrate's grudge with Schlichtmann. They filed one motion after another, complaining that Schlichtmann had not turned over test results when he had promised, that his witnesses would not answer questions, that he had arrived late at depositions and had taken too long for lunch. More often than not, the magistrate granted their motions, but when Schlichtmann made a motion, the magistrate usually denied it. "You're making an oral motion to take a deposition, Mr. Schlichtmann?" asked the magistrate.

"Yes," replied Schlichtmann.

"Denied," said the magistrate.

A moment later, Schlichtmann tried again. He asked the magistrate to compel Cheeseman and Facher to identify their expert witnesses.

"Your motion is denied, whatever it is," the magistrate said.

"Okay," said Schlichtmann. "No sense making any motions, I guess."

"You already did. It's denied."

"No sense even coming here," Schlichtmann muttered under his breath.

"What are you saying, Mr. Schlichtmann?"

"Nothing."

"Apparently not," said the magistrate.

"Your Honor," Schlichtmann said to the magistrate, "do the Rules of Civil Procedure apply equally in this court to defendants as to the plaintiffs?"

"Absolutely."

"Then I make a motion—and we'll see if it's granted or not—that the defendants today tell the court when their experts will be made available so I can depose them."

"The defendant did not choose to be sued," said the magistrate. "You brought suit against them. The party that has to defend against your theories—God knows what theories!—should be entitled to find out what they are first. From the beginning of this litigation, I had no idea what your experts would say. You wanted me to go through a two-volume report. They're trying to prepare a defense."

"That's right," said Schlichtmann. "They don't have one yet. I'm glad Your Honor recognized that."

"I didn't say that, Mr. Schlichtmann! You should be ashamed of—"

"I'm not ashamed of anything I've said today."

"Well, that's your problem, right?"

"There's a double standard in this court," said Schlichtmann angrily. "One rule applies to the plaintiffs, the other rule applies to—"

"If that's your view, Mr. Schlichtmann, I suggest you file a motion for recusal. I will point out the statute to you. Those other motions are allowed," the magistrate added.

"My motion as well?" asked Schlichtmann.

"Not your motion. Your motion is denied."

Schlichtmann muttered something else under his breath.

"You wanted a ruling, Mr. Schlichtmann. You got a ruling."

"Right, I got a ruling, I certainly did," Schlichtmann said.

Nowadays Schlichtmann saw daylight only from his office window or while walking to and from a deposition. His hair was turning gray at an alarming rate. Kathy Boyer attributed this to stress and overwork, although it was probably more a matter of heredity. But he had lost weight and grown pale. His tailored suits hung from his gaunt frame and no longer looked tailored. His hypochondria seemed to blossom under the fluorescent lights of the conference rooms. Sometimes he'd worry about his heart, other times he'd worry about cancer. A prolonged headache started him thinking about brain tumors. He felt as if he were suffocating under the weight of the case. He could not hold all the things he had to do in his mind, and he was afraid of forgetting something crucial. In every other case, he'd always felt confident of his mastery of the facts, but Woburn was much more complex than any other case. After a long day he'd fall into an exhausted slumber and dream of numbers—of T cell counts, blink reflex milliseconds, parts per billion of TCE. He'd awake with a start at five or six in the morning, feeling as if he had worked through the entire night. And then, the moment he opened his eyes, he would begin organizing the coming day. Some days, when things went well, he'd feel that he really was in control after all, but the next day he'd realize that it had just been an illusion. "It's like one of those kiddy cars," he said to Conway. "They give you a steering wheel but it's not connected to anything. You think you're in charge, but you're not."

He tried not to think about money. His credit cards were burdened with debt. Just recently he had attempted to use one at a restaurant and it had been refused. Teresa took him out to dinner and a movie on Saturday nights. She hoped to lure his mind away from the case, but he couldn't let it go, not even for an evening. Once, when she returned from a trip to the Caribbean, she began telling him about where she'd been and what she'd seen. She could see that he was trying to appear interested, but he asked questions in a mechanical way, and then he lapsed into silence. "What are you thinking about now?" she asked. And he looked up as if in a reverie.

One morning that fall, Conway stood at the office window, looking down on Milk Street as Schlichtmann departed for another deposition. He watched as Schlichtmann hurried across the street, directly in the path of a small van. Conway saw the van lurch to a halt and heard the driver blaring his horn, but Schlichtmann did not even seem to notice.

"He never looks," Conway murmured to Kathy Boyer. What would happen if Schlichtmann was injured? Or fell ill? Conway wasn't a trial lawyer. He knew that neither he nor Crowley could take Schlichtmann's place.

Conway also knew that nothing he said would do much good, but he had to try. "You're the only one, Jan, who has control of the facts in this case."

"My brain," Schlichtmann said mournfully. "Facher would crush me like a bug if he could."

Conway was trying to get him to pay attention to traffic, but Schlichtmann couldn't even pay attention to his plea. "One high fever and it's all gone," said Conway, and he smiled.

It was September, the ninth month of discovery. The trial was scheduled to begin on February 18, five months away. When Schlichtmann's fears about money and his own flagging stamina threatened to overwhelm him, he told himself that if he could just survive discovery and get the case in front of a jury, then everything would be all right. Getting to a jury had always meant victory before.

He had to endure only five more months. Provided, of course, that there were no delays. And just now, the prospect of delay appeared imminent. He had to let Facher and Cheeseman begin deposing his expert witnesses if he wanted to keep the trial date. But the medical experts had not finished all their work yet. Just as important, Schlichtmann hadn't found time to prepare them properly for cross-examination. Most were not experienced at giving their opinions under oath. Schlichtmann had to convince them that the rules of evidence were different from the rules of science, that the witness stand was no place to express doubt or uncertainty. They would have to understand that the other side would try to make them say things at their depositions that could be used against them later in the courtroom.

There hadn't been time for any of that yet. The experts were not ready to be deposed, but Schlichtmann did not want to be the one to ask for a delay. He knew that Facher and Cheeseman had no interest in keeping this trial date. They would try to postpone the day of reckoning as long as they could, hoping that he would run out of money. Schlichtmann feared that one delay might lead to endless delay. In his darkest hours of insomnia, he feared that any delay might lead to no trial at all.

So he agreed to let Facher and Cheeseman take the depositions of three experts. Under the terms of this agreement, as Schlichtmann understood it, these "preliminary" depositions would be limited strictly to factual matters—the types of medical tests the doctors had performed on the families and the results of those tests. The doctors would not, according to the agreement, be asked to state their conclusions and opinions. That would come in the second round of depositions, after the experts had completed all their work.

This agreement was, in retrospect, a mistake caused by haste and a burdened mind. Facher and Cheeseman were no more likely to stay within the terms of the agreement than Schlichtmann would have been in their place. Schlichtmann was uneasy and skittish, and this first mistake led him to a series of further mistakes, mistakes of intemperance.

"I thought we were going to restrict the deposition to the doctor's tests," Schlichtmann said to Facher's associate, Don Frederico, five minutes into the first of those preliminary depositions. A few minutes later, Schlichtmann interrupted again. "Correct me if I'm wrong—the sole purpose of this deposition is for you to find out what testing was done so you can determine your own testing program. I know there's a thousand questions you want to ask. You'll have an opportunity to ask a thousand, two thousand questions, but not today. Today's for a very limited purpose."

"Mr. Schlichtmann," replied Frederico, "I'm not sure we have time for all your speeches."

"We don't have time for you to ask questions that you know are beyond the scope of today's deposition," said Schlichtmann hotly.

"We reserve our right to object—"

"You reserve your right to whatever. Don't try to pervert this deposition into something it's not. The purpose is to go over the goddamn tests and reports so you can design whatever testing program you want."

"Please lower your voice," said Frederico. "Are you instructing him not to answer?"

"Don't pull that bullshit with me!"

"There's no need to shout or make accusations," said one of Cheeseman's partners.

"You want to make it look like I'm obstructing this deposition," said Schlichtmann. "You want to push the trial date off. This little game—'Look, Judge, Mr. Schlichtmann is a son of a bitch and not cooperating and we need more time'—I won't play that game. I am cooperating. I've gone out of my way to help you. I'm going to make you abide by these agreements. It's good for the soul."

The lawyers managed to get through the first deposition, although they left behind two hundred and fifty pages of transcript cluttered with long arguments. The second deposition, of Schlichtmann's immunologist Alan Levin, was worse. "I'm here under false pretenses," Schlichtmann shouted at one point. "I've been abused!" A dozen times, he threatened to walk out. Then, instead, he began conferring with Levin before allowing him to answer many of the questions. Coaching a witness in the middle of a deposition is a serious violation, but Schlichtmann didn't care. These depositions, he contended time and again, were not "regular" depositions. "Before you answer that question, I want to talk to you," he told Levin. "Very important point. Come on." He got up and started to leave the conference room, pulling Levin along with him.

"Do you have a problem with the clarity of the question?" asked Cheeseman's partner, a lawyer named Marc Temin.

"I have a problem with the clarity of the question," said Schlichtmann, on his way to the hall.

"Don't leave the room, Mr. Schlichtmann, while someone is speaking!"

"I'm going to leave the room anyway. This isn't a regular deposition. You're going to get a second shot."

"I object to your doing so."

"I join in the objection," said Frederico.

"You all join together and do what you wish," said Schlichtmann.

When Schlichtmann returned from the hallway, Temin said, "Now, Doctor, did you confer with Mr. Schlichtmann again?"

"Oh, get out of here," said Schlichtmann. "Next time you make a comment like that, we're going home. Okay? One more comment like that on the record and we're getting out of here."

"The record is going to reflect what is taking place."

"No, it is not!" shouted Schlichtmann.

"Mr. Schlichtmann, your threats, warnings, and raised voice are totally inappropriate."

"No they're not! I will not be subjected to insulting behavior by you people."

"There was a question pending—"

"There's no question pending!"

"I'd like to complete a sentence without being interrupted. Mr. Schlichtmann conferred with the witness between the question and the witness's answer. I think he has no right to do that."

"The conference had nothing to do with his answer," said Schlichtmann. "If you insinuate it again, I will assume you're bad, ill-mannered, and not worthy of conducting this deposition."

"You can assume what you like about my manners."

"Continue with your question," said Schlichtmann.

"The record will reflect—"

"The record will reflect everything we've said. Continue your examination or we're going right now. This was an agreement with special limitations, done as a convenience for you. Now you pervert it into something else. I resent it. I'm sorry Judge Skinner wasn't a party to the agreement. He won't know who's lying and who's telling the truth. I'm going to pay the penalty for trusting you."

Facher had not attended the first deposition, but he did come to the second one at Frederico's urgent request. He sat at the far end of the table, looking on with pursed lips and narrowed eyes, not saying a word. After an hour he departed silently.

Judge Skinner met with the lawyers in his chambers one week after the first depositions had ended. Just before the conference began, Facher handed Schlichtmann several new motions. Schlichtmann glanced quickly at them. Then he froze. One of Facher's motions asked the judge to censure him. The motion accused him of "undue interference with the orderly taking of depositions, unwarranted disruptions, rude and threatening statements . . . and conferring with the witness while under examination." Attached to the motion were forty pages taken from the deposition transcripts, with his utterances, oaths and all, boldly underlined. Schlichtmann felt a stab of panic. Glancing at this material was like awakening the morning after to the faint, hazy memory of a terrible indiscretion.

Judge Skinner took the bench and looked at the stack of fresh motions before him. "A whole lot of motions came in today," he muttered with disgust. "It looks like a hell of a mass of stuff."

"There are some discovery things," said Schlichtmann warily.

"I will not deal with it," said the judge. "I'll send that down to a magistrate."

Schlichtmann groaned inwardly at the thought of the magistrate. But even that seemed better than facing the judge's wrath now.

Facher spoke up. He wanted the judge to deal with these motions immediately. "We thought the last time you said, 'Bring these discovery things back to me and I will be a nanny in the case.' "

"I now find myself up to my ears," said the judge. "Trials stacked up back to back. I don't think I can perform the nanny function. I'm sorry you need it," he added.

"So am I," said Schlichtmann quickly.

"I am, too," agreed Facher. "But I think we are getting worse and worse. The discovery is getting off the track. We have some conduct that I think we ought to deal with."

Judge Skinner sighed. "I'll send it down to the magistrate with orders to put it at the top of his civil priorities. I don't want to change the trial date."

"Neither do we," said Schlichtmann.

"I want to try this case in February," continued the judge. "I don't think it is going to get any better with age."

Schlichtmann picked up his coat and walked out of the courtroom, down the long corridor to a bank of elevators. He pushed the button and waited. It was five o'clock. Government employees were leaving work, and the elevators in the federal building, old and slow, were long in coming. A minute passed. Schlichtmann began to wonder why

Facher had not appeared in the hallway. Was he still with the judge? Another minute. Schlichtmann paced in agitation. With each passing second he became more certain that Facher was showing Judge Skinner the motion, hoping to anger the judge. Finally an elevator door opened and Schlichtmann, taking one last glance down the corridor, stepped in. At that moment he saw Facher emerge from the courtroom.

Back at the office, Schlichtmann told Conway what he had seen. He was certain that Facher had stayed behind to speak privately with the judge, to convince him to look at the motion for censure. "Facher is trying to poison the judge against me," said Schlichtmann.

Conway doubted this was true. An *ex parte* conference between a lawyer and a judge, in the absence of the opposing lawyer, was a clear violation of the disciplinary rules. Perhaps Facher had tried to talk with the judge privately, but Conway did not think that Judge Skinner would countenance such an act. "You're imagining things," he told Schlichtmann.

Schlichtmann got a phone call early the next morning. It was from Judge Skinner's clerk. "The judge wants to see you in chambers at three o'clock. I've never seen him this angry before."

"My God," said Schlichtmann. "I thought he was going to send all these motions down to the magistrate."

"He's read the motions," said the clerk. "He's threatening to do things to you that I haven't heard him say in fifteen years on the bench."

"My God," said Schlichtmann again. "What's he going to do?"

"I don't know, but whatever it is, it's not going to be good."

Schlichtmann imagined the worst. At the very least, the judge would censure him and order him to pay a big fine. But Skinner could do much worse. It was within the judge's power to remove him from the case, and then to send the matter to the Board of Bar Overseers with the recommendation that his license to practice law be suspended.

Schlichtmann spent the morning pacing the office, cursing and wailing. By noon he had convinced himself that the judge would throw him off the case. His name would be blackened and his work wasted. He resolved that he would not go without a fight. "There'll be blood on the floor," he announced to Conway. An hour before the hearing he rushed out of the office and went home. Tears sprang to his eyes as he changed into his favorite suit, a charcoal-gray pinstripe that he wore only on the most important occasions. He thought of it as his lucky suit. It was the one he had worn for his closing argument in the Carney case. It was, he'd often said, like a "suit of armor," which protected him from "bad karma."

Judge Skinner's chambers consisted of a single large and gloomy room among a warren of other smaller rooms and dark hallways that adjoined the courtroom's vaulted expanse. The judge and his staff of law clerks spent their time in a suite of more commodious offices across the corridor. As a consequence, the judge's chambers had a dusty, uninhabited feel. A single grimy window let in a shaft of sunlight from the canyon of tall buildings along Milk Street. A pan of water, crusted with a white calcified residue, sat on top of a radiator. The judge's contribution to the decor consisted of two framed faded photographs of sailboats, which hung on the government-green walls. Dominating the room was a long wooden table, surrounded by eight ancient oak chairs, padded with horsehair, upholstered in leather.

Schlichtmann arrived at the judge's chambers with an entourage from the office—Conway, Crowley, Kathy Boyer, Peggy Vecchione, and several others—who came along to lend moral support. Facher was already seated in the first chair on the right side of the table, immediately adjacent to the judge's chair at the head of the table. He had come with an entourage, too—Jacobs, Frederico, and another associate— who occupied the remaining chairs on that same side of the table. Across from them sat Cheeseman and his partner Marc Temin and two other colleagues. Schlichtmann and his retinue were the last to enter the room. Schlichtmann took the chair at the far end of the long table. Conway, Crowley, and the others gathered around him on folding chairs. Facher, who seemed in high good humor, said something to Jacobs, who smiled. Facher chuckled. Schlichtmann sat in silence.

Judge Skinner appeared at the door, looking pale and angry. He halted abruptly and glared at the gathering of lawyers, his stooped frame bent at the waist. He waved his arm in an impatient gesture. "Clear it out," he said. "One lawyer for each side."

Facher and Schlichtmann remained seated as the others stood to leave. Kathy Boyer bent down to whisper reassurance in Schlichtmann's ear before she left. Cheeseman and his partners stood and consulted in low voices for a few seconds. Then Temin, who had attended the preliminary depositions, took a chair beside Facher.

The door closed. Judge Skinner looked down the length of the table at Schlichtmann. "I'm going to lower the boom on you, Mr. Schlichtmann."

Schlichtmann cleared his throat. "Judge, if this is going to be a hanging, I want the court stenographer here to record it."

"You don't want a court reporter for this," murmured Facher.

"I will not tolerate behavior of this sort," said the judge. "I've read things in these depositions—outrageous things—that I've never read before, and I've been here quite a while. Swearing on the record, instructing witnesses not to answer, counseling witnesses on their answers . . ."

"Judge," said Schlichtmann, "do you know what this is all about? I'd like to explain what—"

"I know *exactly* what this is about, Mr. Schlichtmann. These are depositions."

"That's not exactly right, Your Honor. These are not regular depositions." Schlichtmann, alone at the far end of the table, felt at a disadvantage. He wanted to move up closer to the judge. He said, "Your Honor, can I come up there and sit next to you?"

Skinner looked momentarily surprised. "Yes, of course."

Schlichtmann stood. He heard a loud rip. He looked down and saw that the lining of his suit had caught on a brass tack in the upholstery of the chair. "My God," he said softly, "that's not a good sign." When he looked up, he saw the barest hint of amusement cross the judge's lips. It passed in an instant and Skinner's expression turned stony again.

Schlichtmann moved to the empty chair beside the judge and tried to explain the circumstances of the depositions. He showed the judge the page in the transcript where he'd said, "I'm sorry Judge Skinner wasn't party to the agreement."

But the judge was not mollified. "There is no excuse, no excuse whatever, for this sort of conduct, no matter what sort of agreement you had. Swearing like that in a deposition."

"I was wrong to do that," admitted Schlichtmann, doing his best to appear contrite. But he could not stop himself from adding, "But I had a reason to swear."

"I warn you, Mr. Schlichtmann, I will deal with this in a way that will make headlines in *American Lawyer* if it happens again."

Schlichtmann nodded, his head bowed, again contrite.

"You are to say nothing—nothing!—in these depositions except to object to the form of the question. Do you understand that?"

Facher spoke again, for only the second time. "Your Honor, I don't see how we can possibly continue with discovery in this way. Mr. Schlichtmann wouldn't even get on the elevator with me as we were coming up here."

This was true. When Schlichtmann arrived at the courthouse that afternoon, he and Conway and the others had encountered Facher and his team at the elevators. An elevator door had opened, and Facher had gotten on. Conway had stepped forward as if to board the elevator too, but Schlichtmann had grabbed him by the arm and pulled him back. They'd stood for a moment, a frozen tableau, facing each other, Schlichtmann glaring at Facher. And then the elevator door had closed.

The judge cast a baleful eye on Schlichtmann. "Mr. Schlichtmann, let's have no more of this. You've got to get along with each other."

Schlichtmann knew now that the judge had done all he was going to do. "You're absolutely right, Your Honor," Schlichtmann said, nodding vigorously in agreement. "I think Mr. Facher and Mr. Temin and I should try to resolve this. Perhaps Your Honor could give us a few minutes to talk about it between ourselves?"

The judge considered this. "I think that's a good idea," he said finally. He gave Schlichtmann one last stern gaze of warning and then rose from his chair and left the room.

The worst had not happened. Schlichtmann felt that he had narrowly escaped disaster, but his sense of relief was mingled with defiance. He looked at Facher and said, "You're not going to knock me out of this case. We're going to trial in February. Your client's property is soaked with solvents." To Temin, who had not said a word throughout the entire hearing, Schlichtmann said, "And your client is going to be indicted by the grand jury. If you're hoping that I'm going to run out of money, you're wrong. We've settled with Unifirst."

In a soft voice, almost as if he were speaking to himself, Facher said, "I suspected something like that was happening."

"I've got enough to go the distance, and I'm going to get a jury in February," continued Schlichtmann. "We better start trying to work together, because sooner or later we're going to have to sit down and talk about whether we want to settle this thing."

4

Facher took to calling the meeting in Judge Skinner's chambers the Woodshed Conference. Whenever he felt that Schlichtmann had transgressed again, Facher mentioned that day to the judge. "I don't have to remind Your Honor of that little meeting back in the Woodshed," Facher would say.

Facher wondered how much money Schlichtmann had gotten from Unifirst. He could have asked, but he doubted that Schlichtmann would have told him. He had other ways of finding out. On the whole, he viewed the Unifirst settlement as an encouraging sign—it meant that Schlichtmann really was willing to settle rather than go to trial. And it seemed to Facher that now, after being taken to the Woodshed, Schlichtmann might welcome the opportunity to settle the case against Beatrice. As for Cheeseman, he would have to look out for himself and his own client. Facher might cooperate with him from time to time, when it suited both their aims, but he owed Cheeseman nothing.

It took Facher one phone call to find out on good authority that Schlichtmann had gotten a million dollars from Unifirst. This, too, seemed propitious. Facher liked to boast that he had never paid more than a million dollars to settle a case, but in this instance he thought it might be worth a million dollars to get Beatrice out of this case. He called Schlichtmann one evening, a few days after the Woodshed Conference. "You got your money from Unifirst?" Facher said.

"Yes," said Schlichtmann.

"You want some more?"

Schlichtmann laughed.

"Come on over. I'll give you some."

Schlichtmann suggested that they arrange a meeting at a neutral place, the Ritz-Carlton, for example, with what he called the "decision-makers"—Beatrice executives and the corporation's insurance agents.

Facher brushed this aside. "That's too complicated. I do it the old-fashioned way. Come over to my office and let's talk."

Facher met Schlichtmann in Hale and Dorr's opulent reception room on the twenty-fifth floor. It was after seven o'clock and the offices were quiet. Schlichtmann had brought Conway and Gordon with him. Facher did not mind that. He motioned for them all to follow him into his office. He sat behind his desk, and Schlichtmann and Conway sat across from him, their coats folded in their laps. Gordon took a chair by the door, near the small refrigerator in which Facher kept leftovers from the firm's weekly buffet. The office itself was small, too cramped for four people. "Some lawyers have very pretentious offices, big and sweeping," Facher said, adding that he had been offered just such an office many times but had turned it down. "I don't like waste," he said.

The office was cluttered with piles of paper and baseball memorabilia. A major-league bat, split at the handle, served as Facher's doorstop, and a ball signed by Red Sox players occupied a prominent spot on his desk. On top of the bookcases and filing cabinets were souvenirs from his previous cases. Facher was in no hurry to get down to business. He noticed Schlichtmann looking around curiously, so he showed Schlichtmann a scale model of a railroad boxcar, a gift from the Southern Pacific Railroad, for whom he'd won a case. On the walls, Facher had hung his diplomas and pictures of himself with clients and colleagues from earlier years. Looking at the photos, Schlichtmann thought that Facher had not changed much. He had the same heavy-lidded eyes and lugubrious face, the same pursed lips. As a young man, Facher had been a bit heavier around the shoulders and chest and slightly fuller of face than he was now. Facher took particular pride in a framed photograph of one of his two daughters, which sat on the credenza behind his desk. The woman in the photograph appeared a few years younger than Schlichtmann. She smiled a thin, wan smile.

"You're married," Schlichtmann said with mild surprise, realizing at that moment that he'd never thought of Facher as having children and a life outside of the law.

"No," replied Facher. His marriage, he told Schlichtmann, had ended a long time ago. Facher picked up a spongy rubber ball, tossed it in the air and caught it. He swiveled his chair around and threw the ball against the wall, catching it with both hands cupped cautiously as it bounced back, like a man catching a raw egg. "This is what I do to relax," Facher said. As he threw the ball he talked. The case against

Beatrice was no good, he told Schlichtmann. The ball thumped against the wall. There was no evidence that the tannery had ever used TCE (thump). Riley had never dumped anything on the fifteen acres (thump). Riley was a victim of midnight dumpers, just as the families were victims (thump). "You've got a lousy case, and you know it."

Schlichtmann admitted that the case against Beatrice was not as strong as the one against Grace. But it was not, he told Facher, a "lousy" case. The fifteen acres were saturated with TCE and other contaminants. "I think Riley dumped tannery waste on the fifteen acres. I've still got time to develop the case."

"You don't want me in this case," said Facher. "You've got Grace, and one deep pocket is enough. I'm only going to hurt you. I'm giving you a chance to get rid of me." Facher added that he could not match the Unifirst settlement. "I don't have that much to give you." He thumped the rubber ball against the wall.

It was obvious to Schlichtmann that Facher had found out how much Unifirst had paid. He thought that Facher was acting in an arrogant, insulting manner, every thud of the rubber ball like a slap. But Schlichtmann didn't let himself feel offended. The first goal in any negotiation was to keep talking, and talking to Facher was the first step to a real negotiation. "We don't have to talk numbers now," said Schlichtmann. "Let's get the decision-makers together first."

"You want the decision-maker?" said Facher. "I'm it. You want Mr. Beatrice Foods? He's sitting right here. Tell me what you want. Make it reasonable, and I'll accept, and we can get on with our lives."

"We can't just throw numbers at each other," said Schlichtmann. "That doesn't work. We need to set aside some time so we can discuss this—your people and my people—in a neutral place."

Facher grunted at this. "Why don't you bring your clients up here? They're the decision-makers, aren't they? Let me hear them say no to a million dollars."

Schlichtmann demurred. They had reached an impasse. Facher began telling stories about his past cases, about the Southern Pacific case, about the Saxon Theatre case. He didn't mention the Baltic Birch case, which he had tried in front of Judge Skinner several years ago and lost, the last case that he had lost. Again he asked Schlichtmann for a number, and Schlichtmann again refused to give him one.

Facher was exasperated. "I don't understand why you won't give me a number, any goddamn number." He reached into his hip pocket, pulled out his wallet, and slapped a twenty-dollar bill on his desk. He leaned back in his chair. "What if I put six zeros on the end of that. Would you take it?"

Twenty million dollars.

Schlichtmann laughed but did not answer Facher's question.

The twenty-dollar bill remained on Facher's desk, directly under Conway's nose. Conway felt tempted to pick it up and put it in his pocket. He had only a few dollars in his own wallet, and not much more in his bank account. Twenty dollars would pay for dinner tonight. It was after eight o'clock and Conway was hungry. It seemed obvious to him that this discussion was going nowhere.

Facher had a warning for Schlichtmann before he left. "You think you're going to put those families on the witness stand and break everybody's heart. You think the jury's going to pull out their handkerchiefs and dab their eyes." Facher shook his head resolutely. "It will never happen. Those families will never see the light of day."

Schlichtmann regarded Facher's parting words as an idle threat. He did not give them a second thought. He could see no possible way that Facher could stop the families from telling their stories once he had a jury impaneled.

He had survived the Woodshed, but the entire episode left him unnerved. There was an enormous amount of work to do in the coming months, and he could not afford another misstep. He had an ominous feeling about the judge. It seemed to him that Skinner treated Facher with more respect and deference than he accorded him. Something the judge had said about Facher at the Rule 11 hearing, three years ago now, had stuck like a burr in Schlichtmann's memory. He recalled the judge saying, "I can't let Mr. Facher's judgment be substituted for mine, although I ordinarily would give it great respect."

The judge and Facher were of the same generation. They had gone to the same law school at virtually the same time. They had the same breeding in the law, and they had both risen to high positions in it. They even seemed to think alike. Schlichtmann had noticed that they had a habit of finishing each other's sentences. Sometimes Schlicht-mann felt as if he were eavesdropping on a private conversation.

"These witnesses are not critical," he'd heard Facher telling the judge at one hearing.

And the judge had said, "It doesn't sound to me as if they're critical."

"They're not critical in the least," Facher said.

"Beatrice is a great big food company," said the judge.

"Tropicana, LaChoy, and some other things," said Facher.

"This rinky-dink tannery represented about what, one percent of their gross income," said the judge.

"An absolutely insignificant acquisition," agreed Facher.

Schlichtmann had suffered in silence through a number of conversations like that. "It's like listening to Tweedledee and Tweedledum," he told Conway. It had merely annoyed him at first, but now it worried him. He knew he couldn't compete with Facher for the judge's respect, especially not since the Woodshed Conference.

Billion-Dollar Charlie

1

A Harvard Law School professor named Charles Nesson had spent many years pondering the nature of judicial proof—proof in the courtroom—and its relationship to truth. Nesson taught evidence and criminal law at Harvard, and one particular riddle involving the use of statistics as evidence had absorbed him for some time. To solve it, he relied on a hypothetical case, which he called the Case of the Blue Bus.

The facts of Nesson's imaginary case were simple: Mr. Smith is driving down a dark two-lane road late one night when he encounters the headlights of a vehicle speeding toward him in the center of the road. To avoid a head-on collision, Mr. Smith swerves off the road and his car hits a tree. In the darkness, he sees that the vehicle speeding by him is a bus. While recovering from his injuries, Mr. Smith learns that the Blue Bus Company owns and operates 80 percent of the buses that drive along the route where the accident occurred. Mr. Smith sues the Blue Bus Company for damages. During the trial, he proves the aforementioned facts but admits that he cannot identify the color of the bus that forced him off the road.

Given this evidence, Professor Nesson asked, can Mr. Smith win his case?

If the Blue Bus case were a criminal trial, where the state has to prove its case beyond a reasonable doubt, Mr. Smith obviously could not hope to win. There is, after all, at least a 20 percent chance that the Blue Bus Company is not guilty. But this is a civil action, where the aim is to resolve disputes in a just manner, and in civil cases the plaintiff's burden of proof is not as onerous. Mr. Smith has to prove only that it is "more likely true than not"—a standard often taken to mean by 51 percent or better—that the Blue Bus Company caused the accident. By that standard, it would seem that Mr. Smith *should* win his case.

But Nesson believed that a verdict for Mr. Smith would be a grave error. "In this case and others like it," Nesson wrote in the *Harvard Law Review*, "the plaintiff will lose; in fact, the case is unlikely even to reach the jury." In the absence of a credible eyewitness or some other tangible piece of evidence—a scrape of blue paint on Mr. Smith's car, for example—a jury could not hope to know the actual truth of the event. A jury might, of course, be willing to bet that the Blue Bus Company was liable, and the odds would greatly favor such a bet. But a verdict based simply on the odds, Nesson argued, even very good odds, has no moral or legal force, and sooner or later the public would find such verdicts and the judicial system that permitted them unacceptable.

Each trial is a drama in its own right, wrote Nesson, a morality play watched by a public audience. "Through trials, society seeks not only to discover the truth about a past event, but also to forge a link between crime and punishment, between wrong and liability." The judgments of the courts are meant to reinforce social rules and values and, at the same time, to deter behavior contrary to those rules and values. To achieve this end, the public has to believe that jury verdicts are statements about the truth of actual events, not mere probabilities. If that belief is ever lost, a society based on the rule of law would ultimately collapse into anarchy. To find for the plaintiff against the Blue Bus Company would be, in this sense, to find for anarchy.

Judge Skinner was a regular reader of his alma mater's famous *Law Review*. So it was, perhaps, not so strange that the Case of the Blue Bus should enter the Woburn case.

The lawyers were gathered for another conference, the first since the Woodshed Conference, two weeks ago. Outside the tall windows of Judge Skinner's courtroom, the slanting afternoon sunlight cast a golden glow on the city. It was unmistakably autumn light, and it reminded Schlichtmann of how little time remained before the trial, and how much he still had to do.

"I have a question about this case," Judge Skinner said at the end of the conference, apropos of nothing he and the lawyers had been discussing. "I was put in mind of it by reading an article by Professor Nesson at the Harvard Law School about the use of statistics in proof. Mr. Schlichtmann, perhaps you can help us out on this."

Schlichtmann rose from the counsel table and listened in an attentive but wary manner, one that evoked memories of schooldays.

"It has to do with the trial itself," continued the judge. "It occurred to me that you may intend to use a statistical analysis to prove causation by showing us the unlikelihood of so many instances of disease in a particular area. The question is whether evidence which would not be the proper basis for a verdict becomes proper because an expert blesses it and says, 'I, as an expert, would be willing to take this bet.' If that's going to be the case, I'd like to have some advance briefing on exactly how it's going to work."

Schlichtmann knew nothing about Professor Nesson or his *Law Review* article, but he surmised that the judge was probably asking about the Harvard Health Study. Schlichtmann certainly hoped to use that study during the trial—it was a valuable piece of the evidentiary puzzle—but he could tell that the judge took a dim view of it. Schlichtmann didn't feel prepared to debate this issue yet. He had to be careful about what he said. A moment passed, and then another as he considered how to answer the judge.

"Is that going to be part of your case?" the judge asked again.

"Obviously—" began Schlichtmann, and then he suddenly changed his mind. "Our case will be proven on clinical grounds, Your Honor." He had almost said, yes, the Harvard study would play an important role, but he decided it was safer to speak about the hard, clinical evidence—Feldman's tests, Colvin's studies, the cardiology results, the physical examinations and medical histories of the families.

The judge did not seem satisfied. "Well, specifically, are you going to use the—"

"I will not use statistics to prove causation," said Schlichtmann.

"Okay, fine. Then my problems for the time being are resolved."

"May I say," Schlichtmann hastened to add, "that epidemiology and statistics will be important in the case."

Facher wasn't present at this hearing, but Cheeseman and Neil Jacobs were both there. Jacobs arose to address the judge. "The more direct question is whether the Harvard Health Study, which is this type of statistical analysis, will be offered as evidence in the case. I can't tell from what Mr. Schlichtmann said how that question will be answered."

Cheeseman was also standing. "Your Honor, we do expect to challenge the admissibility of that study."

But by then the judge had risen from his chair, too. It was getting late and he had already spent a long day presiding over another case. "I'm not inviting a pretrial conference," he said to Cheeseman. "I just wanted to find out if I was going to have to worry about that particular issue, and I wanted to get prepared to worry about it intelligently."

2

Schlichtmann felt exhausted as he left the courthouse that afternoon. He had expected Cheeseman and Jacobs to challenge the Harvard study, and it appeared to him that Judge Skinner was already disposed to rule in their favor. Researching and writing a brief that might change the judge's mind would take him dozens of hours. Imagining the work, he felt as if he'd already been up all night doing it. He had a hundred other things to do—fieldwork in Woburn to oversee, experts to prepare, interrogatories to answer—before actually attending to that problem. On top of everything else, the Woburn families were scheduled to return to Boston that week for a second round of depositions.

Schlichtmann felt it necessary to attend all of those depositions to defend his clients. There were nineteen of them—they included all of the parents and five of the oldest children—and most of them took an entire day. For three weeks Facher and Cheeseman and their assistants questioned the families closely about their use of more than five hundred brand-name household products—cleaning agents and detergents, rug shampoos, cosmetics, nail-polish removers, insect repellents, paints, lawn fertilizers, cold remedies, cough syrups, herbal teas, coffee, even peanut butter.

To Schlichtmann, the strategy behind this exhaustive list was obvious. These five hundred items all allegedly contained a known or suspected carcinogen. Peanut butter, for example, ranked high on the list, right up with cigarettes. The reason: all peanut butter contains trace amounts of aflatoxin B1, a natural but potent liver carcinogen produced by a common peanut mold. Cheeseman and Facher would try to suggest to a jury that inasmuch as the cause of childhood leukemia was largely a mystery to medical science, dozens of substances used by the families might just as likely have caused the Woburn illnesses as the contaminated water.

"Do you eat peanut butter?" one of Facher's young associates asked Anne Anderson.

"No," said Anne.

"Did you *ever* eat peanut butter?"

"I guess everybody living has probably tried it," replied Anne. "I've eaten it, but I'm not a peanut butter fan."

"Do your kids eat peanut butter?"

"Well, the same jar has been sitting there an awfully long time, so I guess we don't eat much."

"What kind is it, plain or chunky?"

"Plain, smooth," said Anne.

"You made your children peanut butter sandwiches?"

"They ate some, when they were small."

"When you say, 'some,' could you quantify that? One or two sandwiches a week for the children?"

Schlichtmann listened to questions of this sort for hours on end, all the while thinking about the other things he had to do. Memories of the Woodshed Conference were fresh, and he acted with greater restraint now. But he sometimes could not resist giving vent to his impatience. "It's now five o'clock," he told Facher's associate. "You're squandering time on absolutely ridiculous questions. The witness is exhausted and I'm exhausted. I urge you to finish your examination by six o'clock."

His complaints had no effect. Do you eat bacon? one of Facher's associates asked yet another of Schlichtmann's clients. (Bacon contains dimethylnitrosamine, a carcinogen.) How often? How many slices? Do you fry it or bake it? Do you have Teflon pans? (Teflon is made of a resin containing acrylonitrile, a carcinogen.) How often do you use them? Do you chew sugarless gum? (Saccharin, a carcinogen in mice.) How often? Do you pump your own gas? (Benzene, a leukemogen.) How often do you bathe? Do you have plastic shower curtains? (Vinyl chloride, a liver carcinogen.) Have you ever owned a cat? (Feline leukemia virus.) Do you drink beer? (Nitrosamines.) Do you use a deodorant? (Aluminum chlorohydrate.) "Of course," said Mary Toomey to that query, mildly indignant. "Since I came of age, I've always used deodorant."

Roland Gamache was dying of leukemia by the time his second deposition began. Neither he nor his wife could admit this to each other. But the lawyers all knew. In early October, Gamache did not have strength enough to get out of bed. His bone marrow had stopped producing red blood cells and, as a result, every cell in his body was slowly asphyxiating. He received a blood transfusion and began a new round of chemotherapy, and he felt well enough to travel to Boston for his deposition. "The last three months have been very difficult," he told his examiner, one of Cheeseman's assistants.

"Are you and your wife able to talk about the situation candidly?" asked the associate.

"It's difficult for her, very difficult," said Roland. "Every time we talk, there's tears in her eyes."

On a Friday afternoon, after a week of these depositions, Schlichtmann left his office early and went downstairs to Patten's Bar & Grill. He found an empty booth in a dark corner of the bar and sat alone in the gloom, drinking a double Scotch. He had finished his first drink and ordered a second when his friend Tom Kiley arrived. He had met Kiley, who was himself a personal injury lawyer, six years ago at the Essex County courthouse, on the day Schlichtmann began the Eaton trial. After the verdict, Kiley had called to congratulate him. Over the years, a mutual regard grew into a friendship. In time, they developed a ritual of getting together on Friday afternoons for a drink.

Schlichtmann valued Kiley's counsel even though he and Kiley practiced personal injury law in very different ways. Kiley didn't feel secure unless he had dozens of cases in his files, most of them small, uncomplicated disputes—his "bread and butter," he called them. He'd won a few big and difficult malpractice cases, too, and he was ambitious, but he ran a frugal office with only two assistants. "He counts the pencils when he leaves the office at the end of the day," Schlichtmann once said of Kiley. And Kiley, watching Schlichtmann risk a small fortune on the Carney case, had said, "I'd wake up in a cold sweat at two o'clock every morning." As for Woburn, Kiley admired Schlichtmann for taking it on, although he personally would not have done so.

Now, in Patten's, Kiley saw in his friend's demeanor all the reasons for avoiding cases like Woburn. Schlichtmann looked wan, almost sickly, and he spoke like a man on the verge of despair. "I feel like I'm drowning," Kiley heard Schlichtmann say. "I'm in too deep. I've got no control over this case, and that scares me."

Schlichtmann told Kiley about the Woodshed Conference, and about the last hearing, when the judge had seemed on the verge of excluding the Harvard Health Study. He felt, Schlichtmann said, as if he were being overwhelmed by the two big law firms (Facher and Cheeseman each had a staff of a dozen lawyers working on the case by now), by their discovery demands, their constant motions, and their personal attacks. The judge's magistrate didn't respect him or his case. Even worse, neither did the judge.

Kiley didn't doubt the truth of any of this. In his own practice, Kiley tried to avoid the federal courts, which he found much less receptive to personal injury law than the state courts. All the same, he tried to reassure Schlichtmann. "You've got to get hold of yourself," Kiley said. "You can do this, but you can't do it by yourself. You've got to get somebody to help you out."

Kiley offered his own services, on a part-time basis. He'd had a successful year and he could spare the time. But, mused Kiley, the best thing might be for Schlichtmann to find a law professor, someone who could render advice on the legal theories of the case, someone who could figure out how to get the Harvard Health Study into evidence. "Maybe you'll have to pay some professor thirty or forty thousand dollars," Kiley said. "You've already spent a million, so what's another thirty thousand?"

Kiley mentioned a professor at Suffolk who might be interested. Schlichtmann wrote the name down on a napkin. The more he and Kiley talked about candidates, the more animated Schlichtmann became. Yes, Kiley was right! A law professor who would sit with him at the counsel table during trial, an éminence grise who would command the judge's respect, whose sentences the judge would be honored to finish. One name led to others. Soon they had compiled a list of half a dozen law professors from Suffolk, Northeastern, and Boston University.

They were working on this list when Rikki Klieman came into Patten's Bar & Grill. She had not seen much of Schlichtmann since the Carney trial, since that morning when he'd called her in a paroxysm of anxiety. But she felt convinced that they were right for each other and that someday they would be together. She had spent her day in court, defending a client accused of smuggling drugs into the country aboard a fishing boat. She wore a conservatively cut gray suit, hemline to the knees, a pearl necklace, and gold-bangled earrings.

She'd come to Patten's hoping that she could persuade Schlichtmann to go to Puerto Rico with her, to the First Circuit Judicial Conference. It was a prestigious event, by anonymous invitation only, and this year's conference, on the beaches of San Juan, promised to be more fun than most. Rikki's invitation, she happened to know, had come from Judge Skinner, for whom she had clerked after law school. She and lawyers from the large, well-connected corporate law firms routinely got invited. Solo practitioners and plaintiff's lawyers, ambulance chasers like Schlichtmann, rarely did. But this year, for the first time, Schlichtmann received his own anonymous invitation in the mail.

Rikki had been trying all week to talk him into coming. She knew that he was still involved with Teresa, but she had a sense that this relationship wouldn't endure. "I saw this as my chance to get Jan alone," Rikki would say later, with a smile.

Kiley and Schlichtmann were working on their list of law professors when Rikki sat down at the table. She listened awhile, and then she made a suggestion that suited both Schlichtmann's needs and her own purposes for being here. "How about Charlie Nesson?" she said. "He's speaking at the conference in Puerto Rico."

Schlichtmann turned to her in astonishment. "The judge just mentioned him," he exclaimed. "You know him?"

Rikki said yes, she'd known Nesson for years. She taught at the Harvard Trial Advocacy Program every January, which Nesson had adopted as his special program. In fact, she and Nesson had gone out to dinner with mutual friends not long ago. "Come to Puerto Rico with me and I'll introduce you to him," Rikki said.

The coincidence seemed at first quite remarkable to Schlichtmann. And then, after a few moments, he decided it was not a mere coincidence at all, but a matter of destiny. Clearly, this Professor Nesson, author of articles that the judge himself cited, was the one whom Providence had chosen.

3

Rikki Klieman flew down to San Juan on the following Friday, November 1. The next morning, she went out to the beach, returning periodically to the lobby of the Dupont Hotel to see if Schlichtmann had arrived. When he finally did arrive, early that afternoon, she was there to greet him. Directly behind him, she saw a porter wheeling in a black litigation bag, its sides bowed out with the weight of documents. Her heart sank. It looked as if the bag contained more reading than anyone could hope to accomplish in a month.

She talked Schlichtmann into going to the beach with her. He brought along a large sheaf of documents. "He carted them around with him everywhere," Rikki would recall later. "He looked so unhappy." She lay in the sun, listening with half an ear as Schlichtmann talked about the case. All around them on the beach were dozens of pale lawyers and their wives—corporate attorneys of distinction, federal prosecutors, bankruptcy judges, magistrates, district court judges, appeals court judges.

Schlichtmann pestered Rikki about meeting Nesson. He had already checked the hotel registration and found that Nesson had not arrived. That evening he and Rikki went to a party at the Old Fort in San Juan. Schlichtmann looked for Nesson and had a lot to drink. He encountered one of Facher's partners from Hale and Dorr. The partner, who had consumed a number of rum punches himself, told Schlichtmann that Woburn was a "career-making" case, one that would no doubt lead to fame and riches. "Are you kidding?" exclaimed Schlichtmann, who spent the next half hour telling Facher's partner how impossible the case was. Rikki wandered off to find a more interesting conversation.

She lost track of Schlichtmann that evening, and she returned to her room late, and alone.

She awoke early the next morning and went to the beach to lie in the sun. Her hopes of kindling a romance with Schlichtmann had not worked out on this trip, but she felt that wasn't the fault of either of them. Woburn absorbed him completely, and she understood that. She had spent the last ten years of her own life completely absorbed in her career. She wouldn't give up on him yet. She decided to go on being patient.

Nesson was scheduled to give his talk before lunch, and Rikki wanted to hear him. She had a professional interest in the subject—government confiscation of the assets of drug dealers. She folded her towel and returned to the hotel just before Nesson's talk began. She wore a loose shift over her swimsuit and took a seat in the back of the room. As Nesson concluded his presentation, Schlichtmann sat down next to her.

"Go speak to him when he finishes," he whispered.

"Not now," she said. "I've got to change my clothes."

"Why? You look fine."

"Jan, just calm down," she said, and she left for her room.

Schlichtmann went to the dais, where Nesson, surrounded by a small audience, was engaged in conversation with an elderly federal judge named Charles Wyzanski. Nesson appeared to be in his late forties, slightly built, with pale, almost translucent skin. He had luminous hazel eyes and a broad and cerebral brow. His light brown hair, which had grown long, over his ears and down the nape of his neck, was turning gray. Schlichtmann elbowed his way through the group around Nesson until he stood beside the Harvard professor. He waited impatiently for a pause in the conversation, for an opportunity to interrupt the old judge who was relating what seemed to Schlichtmann a complicated and interminable story. As he waited he watched Nesson, who listened to the judge serenely in a manner that made Schlichtmann think of Zen-like wisdom. When the judge finally paused, Schlichtmann impulsively thrust his hand out and introduced himself to Nesson. "I'm involved in a case, maybe you've heard about it," Schlichtmann began.

Nesson had already noticed, out of the corner of his eye, this tall young lawyer, head bobbing above the crowd, an intent and anxious look on his face, homing in on him. Nesson recognized the type. Another fresh-faced young member of the bar seeking free advice, he thought. Nesson got paid handsomely to give speeches at conferences such as this, but he got no compensation for the advice lawyers inevitably sought afterward. After nineteen years at Harvard and many of these legal conferences, Nesson had become adroit at getting rid of pests. He shook Schlichtmann's hand and said, "Please meet Judge Wyzanski." Then he turned and began to make his escape. The elderly judge started to say something to Schlichtmann, who ignored him and took a step in pursuit of Nesson.

"You want some advice?" said Nesson over his shoulder.

Schlichtmann nodded.

"My advice is you should never turn your back on a federal judge." And then Nesson disappeared into the crowd.

Rikki, freshly showered and wearing a skirt and blouse, came downstairs to find Schlichtmann looking frantic. He had reservations on a plane back to Boston that afternoon. "Time's running out," he said.

She told him to find a table for the luncheon session, and then she went in search of Nesson. She spotted him in the lobby, among another group of judges and lawyers. She went up to him and put her hand on his sleeve. "Charlie," she said, "have lunch with me. I've got someone I want you to meet."

Leading Nesson back to the conference room, she could see Schlichtmann standing at a table, peering anxiously around for her. She felt like a matchmaker, and the irony of this thought amused her. It also made her a little nervous. She worried that Schlichtmann, in his eagerness, would put Nesson off.

She introduced them to each other. Nesson smiled wryly. "We've already met," he said.

As they took their seats at the table, Rikki between the two men, she leaned close to Schlichtmann and said, "Jan, settle down and let me talk."

Schlichtmann managed to contain himself for several moments while Rikki described the Woburn case to Nesson, who listened and said very little. Schlichtmann mentioned the Harvard Health Study, and Nesson said he recalled reading about it in the newspapers. Waiters came with lunch and by the time the plates were cleared, Schlichtmann had barely touched his food. As Schlichtmann talked, the waiters brought lemon meringue pie for dessert. Rikki watched Nesson pick up a fork and begin to create designs in the meringue. He never took a bite of the pie, but the designs grew increasingly complicated. She couldn't tell if this meant that Nesson was interested in what Schlichtmann was saying, or if he was merely bored.

Up on the dais in the front of the room, someone stood to introduce one of Nesson's famous colleagues from Harvard, Arthur Miller. Schlichtmann kept talking. Miller began delivering the keynote address, and still Schlichtmann talked. Rikki put her hand on his arm, and finally he stopped.

He sat in silent agitation through Miller's speech, not hearing a word of it. As soon as Miller finished, while polite applause rippled through the room, he leaned over to Nesson to resume his disquisition. But before he could get a word out, Nesson stood to excuse himself. He explained that he had made plans to tour the old section of San Juan with friends that afternoon. "Interesting case," he told Schlichtmann.

"Maybe we can get together later today," Schlichtmann said.

Nesson smiled and shrugged. "I'm flying back to Boston this evening."

"So am I!" said Schlichtmann. "We can talk on the plane."

But Nesson merely smiled and walked away.

"Jan, don't try to talk to him on the plane," warned Rikki. "Just let him think about it for a while. Please. Promise me."

Ten minutes after the plane took off, Schlichtmann left his seat in first class and went back to coach to find Nesson. He brought a copy of his summary judgment brief and of the Harvard Health Study. "There's an empty seat next to me in first class," Schlichtmann said to Nesson. "Come on up. We can talk."

Nesson shook his head. "I'm comfortable here," he said coldly.

Schlichtmann pressed the documents on Nesson and then, feeling as if he had done all he could, and perhaps more than he should, he returned to his seat.

Nesson had taught at Harvard Law School for nineteen years. He had known from the age of six that he wanted to be a lawyer. As an undergraduate at Harvard College, he had marked time by studying mathematics until he could enter law school. The subject bored him and he got mediocre grades. In his junior year he took the law school boards, got an almost perfect score, and applied for early admission to

Harvard Law. He was shocked when he was rejected. He appealed to the dean of the law school. He was even more shocked when the dean told him not to bother applying again. High test scores and low grades indicated laziness, the dean said, and Harvard Law did not want lazy students. Nesson framed the rejection letter in a black border, as if it were a obituary, and hung it above his desk. He began studying mathematics in earnest. His grades improved. He applied again to the law school, and this time he was admitted.

The law seemed to Nesson like a series of wonderfully complicated but entertaining riddles involving human behavior. At the end of his first year, when the registrar posted the grades in Langdell Hall, Nesson ranked first in his class of five hundred students. Given his undergraduate record, he considered this "a fluke," as he put it many years later. But at the end of his second year, he again ranked first. In the hotly competitive atmosphere of Harvard, rumors about his brilliance began to circulate. His rivals for the head of the class were determined to dislodge him in the third and final year. They did not succeed. He was a true legal prodigy. At Harvard Law, grades are carried out to three decimal points, and legend has it that Nesson left the law school with the highest grade point average since Felix Frankfurter graduated in 1907.

Harvard has a long tradition of rewarding its best students with teaching positions. Nesson was only twenty-seven years old when the law school invited him back to Cambridge. By then he'd spent a year clerking for Supreme Court Justice John Harlan, and another year at the Civil Rights Division of the Justice Department under John Doar. He accepted Harvard's offer and won tenure within three years. He married one of his law students and bought a home in the most expensive district of Cambridge, not far from the Harvard campus. And then he began to think that perhaps he should have seen more of the world. He took time off from teaching to work on the celebrated Berrigan and Ellsberg cases.

His job carried great prestige and he made a good income, but it was only a fraction of what many of his former law school classmates, and even some of his former students, now made in private practice. Nor had he achieved either the scholarly recognition or the popular fame of colleagues such as Laurence Tribe, Arthur Miller, and Alan Dershowitz.

At lunch in San Juan, Nesson had kept his own counsel while listening to Schlichtmann talk about the Woburn case, but he had not been bored. Now, on the plane, reading the material that Schlichtmann had thrust upon him, he saw that this young lawyer had developed a great deal of evidence in immunology, cardiology, and neurology. Clearly Schlichtmann understood that he could not rely on the Harvard study alone. From what Nesson could tell, Schlichtmann must have invested a fortune in this case. He obviously made a good deal of money, since he dressed expensively and flew in first-class. He wanted help, and Nesson figured he needed it.

Nesson had once written a poem that he handed out to his students on the last day of a class in criminal law. It read in part:

> *Reach for what you want*
> *Want more than you can get.*
> *Reach, and learn what you can let go . . .*
> *To get what you want,*
> *Reach for more,*
> *An adversary premise,*
> *A good premise . . .*
> *What do you want?*
> *More than you can get.*
> *But then how?*
> *Take it in pieces,*
> *Want it all.*

Nesson's gifts clearly lay in the legal, not the poetic, realm, but the poem was a disarmingly candid statement about ambition. He had been looking for a new challenge. The Woburn case seemed like a wonderful riddle, and it had everything he could want in a lawsuit—interesting proof and evidence problems, an important social and environmental issue, plenty of media attention and, not least of all, the potential for making a great deal of money. It seemed, in short, like something worth reaching for.

Nesson left his seat in coach and went up to the first-class section. He tapped Schlichtmann on the shoulder.

Schlichtmann looked up and broke into a smile.

"Okay," said Nesson. "I'm interested. What kind of deal can you offer me?"

4

Conway didn't mind the idea of a law professor joining the team. Conway knew they needed help, and he was prepared to remain open-minded, at least until he met Nesson. But Gordon was opposed. Gordon grumbled about ivory-tower academics who never did any real work and yet always seemed to have exalted opinions of themselves. What would Nesson actually do? Gordon asked. And how much would he want for it? There was no money, not even any loose change around, to pay someone like Nesson. Schlichtmann had already brought Kiley into the case and offered him a share of the fee. The thought of giving yet another share to this Harvard professor, this outsider, appalled Gordon. How much more of the case were they going to give away?

To Schlichtmann, it made no difference what anyone else thought. One evening shortly after his return from Puerto Rico, he brought Nesson over to the office to meet the rest of the team. They assembled around the conference room table—Conway and Crowley, Gordon and Phillips, Kiley and a defense lawyer named Tom Neville, a childhood friend of Conway's who had volunteered his services—to hear the Harvard Law professor.

To his thinking, Nesson told those gathered around, this case should stand for something more than just compensating the Woburn families for their losses and injuries. It was, he continued, the sort of case that could ring alarm bells in corporate boardrooms all across America. How do you stop big corporations like Grace and Beatrice from polluting the earth? How do you send the message that they cannot get away with it anymore? "The only language that corporations understand is money," said Nesson. "Sales, income, earnings, profits, the bottom line. That's their blood."

Then Nesson asked how much W. R. Grace and Beatrice made in one year.

Gordon had collected a large stack of Grace and Beatrice annual reports. He knew these figures as well as he knew his own bank account. W. R. Grace had reported sales of slightly over five billion dollars last year, Gordon replied, with profits of $198 million. For Beatrice, net earnings had come to $436 million.

"What do you think it would take to get Grace's attention?" asked Nesson. "What's the smallest unit that would make a difference to a corporation of that size? Ten million dollars? Fifty million? A hundred million?"

The Harvard professor had everyone's attention now.

"What if," said Nesson, "you took away a full year of profits? I think that might get their attention."

Nesson was talking about something far larger than anything Schlichtmann had dared to imagine. Just a month ago, he had told Uncle Pete at the Bank of Boston that the case might be worth as much as three million dollars per family, a total of twenty-four million. Could Nesson possibly be right? A year of profits from both Grace and Beatrice amounted, in round figures, to more than half a billion dollars.

"You have a whole city poisoned," Nesson was saying. "You have public attention riveted to this case. And you have two multibillion-dollar corporations caught in the net." In the final phase of the case, said Nesson, the judge would have to allow them to tell the jury the net worth of these two corporations. They would ask the jury not just to compensate the families, but to punish the corporations, to send a message in the only language that companies like Grace and Beatrice understood.

"Frankly," admitted Nesson, "I'm in this for the punitive damages."

The law professor had cast an entirely new light on the case. Schlichtmann himself had always maintained that Woburn was a "political" case, but he felt now that he'd never come close to defining it as clearly, as succinctly, as brilliantly, as Nesson just had. And this analysis came from a man who gave lectures to judges and to corporate executives and their high-powered lawyers. Nesson was, to a far greater extent than any of them sitting around the conference table, a part of the very establishment to which he wanted to send a bill for half a billion dollars.

By the time Nesson had finished, no one in the room had any qualms about his joining the team.

"The man *is* brilliant," Gordon conceded.

It was not long before Gordon began conjuring up images of a Palm Beach villa with a large yacht moored outside and two Mercedes-Benzes in the garage. Schlichtmann disliked hearing that sort of talk. He felt it was a jinx, and Gordon refrained from spinning these daydreams in Schlichtmann's presence. But Phillips knew of Gordon's reveries and he knew where they came from. Phillips himself wasn't immune to such fantasies, nor was anyone else on the team, for that matter. But Phillips had a sardonic way about him. Billion-Dollar Charlie, Phillips called Nesson, out of the professor's hearing.

If Judge Skinner was surprised to see Professor Nesson at the next hearing, sitting next to Schlichtmann at the counsel table, he did not show it. He welcomed Nesson with a smile and an amiable nod. Over the years, he had attended several of Nesson's lectures. He genuinely enjoyed a good intellectual discussion, and he looked forward to having several with Nesson in coming months. Nor did the judge seem to take offense when Nesson, rising to address him for the first time, announced: "I consider it my job to get this verdict with no error that can possibly upset it on appeal."

Still smiling, the judge said, "If you can prevent me from making an error, that's fine."

But the smile began to fade from the judge's lips as Nesson went on to explain how he saw this case. The Woburn families, he told the judge, "feel that they're suing on behalf of a broader constituency. They want this case to set an example, Your Honor. They want to send a message, to ring the alarm, if you will, in the corporate boardrooms across the United States."

The judge didn't say anything then. It only became apparent some weeks later at the next hearing, in the midst of another discussion, just how much Nesson had irritated him. "I take umbrage at the entire tone of your presentation," the judge told Nesson, his voice rising in anger. "You were trumpeting away about sending messages to the boardrooms of America. Lawsuits are between parties, Professor. One side seeks compensation and the other side defends against it. If the boardrooms of America happen to notice what's going on, that's an incidental consequence of the process. It's not the purpose of it."

"I apologize for my tone," Nesson said quietly. "You will not hear another trumpet from me."

Still, the idea that the case might actually be worth a monstrous sum of money occurred to the judge himself shortly after Nesson's appearance in his courtroom. "This is really quite an interesting and important case," the judge mused at the end of a less acrimonious hearing. "The amounts of dollars potentially at stake here are astronomical, I suppose."

Astronomical—the sound of that word rang in Schlichtmann's ears.

"I have no idea what a jury might do with it," continued the judge. "Certainly there's the potential for a very substantial award. I wouldn't expect it to knock out the Texaco case as the champion high verdict of the century, but it is obviously an important case."

In the privacy of Schlichtmann's office, Nesson had talked about hundreds of millions of dollars, and now the judge was comparing Woburn—or so it seemed to Schlichtmann—to *Pennzoil* v. *Texaco,* in which a jury had awarded the plaintiff, Pennzoil, eleven *billion* dollars.

Gordon happened to be sitting in the courtroom gallery that afternoon. That's bankable, Gordon thought when he heard the judge's remarks. Gordon planned to take a copy of the transcript to Uncle Pete at the Bank of Boston and try to use it as collateral for a bigger loan.

5

The pace of discovery grew more frantic as the trial date drew near. By December all of the lawyers in the case were working seven days a week. They lived on sandwiches and catered cold cuts and take-out Chinese food, eating meals at their desks or around conference tables. Those who had families saw them infrequently. Conway would arrive home in Wellesley after his wife and two children had gone to sleep, and he'd awake the next morning in the dark winter dawn, before anyone else had arisen. Some nights Schlichtmann never even got home. He'd fall asleep on the couch in his office and awake the next morning at first light. His grandmother died in early December. She was buried on a Saturday, and even then Schlichtmann could spare no more than an hour to attend her funeral.

It was a time of cold, gloomy weather, a time of fatigue and headaches and burning eyes and short tempers. One of Facher's young associates at Hale and Dorr had made plans to get married that winter. Facher told her to delay the wedding until after the trial, and she did, but she also began plotting a transfer out of litigation and into real estate. Over at Foley, Hoag & Eliot, Cheeseman billed W. R. Grace for 115 hours of his time in a single week, an average of sixteen and a half hours a day for seven straight days. He had never billed that many hours in one week before, not even as an associate anxious to impress the senior partners. He hoped never to do it again.

Cheeseman knew nothing about Facher's attempt after the Woodshed Conference to settle the Beatrice case for a million dollars. To all appearances, their informal alliance against Schlichtmann remained intact. But Cheeseman worried about his ally's stamina. One day that winter he watched Facher stand before Judge Skinner to argue a motion that Cheeseman himself had an interest in. Facher looked exhausted, small and old and gray. His voice drifted off into a mumble. It sounded almost as if he were muttering in his sleep. The judge gently reminded Facher to speak up. And then Facher just shrugged and wearily sat down. He's giving up on the motion, thought Cheeseman in alarm. Later, back at his office, Cheeseman remarked to his partners, "Facher's getting old for a trial lawyer. I wonder if he's losing it. I wonder if we can still depend on him."

Cheeseman and Facher and their teams of associates continued throughout the fall and into the winter with the depositions of Schlichtmann's expert witnesses. Schlichtmann had done what he could to prepare his experts, and most stood up fairly well.

There was, for example, the case of Dr. Vera Byers, an immunologist from California who had published some eighty-five articles on tumor immunology in respected journals such as *Lancet.* Last summer, at Schlichtmann's behest, Byers had conducted her own physical examinations of the Woburn family members. After reviewing the work of Schlichtmann's other experts, she concluded that the families were indeed suffering from chronic solvent poisoning. Long-term, low-dose exposure to TCE, she believed, had impaired their immune systems and caused the high incidence of leukemia.

Byers had never testified in court before. This was her first experience as an expert witness. As a rule, Schlichtmann liked inexperienced witnesses. "Virgins," he called them. They were generally impressionable enough to follow his advice and listen to his warnings. They might get frightened under cross-examination, but Schlichtmann felt this was no handicap. "The honest, scared witness is best," he once explained. "They exude honesty when they're nervous. Judges and juries love them."

Byers, who was in her early forties but looked younger, remained a plucky witness throughout the three long days of her deposition. When Facher showed her a list of a hundred scientific studies and asked which ones she had reviewed, Byers said, "Holy Toledo!" When he asked how many different kinds of leukemia there were, she said, "Jeepers! There are many kinds. It depends whether you're a splitter or a lumper." Several times she exclaimed, "Bingo!" and "You betcha!" when she happened to agree with something Facher said.

She grew more sober under questioning by Cheeseman, who began by asking if she'd been a cheerleader in high school. Turning to the substance of Byers's opinion, Cheeseman demanded to know what specific harm Anne Anderson, for example, had suffered from the contaminated well water.

"The systems damaged were respiratory, cardiac, gastrointestinal, neurologic, and immune," replied Byers. "And there was probably damage to cells and other organs."

"Like the skin?" said Cheeseman.

"Like the skin," agreed Byers. "Maybe the kidney."

"Mostly you have the whole human body there, haven't you?"

"True," said Byers. "The thing is systemic."

"Looks like you've found the universal evil in these solvents," remarked Cheeseman. Item by item, he led Byers through Anne Anderson's medical records. His tone grew mocking. "You wrote on the physical exam that she's a well-developed, well-nourished woman in no apparent distress. Does that mean at the moment you were examining her she was not experiencing cramping, irritable bowel, rhinitis, sinus headache, migraine headache, et cetera?"

"That's correct."

"So," said Cheeseman, "you caught her at a good moment, huh?"

The depositions of Schlichtmann's twelve medical and three geological experts would ultimately consume fifty-three days and fill ten thousand transcript pages. Those whose opinions were based on quantifiable, objective measurements—the blink reflex tests and the cardiology exams, for example—fared best. The expert who fared worst was Dr. Alan Levin, another of Schlichtmann's immunologists. On the third day of his six-day-long deposition, Facher began by asking the doctor in a mild, almost friendly manner how much time he spent on legal matters.

Levin said that consulting work occupied only 10 to 15 percent of his time. He added that he much preferred seeing patients in his clinic, work that he found more personally satisfying.

"Well," said Facher, "how many lawsuits are you currently involved in?"

Levin replied that he'd been retained in two other cases, one in Sacramento, another in Texas.

"Tell me about the case in Texas," said Facher. "Have you given an opinion?"

"I haven't given an official opinion. I don't have all the data, but based on what the defendant's immunologist did, there's clear evidence of immune dysregulation."

Facher looked at notes prepared by one of his associates. "There's some case in Iowa?" he said.

"I'm sorry," said Levin. "You're right. Mr. Carpenter. He's suing a bunch of pesticide people."

"I have a note here involving someone named Johnson. Does that mean anything to you?"

Levin shrugged. "Could have been," he said.

"Millie is the first name? 1983?"

"Millie Johnson—she developed asthma after being exposed to Raid," said Levin.

"Raid? The insecticide? Did you render an opinion of immune dysregulation?"

"I believe that's what I did, yes."

"I have a note here about Times Beach. What is that?"

"I'm involved in Times Beach, too," Levin answered, "and I was involved in Three Mile Island."

Facher smiled. "I seem to be helping your memory. Any others?"

"I can't recall right now."

"I have a note, Aircraft Stamping."

"That went to the jury," said Levin.

"And your opinion was what?"

"That the chemicals caused immune dysregulation in that population."

"Do you have any criminal record, by the way?" said Facher.

Schlichtmann, seated next to Levin, held his tongue.

"No," said Levin.

"What about Schuller?" asked Facher, getting back to Levin's professional history. "Does Schuller mean anything to you?"

"Schuller was a patient of mine who was exposed to chlordane. That was an interesting case."

"Your opinion, again, was immune dysregulation?"

"Right," said Levin.

"Fiberite Corporation," said Facher. "Does that mean anything to you?"

And on it went. Cheeseman, too, had done some research on Dr. Levin. Cheeseman's medical experts had told him that "clinical ecology," a branch of immunology championed by Levin, was "a screwball science." Cheeseman thought Levin was a charlatan, and he finally said so on the sixth day of Levin's deposition, when the doctor asserted that the T cell tests led him to believe that Anne Anderson was "a sick lady," at risk of developing serious illness in the future. In a voice heavy with sarcasm, Cheeseman said, "That's sort of like reading entrails, isn't it? Tarot cards. You throw the cards down and look at them and you see the future from that?"

It had been a difficult week for Levin, and almost as difficult for Schlichtmann. He admired and trusted the immunologist, and he owed him a debt of gratitude as well. Levin had been his first expert, his guide and tutor on the medical part of the case. "Cheeseman doesn't want to believe that this is a legitimate case," Schlichtmann said after Levin's deposition. "He wants to believe that I'm a charlatan. But I believe these people have been injured, and the more I find out, the more I believe that. I believe these chemicals can cause harm. I don't want any of them in my body."

6

Schlichtmann got his chance in the final two weeks of discovery to hear the opinions of the medical experts hired by Cheeseman and Facher. Together they had assembled a roster of twenty-eight specialists, many with impressive résumés, several from the nearby Harvard Medical School. There were six toxicologists, five epidemiologists, three neurologists, a molecular biologist, a pediatric hematologist, a cardiologist, a psychiatrist, and several immunologists, chemists, and pathologists. Schlichtmann had no time to take leisurely six-day-long depositions, as Facher and Cheeseman had. One day during the last week of discovery he took eight depositions, walking into conference rooms to confront expert witnesses whose specialties—whose very names—he did not know.

He found that several of these doctors knew his own experts, sometimes personally, sometimes only by reputation. One physician, a specialist in occupational medicine, told Schlichtmann that he had often referred patients to Dr. Robert Feldman's clinic.

"What's your opinion of Dr. Feldman?" Schlichtmann asked this expert.

"He strikes me as a good neurologist," replied the doctor. "I depend on his judgment considerably."

Schlichtmann planned to use this in front of the jury, even though this same doctor stated that he did not believe the Woburn families had suffered any ill health from exposure to TCE. "I've seen individuals working with levels of exposure a thousand—ten thousand— times the levels you have quoted without suffering any ill effect," the doctor said.

A neurologist, a professor at Harvard, agreed that Feldman was, in his words, a "competent" neurologist, but he, too, disagreed with Feldman's conclusions. He thought Feldman had completely misinterpreted the results of the blink reflex tests. "I think the normal ranges, as construed by Dr. Feldman, were excessively low," said this neurologist. Another Harvard professor, a pediatrician, said much the same thing about Colvin's T cell tests. This expert acknowledged that Colvin had an "impeccable" reputation, but he thought Colvin had used "rather low" laboratory normals in assessing the Woburn families' T cell values.

The cardiologist hired by Facher and Cheeseman was an eminent doctor by any measure. His name was Gilbert Horton Mudge, Jr., a professor at Harvard and director of the heart transplant program at Brigham & Women's Hospital. Schlichtmann asked Dr. Mudge if he had reviewed the cardiological exams of the Woburn families. Mudge said that he had.

"Were any of those people suffering from cardiac arrhythmia?" asked Schlichtmann.

"I believe all those patients were normal," replied the doctor.

"Are any of them suffering from cardiac arrhythmia?" Schlichtmann asked again.

"Their rhythm disturbances are within normal limits," said Mudge.

Mudge still had not answered the question. Schlichtmann asked it again, for a third time: "Are any of these people suffering from cardiac arrhythmia?"

"Yes," said Mudge.

"How many of them are suffering from cardiac arrhythmia?"

"As I remember, virtually all of them had some cardiac arrhythmia. But it's my opinion that such rhythm disturbances are entirely consistent with a normal patient population."

Near the end of the deposition, which lasted less than an hour, Mudge said he would like to take echocardiograms of the Woburn people. "I'd like to look at their echocardiograms to see if there's any objective evidence to suggest a structural abnormality of the heart."

"Why would that be important?" asked Schlichtmann.

"To make absolutely sure that there's no reason to be concerned about these extra heartbeats."

Schlichtmann liked Dr. Mudge. He looked forward to seeing him again, in front of a jury. Schlichtmann smiled at him. "We're all done, Doctor. Go forth and heal."

None of the six toxicologists hired by Cheeseman and Facher believed that the small amounts of TCE found in Woburn wells could have affected the health of the plaintiffs. One of them, from the University of California at Berkeley, agreed that TCE could damage the heart, the central nervous system, and the immune system, but not at the "infinitesimally small levels" reported in Woburn.

Schlichtmann asked how much TCE it would take to cause such damage, and the toxicologist said, "Very, very high levels."

"How high?"

"I don't think people would drink the water at levels high enough to cause toxicity," said the toxicologist.

Schlichtmann asked the toxicologist if he would consider the levels in the Woburn water to be safe.

"There is no such thing as complete safety," replied the toxicologist. "Everything poses a risk. Walking down the street is not safe. Sitting here in this room, being bombarded by cosmic rays, is not safe. What

I'm saying is, the risk is acceptable to the human population because it is so infinitesimally small."

By way of illustration, continued this expert, the risk of getting cancer from the Woburn water would be roughly equivalent to spending thirteen minutes in a canoe on a placid lake, or to smoking three cigarettes.

"Three cigarettes a day?" said Schlichtmann.

"Three cigarettes in a lifetime," said the expert. "Absolutely negligible risk, insignificant."

Schlichtmann deposed a pediatric hematologist from Chicago, a renowned specialist who had treated hundreds of children with leukemia. The hematologist agreed that there was indeed a high incidence of leukemia in Woburn, but he also stated that "all previous clusters of childhood leukemia were related to statistical coincidence and not to any specific exposures." In his opinion, the Woburn water had nothing to do with the Woburn leukemias. Both animal and epidemiological studies, he said, indicated that TCE was not a carcinogen in man.

If that was so, asked Schlichtmann, then what did cause the Woburn leukemias?

"I don't think anyone in the world knows what causes acute lymphocytic leukemia in children," said the hematologist. "It's evolving. The molecular biologists are going to tell us the answers, but no one knows the answers yet."

The molecular biologist, a professor at Tufts University School of Medicine named Dr. John Coffin, admitted at his deposition that he did not know the answers yet. But he had a theory. He had spent much of his professional life studying tumor viruses, and he believed that a virus was most likely responsible for many cases of acute lymphocytic leukemia in children. That was, at least, a "plausible" explanation, Coffin maintained, more plausible than the contaminated well water. "My opinion," Coffin told Schlichtmann, "is that the compounds in this case are not at all likely to be human carcinogens."

"Are you aware," asked Schlichtmann, "that the EPA has determined that trichloroethylene is a probable human carcinogen?"

"Is that their exact phrasing?" replied Coffin. "My memory is that the EPA did not conclude that it was a probable human carcinogen."

In this instance, Coffin's memory was wrong. "If I told you they had," continued Schlichtmann, "would that be news to you?"

"It is a question of phrasing," said Coffin. "I don't remember the phrasing."

Schlichtmann sensed that he had Coffin in retreat. He decided to push him further. "In your opinion, Doctor, does trichloroethylene pose a health hazard in the domestic water supply?"

This was a tricky question to answer. If Coffin answered yes, the rational, sane reply, then Schlichtmann would turn this admission to his benefit. He would, in effect, turn Coffin into his own witness. And if Coffin answered no, he would make the doctor look biased and untrustworthy.

Coffin considered the question for a moment. Then he said, "I am not an expert in domestic water supplies, so I don't think I can answer that question."

This was the rehearsed answer that Schlichtmann had expected. "Well," continued Schlichtmann, "based on your study of the toxicological effects of trichloroethylene, do you consider that it poses a potential health hazard and should not be allowed in a community's domestic water supply?"

"The question is very broad. I'm not an expert on water supplies."

"Are you an expert on trichloroethylene?"

"I've reviewed the literature on trichloroethylene relative to its carcinogenesis."

"Based on your review, does trichloroethylene pose a potential health hazard? And for that reason, should it be not allowed in a community water supply?"

Coffin finally relented. "I don't believe any foreign material of that sort should be allowed in a community's water supply."

Schlichtmann had him now. "Why?" he asked.

Prolonged silence. Schlichtmann looked intently at Coffin. At last Coffin said, "You are now getting into an area which is my personal opinion rather than my expert opinion. My personal opinion is that foreign compounds do not belong in the domestic water."

"Why?" asked Schlichtmann again.

"Where does one draw the line?" said Coffin. "If one allows one foreign compound into a public water supply, they would be allowing others. But this is getting very far afield from areas of my expertise. I don't feel comfortable talking along these lines."

Schlichtmann believed that most of the experts hired by the defense were able, even distinguished, doctors who simply happened to disagree with his own able, distinguished doctors. "Most of their experts concede that TCE can cause cardiac, neurological, and immunological problems," said Schlichtmann late one evening, after taking five depositions in one day. "The only difference between their experts and my experts is that theirs don't think there was enough TCE in the water to cause problems."

Schlichtmann also found among the defense experts some whom he regarded as charlatans, much in the way that Cheeseman regarded Levin. One doctor told of a study he'd done with workers exposed to TCE. "There was, in fact, less deaths from cancer than one would have expected," this doctor explained at his deposition. "There were fewer deaths from heart disease. I would begin to entertain a serious hypothesis that trichloroethylene in these quantities, rather than being harmful, is quite beneficial with respect to heart disease."

Conway had deposed this witness while Schlichtmann was busy at another deposition. The study, the doctor admitted under questioning from Conway, had been financed by the very same company that had exposed its workers to the solvent.

That evening, Schlichtmann asked Conway how the deposition had gone.

"He says TCE is good for you," said Conway.

7

Out in Woburn, the Environmental Protection Agency began its long-delayed test of the Aberjona aquifer. Wells G and H were cleaned and oiled, and then started up for the first time in almost seven years. The test was designed to re-create groundwater conditions during the 1960s and 1970s, when the wells had pumped water into the city mains. Although it was widely believed that W. R. Grace and Beatrice Foods were responsible for contaminating the aquifer, this belief was based largely on circumstantial evidence and unproven theory. The EPA felt it necessary to test that theory in the field before filing its own lawsuit demanding that Grace and Beatrice pay the cleanup costs.

Schlichtmann had eagerly awaited the EPA test. He needed the results for his own case. He had no doubt that it would prove the two companies were responsible for contaminating the wells. On a frigid morning in early December, the day the wells were activated, he was out on the Aberjona marsh along with an army of a hundred geologists, engineers, hydrologists, well diggers, and lawyers from the EPA, the U.S. Geological Survey, and the environmental consulting firms hired by each of the three parties to the lawsuit.

The test was scheduled to last an entire month, until January. The workers had to keep track of the fluctuations of the groundwater in more than a hundred small monitoring wells that had been drilled into the aquifer. They set up shanties to shelter themselves from the snow and freezing rain during the cold winter days. Gordon organized a coffee brigade for these people, and extended his magnanimity even to the Grace and Beatrice consultants. He drove out to the Aberjona in the gray winter dawns, carrying a hundred cartons of coffee and two hundred doughnuts in the trunk of his Mercedes. From their stations at the test wells on the marsh, men and women bundled in parkas, looking like refugees from an Arctic expedition, would tramp across the wooden planks that spanned the ice-covered grassy tussocks and assemble at the trunk of the Mercedes for Gordon's coffee and doughnuts. Gordon would return in the afternoon, the trunk filled this time with sandwiches and more coffee.

When an electrical cable connecting a trailer full of computer equipment was severed two days into the pumping test, it was Gordon who, suspecting sabotage, arranged for security. He hired the entire Woburn police force to patrol the area in shifts, during their off-duty hours. When a critical device, a capacitator, broke down on a Saturday and the EPA said it would take at least a week to replace it, Gordon had the part flown in from Denver on Sunday, on a specially leased jet. In his spare moments he stood on an outcropping of bedrock near the Beatrice property, surveying the icy scene with binoculars, keeping in touch with the EPA and Schlichtmann's engineers by walkie-talkie.

The pump test was costly for everyone concerned. But for Schlichtmann, at least, the results were worth the money. His specialist in groundwater, a Princeton hydrogeologist of great renown in his field, studied the data and reported that the pump test had confirmed

Schlichtmann's fondest suspicion—Wells G and H were contaminated by groundwater coming from the Beatrice and Grace properties.

One evening in late December, after a day on the marsh, Gordon sat in his office and calculated how much money the firm was spending on Woburn each day. Only three months ago, he'd estimated that it would cost a quarter of a million dollars for the pump test and the groundwater consultants. The actual costs were now more than twice that, and the work still was not done.

Gordon spent the entire weekend in his office, adding up the bills. By the time he finished on Monday morning, he had a precise total of the cost to date: $1,803,195.84. Interest alone on the debt to the Bank of Boston and other creditors amounted to several hundred dollars a day. They were now half a million dollars over the budget he and Schlichtmann had given Uncle Pete three months ago. And the trial was still several weeks away.

Gordon figured they could make it until the trial. Once they began selecting a jury, anything could happen. They might settle with Beatrice, perhaps even Grace. And if that didn't happen, he'd find a way to get through the trial, even though the creditors might be banging on the courtroom doors.

The only thing they could not afford, Gordon figured, was a postponement of the trial. He could not imagine any way of financing Schlichtmann through a long delay.

Facher's Plea

1

Late at night Facher would sit in his war room, in the cavernous space on the twenty-first floor that Hale and Dorr used for storage. From his chair at the wooden table in the center of the room, in a pool of lamplight, he could look out the windows and into the darkened offices of the skyscraper across the street. He had just turned sixty. One of his cats, his only and beloved companions at home, was dying of diabetes. "Life is so short," he said not long after his birthday. "It seems foolish to devote it to motions to dismiss, but that's what I've done."

Sometimes he'd leave the war room and wander the dimly lit corridors of the firm, going from floor to floor past the dark, deserted offices. He'd stop in one of the kitchenettes and peer in the refrigerator, looking for something to eat. If he saw a pile of dirty dishes and coffee cups, he might roll up his sleeves, fill the sink with soapy water, and begin washing. "That's a good day's work," he'd say when he finished.

One of Cheeseman's partners had called Facher last fall and explained a plan to hire Litigation Sciences, a firm that specialized in jury research. Was Facher interested in sharing the costs? Against his better judgment, Facher had reluctantly agreed to contribute twenty-five thousand dollars for a telephone poll of five hundred potential jurors in the Boston area. Facher personally regarded "scientific" jury research with skepticism, although the field had become quite fashionable among many trial lawyers and his own partners at Hale and Dorr. A month later, Facher went to a meeting at Cheeseman's firm, where he received several pie charts based on the telephone interviews. The pie charts told him that he could not hope to win the Woburn case. Eighty-two percent—409 of the 500 people interviewed—felt that large corporations should, as a general rule, be held responsible for damages in toxic waste cases. Among those people who knew of the Woburn case from newspaper articles or the television news, 77 percent had already decided that both Grace and Beatrice were responsible for the leukemia deaths. Given responses like these, the jury research expert told the lawyers, the best the two defendants could hope for was simply to "contain" the damages.

"I didn't need to pay twenty-five thousand dollars to be told that," Facher grumbled.

A few weeks later, Cheeseman's partner had called again, this time to inform Facher that they planned to stage a mock trial and watch several panels of "jurors"—people selected at random off the street—deliberate from behind one-way mirrors. Facher had refused to contribute. "I wouldn't pay another nickel after those pie charts," he said. "I think it's pissing money away." Facher later estimated that the jury research had cost Cheeseman's client at least a hundred thousand dollars. "The gold-plated defense," Facher called it in disgust. "Some clients think the more money you spend, the harder you're working."

Facher heard that one of the mock jury panels had awarded the Woburn families enormous sums of money, as much as two hundred million, according to one account. Facher shrugged. He didn't believe in mock jurors anyway.

In three weeks they would begin selecting a real jury. Facher had never expected Schlichtmann to get this far. He opened a cabinet drawer and saw thick files containing the results of Colvin's blood tests. He took out a file, looked at page after page of numbers, columns of numbers each labeled at the top with words like "blastogenesis" and "Dim 8's" and "helper-suppressor cells." He realized that he did not understand what he was looking at. He put the file back and opened another drawer, this one filled with hydrogeological studies, thousands of pages of well logs and more numbers—water levels, pumping rates, traces of chemicals measured in parts per billion. He went at random from one drawer to another. He opened a drawer that contained the medical records of two of the children, both dead before age twelve— six thousand pages of nursing notes, lab reports, chemotherapy treatments, bone-marrow aspirations, and notes from consulting doctors. Other drawers held the medical histories of the twenty-eight living plaintiffs, their cardiological tests, psychomotor tests, electromyography tests, psychiatric profiles. Facher began counting the number of file drawers. He had an associate count the deposition transcripts. There were 159 bound volumes totaling 23,337 pages. There were forty-three expert witnesses in the case. Facher didn't even know some of their names, never mind the substance of their opinions. He had not had time to sit down and read those depositions, and there were thirty-six more that had not even been transcribed yet.

He was, he realized, not ready to try this case. He felt he needed at least another six months to prepare. He had already asked Judge Skinner for a continuance once, two months ago, but the judge hadn't taken his request seriously. Facher thought perhaps he hadn't been forceful enough. He'd made only an oral argument—"lawyer's words," as he put it, "and they come cheap."

He decided to ask again. This time he would put his request in the form of a personal affidavit to the judge, one in which he could invoke the weight of his reputation and career. Facher did not, as a rule, like lawyers' affidavits. "The New York style of personal affidavits that flood the courts," he once called them. "I think they're undignified and unprofessional." But on this one occasion, he felt justified.

"I am Jerome Facher, a senior partner in Hale and Dorr," his affidavit began. "I am chairman of the Litigation Department at Hale and Dorr and have held that position since 1976. I have had extensive trial experience in complex litigation of all types, including securities regulation, trade regulation, anti-trust, product liability, trade secrets, high technology, patents, banking. . . ."

The trial, wrote Facher, would be "the single most complex medical and scientific case ever tried by any counsel in this case." He estimated that it would take "from seven months to a year or more." Facher himself had measured the size of the file drawers and added the numbers together. "A rough estimate of the magnitude of medical, technical and legal materials amassed thus far, stacked vertically, would exceed sixty feet, or the equivalent of a three-story building."

He asked for a postponement of seven months, until September, and he ended his twenty-page affidavit by telling Judge Skinner that he had written it reluctantly "after much thought and deliberation, by trial counsel whose experience and tradition has been opposed to seeking trial continuances and who has been consistently ready for trial in state and federal courts. This is the first occasion I have made an affidavit which supports a continuance of a trial date. I do not expect to make such an affidavit again."

It had taken him a week, working off and on between depositions, to complete the affidavit. It was a personal plea, but he felt it was a dignified one. He felt proud of it. He finished it on Sunday night in late January, in plenty of time for the judge to read it before the pretrial conference on Wednesday afternoon.

Judge Skinner had not read Facher's affidavit by the time the lawyers convened in the courtroom on Wednesday. The judge could not, in fact, even find the affidavit among the piles of motions on his desk. He rooted around for a while and finally unearthed it.

"I do pause to give Your Honor a moment to peruse it," Facher told the judge with evident dismay.

Schlichtmann sat at the plaintiff's counsel table with Nesson on one side of him and Conway on the other, waiting in silence as the judge read to himself. Gazing out the courtroom windows at the dull winter sky, Schlichtmann noticed that it had begun to snow. If Facher succeeded in persuading the judge, summer would come and go before the trial finally got started. Schlichtmann knew he could not survive until September. The case was costing his firm thousands of dollars every day, and it would keep on costing until the trial began.

"Seven months to a year or more?" exclaimed the judge, looking up from the affidavit. "No, the trial will not take that long. Some of you may be used to patient judges. I am not one of those. I will not let testimony go on and on."

Judge Skinner went back to the affidavit. When he finished, he looked thoughtfully at Facher and said, "I know it's hell to be under the gun from some cockamamie judge who wants to go to trial all the time. But it also raises hell with your time to get all cranked up for a case and then drop it for half a year. It's just a terrible waste."

Entering the judge's courtroom that afternoon, Facher had felt almost certain that his affidavit would persuade the judge to delay the trial. Now he realized that he'd have to do more.

"I'm asking you, practically begging you," Facher said. "I'm not in the least cranked up. That's the God's truth. We've had a schedule that was just absolute insanity. We have to bring people in, we have to prepare them. We have a number of novel theories, and it ain't easy."

Facher's plea—the old lawyer actually *begging* the judge—amazed Schlichtmann. Nesson was busy taking notes on a yellow legal pad, and Schlichtmann glanced at them. Nesson had written: " 'It ain't easy'— Jerry Facher, Jan. 29, 1986."

Schlichtmann picked up a pen and wrote on Nesson's pad: "Are we okay?"

"So far," wrote Nesson back. Then he added: "Do not assume that we have a Feb. trial date."

"I'm working night and day, weekends," Facher was telling the judge. "I've canceled all my other obligations. I thought maybe once in my career I would say to you that I'm not ready. This is not a case of some lawyer's grandmother dying for the third or fourth time. Nobody has slacked off."

"I'm not suggesting anybody has," said the judge.

Schlichtmann decided it was time he said something. "The plaintiffs are prepared to go forward, Your Honor. We've made good use of the time. Mr. Facher says that he hasn't been able to read the material, but I have. I deposed eight expert witnesses in one day—"

Facher made a face. "Jan, the way you did them, you might as well not have done them. It's not the kind of careful point-by-point examination that I—"

"Oh, I don't know," said Schlichtmann. "I got a lot out of them."

"If you delay," the judge said to Facher, smiling, "you may give Mr. Schlichtmann a chance to get better prepared."

"Exactly," agreed Schlichtmann. "It's time to say enough is enough and try the case. I know the defendants are just as ready as I am. They are very excellent trial lawyers. You'll not see any better. I'm honored to go against them."

Facher ignored this shallow compliment. "I'm proud of the way I prepare cases," he told the judge. "I am not able to prepare this one. Is it right to force a party to trial if a lawyer says to you, 'I just can't do it. Don't make me do it'? As bad as it sounds on the record, that's what I'm saying. Believe me, it hurts to say that because I'm a proud lawyer."

"What do you think about this," the judge said. "We go ahead and empanel the jury as scheduled and at least get them insulated to the extent we can. Then we'll commence trial in March instead of February. How does that sound?"

"I have to say it doesn't help me," replied Facher. "I am not a lawyer who tries to bargain with the Court. I don't happen to be one of those lawyers who exaggerate."

"I'm not suggesting I don't believe everything you're saying," said the judge. "If it was a matter of a week or two, I could deal with it. But I think we really have to get started. The only thing to do is to bite the bullet and go." The judge paused for a moment, and then added, speaking to no one in particular, "I'm very sympathetic to Mr. Facher's point of view. I'd hate to be in his position."

Facher said softly, "I'm more than a little disappointed."

"I can tell that you are," said the judge, just as softly. "I'm sorry."

Facher had one last hope of stopping the trial. He said to the judge, "I would like to get Your Honor involved in a possible settlement of this case. That's a very important and neglected issue that needs the Court's intervention. It really does, and I'm not a big one for judicial intervention."

"If there's any possibility of settlement," said the judge. "I don't want to talk to people who don't want to settle." He looked at Schlichtmann. "Do you want to settle?"

"Of course," replied Schlichtmann. "Plaintiffs always want to settle in a reasonable and fair manner."

"Ask him how much he wants to settle for," said Facher sarcastically. "See if you get an answer, because I haven't gotten one yet."

"You do have to start with a figure," the judge said to Schlichtmann. "You can't expect the defendants to bid against themselves. Are you in a position to generate a realistic—not a pro forma—demand for the whole case?"

"Certainly," replied Schlichtmann.

"Why don't you do that tomorrow? Sometimes," continued the judge, musing, "if you examine what people really want, it's surprising how quickly a case will settle. The main fuel, I think, in lawsuits for the death of children is an overwhelming sense of personal guilt. Mostly, I don't think parents really want money. They may indeed be offended that money is an equivalent for life. What they do want is to have it said clearly that this wasn't their fault."

2

It was dark when Schlichtmann left the courthouse that evening. He walked with Conway, his Sancho Panza, and Nesson, his Harvard law professor, down Milk Street in the frosty January air, his coat open, feeling elated. He had survived Rule 11, summary judgment, the judge's wrath in the Woodshed, and the magistrate's petty scorn. He had survived discovery and Facher's plea for a continuance. He was going to get a jury at last.

Back at the office, he shouted in jubilation. The secretaries and paralegals gathered around to hear what had happened. He told it all again when Phillips and Gordon dropped by that evening, and once more to Kiley and Neville when they showed up. " 'I'm a proud lawyer, I'm practically begging you,' " Schlichtmann crowed. "Imagine that! Facher begging the judge!" To his colleagues that evening, he said, "The only question now is how big we'll win."

That night, Schlichtmann and his team went out to the Hampshire House, to a private dining room, to work on a settlement proposal over dinner. Schlichtmann had assured the judge he was ready to deliver a reasonable demand by tomorrow, but no one had given any thought to what they might actually ask for, not since Nesson had arrived and suggested that twenty-four million for this case was mere pocket change.

Midway through the evening, after much debate, they decided that a hundred million dollars seemed like a reasonable figure. On that evening, at least, after listening to Facher beg, it did not seem like an outlandish sum.

Kiley argued for more. "They're the landed gentry and we're the warriors," he said. "We're walking in and putting our sword on the table."

Some others also thought a hundred million might be too little. They might "lose opportunity," as Gordon put it. "We don't want to cap ourselves," he said.

So in the end, they compromised. They decided to ask for a hundred and seventy-five million. That would allow room for negotiation down to a hundred million, if that should become necessary. But they wouldn't be so crude as to ask for such a sum outright. They would present a package of demands and a payment schedule.

Schlichtmann recalled the judge mentioning a settlement in which a company had established a scholarship in the name of a boy killed by one of its outboard motors. What about setting up several scholarships? Better yet, what about demanding that Grace and Beatrice put up the money for a foundation for leukemia research, perhaps at the Dana Farber Cancer Institute in Boston? Or maybe endowing a university chair in environmental health?

Gordon liked the last idea. "They all went to Harvard," he said, referring to the defense lawyers. "They'd love that."

"Give somebody else a chance," said Kiley. "Give it to Boston University."

After some discussion, they settled on twenty-five million for a leukemia foundation, another twenty-five million in cash, and the rest to be paid out in installments to the families over thirty years.

Gordon shed his jacket, rolled up his sleeves, and went to work on the calculator. Soon he had piles of paper next to him. He had worked on plenty of structured settlements involving a million dollars, and even some for two and three million dollars, but never one with so many millions to disburse. A million dollars a year to each family for thirty years? That sounded like too much. Gordon tried dividing it into a monthly sum, but that sounded even worse—$83,333 a month for thirty years. Maybe a larger cash payment up front?

"Come on, Gordon," said Schlichtmann. "It's not that difficult. Just make it look good."

Conway got up and walked around the table. He leaned over Gordon and looked at the figures. He lit a cigarette and sighed deeply, turning to Schlichtmann. "This is ridiculous, Jan. You're going to give them this demand and they're going to laugh at us. They're going to get up and leave."

Schlichtmann expected just such a comment from Conway. "Are you kidding?" he said to Conway. "We're going to be there all day negotiating."

Conway had his reasons for worrying. The deed to his house in Wellesley was now at the Bank of Boston, in Uncle Pete's files. Gordon had gone to Uncle Pete for more money, and this time Pete had said he would need collateral. Gordon had pledged Schlichtmann's condominium and the houses of both Conway and Crowley.

What about what they had told Pete four months ago? Conway wanted to know. They'd said the case was worth twenty-four million dollars then. Now they were at a hundred and seventy-five million. "It's crazy, Jan," said Conway.

Schlichtmann laughed. He called Conway "the soft underbelly." He shook his head and said, "You're being negative, Kevin."

Conway felt completely alone in the room. He could not talk to Schlichtmann, who was surrounded by others and who no longer seemed to listen to him, anyhow. Nesson and Kiley had his ear now. Conway felt as if he'd lost his bearings. Even his friend from childhood, Tom Neville, the cynical defense attorney, seemed gripped by the frenzy of the evening. Neville was talking big numbers, too.

Conway wondered if he was the one who was crazy. Why didn't he feel the way everyone else did? He kept thinking about the deed to his house in Uncle Pete's files. He got another cigarette from Gordon and sat at the end of the table, smoking, watching the group talk excitedly among themselves. Nesson sat next to Schlichtmann and Kiley, and Phillips hovered over Gordon, who was chain-smoking Marlboros while he worked on the calculator.

After a moment, Phillips came to sit next to Conway. "Well?" said Phillips.

"I can't believe this is going on, this talk about numbers," Conway said bitterly.

"It'll pass, it'll pass," said Phillips in a soothing voice.

Conway wasn't sure what Phillips meant. Phillips had seemed infected by the delirium of money, too, talking about Grace's two-hundred-and-fifty-million-dollar environmental insurance policy and the leveraged buyout of Beatrice, going on at that very moment, for seven billion.

"This is insane, Mark," Conway insisted to Phillips. "You know it's crazy. They're never going to give us this kind of money. Facher's going to say, 'Fuck you,' and walk out."

But nobody was listening to Conway tonight.

At the end of the evening, they discussed the seating assignments for the negotiation. Gordon had already reserved a private conference room, the Wendell Phillips Room, at the Four Seasons Hotel. The room, adorned with crystal chandeliers, overlooked the Public Garden adjacent to the Boston Common, and a statue of Wendell Phillips, Mark Phillips's great-uncle. Schlichtmann and Conway, along with Gordon and Phillips, had once negotiated another settlement there, with the insurance adjusters for a Boston hospital. They'd sealed that settlement by sharing a fifty-dollar bottle of single-malt Scotch whiskey with the adjusters. Afterward, they had walked out to the Public Garden and Phillips had climbed the statue of his ancestor, frozen in heroic oratorical pose, and planted a kiss on the bronze cheek.

Gordon instructed the Four Seasons to provide breakfast—freshly squeezed orange juice, melons, coffee, and croissants and other pastries, along with fresh flowers and sterling-silver water pitchers. If it all went as expected, Gordon wouldn't have to worry about being able to pay for it. He wouldn't have to worry about paying for anything ever again. He also made arrangements for lunch, accompanied by an "upgraded" wine (as Gordon called it), and for dinner as well, if that should become necessary.

Schlichtmann decided that they would all sit on the side of the long, oval table that faced out to the Public Garden. He didn't want Facher and Cheeseman and their partners to feel uncomfortable with the glare of the sun in their eyes. Schlichtmann would sit in the middle, flanked by the two money men, Gordon and Phillips. Conway and Crowley would sit on one side, Nesson and Kiley on the other.

These plans delighted Nesson, who'd never before attended a big-money settlement. "This is scripted like a Hollywood production," Nesson said in amazement.

According to the script, Schlichtmann would talk first about the process of settlement, about involving insurance companies and corporate decision-makers. He'd tell the defense lawyers that as a condition of settlement their clients had to agree to clean up the Aberjona aquifer and admit their responsibility. Then Gordon would take over and explain the details of the $175 million deal.

"What are you going to wear?" Gordon asked Schlichtmann.

"Black suit and red tie," said Schlichtmann. "Red for passion."

"Black is your trial suit," said Gordon. "This is a business meeting. Gray is for business. You going to wear your blue suit tomorrow, Mark?" he asked Phillips. "My blue's better than yours. What about you, Kevin?"

Conway hated this talk about apparel. "I'll come up with something special," he said.

"Not the wolf's head tie with the gravy stains," warned Schlichtmann. "Not the suit you got ice cream all over, the one your wife put through the wash."

3

Cheeseman and two of his partners arrived at the Four Seasons promptly at ten o'clock. Schlichtmann greeted them as they came in and exchanged a handshake with Cheeseman. It seemed faintly ridiculous, since he and Cheeseman had seen each other almost every day for the past year and had never shaken hands on those occasions. They stood by the buffet table, near the silver coffee urn and the croissants and fruits, and made an effort to chat, but the conversation ended lamely.

Conway gazed out the window at the snow-covered Public Garden and the statue of Wendell Phillips, and thought again about the deed to his house in Uncle Pete's filing cabinet. He really should have told his wife that he'd surrendered the deed, but he couldn't figure out how to say it.

Facher was ten minutes late. He entered the room with Frederico, smiled agreeably, and he, too, shook Schlichtmann's hand, then Nesson's. They were late, Facher explained, because they had walked all the way from the office. Facher didn't like paying for taxicabs. As he took off his coat, he told Nesson that he had just been given "a chair" at Harvard.

This news shook Nesson. Facher with an endowed chair? Nesson had never imagined that Facher was such a distinguished scholar. "Which chair?" asked Nesson.

"A black chair, with arms," said Facher. It had his name inscribed on a brass plate on the back. His law students had given it to him.

Nesson laughed and congratulated Facher.

After a few minutes, the lawyers took their assigned seats at the table. Schlichtmann began talking about how he and his partners took only a few select cases and worked to the exclusion of all else on those. (This was Schlichtmann's way of saying there was no stopping them.) He said he wanted a settlement that would provide for the economic security of the families, and for their medical bills in the future. The families, he continued, weren't in this case just for money. They wanted an acknowledgment of the companies' wrongdoing, Schlichtmann said, a full disclosure of all the dumping activities.

"Are you suggesting there hasn't been a full disclosure?" Facher asked.

"No," said Schlichtmann, who was suggesting exactly that, but now made an effort to avoid confrontation. "But as part of a settlement, we want a disclosure that the judge will bless." Another condition of settlement, he added, was an agreement that the companies clean their land of the toxic wastes, and pay the costs for cleaning the aquifer.

None of the defense lawyers had touched any of the food or drink. As Schlichtmann spoke, he saw Facher reach for a bowl of mints on the table and slowly unwrap the foil from one. Facher popped the mint into his mouth and sucked on it, watching Schlichtmann watch him.

Schlichtmann talked for fifteen minutes. Then Gordon laid out the financial terms of the settlement: an annual payment of $1.5 million to each of the eight families for the next thirty years; $25 million to establish a research foundation that would investigate the links between hazardous wastes and illness; and another $25 million in cash.

Cheeseman and his partners took notes on legal pads as Gordon spoke. Facher examined the pen provided courtesy of the Four Seasons, but he did not write anything on his pad. Facher studied the gilt inscription on the pen. It looked like a good-quality pen. These figures, he thought, were preposterous. They meant that Schlichtmann did not want to settle the case, or else he was crazy. Maybe Schlichtmann simply wanted to go to trial. This opulent setting, and Schlichtmann sitting at the table flanked by his disciples like a Last Supper scene, annoyed Facher. Where was Schlichtmann getting the money for all this?

When Gordon finished, silence descended.

Finally Facher stopped studying the pen. He looked up, and said, "If I wasn't being polite, I'd tell you what you could do with this demand."

Cheeseman had added up Gordon's figures. By Cheeseman's calculations, Schlichtmann was asking a total of four hundred ten million over thirty years. "How much is that at present value?" Cheeseman asked Gordon.

Gordon replied that he would rather not say. "Your own structured-settlement people can tell you that."

Facher took a croissant from the plate in front of him, wrapped it in a napkin, and put it into his pocket. That and the mint he had consumed were the only items the defense lawyers had taken from the sumptuous banquet that Gordon had ordered.

Cheeseman and his partners asked a few more perfunctory questions about the terms of disclosure, which Schlichtmann answered.

Facher had gone back to studying the pen. "Can I have this?" he said abruptly, looking at Schlichtmann.

Schlichtmann, appearing surprised, nodded.

Facher put the pen into his breast pocket. "Nice pen," he said. "Thank you."

Then Facher got up, put on his coat, and walked out the door. Frederico, who had not uttered a word, followed him.

Cheeseman and his partners stood, too, and in a moment, they followed Facher.

Schlichtmann and his colleagues sat alone on their side of the table. Gordon looked at his watch. The meeting had lasted exactly thirty-seven minutes, he announced. "I guess we're going to trial," Gordon added.

Schlichtmann was surprised, but only for a moment. He looked at his colleagues and shrugged. "We're going to get a jury in two weeks," he said. "The pressure's on them."

Conway got up and paced the room and smoked a cigarette. He didn't feel like talking. There was nothing to discuss. They'd gotten nothing out of this so-called settlement conference, not even information from the other side. He put on his coat and, along with Crowley, walked up Tremont Street back to the office. He kept wondering if Facher had actually said, "Fuck you," or if he'd just imagined it.

"I thought I heard Facher say 'fuck you,' " Conway said to Crowley. "Did he say that?"

"He didn't," said Crowley. "But he might as well have."

Judge Skinner learned later that day that the meeting had not produced a settlement, but he didn't inquire about the specifics of Schlichtmann's demand, which was probably just as well for Schlichtmann. "It's a very complex proposal" was all that Facher told the judge. "I won't go into the details, but I, personally, am not thrilled with it."

No one brought up the subject of settlement again until two weeks later, on the first day of jury selection. That morning, on the bus coming in to work, the judge read a *Boston Globe* article in which Anne Anderson was quoted as saying that money wasn't important to her. "To me, it would be blood money in the strictest sense," the *Globe* quoted Anne as saying. "I would just like them to say, 'Yes, we made a mistake.' "

In his chambers, the judge said to Schlichtmann, "Mrs. Anderson is trumpeting in the newspapers. She says she doesn't care about money. But if she doesn't care about money, I think this case can be settled."

Schlichtmann laughed politely, but it came out sounding as if he'd just heard a bad joke.

"Ha, ha," replied the judge, mocking the thinness of Schlichtmann's laugh. "Somebody cares about money."

"Corporations care about money," said Schlichtmann, who suspected then that the judge had learned the details of his settlement proposal.

"But if *you're* not arguing money, you can probably settle this case."

Schlichtmann shook his head ruefully.

"Well, then, somebody ought to tell Mrs. Anderson," said the judge. "Because she doesn't think it's about money."

4

Jury selection began on schedule, at nine o'clock on a Tuesday morning in mid-February. It was, of course, preceded by the usual maneuvering. Cheeseman and his partners claimed that W. R. Grace could not get a fair trial in Boston because of all the adverse publicity. They wanted the case moved to another venue. They suggested Bangor, Maine.

"Are you serious?" muttered the judge. "One of those big Superfund projects is up there. I think you're out of the frying pan and into the fire, going to Bangor."

Schlichtmann didn't even have to argue against this motion. But there *had* been a great deal of publicity about the case. The most widely watched show in America, *60 Minutes,* was about to air its own pretrial version within the next few weeks, a version based largely on what Schlichtmann had told the show's producer, David Gelber. Out in Woburn, *60 Minutes* correspondent Ed Bradley had taken a walking tour of the Pine Street neighborhood with Anne Anderson, a camera crew trailing all the way, and then Bradley had interviewed Al Love and his wife around their kitchen table.

So Judge Skinner took special care in selecting a jury. Usually he questioned an entire jury pool, some fifty people, en masse in his courtroom. But for this trial he chose to conduct an individual *voir dire* of each prospective juror in the privacy of his chambers. The lawyers would be present, of course, but the judge alone would pose the questions.

In Schlichtmann's mind, the ideal jury would consist of twelve housewives much like Anne Anderson, all mothers with young children. Facher didn't want any jury to hear the families' sad stories, but he especially did not want mothers with young children. As it happened, one of the first prospective jurors to enter Judge Skinner's chambers was a comely, well-dressed young woman who had two children, ages four and six. It took the judge ten minutes to pose all his questions to the woman: Did she know anyone who lived in Woburn? Had she ever worked with chemicals? Had anyone in her family ever had leukemia? Had she ever lived in a town where the wells had been closed because of pollution? Had she read or heard anything about this case? The woman answered with a string of negatives.

The judge told her that the case involved the death of several small children from leukemia, for which the plaintiffs blamed two large corporations. Was there anything about these circumstances that would make it difficult for her to view the evidence fairly and impartially?

The woman looked thoughtful for a moment. "No, I don't think so."

"You have small children of your own," said the judge. "Would that be a problem?"

"I don't think so."

"You think you could handle the evidence impartially?"

"Yes."

The judge asked the woman to step outside for a moment. "Any problems?" he asked the lawyers.

Facher replied, "Whether she says so or not, I think it's very difficult for any woman with small children to decide the case on the evidence rather than emotion. I think it's almost an impossible task."

"Well, would you exclude a father with small children?" asked the judge.

"No," said Facher. "But I think a woman who carried a child for nine months is a special class."

A very large special class, indeed. "The death of children produces an emotional response," the judge said. "There's no way to avoid it. She seems like a very intelligent young lady. I will seat her."

The woman did not remain seated for long. Facher used the first of his six peremptory challenges on her.

Many people in the jury pool readily admitted—all too readily, in some cases—that they believed big corporations were untrustworthy and acted with reckless disregard when it came to the environment. Some people clearly said so just to avoid jury service. Others seemed to mean what they said. A woman in her early thirties, married with no children, told the judge that she lived in a town where the wells had been contaminated by a large oil company. "The stuff is just pouring into these people's wells, and nothing's happening. I just feel like they're so small compared to this big company."

Excused.

A college administrator whose sister-in-law had developed aplastic anemia after working with chemicals in an auto plant told the judge, "I feel funny about large companies maybe not being honest."

Excused.

A woman in her sixties, a department-store clerk with five grown children: "I think I would be a little biased against the companies."

"Why?" asked the judge.

"I just think that companies are—they're too big, and they really sort of do what they want to, regardless of what the law says."

Excused.

And then there was the woman in her mid-fifties, well dressed and obviously affluent, who told the judge that her husband once had "some dealings" with Facher's firm.

"Would that lead you to favor Hale and Dorr's claim?" the judge asked.

"Not necessarily," replied the woman. "They charged my husband too much money."

Excused.

Schlichtmann regretted losing all these candidates. But the judge also excused those who obviously favored Grace and Beatrice. The retired Boston transit worker, for example, who said of J. Peter Grace, chairman of W. R. Grace, "Well, I admire him. I have the greatest respect for the man. I would never want to see any harm come to him."

The judge and the lawyers greeted this statement with stunned looks and a moment's silence.

"You wanted an honest answer," said the man, sounding defensive.

Excused.

On a good day the judge would question as many as eighteen prospective jurors. Some days he got through only ten. By the fifth day Facher and Cheeseman had used all of their peremptory challenges, all but one on women with children. Schlichtmann, too, had used all of his, all on men—on accountants, engineers, and bankers. Then, on the sixth day, Schlichtmann had a scare. Into the judge's chambers came a man who manufactured chemical reagents for medical labs. The chemist said he had followed reports of the Woburn case in professional journals with great interest. "I don't think they'll be able to prove that the materials these two companies disposed caused leukemia."

The judge thanked the man for speaking forthrightly and excused him. Then he looked at Schlichtmann and chuckled. "Having that fellow and no peremptories left!"

Schlichtmann smiled gamely. "I was naked before the world."

Schlichtmann was still naked when the next man, a telephone company executive, said that he used to go sailing with an executive vice president at W. R. Grace.

"Were you close friends?" asked the judge.

"We were just sailing buddies. I doubt very much it would affect me."

Judge Skinner seated the man. Then he glanced at Schlichtmann and saw his despondency. "Well, you never know," said the judge, not unkindly. "Maybe he's harboring a grudge. Maybe the Grace fellow cut him off at the buoy."

Facher and Cheeseman got the telephone company executive, but Schlichtmann got a retired social worker who belonged to the Audubon Society and received Sierra Club literature, with which, she admitted, "I more or less agree." In the end, however, most of those chosen were essentially compromise candidates. The forklift lady, for example—a woman in her sixties, gray-haired, plump and ruddy-cheeked, the image of a good-natured grandmother. True to the image, she had six grandchildren. She also worked in a department-store warehouse. "Believe it or not, I drive a forklift," she said.

When the judge asked if she'd formed any impressions about the case, the woman hesitated before finally saying no. A long pause followed her answer.

Judge Skinner waited in silence.

"If you want an honest opinion?" said the woman at last. The judge nodded. "I thought maybe the lady was looking for extra money, and it was a big company . . ." her voice trailed off.

The judge seated the woman despite this comment. Schlichtmann had a peremptory challenge remaining at that time, but he decided not to use it. He liked the fact that this forklift operator had six grandchildren. And Facher and Cheeseman didn't challenge her, either. They liked what she'd said about "the lady looking for extra money."

It took six days and the *voir dire* of seventy-nine citizens to empanel six jurors and six alternates. The oldest was in his late sixties, the youngest in her early twenties. Only one woman had young children, but she was an alternate and would not actually deliberate unless one or more of the regular jurors had to be excused during the trial. There were three men on the regular jury—a utility foreman, a self-employed house painter, and a postal worker. Among the three women of the regular jury, one was the forklift lady. Another, a church organist, had four grown children. And the third, a clerk for an insurance company, was in her late twenties, unmarried and childless.

The lawyers really did not know much about any of these people. Superficially, at least, it wasn't the jury of Schlichtmann's dreams, and it wasn't Facher's or Cheeseman's, either. The judge, of course, was aware of this. He brought these proceedings to a close by telling the lawyers, "You're not entitled to a jury of your liking. You're only entitled to an impartial jury."

5

The nuances of jury selection engaged Schlichtmann during the day. In the evenings, back at the office, he allowed himself to relax for brief moments, and it was delicious relaxation to reflect on how far he had come. Now that the trial was about to begin, Woburn was attracting attention across the entire nation. An article in *The Washington Post* called it a "bellwether case," and *The New York Times* quoted legal experts who said that it would make "the court a forum for a national debate" on toxic waste and cancer. Articles appeared in *Newsweek, Time,* and *The New Republic,* nearly all of them citing Judge Skinner's comment about the potential for an "astronomical" verdict. According to *Business Week,* Woburn promised to become a "landmark case" with "major implications for companies."

But the case, of course, was not a landmark yet. The trial was still to come, and just before it began Judge Skinner made an important decision about the way Schlichtmann would have to present his evidence.

It occurred when the judge mentioned that he'd been pondering the question of a trial plan. "I've been trying to picture what this trial is going to look like," the judge told the lawyers. "You've got thirty-three plaintiffs, and to submit all thirty-three of these causation and damage issues in one trial may be unbelievably cumbersome. It's very complicated." The judge asked the lawyers to submit briefs with their suggestions for a trial plan.

Schlichtmann had assumed all along that he would be allowed to present witnesses in the order and manner in which he saw fit. That had always been the plaintiff's prerogative. But the judge clearly had doubts about the traditional way.

Schlichtmann and Nesson talked it over. Nesson proposed the idea of a "test case" involving only one family. The trial could begin, Nesson suggested, with Anne Anderson's telling the jury about the onset of

Jimmy's illness, about her trips to Dr. Truman's clinic at Mass. General, where she'd seen other mothers from Woburn, and about her growing suspicion that something in the environment was causing an epidemic of leukemia. After Anne, they would present evidence that Grace and Beatrice had contaminated the city wells. And then the medical experts would explain how the toxic solvents had caused leukemia and other illnesses.

Schlichtmann liked this approach. Nesson thought it would appeal to the judge for several reasons. It answered the judge's concern about the jury keeping straight all the family members. Moreover, Nesson recalled that Skinner, ruminating aloud on the subject, had first mentioned "trying the plaintiffs *seriatim*," an idea very similar to a test case.

Nesson's plan incorporated Facher's greatest fear. Ever since hearing Richard Aufiero tell the story of his son's death, more than a year ago now, Facher had been vowing—to himself and even once aloud to Schlichtmann—that no jury would ever hear the families' stories. He had tried several times to make good on this vow. He had offered Schlichtmann a million dollars to drop Beatrice from the case; he'd gotten the judge to take Schlichtmann out to the Woodshed; and then he'd tried to postpone the trial in the hopes that a long postponement would leave Schlichtmann too much in debt to proceed.

Now, on the eve of trial, Facher saw another chance to keep the families off the witness stand and away from a jury's sympathetic eyes. He suggested to the judge that the trial should deal first with the question of whether any "poisons" ("If Jan likes that term, I'll use it," Facher said) had gotten from the Beatrice property to the city wells. If a jury were to decide that Beatrice had not contaminated the wells, that would end the case for Beatrice. "You wouldn't need thirty-three plaintiffs telling us how they lost their children and how they've suffered," Facher told the judge.

As for Cheeseman, he didn't want the families on the witness stand, either. He and his partners had several different ideas, the first of which involved a trial just on the issue of whether TCE could cause leukemia, the issue he believed would be the weakest part of Schlichtmann's case.

Judge Skinner took a week to consider these various suggestions. He finally decided on a plan virtually identical with Facher's. The first stage of the trial, the judge announced to the lawyers, would deal with the question of whether Beatrice and Grace were responsible for conraminating the city wells. The "waterworks" phase of the case, the judge called it. "Unless you get the product being dumped on the property and getting into the water, there's no case. There's no point in going any further."

If, however, the jury *did* find Beatrice and Grace liable, continued the judge, the second stage of the trial would address the medical question—had the chemicals in fact made the surviving family members sick and killed the children? "If the jury decides that favorably," continued the judge, "then you have to ask, 'How much is that worth? How much compensation do you give somebody for the loss of a child?'" The judge paused, and then he said in a low voice, "What a question!"

Facher was happy to let Judge Skinner take credit for this plan. Facher suspected the judge was trying to make amends for denying his plea for a six-month delay. And the judge, in fact, as much as acknowledged so. Announcing the waterworks plan to the lawyers, Skinner said, with an eye to Facher, "You won't have to master everything at once. You can take a breather between phases."

On the face of it, it did make sense to divide up the trial in this way. Nesson saw the logic of it, but he also saw the danger. The jurors would come into the courtroom expecting to hear a human drama about the poisoning of the Woburn families. Instead, they'd first have to sit through a case about geology and groundwater movement.

Nesson tried to change the judge's mind. "This is the defendants' plan," he began, but the judge quickly interrupted him.

"No, it's *my* plan," the judge insisted.

"It's your plan," conceded Nesson. "But when you start the trial with essentially a bloodless issue, where you don't have the families, that's very advantageous to the defendants."

But the judge was adamant. "I've given this a lot of thought, Mr. Nesson. I appreciate your problem. I didn't come here directly from law school, you know, and I'm perfectly aware of the necessity for getting a little pizzazz into it. If it's as you say—all these dreadful people are wickedly and heartlessly dumping known poisons into the water system—holy moly, what more of a hair-raising opening do you need?"

To Schlichtmann, the structure of the trial didn't matter as much as the fact that there would be a trial. He would have preferred starting with Anne as the first witness, but he was in an especially optimistic frame of mind nowadays. He could even see an advantage in this plan devised by Facher and adopted by the judge. After all, both the Grace and Beatrice properties were contaminated with TCE. Wasn't it obvious that they had contaminated the wells, too? A jury would surely see that. The waterworks, Schlichtmann told Nesson, was actually the easiest part of the case. In winning it, they would gain credibility with the jury, credibility they might need later, for the leukemia part of the case.

Nesson remained worried, but Schlichtmann wasn't particularly worried about Nesson being worried. Schlichtmann had his jury at last, and he had never lost in front of a jury. Nesson was, after all, only a law professor. He didn't have much trial experience.

Then again, compared with Facher, Schlichtmann didn't have much, either.

6

Judge Skinner gave the lawyers two additional weeks after jury selection to prepare for the trial. On Tuesday afternoon of the second week, Schlichtmann got a call from Facher's lieutenant, Neil Jacobs. Over the phone, Jacobs said he wanted to make another attempt to settle the case against Beatrice. Schlichtmann thought it odd that Jacobs, not Facher, would make this call, but he was happy to talk settlement with Jacobs anyway.

They met for drinks that evening at the Bay Tower Room. Schlichtmann told Jacobs that if he really wanted to negotiate, he would bring in someone from Beatrice, a "decision-maker," who could authorize settlement. Jacobs agreed to have Beatrice's assistant general counsel fly in from Chicago. But Jacobs seemed nervous. He asked Schlichtmann for some assurance that the assistant general counsel wouldn't come to Boston just to hear another outrageous demand. "This won't be another Four Seasons type of demand?" asked Jacobs.

"You won't be embarrassed," said Schlichtmann.

There were no elaborate preparations for the negotiation this time, no rented suites or silver service, and the sums discussed were not, as Schlichtmann had promised Jacobs, fantastical. On Friday morning Schlichtmann, Conway, and Gordon went over to Hale and Dorr to meet the Beatrice assistant general counsel, a thin, chain-smoking woman in her mid-forties named Mary Allen. She responded with hostility to Schlichtmann's opening demand for thirty-six million dollars. She threw down her pencil and called it "extortion." She told Schlichtmann that Beatrice was a big company and that he was "just a mosquito to us."

Jacobs, looking worried, escorted Mary Allen from the room. A few moments later he returned alone. Mary Allen was upset, he said. The demand was much larger than either he or she had expected. He was, however, prepared to make Schlichtmann a counteroffer: Half a million dollars for each family, four million in total. "Will that do it?" Jacobs asked.

There was, it seemed, no question that Jacobs—and hence Facher— were genuinely interested in settling the case against Beatrice. Schlichtmann told Jacobs that the only way to bridge the gap between them was to talk about their respective positions.

Jacobs said that there was no time for that. It was Thursday afternoon now. The trial was about to start on Monday morning. "You've got to give me your bottom line," said Jacobs.

Schlichtmann shook his head. "It never works that way. My bottom line will always be too high, and your top will always be too low."

Jacobs left the room again. When he returned, he had another proposal. He told Schlichtmann he was not authorized to make this offer yet. "But if you accept it, I'll see if I can get it. It's in the vicinity of a million dollars per family. Is that in the ballpark?"

In spite of all the talk about billion-dollar settlements and "astronomical" verdicts, this was an offer that Schlichtmann had to consider carefully. His firm was deeply in debt. He could use the Beatrice money to finance the trial against Grace, and at the same time put a substantial sum into the hands of the families. Furthermore, getting rid of Beatrice also meant getting rid of Facher, who had proven to be his strongest adversary. Without Facher to complicate matters, the trial against Grace would no doubt be simpler, and probably clearer and more compelling for a jury of ordinary citizens.

Then again, thought Schlichtmann, it wasn't as if he had no case against Beatrice. The land *was* contaminated with TCE, and he could prove it. True, Riley had claimed at his deposition that he had never used TCE, but Schlichtmann was convinced that Riley had been lying. He had learned from that encounter that Riley was a man of violent and erratic temper. Back then, Schlichtmann had told himself that when he finally got Riley on the witness stand in front of a jury, he'd taunt the old tanner into losing his temper, and perhaps even exposing his lies.

Maybe Jacobs and Facher were afraid of this very thing. Whatever the reason, Jacobs was obviously worried. After all, he had initiated this discussion. He had offered four million, and then, within a matter of minutes, he had doubled his own offer.

That afternoon, as Mary Allen left for the airport, Schlichtmann promised Jacobs that he would call back that evening with a final figure, one "cut to the bone."

At the office, he and Conway and Gordon debated what to do. Schlichtmann wondered if he was ethically obliged to inform the families of Jacobs's offer. Doing so might create problems. What if some of the families wanted to take the money and others insisted on going to trial?

But Jacobs had not actually offered eight million dollars—he'd said only that he would "try" to get it. Moreover, the negotiation was still going on. Schlichtmann owed Jacobs a call.

For the moment at least, Schlichtmann decided to discuss the matter only with his partners. They talked into the evening before they decided upon a sum. In his office, with the door closed and Conway, Gordon, and Crowley sitting around his desk, their eyes all on him, Schlichtmann made his call to Jacobs. "The figure," he said into the phone, "is eighteen million."

Schlichtmann listened for a moment, and then hung up the phone.

"What did he say, Jan?" Gordon asked.

Jacobs had thanked him, replied Schlichtmann, and said he would call back with a response.

Schlichtmann expected Jacobs to call on Friday, but Jacobs didn't. He waited over the weekend, expecting to hear from Jacobs at any moment, but Jacobs never called back.

The Trial

Schlichtmann stood silently in the well of the courtroom, facing the six jurors and six alternates. He wore his charcoal-gray suit with the faint pinstripes, his lucky suit, and a new red Hermès tie that Teresa had given him. He stood before the jurors, but he didn't look at them. His head was bent, his gaze fixed on the floor, his left hand cradling his chin as if he were deep in thought, his tall, slender form a study in angles.

Opening statements in well-publicized jury trials are among the law's more theatrical moments. A moment ago, Judge Skinner had taken the bench and peered out at the gallery, where people sat wedged on the long pews like subway commuters at rush hour, briefcases, coats and purses perched on their knees. More people stood at the back of the gallery and along the walls between the tall marble columns. "We can't have standees," the judge had said. "Those of you who can't find seats, I'm going to ask you to leave."

Two hundred spectators remained, seated in rows behind the stout oak railing that separated them from the well of the courtroom.

Reporters and courtroom sketch artists from television had the best front-row seats. Behind them, among the sea of faces, was Schlichtmann's mother, her gray hair freshly coiffed, and Kathy Boyer and Teresa and, several rows distant, Rikki Klieman. Uncle Pete was there, keeping an eye on his collateral, and Gordon and Phillips and their wives, and everyone else from Schlichtmann's office, down to the part-time receptionist. And so, too, was Reverend Bruce Young, in a worn black suit and white cleric's collar. An entourage of dark-suited W. R. Grace executives from corporate headquarters in New York claimed several excellent seats near the front of the gallery. Among them was the Grace general counsel, a trim, handsome man in his mid-sixties with a full head of white hair. Across the aisle from him sat his counterpart at Beatrice Foods, Mary Allen, just in from Chicago. Even one of Facher's daughters had come to hear her father in the biggest case of his long career.

The only faces missing from this crowd were those who arguably had the greatest interest in the progress of the case. Schlichtmann had prevailed upon his clients, the Woburn families, not to attend the trial. This had been a tactical consideration. The entire trial, both phases, would surely last several months and if, sitting in the gallery, they should laugh or smile at the wrong time, or look bored, or come only sporadically—well, he'd asked them, think what impressions the jurors might form.

The night before, Schlichtmann had not slept at all. Teresa had stayed with him, and when she fell asleep at midnight, Schlichtmann had been making notes in the margins of his speech. At four A.M., she had awakened to find his reading light still on, his voice a low murmur as he rehearsed.

In the courtroom the old steam radiators hissed and emitted a prodigious heat. The audience seemed to hum with anticipation, a susurrus of excited voices. The sound quickly faded away when Schlichtmann rose from the counsel table. But still Schlichtmann waited, looking at the floor. He waited for such a long moment that his friends in the gallery began to worry.

At last, he took a deep breath and looked up at the rain-streaked windows above the jury box. "Ladies and gentlemen of the jury," he began in a low voice. "There's a city north of Boston. The name of that city is Woburn. Woburn is like many other cities. It has homes, schools, churches, industry. But Woburn has something else. It has more than its share of sickness and death."

He spoke to the jurors as if he were alone with them, the way two people can be alone in a crowded public park. His notes were at the counsel table, a few paces to his right where Nesson, Conway, Crowley, and Kiley sat, but he never paused to look at them. He told the jury about the tragedies the Woburn families had endured, and then, the tone of his voice growing harsher, about W. R. Grace and Beatrice Foods. He would prove, he said, that these two companies had dumped toxic solvents on the ground, and that these solvents had been drawn into the city wells and then pumped into the homes of east Woburn. "Industrial waste has been dumped by corporations that didn't care, by corporations that knew what they were doing could hurt people. But these corporations chose to do it anyway."

When Schlichtmann was done, the crowd in the gallery remained quiet for a long moment. Judge Skinner broke the spell by calling a brief recess. The crowd, elbow to elbow in their seats, seemed to let out a collective breath, and began talking among themselves as they shuffled out to the corridor. Schlichtmann sat at the counsel table, his back to the gallery, his face flushed. His partners gathered around him, touching him on the shoulders and smiling.

The counsel tables—there were three, one for each party—were arranged in such a way that the lawyers for the two defendants sat behind and to either side of Schlichtmann, counsel for Beatrice on his left shoulder, Grace on his right. Next to Facher at the Beatrice table, Jacobs paused to watch Schlichtmann receive congratulations. Then Jacobs followed the crowd out into the corridor in search of Mary Allen. He found her smoking a cigarette by the pay phone.

"My God," Mary Allen said to Jacobs. "He accused us of *murdering* children! What the hell are we going to say to that?"

Schlichtmann's speech had unnerved Jacobs, too. He would recall later that he could "almost hear the jurors' minds snapping shut." But he did not say this to Mary Allen. "Just wait," he reassured her. "This was Schlichtmann's finest moment. From here on, it's all downhill for him."

It is in the nature of disputes that a forceful accusation by an injured party often has more rhetorical power than a denial. Partly for that reason the opening statements—the denials, as it were—made on behalf of W. R. Grace and Beatrice Foods struck many observers in the gallery as anticlimactic.

A lawyer named Michael Keating, one of Cheeseman's partners, gave the opening statement for Grace. Cheeseman sat at the Grace counsel table, but he was no longer in charge of the conduct of the case. The firm had turned that job over to Keating. Cheeseman didn't mind. Quite the contrary, he had welcomed Keating, a friend and fellow Harvard Law graduate who was also the firm's most experienced trial lawyer. Keating had a wonderful courtroom voice. It was strong and clear and resonant, a forthright, honest voice of the sort that seemed incapable of whispering secrets or bearing falsehoods. Standing before the jury, Keating frankly admitted that yes, some Grace employees had spread small amounts of TCE on the ground to evaporate—*but* it was just small amounts and it had *never* gotten to Wells G and H, and he, Keating, promised he would prove that to them. And even if it had gotten there, it could not possibly have caused anyone any harm, and he would prove that, too. There wasn't much more that Keating could say, except to reply to Schlichtmann's accusation that Grace did, too, care.

For those in the cramped seats of the gallery, Keating's opening statement was mercifully brief. Facher's was not. Facher stood before the jury and patted the pockets of his suit coat as if he'd just discovered that he'd lost his keys. He fixed his gaze on the high vaulted ceiling of the courtroom and turned his head slowly as if he were following the flight of an insect. He often looked squarely at the judge as he spoke, but rarely at the jury. When he tried to erect a large map of Woburn on an easel, he almost toppled it back onto Jacobs and Frederico. And when he finally got the map in place, Judge Skinner interrupted him. "Turn it so the jury can see it," the judge ordered. "You're talking to them, not me."

It wasn't that Facher had no points to make. Schlichtmann had no proof, Facher told the jury, that the Beatrice tannery had ever used TCE, or had ever dumped toxic waste of any kind on its fifteen acres. It was true, he acknowledged, that the land was contaminated today, but there was "not one single piece of scientific evidence" that it had been contaminated in the 1960s and 1970s, when the wells G and H were pumping water into the homes of east Woburn. Moreover, no doctor had ever suggested that the chemicals in the well water could cause leukemia, not until Mr. Schlichtmann found an expert to say so, "a California doctor, a professional expert" who had testified "dozens of times."

It appeared that Facher had said everything he intended to say. He had spoken for an hour and a half, but he seemed reluctant to sit. He had worked hard to prepare his opening. He had rehearsed on the way to work for the past week, bundling himself in a heavy winter coat and a snap-brimmed cap with the earflaps pulled down, walking from his apartment in Arlington to Harvard Square, a distance of three miles—a small, gray, undistinguished-looking figure with a lugubrious face, talking to himself. It wasn't a bad speech, but now, in the courtroom, as he said for the third time that the tannery had never even used TCE, the crowd in the gallery shifted in their seats.

Facher knew he was not a skilled orator. He did not even like the sound of his own voice, which he knew became more nasal and mumbly the louder he tried to speak. But he had won most of his cases, more than sixty in all, in spite of his voice. He knew that some trial lawyers claimed a strong opening statement like Schlichtmann's could win a case outright. In Facher's experience, this was sometimes true, but only in short, uncomplicated cases. In the lengthy cases he'd known, openings didn't matter that much. They were soon forgotten. Facher didn't know how long Schlichtmann expected this first phase, the waterworks, to last. But he, Facher, had no intention of letting it be brief.

2

Schlichtmann figured it would take him four or five weeks to complete the waterworks phase of the trial. In broad outline, his task was quite simple. He had to prove that the Grace and Beatrice properties were contaminated with TCE and other toxic solvents, and that these solvents had seeped into the groundwater and migrated to the city wells by the late 1960s.

He would call as many as thirty witnesses, but he intended to rely chiefly on the testimony of two expert witnesses. The first, a geologist, would describe to the jury the extent of the TCE contamination in the soil of the Grace and Beatrice properties and the time at which, in his opinion, it had occurred. The second expert, a Princeton professor, an authority on the subject of groundwater flow, would explain how the TCE had percolated into the aquifer and was then drawn by the pumping action into Wells G and H.

The timing of these events was critical to Schlichtmann's case. He had to show that TCE had gotten into the wells *before* the leukemias and assorted other ailments began to show up. With Grace, that was easy. He would call Tom Barbas and his fellow employees to the witness stand and have them testify about dumping TCE throughout the 1960s. Beatrice was more difficult. Schlichtmann did not have eyewitnesses who could implicate John J. Riley in the contamination of the fifteen acres. He would have to rely on circumstantial evidence and the testimony of his expert witness, the geologist, to date the contamination.

"Facher thinks all expert witnesses are whores. He'll say to you, 'You're making it up, you're a charlatan!'"

"Can I laugh at him?" asked the geologist.

They were in the conference room at Schlichtmann's office. It was late in the evening. The geologist, a courtroom virgin, was getting a final lesson in witness-stand etiquette on the eve of his appearance. "Do you tend to get nervous?" Schlichtmann asked. "You will never—ever!—put your hands to your face."

The geologist smiled. "How about scratching my crotch?"

Schlichtmann didn't smile. "Just keep your hands clasped in front of you," he said. "Don't leave them free. Do you cross your arms like this?" Schlichtmann folded his arms tightly across his chest and drew his shoulders forward. "Don't do it. It looks hostile and withdrawn. Now you're slouching! Don't slouch."

"I'm a sloucher by nature," said the lanky geologist, sitting more erect.

"Sit on the edge of the chair. It keeps you alert. And keep your eyes on whoever is talking. When Facher and Keating start cross-examining you, never look at me." Suddenly Schlichtmann jumped up and pointed an accusatory finger. "Ahhhaa! Your hands are in front of your mouth now! You just went from slouching to lip holding!"

The geologist drew his shoulders back and sat erect, hands folded in front of him, as motionless as an artist's model. He held the pose for a moment and then he collapsed into laughter. He was punchy from long hours of work.

Schlichtmann went on: "They're going to ask, 'Are you being paid for your testimony?' What do you say to that?"

The geologist hesitated. "Yes . . . ?" he ventured cautiously.

"No, no, no! You're being *compensated* for your time. By the way, do you own a burnt-orange sports coat? A puke-green tie? For God's sake, don't wear it. I want you to wear a conservative suit."

The geologist's name was John Drobinski. He and Schlichtmann had already spent many days before the start of trial going over the substance of his testimony. During the past year Drobinski had led a team of other workers in mapping every foot of the Beatrice and Grace properties. They had drilled more than two dozen test wells in the Aberjona marsh, conducted seismic refraction studies of the underlying bedrock contours, and collected samples of contaminated soil. On the fifteen acres owned by Beatrice, Drobinski had dug into piles of debris and rusted 55-gallon drums, piles saturated with TCE. He had found a Woburn campaign sticker from 1963, a prescription bottle dated 1967, and Budweiser beer cans with tab tops of the sort that Budweiser said they had stopped making in 1970. He had chopped down a stunted tree growing out of one pile and sent cross-sections to a botanist, who determined that the tree, eighteen years old now, had started growing in 1967. Based on these discoveries, and especially aerial photographs from the 1950s and 1960s that clearly showed the piles of drums and debris, Drobinski would take the witness stand tomorrow and testify that the Beatrice property adjacent to the tannery had been contaminated for at least twenty-five years.

Schlichtmann thought it would take him about three days to guide Drobinski through his testimony against Beatrice.

"A plaintiff's case depends on momentum," Facher once told his Harvard class. "The fewer objections you get, the better your case will move along. Objections break up the rhythm of an examination."

And so Facher objected, and kept on objecting. On the second day of trial, the morning Drobinski was supposed to take the stand, Facher demanded an audience at the judge's bench. He objected to documents that Schlichtmann planned to put into evidence on the grounds of relevance, hearsay, authenticity, best evidence, and undue prejudice. "It is a dreadful piece of work," Facher said of one report by a state environmental agent. "The most outrageous report you've ever seen." He objected to Drobinski's soil-test results, and again when Drobinski, on the stand at last, tried to show the jury photographs he had taken on the fifteen acres. "They've got these giant blowups of everything!" Facher complained in a whispered conference at the judge's bench.

"Of course," said the judge. "If you're going to present a case to the jury, you blow up the photographs. You're not shocked by that, are you?"

"But these blowups, they're distortions," insisted Facher. "When you see them you'll agree. They have a hand the size of a tennis racket in this photograph."

"If you want to point out that nobody has a hand that big, you're entitled to do it," said the judge.

Facher objected when Schlichtmann tried to bring into the courtroom a large diagram depicting the fifteen acres. "The King Kong exhibit," Facher called it, "a gigantic piece of demonstrative evidence, I would say ten feet high because it's bigger than Jan, and Jan is about six feet four. They've drawn little pictures of barrels on it, and they've got a hinge on it and then there's a big index, and I will object to it."

The proceedings ground to a halt as the judge left the bench and went out to the corridor to examine the King Kong exhibit. He permitted Schlichtmann to use it, but that didn't deter Facher. A few moments later, Facher objected to a photograph of the tannery's sludge lagoons. "It's a false photo," he told the judge.

Schlichtmann turned to stare at Facher. "It is, is it?"

"Absolutely," said Facher.

"It's your photo," said Schlichtmann, "from your own engineer. Did your engineer falsify it?"

Throughout the first week of trial, every morning began with Drobinski taking the witness stand and then sitting mutely, hands properly clasped before him, as the lawyers gathered at the judge's bench to dispute one matter or another. The interruptions would continue throughout the day. Facher would rise to object and ask to speak to the judge, and then all the lawyers, including Cheeseman and the other Grace lawyers, would rise and troop up to the bench for a conference in low but urgent voices that could last from a few seconds to half an hour. On the fourth day of trial, Facher's objections resulted in twenty-two trips up to the judge's bench. Drobinski, meanwhile, sat on the witness stand, and the jurors sat in the jury box, looking bored and sleepy. They were forbidden to bring newspapers or other reading material into the courtroom. They gazed numbly at the vaulted ceiling or at the gallery, where the crowd had by now dwindled to fewer than a dozen people.

Nesson, the expert on the Federal Rules of Evidence, the one who knew more about their arcana than anyone else in the courtroom and perhaps in the entire First Circuit, would stand beside Schlichtmann at the bench conferences and argue in opposition to Facher. He overcame most of Facher's objections, but even so he grew increasingly frustrated. "Your Honor," he told the judge, making no effort to conceal his anger, "I'd like to put on record an objection to Beatrice's efforts to break up the flow of the case and to delay this trial in every conceivable way."

"I would agree," replied the judge, "except that I think you invited this kind of thing by pushing for trial when you weren't ready."

Judge Skinner, of course, had also been anxious to keep the trial date. Perhaps because of this, the judge seemed willing to tolerate some of Facher's more frivolous objections. And not all of the objections were frivolous. On the seventh day, just as Drobinski was about to utter his expert opinion on the time of contamination, Facher asserted that there was no proper scientific foundation for this opinion, which was based on nothing more than digging up old beer cans, chopping down a tree, and looking at aerial photos. Maybe those piles of debris and drums had been there for thirty years, Facher allowed, but no one could say with scientific certainty that they had been contaminated with TCE back then. Someone could easily have come onto the property in 1979, after the wells had closed, and dumped TCE onto those piles. For this reason, Facher asked the judge to exclude Drobinski's opinion and thus end the case against Beatrice then and there.

Judge Skinner seemed tempted to do so. Nesson warned that such a ruling would be a grave and costly mistake that would surely be reversed by the Court of Appeals. Under Rule 702 of the Rules of Evidence, Drobinski met all the proper qualifications as an expert, Nesson argued. It was therefore up to the jury, not the judge, to decide whether they believed Drobinski's testimony.

That debate went on for an entire morning. The twelve jurors, meanwhile, sat upstairs in the small, overheated jury room. At noon, Judge

Skinner retired to his chambers to ponder the matter. Upon his return, he told the lawyers that his decision was "a very close one." Drobinski's opinion could not rightly be called "scientific"—"He eyeballs the soil the way anybody who has ever dug a hole eyeballs the soil," said the judge. Nonetheless, on the basis of Nesson's argument, the judge decided he would permit Drobinski to state his opinion to the jury.

Nesson had just earned his keep. He had single-handedly saved the case against Beatrice. Back at the office that afternoon, Schlichtmann was exultant. "Charlie, you got inside the judge's perimeter!" Schlichtmann crowed gleefully, splaying his fingers out like a mystical masseur. "You were touching the old bastard's brain!"

But Drobinski's time on the witness stand was not over. In fact, his true ordeal was just beginning. On Friday afternoon, at the end of the second week of trial, Facher began a cross-examination that would last the entire third week. He sought to portray Drobinski as a biased and untruthful witness, handsomely paid for his testimony, who had looked only for information harmful to Beatrice. Wasn't it true, Facher demanded, that most of the fifteen acres was "pristine," full of "pretty little blue wildflowers"? Wasn't it true that only six of Drobinski's nineteen auger samples had contained TCE? Why hadn't Drobinski told the jury that fact? Wasn't it true the highest levels of TCE occurred at the surface of the soil? And that the levels declined the deeper Drobinski dug? This meant the contamination had to be recent, not twenty years old, didn't it? Wasn't that plainly obvious to anyone?

"People are greedy," Facher once told his Harvard class. "The biggest problem with witnesses is that most of them exaggerate." In Drobinski's deposition testimony, Facher had found an exaggeration, and now he drew it forth for the jury to see. Drobinski had claimed he'd gotten his master's degree in geology in 1976, but Facher, taking nothing for granted, had learned that the degree had actually been awarded in 1979. "Didn't you tell me under oath, at your deposition, that you had a degree in 1976?" Facher asked.

"Sir," replied Drobinski, "I was told by my thesis committee and the geology department that I did have my degree."

"You were *told*? You're saying you had a *verbal* degree in 1976?" Facher's voice was full of incredulity. "Is that what you want the jury to believe? Do you know of any university in the world that grants oral degrees?"

Then Facher showed Drobinski a copy of his application to the state of Oregon, also made under oath, for certification as a geologist. "Did you swear under penalties of perjury that you had a degree in 1976?"

Drobinski studied the application. "Yes, sir, that's what it says."

"You were trying to get your license in the state of Oregon by filing a paper that contained false information, isn't that right?"

"I would not characterize it that way," said Drobinski.

"It was under oath, wasn't it?"

"Yes, sir."

"It says '1976' opposite 'master's degree,' doesn't it?"

"Yes, sir."

"You were trying to tell the state of Oregon you already had your master's degree when you didn't, isn't that right?"

And so it went for a long while that day, Facher brandishing this small, but perhaps telling, inconsistency in an effort to cast doubt on the veracity of everything Drobinski had said.

Schlichtmann sat quietly at the counsel table. He looked completely calm, his features bland and inscrutable, but he was seething inwardly. If this were a deposition, he would have interrupted a dozen times and fought bitterly with Facher. But now, in the courtroom, he rarely objected to any of Facher's questions, even when he had legitimate cause. He disliked objecting in front of jurors. He didn't want any juror to get the idea that he was trying to conceal something under the cloak of a legal technicality.

Schlichtmann had his head turned slightly to his right so that he could see, out of the corner of his eye, Drobinski on the witness stand. The geologist was lean and wiry, with a broad forehead and a thick mustache. He sat forward on the edge of his chair, just as Schlichtmann had instructed, his hands clasped lightly together on the small wooden desk in front of him. Schlichtmann thought Drobinski was holding up well, all things considered. Drobinski answered Facher politely, always calling Facher "sir," and never once raising his voice or betraying any irritation. Schlichtmann could also see Facher standing splayfooted before the geologist, his arms crossed over his chest, his shoulders hunched, a gray wisp of a man with heavy-lidded eyes and thick glasses. His lips were pursed in a manner suggesting profound skepticism.

After a while, Schlichtmann noticed something curious. When Facher turned away from Drobinski to pace in the well of the courtroom, Schlichtmann saw the geologist glance down at his cupped hands. Drobinski quickly looked up when Facher turned back to face him. And then, when Facher asked Drobinski to approach the jury box to explain an exhibit, Schlichtmann saw the geologist slip something from his hand into his coat pocket.

It seemed peculiar to Schlichtmann. After court that day, on the walk back to the office, Schlichtmann asked Drobinski about it. Drobinski took from his coat pocket a snapshot of his family—his wife, his young son, and his daughter. The snapshot was creased and dog-eared and stained with sweat from the palm of Drobinski's hand.

Schlichtmann smiled and shook his head sadly.

Drobinski put the photo back into his pocket and apologized for the problem his degree had caused.

"Don't worry about it," said Schlichtmann. "The jury won't care about that."

Schlichtmann believed this. After all, Drobinski did have the degrees he claimed to have earned. Schlichtmann thought that Facher's personal attack might even have won Drobinski some sympathy. He found himself more worried about the effect of Facher's interminable objections. Facher had managed to prevent Drobinski from giving a clear, crisp presentation. But had he succeeded in fragmenting the testimony to the point where a jury of twelve average citizens couldn't reassemble the pieces? Schlichtmann had no way of knowing what the jury thought, but he could not afford to fall prey to doubts now. He told himself that the jurors had understood Drobinski.

3

Schlichtmann dreamed that his firm—he, Conway, and Crowley—had purchased a sailboat. The sailboat was frozen in a sea of ice, which became, in the peculiar way of dreams, a vast glacier. In his dream, Schlichtmann fell from the deck of the boat and careened down the glacier's icy surface. He could see looming before him a dark crevasse in the blue ice. An instant before he tumbled down into the crevasse, he awoke, the bedsheets knotted and wet with perspiration.

The dream was so vivid and unsettling that he felt compelled to tell everyone at work about it the next morning, as if by doing so he could exorcise its apparent prophecy. His dreams were not always so richly metaphorical. To his dismay, he usually dreamed about the trial—the courtroom, the judge, the witnesses—in painfully realistic detail, awakening at the first light of dawn and feeling as if he'd worked throughout the night.

The trial was moving more quickly now. Schlichtmann was still presenting evidence against Beatrice, leaving Keating and Cheeseman little to do for the time being. He called to the witness stand several Woburn residents who told of seeing piles of debris and dozens of barrels strewn across the Beatrice land from the late 1950s to the 1970s. One witness, now in his mid-thirties, described how he and others had played on the land as children, fashioning rafts by lashing barrels together. This witness recalled seeing "a constant spray of whitish, grayish stuff being blown out the back door" of the tannery, and men dumping "wheelbarrow loads of some sort of sludge" down the side of the hill. "All us kids, we called that area Death Valley because there were dead trees covered with a whitish powder." Another witness told of seeing flatbed trucks laden with barrels drive onto the land. "They didn't want me to be around there," said this witness. "They would throw things at me, scare me, chase me out of there. Afterwards, it would be wet and it would smell, too, like rotten eggs. I know it was some kind of chemicals, it had to have been."

For the past several days, during breaks in the testimony, Schlichtmann had seen John J. Riley waiting in the corridor outside the courtroom doors. The old tanner had tried to take a seat in the near-empty gallery, but the judge had ordered all witnesses sequestered, and Riley had been banished to the corridor. Riley sat alone on the bench near the stenographer's office, the fabric of his expensive dark blue suit stretched tightly over his massive shoulders and meaty thighs. During the morning recesses, when Schlichtmann gathered with Conway, Nesson, and Kiley in the corridor, Riley would rise from his bench and stare balefully at Schlichtmann from afar, his thin lips compressed and turned down in a look of bilious hatred.

Schlichtmann never met Riley's stare. He acted as if the old tanner wasn't there. But he felt the heat of Riley's anger, and to Schlichtmann it was like a sunny warmth. He wanted Riley angry. He wanted to stoke

Riley into a rage on the witness stand. He had anticipated this moment for months, ever since Riley's deposition, when the tanner had contemptuously emptied a glass of water on the bird's-eye-maple conference table. "If I choreograph it right," he told Conway, "Riley will crack. He'll demonstrate to the jury that he's an utter and complete liar."

The old tanner ascended to the witness stand and swore to tell the truth on the afternoon of April 19, at the end of the fourth week of trial. As Schlichtmann questioned him, it became apparent that he had been well prepared by Facher and Jacobs. In a benign, almost courteous manner, he steadfastly denied ever dumping tannery waste or barrels on the fifteen acres. "We had our well on that land," said Riley, referring to the tannery's production well. "It was our livelihood, our lifeblood. We're not going to run a dump where our well was." In thirty years, from the early 1950s up to 1980, he himself had never seen any barrels or industrial waste on the property. "Maybe a tire or two," he said with a shrug. "Some old timbers from a shack that was there."

These denials didn't surprise Schlichtmann. He had, in fact, counted on eliciting them to set up his confrontation with Riley. He produced what he liked to call his "killer document"—the 1956 report by state health agent A. C. Bolde, in which Bolde had ordered Riley to remove six hundred feet of tannery sludge from the edge of the Aberjona marsh. That report told, in black and white, how Riley had refused, claiming that he owned the land and could do what he wanted on it. Now, as Schlichtmann placed this document in front of Riley, he had high hopes. He didn't really expect Riley to confess, but he did expect the tanner to falter, and even better, to lose his temper.

But Riley did neither. He denied ever meeting Bolde, and he did so with majestic serenity. "No, sir," he said, shaking his massive head, "I've never been on the fifteen acres with anybody from any body of public health."

Schlichtmann pressed Riley. "Didn't you go down the access road with an investigator from the state Department of Public Health?"

"No, sir, I did not," replied Riley calmly.

Direct examination of a hostile witness is the most difficult of all the trial lawyer's skills. Schlichtmann's examination proceeded fitfully, interrupted by Facher's objections and the inevitable bench conferences. When Schlichtmann tried repeatedly to press Riley, the judge grew annoyed. "You've asked that question twice, and he's answered it," the judge told Schlichtmann in front of the jury. "Let's move on."

At times that day, Schlichtmann seemed to lose the mechanics of his craft. He phrased questions in ways that violated the Rules of Evidence and standard courtroom procedure. Time and again, Facher rose to object, and when the judge sustained these objections, a small smile crept over Riley's face. At one point the judge said, "This is an awkward way to do this, Mr. Schlichtmann."

Nesson tried to rescue Schlichtmann. "If I could be heard on this point—"

But the judge curtly silenced Nesson. "You're not entitled to be heard on every nit-picking point. Let's get on with it."

Schlichtmann stood facing Riley, but he was staring down at his notes, trying to figure out how to phrase a question in a way that would overcome Facher's certain objection. The courtroom was silent, and the silence grew longer and longer, broken only by the distant wail of an ambulance from the streets below.

At the far end of the plaintiffs' counsel table, seated next to Conway in the shadow of the judge's bench, Tom Kiley grimly watched this scene. He longed to jump up and question Riley himself. Six months ago in Patten's bar, when he had offered to help Schlichtmann with the case, Kiley had imagined that he and Schlichtmann would sit side by side, sharing the duties of direct and cross-examination. But now it was Nesson who sat by Schlichtmann's side. "I keep thinking to myself, 'I can't fucking believe I'm just sitting here," Kiley would say later. In the first weeks of the trial, he had written out questions for Schlichtmann, lines of examination he thought might prove fruitful. But Schlichtmann had his own way of doing things. Kiley found himself watching his friend and thinking, I'd do that differently. Sometimes Kiley thought, I could do that better. He'd steal glances at the big gold Rolex on his wrist and try to stifle yawns. For a time, he had considered no longer coming to the trial. He had a big case of his own, an accidental electrocution, to work on, and he was losing money sitting here. But he had offered to help, and even though the situation hadn't turned out the way he'd expected, he felt obliged to stand by his offer. Besides, if something were to happen to Schlichtmann, he'd have to take over. Nesson and Conway weren't trial lawyers, and Crowley lacked the experience for a case of this complexity. Kiley had decided he would stay, but he wouldn't try to compete with Nesson for Schlichtmann's attention. There's enough going on without my ego getting in the way, Kiley thought. If Jan wants my advice, he can ask.

Schlichtmann looked up from his notes and began questioning Riley again, trying to insinuate that the tanner knew full well others had used the fifteen acres as an industrial waste dump. Riley smiled tolerantly, as if Schlichtmann were a schoolboy who had to be set straight, and shook his massive head. "If I had been aware of that, I would have stopped it immediately."

"Why?" asked Schlichtmann.

Kiley winced at this question. Every trial lawyer learns early in his career that he should never ask a hostile witness "Why?" and thereby invite the witness to make a self-serving speech.

Riley readily accepted the invitation. "Because it was our land," the tanner explained. "No one has the right to dispose of anything on our land."

Schlichtmann sat in the conference room that evening, his head cradled in his hands. "God, that was exhausting," he said to Conway. "I looked at the clock and it said noon but it felt like it was five o'clock."

Nesson sat across the table from Schlichtmann. "I think the problem is you're giving Riley too much leeway. It makes the examination seem meandering."

"The judge was being petulant," muttered Schlichtmann. "He wanted to hurt us today."

Gordon came into the conference room and settled into a chair. He'd spent most of the day in the courtroom gallery and he hadn't liked what he'd seen. The one good thing, he told Schlichtmann, was that Uncle Pete hadn't come to court today. "You've got to get some direction," Gordon said. "It wasn't as crisp as you usually are."

Schlichtmann sighed and rubbed his eyes. "Was the jury against me?"

Gordon shrugged. "Vogel's attention was wandering," he said, referring to the jury foreman.

"I shouldn't worry about the jury," Schlichtmann murmured softly. "I should just do my job and not think about them."

The tall, willowy figure of Patti D'Addieco appeared at the door, behind Schlichtmann's shoulder. She leaned against the doorframe and listened to the conversation. Schlichtmann, sensing her presence, looked over his shoulder. "Well," he said to her, "what did you think?"

"Can I be completely honest?" she asked.

Schlichtmann gave her an exasperated look.

"Riley didn't come off as slimy as I thought he would." She smiled sadly. "Sorry, Jan."

Nesson looked at Schlichtmann for a moment—a sober, appraising gaze. "I'm worried about you. You're tired, and I am, too. Somehow, between now and tomorrow, we've got to get the energy level up. This is *the* case against Beatrice."

The lights along Milk Street came on, casting their glow into the conference room. Crowley turned on the TV to catch the evening news. A reporter from a local station had spent the day in the gallery listening to Riley's testimony. Nesson left for Harvard, promising to return later that night. Schlichtmann, Conway, and Crowley were sitting around the table, debating how to get a certain document into evidence over Facher's objection, when Kiley arrived. "The question is relevance," Schlichtmann was saying. "How can I set it up so the judge doesn't have a problem with relevance?"

Kiley sat down at the conference table and listened. He offered no advice. He stared at the television.

"Why aren't you guys helping me, goddamn it?" said Schlichtmann.

Conway shook his head wearily. "I don't know what to say."

"I don't think you need it," Kiley said at last, referring to the document with the relevance problem. "You want to dot all the *i*'s and cross the *t*'s, but that stuff doesn't matter to the jury."

"I spent all weekend getting this stuff together!" cried Schlichtmann, lifting the stack of paper and letting it drop with a thud onto the table. "If Riley's going to lie, I want to have a document that proves he's lying."

"Let me put it this way," said Kiley. "Anything you can put in smoothly, quickly and efficiently, you should use. Anything else is going to be a debacle. The jury just won't understand what you're trying to do."

From the television across the room, the anchorman announced, "Big day in the Woburn toxic waste trial."

Crowley rose and turned up the volume. An artist's rendering of Schlichtmann appeared on the screen, his arm raised, his mouth open, standing beside Riley on the witness stand. In the background the judge frowned. The reporter's voice said, "The families' lawyer, Jan Schlichtmann, asked Riley, 'Did you ever see any drums or barrels on your property?' Riley said, 'I don't recall seeing any drums.' The jury has already seen aerial photographs showing the property littered with what seemed to be drums and barrels."

Schlichtmann blinked as if coming awake. "That was a good report," he said.

"Better than I remember it," said Conway.

Schlichtmann clapped his hands together and said, "Okay, everybody, let's go to work."

At that moment, Conway's friend Tom Neville appeared at the door of the conference room. Neville made his living as a defense attorney for insurance companies, but he came by the office most evenings to play the devil's advocate for Schlichtmann. In his line of lawyering, Neville took few personal risks. He enjoyed watching the way Schlichtmann walked on the edge, and he didn't mind taking Schlichtmann out after an evening of work and buying him dinner at an expensive restaurant.

Schlichtmann glanced up at Neville but offered no greeting.

"Well?" said Neville in a hearty, good-humored voice.

"The judge is pissed off," said Kiley.

"What's he pissed off about?"

"Jan's trying to get all this shit in," Kiley lifted his chin to the pile in front of Schlichtmann, "and Skinner's jumping all over him on relevance."

"Did you use that 1956 report about the tannery waste?" Neville asked.

"I did," said Schlichtmann.

"And that didn't crack Riley?"

"He just denied it."

"The jury wants you to kick the shit out of this guy," said Neville.

Schlichtmann looked around the room. "Where's Charlie? We need him now, damn it."

This was too much for Kiley to endure in silence. He stood and planted his hands on the table, the thick muscles of his shoulders and arms bunching under his white shirt. He thrust his face toward Schlichtmann, who drew back in his chair. "You take Riley through a logical sequence," Kiley said with exaggerated patience. "You state the facts in simple declarative sentences. You get him up in front of the photographs and you say, 'Mr. Riley, you saw all those barrels on your land. Isn't it true that there was a pile here, and one here, and here? That pile was there in 1964, wasn't it, Mr. Riley? You never once threw any of your barrels on that land? Never once?' " By now, Kiley was shouting. "You get him to say no, no, no! And then if he says yes just once, he'll crack!"

Neville jumped up, too, and hovered over Schlichtmann from the other side. "You got to manhandle him!" said Neville.

"Yeah, great," said Schlichtmann, his head bowed, his voice soft. "That's good showmanship, but I've got to get evidence in."

"My God, this is the guy who killed your kids!" yelled Neville. "You should be attacking him with a fucking baseball bat! You shouldn't be asking him"—Neville adopted a mincing tone—"And then what did you do next, Mr. Riley?"

Schlichtmann slouched deeper in his chair, until he was almost supine. He stared vacantly past Kiley and Neville to the television, which still droned on.

Kiley grabbed one of the documents and brandished it in front of Schlichtmann's face. "Did you ever receive a letter in 1980 from the city about barrels all over your property, Mr. Riley? He says no and you drop this in front of him"—Kiley flung the letter down in front of Schlichtmann—"and you say, What's this, Mr. Riley?"

"Yeah! You're better off making your point and not getting the document in," said Neville.

"What's he going to say?" repeated Kiley, his lips curled in a sneer. "It doesn't matter what he says! He's fucked!"

Then Kiley took a deep breath and sat down. He gave Schlichtmann a puzzled look. "In my eleven years of trial experience, you've got more shit to use on this guy than I've ever seen before. You can fucking destroy him. What does it take to get you mad?"

Schlichtmann and Conway were the last to leave the office that evening. It was near midnight. "What do you think, Kevin?" Schlichtmann asked as they walked out the door together. "Should I have been more haranguing?"

Conway looked thoughtful but he didn't answer directly. "Riley surprised me today," he said. "He came off looking better than he should have. He was so arrogant and combative in his deposition."

"He's a liar but he's not stupid," said Schlichtmann.

Conway nodded as he put on his coat. "I think you've got to get angry, Jan."

Schlichtmann got angry the next day. Some thought it went better than the day before. Schlichtmann himself announced after court that he felt pleased, and when he asked Kathy Boyer her opinion, she said, "I thought it was stronger today."

But Tom Kiley had seen no great improvement. If anything, thought Kiley, the old tanner had looked even more at ease on the witness stand. When Schlichtmann, trying to "manhandle" the witness, had interrupted Riley with a brusque "Is that correct, sir? Yes or no," the judge had intervened. "Wait a minute, let him answer." Riley had smiled confidently and embarked on a long monologue, telling the jury again that the tannery had never used TCE and had never dumped its waste on the fifteen acres. When Schlichtmann stood Riley up in front of the jury and took him on a tour of the fifteen acres, showing him a map of the land and the photographs taken in 1985 of old, rusted barrels, Riley said time and again, in a placid and serene manner, "No, it did not look that way to my eyes in 1980. . . . No, I don't remember any debris pile there. . . . That, to me, doesn't look like the site. . . ."

And Facher had repeatedly objected to Schlichtmann's questions as repetitious and argumentative. The judge had agreed. "Yes, you're simply arguing with the witness," the judge had told Schlichtmann in front of the jury.

These rebukes were just the sort Facher liked to hear the judge utter, especially in front of the jury. At the morning break, downstairs on the third floor in the federal cafeteria, Facher was in high spirits. "A case depends on momentum and Schlichtmann doesn't have any," Facher told the young associates who gathered around him, coffee cups in hand. "He doesn't know how to ask a proper question. Just from a craftsman's point of view, I feel bad for him." Facher's young associates all smiled.

Facher had worried about Riley. He knew the tanner to be a temperamental man, the sort of witness who was dangerous to himself. But Facher thought Riley had acquitted himself well, and that the danger had passed.

Facher was wrong. The next morning, the first small crack in Riley's composure appeared. It happened, oddly, when Facher began what was supposed to be a friendly cross-examination. Facher asked the tanner if there had ever been, to his knowledge, sludge of any kind dumped on the fifteen acres.

Riley seemed resentful at being asked this question again. He seemed even to forget that Facher was his lawyer. "I have told you," Riley replied sullenly.

"Just tell us again," Facher gently prompted.

"No!" said Riley, his jowls flushing. "Never. Never in my knowledge. Absolutely never."

"Even assuming that sludge was deposited at any time on the fifteen acres, would that sludge contain any of the chemicals in this case?"

"No!" said Riley, his voice growing louder. "Absolutely not! Without question! And I will go to my grave with that story!"

The vehemence in the tanner's voice startled Facher. His sleepy eyes came fully open and he looked at Riley curiously for a second. Then he laughed a soft, deprecating laugh. "I don't want you to do that, sir," he said. "I want you to stay well and happy."

At the Grace counsel table, Keating had not uttered a word in the courtroom for many days. But he had the right to cross-examine all witnesses, even if they were testifying only about Beatrice. He chose to exercise that right with Riley, embarking on a little friendly cross-examination of his own. "Isn't it true," Keating said to Riley, "that the tannery has been a good citizen of Woburn, a supporter of civic activities, supporter of a local baseball team and the like?"

The question appeared to have a soothing effect on Riley. "We took a lot of pride in Woburn," said the old tanner. "We loved Woburn, and still do."

"You were born and brought up in Woburn, and your children were born and raised there?"

"Yes," said Riley.

"You consider Woburn your home, don't you?"

"Yes, I do."

And then Keating asked Riley about the fifteen acres. "That land is now owned by a nonprofit corporation called the Wildwood Conservation Corporation, of which you are the sole trustee?"

"Yes," said Riley.

"And that corporation has dedicated the fifteen acres for conservation purposes, for the use and enjoyment of the citizens of Woburn?"

There was no barb in Keating's voice. A look of mild suspicion came over Riley, but he replied in a neutral tone. "It is a conservation commission for the preservation of wetlands, yes."

"No further questions, Your Honor," said Keating.

Schlichtmann looked at the jurors. He wondered if they saw the hypocrisy in Riley's dedication of some of the most grotesquely polluted land in New England for the "use and enjoyment" of Woburn's citizens. But the jurors' faces remained a collective mask.

It was Schlichtmann's turn to question Riley on redirect examination. He considered exploring the subject of Riley's "conservation commission" at greater length, but he decided that the jurors could not have failed to miss the irony. There was only half an hour left in the day, Riley's last day on the stand, and Schlichtmann wanted to use the time differently. He knew exactly how he wanted the day to end, but he had to occupy some time first. He began by questioning Riley once again about his dealings with the public health authorities and the barrels on the fifteen acres. Riley answered brusquely. Facher objected and accused Schlichtmann of simply "running out the clock."

A few minutes before adjournment, Schlichtmann returned to the subject of the tannery's records. "Mr. Riley," said Schlichtmann, "you do not have any records from the 1960s and 1970s indicating what chemicals the tannery used, do you?"

"No," said Riley. "Only my memory."

"Those records have been destroyed, is that right?"

Riley's reply was curt. "Yes."

"Your records go only to 1979, the year the Wells G and H were closed?"

"Yes."

"Mr. Riley, when did you destroy those records?"

The tanner was instantly enraged. This question worked just as Schlichtmann had hoped. In a loud, angry voice, Riley said, "I don't know when those records were destroyed, but I will repeat to you, sir, again and again, we never used trichloroethylene—"

"No, no, no," interrupted the judge. "You're not being asked that. You're being asked when the records were destroyed. You say you don't know. Next question, Mr. Schlichtmann."

"That's all," said Schlichtmann, smiling.

Walking down Milk Street with Nesson and Conway, Schlichtmann laughed out loud. "It was great, wasn't it, Charlie! Why would Riley immediately make the connection between TCE and destroying records? Because he was covering up! The jury understood that, didn't they? Did you see Facher? How totally crumpled he was? He was walking out and Frederico said something to buck him up, and Facher said, 'I don't want to feel better.' God, it was just great! It felt so good!"

The point, once elucidated, seemed cogent. Why *had* Riley made that connection all on his own? But to Nesson, it seemed as if Schlichtmann had not hammered home this point for the jury. Perhaps, thought Nesson, Schlichtmann understood the case too well. He expected everyone to be a master of its subtleties.

But Nesson was glad to see Schlichtmann in high spirits again. And maybe Schlichtmann was right in thinking that he'd exposed Riley as a liar in the eyes of the jurors. In the enclosed, ritualistic world of the courtroom, where judges wore black robes, witnesses were sworn to tell the truth, and panels of silent strangers held one's fate in their hands, reality was often a mere shadowland.

4

Every morning Kathy Boyer sent eight copies of the previous day's trial transcript out to Woburn by courier. The courier would drop off the transcripts at Donna Robbins's small apartment on North Main Street, and someone from each of the families would come by in the late afternoon or early evening to pick up their copy. Usually they would linger for a while to chat and hear Donna's account of her daily telephone briefing with Schlichtmann, coming away from their evening ritual with a sense of solidarity and purpose.

In the beginning, all of the Woburn adults tried to keep abreast of the growing pile of transcripts. But they found the reading laborious and full of confounding legal arguments. Most tended to rely instead on the reports in the *Woburn Daily Times,* which were more easily digested than the raw transcript testimony.

Richard Toomey was one of the few who continued to read the transcripts faithfully every evening. After dinner and a long day at the metal shop, he'd sit in the recliner in his living room, a transcript in his lap. He'd found the reading difficult at first, but he'd persisted. Now he found himself looking forward to the next day's episode. He felt drawn to the transcripts, he said, in the way he imagined some people got addicted to soap operas. The bench conferences, where the lawyers argued among themselves and with the judge, particularly engrossed him. He had despised Facher initially, but in time that had turned to a grudging respect. "His attack on John Drobinski was a terrible thing," Richard said one evening at home, surrounded by transcripts. "The judge let it go on day after day. Facher dominates everybody, including Jan and the judge. It's almost like Facher's giving lessons to the judge."

One of the eight families, the Gamaches, paid almost no attention at all to the details of the trial. Six months earlier, Roland Gamache had entered the fulminant end-stage of leukemia, what his doctors called a "lymphoid blast crisis." He was treated with an aggressive round of chemotherapy, but that failed to induce a remission. His only hope for survival lay in a bone marrow transplant from a compatible donor. None of his immediate family, however, proved compatible. On the advice of his doctors, Roland elected to have a transplant from a non-related donor. He and his wife, Kathryn, flew to Iowa City for the operation. There Roland suffered multiple complications from the bone marrow transplant and his hospitalization was, according to the records, "stormy." He died on April 17, in the sixth week of trial. His body was flown home for burial. A gathering of mourners that included several of the families attended a private service at St. Joseph's Church in Woburn.

All the families had felt a flurry of excitement and high expectations at the start of trial. But now, as the weeks dragged on and the daily transcripts mounted into a towering pile, their lives settled back into the normal daily routine of work and school. The trial—their trial— became a distant echo.

In the courtroom, Schlichtmann had begun his case against W. R. Grace. Nesson couldn't understand why he had bothered to call a former Grace worker named Frank McCann to the witness stand. McCann admitted using TCE to clean fingerprints and grease off conveyor belts, but he insisted that he'd never dumped any waste solvent behind the plant, nor had he ever seen anyone else doing so. Nesson shook his head in consternation over McCann. "I thought he was a net loss. I don't understand why you called him."

"Charlie, Charlie!" exclaimed Schlichtmann, his eyes wide in astonishment. "Don't you see what I did? This guy said he used a half-gallon of TCE a day. Half a gallon! He said the conveyor belt bubbled if he left it on too long. If the jury hears that often enough, they'll damn well remember it."

Nesson had to agree this was true, but if he had missed that point, he wondered how Schlichtmann could expect the jury to get it. Nonetheless, the case against W. R. Grace was moving swiftly, and despite some misgivings Nesson told Schlichtmann one afternoon, "I think it's going fabulously well against Grace."

Schlichtmann managed to get six witnesses, all former Grace employees, on and off the stand in one day, a record for this trial. In large part this happened because Facher was, for the time being, just a spectator. Schlichtmann's examination of Tom Barbas took a day and a half, but it went smoothly. At first Barbas sat erect in the witness stand, in a blue blazer and red tie, but as the hours passed his shoulders sagged and the judge had to urge him repeatedly to keep his voice up. "Shout as if you are outdoors, Mr. Barbas," urged the judge.

Schlichtmann asked Barbas to describe what he did at the end of work each day with the tray of paint sludge and waste solvent, and Barbas said, "I would take the tray out to the rear of the plant and place it on the ground."

"You dumped it on the ground, didn't you, Mr. Barbas?" said Schlichtmann.

"I don't think I said 'dumped,' " replied Barbas cautiously. "I said I used to *place* the material on the ground and let it dry."

Barbas, of course, had spent hours with the Grace lawyers preparing for every nuance of his testimony. This answer sounded like one the lawyers had drummed into him. But Barbas found himself trapped time and again by his deposition testimony. When Schlichtmann asked Barbas how often he'd seen Joe Meola, the maintenance man, dump pails of solvent on the ground, Barbas said, "I believe I only saw him a few times."

"Didn't it happen at least once a week?" Schlichtmann asked.

"I don't know if I saw him doing it once a week."

Schlichtmann picked up Barbas's deposition and flipped it open. "At your deposition, didn't I ask you how frequently Mr. Meola poured waste liquid into the trench? And didn't you answer, 'At least once a week'?"

"Yes," said Barbas.

"And isn't that the case?"

"I believe it to be, yes," conceded Barbas.

After a while, when Barbas balked, Schlichtmann would simply pick up the deposition and start toward the witness stand, and Barbas, seeing this, would turn docile and give the answer Schlichtmann sought.

During the morning recess, Tom Kiley lingered in the corridor outside the courtroom, watching from afar as two Grace lawyers escorted Barbas into a small alcove. He saw Barbas standing mute, looking sadly at his shoes, while the lawyers pressed close and whispered to him. Kiley smiled. "There's a pool of blood on the floor," he told Schlichtmann afterward.

Schlichtmann always spoke of the jurors with respect, almost reverence. He believed they could sense negative thoughts, and so he made an effort to think pure thoughts about them and to extol their virtues. He especially liked the jury foreman, William Vogel, a utility company manager in his early sixties. To most observers, Vogel appeared thoughtful, attentive, and somewhat reserved, but in Schlichtmann's mind these qualities became elevated to a higher plane—to wisdom, probity, and dignity. He recalled that Vogel had once thanked him when he'd handed the foreman a document. Schlichtmann sat close enough to the jury box to know that Vogel had never thanked Facher, and from this gossamer piece of evidence Schlichtmann concluded that Vogel must be on his side.

One morning during the sixth week of trial, Schlichtmann decided for the first time in his life not to wear a suit vest to court. He felt constricted by the rituals of the courtroom and he sought relief by shedding clothing. The next day the court stenographer told him he looked better without the vest. "I heard one of the jurors say so, too," she added. From that day on, Schlichtmann never again wore a vest in the courtroom.

The lawyers, of course, watched each other as closely as they watched the jurors. One afternoon, a Grace lawyer named Sandra Lynch, one of Cheeseman's partners, approached the judge's bench with a serious complaint about Schlichtmann. "I'm told that as the jury started to leave, Mr. Schlichtmann had a little colloquy and suggested they take an exhibit up with them."

The judge's eyes widened. "Oh?" he said to Schlichtmann.

Schlichtmann glared at Lynch. Any improper contact with the jury could result in an immediate mistrial. "Your Honor," Schlichtmann began, trying to explain.

But the judge was already angry. "Absolutely no colloquy with the jurors—"

"It was no colloquy," interrupted Schlichtmann hastily. "The juror looked at me and was about to say something. He had the exhibit in his hand. I turned away from him. I've had no colloquy, no contact whatsoever." Schlichtmann took a deep breath. "That's all I need," he added, more to himself than the judge.

"All right," said the judge, still looking stern.

The next morning, during a break in the proceedings, the second juror, Linda Kaplan, started coughing. Schlichtmann stood at his counsel table, only a few feet away from Kaplan. He had a pitcher of water and paper cups on the table, within easy reach. He glanced at Kaplan, debating whether he should offer her a cup of water, and then decided he could not risk it. Facher, a dozen paces distant, poured water from his own pitcher and started toward Kaplan. Then one of Cheeseman's partners briskly crossed Facher's path and reached Linda Kaplan first with his own cup of water. Facher, intercepted in midstride, stood in contemplation for a moment and then raised the cup to his lips and took a sip.

Schlichtmann witnessed this scene in pained silence. He would have liked to explain to Kaplan why he had ignored her distress, but that was impossible. Had it made any difference? Of course not, thought Schlichtmann, but it made him shudder to think of turning a cold shoulder on a juror.

Schlichtmann returned from court one afternoon to find that the telephone had been cut off. Without the warble of the phone, the office was eerily silent until Gordon arranged to pay the phone company. The first call came from a lawyer in New Mexico who wanted Schlichtmann's advice on a toxic waste case. "Do you want to talk to him?" asked Kathy Boyer.

"No," said Schlichtmann. He added, "Tell him not to take the case," he added.

The next call came from Schlichtmann's mother. He didn't want to talk to her either, but Kathy said, "I think you'd better."

"Is she all right?" asked Schlichtmann.

"You don't want to talk to her," said Gordon, grimacing and shaking his head.

"Why not?" Schlichtmann looked at Gordon suspiciously. "Did she get an eviction notice?"

"Probably," said Gordon.

"James!" he shouted at Gordon. "How come you didn't take care of it?"

Gordon shrugged wearily and said that it had slipped his mind. He promised he would talk to the landlord tomorrow.

Back from court, Conway went to the kitchenette for a cup of coffee and found the pot empty. He searched for coffee filters and found only an empty box. He dumped out the old coffee grounds, carefully rinsed the used filter, put it back into the coffee maker and then looked for coffee. He found only an empty can. He asked Peggy why no one had bought coffee. "There's no petty cash," said Peggy.

Schlichtmann, consulting with his expert on courtroom graphics, an MIT graduate named Andy Lord, wanted new exhibits to replace ones the judge had thrown out because of Facher's complaint that the perspective was "distorted."

"When do you want them?" Andy Lord asked Schlichtmann.

"Tomorrow morning," said Schlichtmann.

"Tomorrow morning? Impossible! I can't do it by then."

"Of course you can," said Schlichtmann. "What the hell am I paying you for?"

"Jan, I haven't been paid since November," said Lord, who was, in fact, owed more than forty thousand dollars.

"Talk to Gordon," said Schlichtmann.

A moment later, Patti D'Addieco appeared at the conference room door. "Andy says he needs some money for supplies."

"Get it from petty cash," said Schlichtmann.

"There is no petty cash anymore," said Patti, not for the last time.

Schlichtmann would gather in the office kitchenette for lunch at one o'clock every afternoon with Conway and Crowley, Nesson and Kiley, and often Gordon and Phillips. They would lean against the counters or sit on the stools and conduct a postmortem of the morning's events while the secretaries and paralegals listened in and sometimes offered their opinions. Schlichtmann, who rarely ate anything for breakfast, looked forward to these lunches. He liked Chinese food, but the secretaries tried to keep costs down by ordering sandwiches. They didn't always succeed. "Sandwiches again?" Schlichtmann would cry in dismay. "My God, even laboratory rats get a change in their diet. Can't we have Chinese?" So Kathy or Peggy or one of the other secretaries would order Chinese. The bill would come to Mary Zoza, the firm's bookkeeper, a middle-aged woman who lived alone with three cats and kept her graying hair in a tight librarian's bun. Mary Zoza nearly fainted the afternoon, seven weeks into the trial, when she got a Chinese lunch bill for $124. She began cooking lunches at home— roast chickens, big bowls of salad, spaghetti and meatballs—and bringing them in to work. Schlichtmann would exclaim in delight when he saw one of these meals, and this in turn seemed to delight Mary Zoza.

Gordon tried to cut costs by instructing Mary Zoza to pay only those expenses that were absolutely necessary to keep the office running. He told her to cancel all newspaper and magazine subscriptions. No more membership dues to the American Bar Association, the Boston Bar Association, or Trial Lawyers of America. No more lawbooks or journals from West Publishing or Martindale-Hubbell. Gordon put a stop to the twice-a-week fresh flower arrangements from Fleural Lis. He saved another two hundred dollars a month by canceling the contract with the Greening Touch Company, which pruned, watered, and fed the office's potted ferns and ficus trees. ("It's fucking ridiculous," Gordon said of that contract.) He stopped paying Schlichtmann's student loan from Cornell Law School. He stopped paying the bank loan on Schlichtmann's Porsche, and he let the insurance lapse. He told Kathy Boyer that henceforth all employees should take public transportation instead of taxicabs when on office business.

But all of these economies added up to only a small fraction of the trial expenses. They didn't even cover, for example, the fee charged by the court stenographer who typed up each day's trial transcript and delivered it to Schlichtmann's office that same evening. The "expedited" transcripts, as they were called, cost about a thousand dollars a week, depending on the number of pages of testimony. On top of that, there was the additional expense of making eight copies for the Woburn families.

Gordon believed he could go to Pete Briggs at the Bank of Boston for money one more time, but he was loath to do that until matters became truly desperate. Uncle Pete showed up at trial occasionally, and Gordon thought he had detected a change in the banker. Pete seemed more distant and aloof. "Something's wrong with Pete," Gordon told Schlichtmann one afternoon.

"Is he upset by the way the trial's going?" asked Schlichtmann.

Gordon shook his head in puzzlement. "I don't know what's bothering him. He won't tell me."

For the time being, Gordon put his hopes in settling a medical malpractice claim that Bill Crowley had been working on. The case concerned a thirty-five-year-old woman who'd gone to the hospital for a standard surgical procedure, a dilatation and curettage, to remove a benign growth on her cervix. Ten minutes into the operation, the woman, whose name was Helen O'Connell,* complained of difficulty in breathing and then lost consciousness. She awoke in the recovery room unable to move her legs. Over time, she regained sensation in her legs, but she continued to suffer from partial incontinence.

Schlichtmann had settled a similar case several years ago for nine hundred thousand dollars. The damages in that instance had been

*A pseudonym.

more severe than Helen O'Connell's, but all the same, Schlichtmann hoped to settle this new case for close to the same amount. Gordon awaited the settlement with impatience. The fee, potentially several hundred thousand dollars, would provide cash for operating expenses and enable him to make partial payments to creditors who'd already begun threatening legal action.

On a rainy afternoon in late April, in the seventh week of trial, Crowley went with Mark Phillips to meet the insurance agents in the O'Connell case. They had decided to ask for eight hundred fifty thousand dollars. No one expected this initial meeting to result in a settlement. But the insurers would make a counteroffer, revealing their own assessment of the case value, and the size of that offer would indicate how quickly the case might resolve.

Crowley and Phillips returned to the office around six o'clock. Schlichtmann spied them from his desk. He came to greet them in his stockinged feet. "How much?" he asked.

Phillips, still wearing his raincoat, his lank blond hair damp on his forehead, lit a cigarette and reached for the phone on Peggy Vecchione's desk. He punched the button for the direct line to Gordon on Newbury Street. Crowley shook out his umbrella and disappeared into his office. The secretaries all watched, waiting to hear what Phillips had to say.

"How much?" asked Schlichtmann again.

Phillips cradled the phone on his shoulder and looked at the ceiling. He took a deep drag on the cigarette.

"Jesus Christ, am I invisible?" muttered Schlichtmann. At the top of his lungs, he screamed, "*How much?*"

This time Phillips glanced at him, a sour look on his face. "One seventy-five."

Schlichtmann turned on his heel and went back into his office. Conway heaved a sigh and thrust his hands deep into the pockets of his pants.

In the conference room later that evening, Phillips explained that the insurance agents had admitted liability. "They didn't even want to talk about that," said Phillips. But the agents also believed the surgeon's claim that all of Helen O'Connell's problems had cleared up. "I think it was a jive offer," continued Phillips. "They're testing us. They know we're wrapped up in Woburn, they know we need the money."

Gordon groaned.

They would have to send Helen O'Connell to a second urologist, continued Phillips, and perhaps even another neurologist, for a new round of complete workups. "If that doesn't convince them," Phillips told Schlichtmann, "we'll have to put the case on the trial calendar for next fall and hope you're finished with Woburn by then. We can't sell out. We've got to settle for fair value or we won't settle."

Gordon groaned again.

After eight weeks of trial, the days in the courtroom had begun to blur into one another, like the countryside seen from a train window. A shaft of spring sunlight would find its way into the court and strike the brass lamp on the judge's bench, a flash of brilliant yellow in the cavernous, gray, dismal room. The fluorescent lights overhead made everyone appear pale and sickly. Thick volumes of legal papers had grown on the counsel tables and more thick volumes lay underfoot in cardboard boxes on the floor. The lawyers' overcoats, damp from a morning rain and smelling of wool, hung over the gallery railing. The radiators hissed gently. Distant, muted sounds of city traffic, a siren, an unmuffled truck, would float up into the courtroom from the streets fifteen stories below. The atmosphere felt heavy and dense. One of the alternate jurors regularly fell asleep. On particularly dull days, such as the one when Schlichtmann read Grace's answers to interrogatories into evidence, Judge Skinner himself seemed to doze at the bench, the flesh of his cheeks slack and his mouth slightly parted, his head rolling back onto his chair.

Facher always used to warn his students at Harvard that if they fell asleep at the counsel table, upon awakening they should come to their feet objecting. "In the time it takes to reach your full height, think of a reason for your objection."

Facher was being facetious, of course. He never really expected any of his students to fall asleep at the counsel table. But one day, eight weeks into the trial, Facher himself fell into a doze during Sandra Lynch's slow and methodical examination of a Grace executive. He awoke when the microphone on the witness stand emitted a harsh squeal.

"Perhaps we can fix the microphone," suggested Lynch.

"Mr. Nesson seems to have the touch," said the judge.

Facher came to his feet at the mention of Nesson's name. "I object," Facher said in a thick, cottony voice. Then he looked around, blinking his eyes, and sat back down.

5

On a morning in early May, Kathy Boyer opened the windows in the conference room for the first time since last fall, and there was fresh air in the offices of Schlichtmann, Conway & Crowley. Across from the courthouse, in Post Office Square, the tulips had burst into flower and the swollen buds on the linden trees had split open into a lacy green filigree of new leaves. Schlichtmann noticed that it was spring, but that didn't cheer him. This part of the trial should have ended long before tulips.

On the other hand, he was making progress. He had one final witness to call in this phase of the trial. This was his expert in hydrology and groundwater movement, one George F. Pinder, Ph.D. Pinder would testify against both Grace and Beatrice. He would, if all went well, make manifest the claim that TCE and other solvents on the properties of both defendants had indeed migrated to the city wells, and that the chemicals had gotten there before the leukemias and other illnesses began occurring.

Schlichtmann felt fortunate to have Pinder. Every geologist who knew anything about groundwater had heard of Pinder. He was preeminent in his field, chairman of the civil engineering department at Princeton University and the person who, fifteen years ago, had developed the first computer model of groundwater flow. Schlichtmann put him up at the Ritz-Carlton, in a suite of rooms.

Pinder was in his late forties, a dapper, diminutive man, nearly a foot shorter than Schlichtmann. His thin brown hair, as soft and silky as a baby's, had receded high on the dome of his head. He wore gold-rimmed spectacles that made his round face look owlish and cerebral. He had a precise, methodical manner, but he was not in the least aloof or self-important. On the morning of his first day in court, he arrived at Schlichtmann's office early and cordially greeted all the secretaries. Schlichtmann saw that Pinder was wearing a blue blazer, a woolly brown tie, brown pants and argyle socks. Schlichtmann always asked his experts to dress conservatively, in dark suits. To his eyes, Pinder was a sartorial nightmare, but he took it calmly. "George is the world's leading expert on groundwater," he told Conway privately before they left for court. "He can get away with dressing like that."

Pinder performed ably on his first day, under direct examination by Schlichtmann. He came to the courtroom equipped with charts and diagrams to educate the jury in the science of hydrogeology. He set up a fish tank filled with kitchen sponges and placed drops of ink on the sponges. "Just think of each drop as being some event of contamination on the ground, entering our aquifer," Pinder told the jury. He talked about saturated and unsaturated zones, capillary fringes, cones of depression. He held forth for the entire morning, confident, jaunty, and full of good humor, as if he were lecturing to a freshman class at Princeton.

Both Facher and Cheeseman knew Pinder's reputation. Two years ago, Cheeseman himself had tried to recruit Pinder as an expert witness for Grace, but he found that Schlichtmann had gotten to Princeton, and to Pinder, first. Facher wasn't worried, though. "They tell me Pinder's the leading expert on this subject," remarked Facher out in the corridor, during the morning break. "They say he's a home-run hitter in any ballpark. But he's in *my* ballpark now."

Indeed, things did not go quite so smoothly after the recess, although that was no fault of Pinder's. The closer Schlichtmann brought Pinder to implicating Beatrice and Grace, the more Facher and Keating began to object. Nevertheless, by the end of the day, Schlichtmann had gotten into evidence the first part of Pinder's opinion—that both Beatrice and Grace were responsible for the contamination of Wells G and H. The second part, the arrival times of TCE and the other solvents, would have to wait until tomorrow.

In the office that afternoon, Schlichtmann clapped his hands and danced on his toes in glee. "You got the opinion in, George!" he shouted. "They tried to stop you, but it didn't happen. It was a great day, today, George! It could not have gone better!"

Pinder smiled indulgently. "This jury looks like a pretty attentive group," he said.

Pinder made his first mistake the next morning. It was a small mistake, but Schlichtmann caught it in an instant. It happened when he asked Pinder how long it would take, in his opinion, for TCE and the three other solvents to migrate from the Beatrice and Grace sites to the wells. Schlichtmann had gone over these calculations with Pinder the night before, but that morning, Pinder gave different times for the solvents, different by a matter of days for one, a few weeks for another, and a year for the third.

Schlichtmann wondered for a moment if he himself was wrong, if he had remembered the times incorrectly. He felt confused, but he had no chance to find out at that moment why Pinder had changed the times. And when the recess finally came, Schlichtmann decided not to broach the subject. He did not want to shake Pinder's confidence in the middle of the day.

That evening, in Pinder's room at the Ritz-Carlton, Schlichtmann found out what had gone wrong. Pinder, feeling overly confident, redid the calculations in his head and forgot to factor in the porosity of the soil. The mistake made no difference to the substance of Pinder's opinion. The solvents had still reached Wells G and H long before the leukemias began occurring. But Schlichtmann knew that Facher and Keating would not miss this mistake, and that they would use it on cross-examination to attack Pinder's credibility.

Schlichtmann decided to wait until the closing minutes of the next day, a Friday, to have Pinder correct the mistake. He'd make it appear as almost an afterthought, of small consequence but requiring mention nonetheless. That would give the jurors the entire weekend to digest the substance of Pinder's opinion before cross-examination could begin on Monday morning.

The next day all went as planned for a while. When only twenty minutes remained before court adjourned for the weekend, Schlichtmann brought up the travel times, and Pinder explained that yesterday, on the witness stand, he had done the calculations in his head. "I was just contemplating my testimony," continued Pinder in a pleasant, untroubled voice, "and it suddenly occurred to me that I'd made a mistake. I'd be very pleased to try and correct that mistake."

"What was the mistake you made?" asked Schlichtmann.

"I left off the constant for the porosity of the soil when I was doing the multiplication in my head."

"Does that affect the travel times in some way?"

"It affects the travel times," said Pinder, nodding. "Not catastrophically but, I think, significantly."

Schlichtmann asked Pinder to tell the jury the new figures. When Pinder finished doing so, Schlichtmann glanced at the clock on the back wall of the courtroom, above the gallery. He still had twelve minutes to occupy until court recessed for the weekend. He planned to end the day by bringing out the fact that the research done in east Woburn—twelve thousand pages of data, 157 monitoring wells, and dozens of volumes from technical consultants—made the Aberjona aquifer one of the most thoroughly studied aquifers in history. He asked Pinder to compare the east Woburn research with other projects that Pinder had worked on, but both Facher and Keating objected. "Sustained," said the judge. Schlichtmann rephrased his question, but again the judge sustained the objections.

"May I have a moment, Your Honor?" Schlichtmann asked.

The judge nodded. Schlichtmann took a deep breath. He studied his notes. He needed another question but he couldn't think of one. He went to the counsel table and bent down to consult with Nesson, who hurriedly scribbled out a question. Schlichtmann turned and asked the question, but Facher objected, the judge sustained the objection, and Schlichtmann gave up. There were only seven minutes remaining. He said, "No more questions, Your Honor."

The judge peered at the clock. "This is probably a good place to stop, since we will begin cross-examination on Monday morning."

The little skirmishes of lawyers are sometimes consequential. Schlichtmann's strategy was obvious enough, and Facher had no intention of letting him get away with it. Facher stood and said to the judge, "Would you give me the seven minutes?"

"You want to start your cross-examination now?" said the judge, looking surprised and not particularly happy.

"Yes," said Facher, his eyes on Pinder as he walked across the well of the courtroom.

Pinder flew home to Princeton that Friday evening. After his seven minutes with Facher, he didn't relish the prospect of returning to Boston on Monday. Facher had treated him in a most contemptible manner, addressing him in an insulting and scornful tone that Pinder, for one, had never before experienced in his adult life. "Are you telling this jury that you came in here yesterday, as a Ph.D. and the chairman of a department, and made a *little* mistake in an opinion you've been preparing for the last year and a half?" Facher had said. "You're telling us, as a professor of geology, that you *forgot* to take into account *porosity?* Didn't you lecture in front of this jury for an hour about making these calculations? Today is true and yesterday was not? That is what you want this jury to believe?"

Pinder felt he'd kept his wits and replied calmly, but the brief ordeal had shaken him. He had testified before, in the Love Canal and Velsicol cases, but on those occasions he'd been on the witness stand for only a short time and his opinions had gone virtually unchallenged. Pinder's wife, Phyllis, took an interest in her husband's work. She knew about Facher from reading the trial transcripts of Drobinski's testimony, which Schlichtmann had sent down for Pinder to peruse. "Watch out for Facher," she warned her husband before he returned to Boston. "You should read your deposition so you won't contradict yourself."

Pinder didn't take his wife's advice. His deposition had gone on for five days and amounted to almost a thousand pages. He didn't bother to read it, but Facher did. Facher read every page.

On Monday morning Facher asked Pinder if he recalled saying at his deposition that the contaminants from Beatrice would have reached the wells within eighteen months. Pinder replied that he didn't remember exactly what he'd said. "But I think that is reasonable, and what I was likely to have said."

"When you testified here in court last week, you said the contaminants had reached the well field within a year. Do you remember that?"

"I don't remember the details," said Pinder. "But if you say that's what I said, I'll accept that."

"You don't consider that a change from eighteen months?"

Pinder replied slowly, choosing his words with care. "It depends on what context I was thinking of the word 'contaminants' when you were using it. That is why it's a little difficult for me to try to be more precise."

Facher suggested that Pinder had formed his opinion before even seeing any data from the pump test. Pinder denied this.

"But you had a hypothesis as to the source of the contamination, right?" asked Facher.

Pinder, thinking that he might have said something like that at his deposition, replied, "I think that is not an unreasonable statement. I think I probably would be prepared to say that I may have said that."

"You *may* be prepared to say that you *may* have said that?" repeated Facher in an incredulous voice.

"Well, I'm a cautious man," said Pinder.

"Very cautious," said Facher. "You use words carefully, right?"

"I try to be as precise and accurate as I can," said Pinder.

Pinder's attempt to be precise and accurate led to dense thickets of confusion and imprecision. Pinder was wary of Facher. He looked for a trap in every question Facher asked. To avoid being trapped, he refused to answer even the simplest questions in a simple way. When Facher asked him about Drobinski's work on the fifteen acres, Pinder said, "I'm not really familiar with what he did in detail. I think in spirit he went back and found some additional things."

"In *spirit* he went back?" said Facher in a mocking voice.

"In the spirit of your question, he went back," replied Pinder. "I have no particular, precise knowledge of the whole matter."

"You didn't even know who Mr. Drobinski was back in December of 1985, did you?"

"Oh, yes, I knew who he was," said Pinder with certitude. "We had talked together many times."

Facher picked up Pinder's deposition. He opened it and flipped through the pages until he found what he was looking for. "At your deposition on December tenth, I asked if you had worked directly with any Weston geologist, and you said yes. I asked, 'Can you identify them by name?'" Facher, standing near the witness stand now, placed the deposition in front of Pinder. "What was your answer?" Facher asked, pointing to the line he wanted Pinder to read.

Pinder leaned over his deposition and adjusted his spectacles. Facher gazed at the ceiling. It took Pinder a long time to answer. He was reading, it seemed, the entire page. " 'No,' " Pinder read aloud at last.

"You wouldn't have known Mr. Drobinski unless he stood in front of you with one of those little 'Hello, I'm Mr. Drobinski' tags on him?"

"At that time I didn't know who he was," said Pinder. "I'd spoken to him. There were several people, and I couldn't distinguish one from the other. That is the spirit of my answer."

"That's the spirit and the fact of your answer?"

Pinder soon abandoned "the spirit" and adopted new phrases. Everything became "in the context of what you're talking about," or "in the sense of what you're asking me." Facher didn't let these slip by. "I didn't put any sense in the question," he told Pinder. "I just asked a simple question."

The judge called the lawyers up to his bench. He said to Schlichtmann, "I'm beginning to get the impression that this fellow has either got a very loose grasp of the language, or he will say anything that comes into his head."

"I don't think that's a fair characterization of his testimony," said Schlichtmann, who knew perfectly well that it was going very badly.

After court that day, Conway saw Schlichtmann alone in his office, sprawled on the couch. Schlichtmann's arm covered his face as if he were shielding his eyes from a bright light.

"Boy, you look like shit," Conway said, standing in the doorway.

Schlichtmann lifted his arm from his eyes and glanced up at Conway. "This is going to be the worst fucking week of my life."

Conway nodded. "What the judge said about Pinder was very disturbing."

"That arthritic old bastard," murmured Schlichtmann.

"There's nothing worse than watching your witness being raped," said Conway. "It's awful to sit there and not be able to do anything."

"Are we going to survive the week?" asked Schlichtmann. "Four more days of this?" He gave a weak, dispirited laugh.

"We'll survive, Jan," Conway said, playing his part once again. He hitched up his pants. "George is the guru, the world's main expert. He knows more about that aquifer than anyone else in the world." Conway paused, and then he added, "Besides, I don't think anything could be worse than today."

At this, Schlichtmann sat up. He looked soberly at Conway. "Do you think it was really that bad?" Schlichtmann laughed again, the same weak laugh. "George actually told me he felt good today. Can you believe it? Ah, it's not George's fault. He's a brilliant guy, but he's not the sort of person who can move others. It's just not the way he is."

Gordon and Phillips walked into Schlichtmann's office. Gordon settled his heavy frame in the chair behind Schlichtmann's desk, put his feet up and lit a cigarette. Phillips sat in the armchair next to the couch and tried his hand at cheering up Schlichtmann. "Facher's little clinic today was great for lawyers, but it doesn't mean shit with the jury."

Phillips hummed nervously. "Just remember, Jan, the biggest victories are won by the slimmest margins."

There was a moment of silence. Everyone seemed to ponder this bit of wisdom. Finally Gordon said, "What exactly does that mean, Mark?"

Schlichtmann departed for the Ritz-Carlton and an evening of work with Pinder. He consoled himself by reasoning that although Facher might have tarnished Pinder's credibility, Facher had not succeeded in damaging the substance of Pinder's opinion. Schlichtmann felt he could make Pinder shine again on redirect.

Meanwhile, Schlichtmann had other concerns. He knew that Facher would try to use the Aberjona River, which flowed between the Beatrice property and the city wells, as a defense. According to Facher's theory, the pumping action of the wells would draw water directly out of the river, satisfying the wells' demand while at the same time blocking the flow of contaminated groundwater from Beatrice.

This theory had some merit. A year ago last spring, Pinder himself had warned Schlichtmann that the river might be "a very profound barrier," although Pinder personally doubted this would prove true. His computer model of the east Woburn aquifer predicted that the city wells would, in point of fact, draw contaminated groundwater from under Beatrice, along a highly permeable stratum of sand and coarse rock that lay under the riverbed. Nonetheless, Pinder told Schlichtmann, he wouldn't know for certain until he saw the field data from the EPA pump test. Then, on December 4, when the EPA activated the city wells and started the pump test, Pinder stationed himself at a monitoring well on the Beatrice property. He saw the water level at this monitoring well decline more than a foot in four hours, exactly the amount his computer model had predicted.

As far as Pinder was concerned, this and similar measurements from other monitoring wells proved beyond a doubt that groundwater from Beatrice was drawn under the river and into the city wells. It also proved that the Aberjona River played almost no role in satisfying the demand of the wells for water. Pinder reasoned that the thick layer of peat that formed the riverbed—twenty or more feet of decomposed leaves, roots, and branches—acted as a nearly impermeable lining. The river, in other words, was not a barrier. It wasn't even relevant.

This all seemed reasonable to Schlichtmann. But one detail troubled him. He and Pinder had both seen the ice on the river's surface that December. After the wells began pumping, the river's surface grew steadily lower, leaving shards of ice along the bank. Obviously the river had lost water. If it wasn't going to the wells, then where was it going?

At the Ritz-Carlton, Schlichtmann tried to get an answer to this question. Pinder had several explanations. Some water had been lost to evaporation. And some of it was being slowly drawn out of the river by the pumping action of the wells. But Pinder felt certain, based on the thickness of the peat layer, that it would take ten to twenty years for any river water to reach the wells.

It still didn't make sense to Schlichtmann. The river, he pointed out, had declined by six inches. That seemed like a lot of water. Pinder's explanations would not account for that much water.

Pinder, himself troubled now, agreed that this was true.

So where had the water gone? Schlichtmann asked.

Pinder didn't know.

They worked until after midnight, but Pinder could not come up with an explanation for the missing river water. He was tired and it was late. He insisted on going to bed. He wanted to have his wits about him tomorrow. He didn't want to face Facher without getting a good night's sleep.

Schlichtmann wouldn't leave. "We've got to figure this out, George. Let's go over it one more time."

"No," said Pinder stubbornly. "I'm going to sleep right now."

Schlichtmann, just as stubborn, refused to go.

"If you don't leave me alone," said Pinder angrily, "I'm going back to Princeton tomorrow morning."

Schlichtmann departed, feeling very worried.

Schlichtmann was waiting apprehensively when Pinder walked into the office early the next morning. He saw at once that their spat of last night had been forgotten. Pinder looked confident and happy. "In a moment of brilliance this morning, Jan, I figured out the river," Pinder said. "I don't know why it didn't occur to me before. It's really very obvious."

Schlichtmann listened carefully as his star expert explained the obvious. Under normal conditions, said Pinder, groundwater in an aquifer discharges into a river, thereby increasing the river's volume. Nearly all rivers, except those in deserts and on mountains, function in this way. Indeed, groundwater discharge is what creates most rivers, and this was the case with the Aberjona in east Woburn. But when Wells G and H began pumping, the aquifer was forced to satisfy the demand created by the wells and could no longer discharge into the river. "You see, Jan?" exclaimed Pinder. "The river's not *losing* water to the wells. It's just not *gaining* what it normally would from the aquifer."

"Are you sure about this, George?" Schlichtmann asked.

Pinder beamed. "I figured it out when I was taking a shower this morning."

"George, don't say that on the witness stand."

"Well, that's what happened."

Peggy Vecchione poked her head around the conference room door. "Jan, it's five minutes of nine. You've got to hurry."

Schlichtmann hovered over Pinder, indulging in a last moment of frenetic activity, the sort of nervous energy that he expended every morning before trial. Pinder's explanation seemed logical enough, but Schlichtmann had no time now to explore it for flaws. "You've got the well logs, George?" he asked. "The ones that are highlighted in yellow marker? You've got those, right?"

Pinder compressed his lips and drew his shoulders up. He hated these chaotic moments just before court. They threw him off balance just when he wanted most to compose himself.

Schlichtmann brushed lint from the shoulders of Pinder's blue blazer, and then he stood back and looked appraisingly at the geologist, at the tie with a faint pink hue and the argyle socks. "You look great, George," Schlichtmann lied. "Are you feeling okay?"

"I was feeling fine until I started talking with you," muttered Pinder.

"You'll do just fine today," said Schlichtmann in a soothing voice.

Together they walked briskly up Milk Street to the courthouse, Pinder taking two quick steps for each of Schlichtmann's long strides. The day was sunny and warm and fresh, sweetened by an easterly breeze off the ocean, but Schlichtmann was oblivious to the beauty of the morning. He thought Pinder was showing some pluck, and he admired him for this. But he feared what Facher might do to him today.

. . .

Pinder did not do fine that day. But he did not do badly, either. "In the spirit" escaped his lips twice early that morning. Facher turned to stare at him. "Why do we have to keep talking about the spirit? I'm just asking you for a date." And when Pinder embarked on a convoluted response to one of Facher's questions, the judge abruptly cut him off. "Listen, Professor, the question is very easy," the judge said. "It does not require any more dissection. Let's try talking in plain English."

At the counsel table, Schlichtmann tried to make himself look calm.

It wasn't until late morning when Facher finally got around to the river and the subject of the missing water. How much water, Facher asked, had been pumped out of the Aberjona River during the test of Wells G and H?

Pinder had eagerly awaited this question. "I think very little, if any at all."

"Didn't the river lose approximately six hundred gallons a minute, according to measurements taken by U.S. Geological Survey?" Facher asked.

"No, sir," said Pinder. "You're wrong about that. And I was puzzled by it until I started thinking carefully about it and I realized—"

Facher interrupted. "Before you answer a question I haven't asked," he said.

"I'm just so anxious to try and inform you," said Pinder.

"You're anxious to help me?" said Facher, amused.

"I am, very much, sir," smiled Pinder.

"And I'm anxious to help you," said Facher. "Now, you apparently saw some phenomenon which the untrained eye might interpret as six hundred gallons a minute being pumped out of the river?"

"That's right," said Pinder.

"But the trained eye who had been hired to give an opinion in this case had a ready explanation, right?"

"Not then," said Pinder. "But I do now. I wasn't actually working on the problem when I came up with a solution. It was more like the sort of thing you think about in the shower."

"Shower thoughts?" said Facher with a raised eye. "Before we get to your shower thoughts . . ." Facher calculated that six hundred gallons a minute amounted to 864,000 gallons a day. "Eight hundred and sixty-

four thousand gallons a day, water that's going somewhere, that's leaving the aquifer—"

"No, sir, that's where you're wrong," said Pinder.

"Well, where did it go?" asked the judge impatiently.

"That's the question!" said Pinder happily.

"All right," said Facher, "tell His Honor, tell the jury, tell us all—
where did the eight hundred and sixty-four thousand gallons go?"

"I'd be very pleased to do that." Pinder got off the witness stand and
walked toward the jury box, to an easel that held a diagram of the
aquifer.

Schlichtmann stood, too, and went slowly to one wall of the courtroom, between a filing cabinet and the jury box, where he could see
Pinder at the diagram. Schlichtmann had his hands in pockets, an
informal pose he normally disapproved of in the courtroom, and his
head was down, bent at the neck, his eyes intently studying his shoes.
Without raising his head, his eyes glanced up occasionally at Facher
and Pinder, but mostly he stared at his shoes. He imagined, he said
later, Facher holding a knife up to the light to study its edge, Facher
testing the keenness of the blade on his thumb, Facher vigorously
stropping the knife, Facher testing the blade again. He imagined
Facher whistling pleasantly at his work.

Facher interrupted Pinder's explanation several times to ask questions. And when Pinder finally finished, Facher said, "Your view, then,
is that the river is not losing any water, it's just not gaining from the
usual sources. It's not that you're losing any money, it's just that you
haven't gotten paid this week, is that right?"

"That, in essence, is what I'm trying to express," agreed Pinder.

"Well now, sir," said Facher, "is there anything else you want to add
to that? This is going to be memorialized and I'm going to be looking
at it tonight."

"I'm sure you will," said Pinder.

"Goddamn, George, you kept him at bay!" exulted Schlichtmann on
the walk back to the office. "I could kiss that little bald head of yours!"

Pinder had looked quite pleased with himself until this comment,
which caused him to frown.

But Schlichtmann still felt worried, the worry of a person who knows something is wrong but can't put his finger on it. That evening, when he settled down to work with Pinder in the conference room, he said, "George, about this cockamamie theory of yours—"

"I beg your pardon," said Pinder.

"We've got to talk about it."

"It's very simple, Jan."

"I know it's simple, but is it right?"

By the end of the evening Schlichtmann knew that it was not right. The proof of Pinder's error lay in measurements taken by the U.S. Geological Survey. The Survey had measured the Aberjona's flow at two spots—at a bridge that crossed the river north of the city wells and, a thousand yards downstream, at another bridge south of the wells. If, as Pinder claimed, the river was not really losing water but was simply not gaining any from the aquifer, then one would expect the flow at the upstream measuring device to equal the flow at the downstream device.

But that, Schlichtmann discovered, was not the case. The two measurements were not equal. They showed that the river's flow did indeed decline by six hundred gallons a minute.

Schlichtmann blamed himself. He had sent Pinder the U.S. Geological Survey's measurements along with several boxes of other documents. He'd been too busy with the medical part of the case to pay close attention to Pinder's work, and Pinder had simply overlooked the measurements.

Pinder was trapped. He could not admit to Facher that he'd been wrong on such a fundamental point without calling into question his entire opinion. And he still believed that his opinion was basically sound—the wells *did* draw contaminated groundwater from Beatrice. Nothing else could account for the one-foot drop in the water table that he had seen with his own eyes.

All Pinder could do was bob and weave, and hope for the best.

The next morning, when Facher asked if he recalled saying that no water left the river, Pinder replied, "No, sir, I don't believe I said that, sir."

Facher picked up a copy of the trial transcript. "You said yesterday, 'Water that would normally go into the river is not going into the river anymore. It doesn't mean it's *leaving* the river, it just means it's not going in.' Do you remember that?"

"Yes, sir, I think that's a fair statement. There's going to be a signal to the water molecule that says, 'Stop! Don't go into the river, think about going back to the well.' And that was the spirit in which I answered that."

"Well, the spirit and the words in which you answered it were, 'Water that would normally go into the river is not going into the river anymore.' Could anything be clearer than that? Is that plain English?"

"Yes," replied Pinder. "In the context of what I said, that is what I meant to say."

Pinder bobbed and weaved tirelessly all morning long, a numbing, hypnotic exercise. To one of Facher's questions he shook his head ruefully. "I'm sorry, sir," he said. "The things you're saying are awfully difficult for me to come to grips with because, in many ways, they're contradictory."

Facher looked at the judge and sighed. "I guess I'll have to start all over again."

The judge looked disgusted. "We're approaching hopeless confusion. I'm going to call a recess and suggest very strongly to Dr. Pinder that he take the transcript of his testimony yesterday and read it."

As that day wore on, Judge Skinner had a few more observations to make about Pinder. "You have a hopeless witness who changes from A to B," the judge told Schlichtmann at one bench conference. "The spirit of his answers doesn't change from day to day, but the form certainly does."

"Expert witnesses are born, not made," Schlichtmann said in a low voice, more to himself than anyone else.

"But *you* made him an expert," replied the judge.

Pinder sat at the witness stand while the lawyers huddled a few feet away at the side of the judge's bench for these whispered conferences. Pinder wasn't privy to the comments the judge was making about him, and Schlichtmann, worried about Pinder's already fragile self-confidence, certainly wasn't about to tell him. By now, the fourth day of Facher's cross-examination, Pinder had lost his appetite and developed insomnia. He felt the burden of the case—the Woburn families, all the other experts, Schlichtmann and his partners and their financial investment—entirely on his shoulders. At night he would lie awake in his bed at the Ritz-Carlton thinking about Facher and plotting escapes from Facher's traps. He felt lucky if he got four hours' sleep. He called home to Princeton every evening and talked to his wife. "You can't imagine the pressure," he told her. "There's no relief from it. I've never had anyone try to discredit me as a human being, which is what Facher is trying to do."

Relief finally did come for Pinder on Friday, the sixth day of Facher's cross-examination, when the judge summoned Facher up to the bench and told him enough was enough. "You and the professor are a pair," the judge said wearily. "I detect signs of incipient coma on the part of the jury."

Pinder flew home to Princeton that Friday evening. His wife met him at the airport. She was shocked by his appearance, by his pallor and the dark circles under his eyes.

Pinder returned to Boston the following Monday, but the worst had ended with Facher's cross-examination. Keating spent two days interrogating Pinder, but Keating did not have much to work with. The Grace plant was situated on a promontory northeast of the wells, and no river intervened to complicate matters. Contaminated groundwater from Grace clearly flowed down the bedrock contour the way a marble would roll down a slope, directly to the well field.

Schlichtmann believed that Pinder's opinion was basically right, even if his shower epiphany was not. "The defendants are trying to find salvation in river water, as people have for centuries," Schlichtmann told the judge near the end of Pinder's testimony. "It has very little to do with this case." He tried to rehabilitate Pinder on redirect examination, but he could not erase the damage that Facher had caused. Under questioning from the judge, Pinder conceded that the wells would draw water from the river after a few months of pumping. But Pinder stuck to his opinion that the wells also drew large quantities of contaminated groundwater from the Beatrice land.

As it later turned out, Pinder was generally right. In its final report, released two years after the trial, the EPA concluded that the Beatrice property "contains the most extensive area of contaminated soil" and "represents the area of highest groundwater contamination at the Wells G & H site." The report may have vindicated Pinder, but it came out too late to do Schlichtmann any good.

The great legal scholar John Wigmore wrote in his treatise *On Evidence* that "cross-examination is beyond any doubt the greatest legal engine ever invented for the discovery of truth. A lawyer can do anything with a cross-examination. . . . He may, it is true, do more than he ought to do; he may make the truth appear like falsehood."

"The truth?" Facher said, smiling, one day after court. "The truth is at the bottom of a bottomless pit."

6

The jurors presented Judge Skinner with a gift in the twelfth week of trial, at the end of Pinder's testimony. They had apparently noticed the judge, white-haired and looking somewhat frail, struggle with the heavy leather-padded door that opened from his chambers onto the bench. So the jurors gave him a doorstop made from a piece of polished granite to keep the door propped open. The judge told the lawyers about the gift ("Perhaps it's from the Aberjona," he said, showing them the rock), and no one suggested that anything improper had occurred.

But Schlichtmann found the gift disturbing. That evening he went out to dinner with Phillips and his wife, Julianna. After a bottle of wine, the talk turned to the judge. "That gift shows the jury's got a lot of respect for Skinner," mused Schlichtmann. "But you don't think they're looking at him as if they're asking, Judge, what should we do?"

"Sure they are," said Phillips. "He's an authority figure. The courtroom is a whole different world for them, and Skinner is their guide."

"That frightens me," said Schlichtmann. "If the judge has become a father figure, what happens if they see me as the outcast, the wayward son?"

"Who's Facher in that scenario? The nasty uncle?"

Schlichtmann laughed, and then he turned pensive. "Facher has the strangest mannerisms," he said. "You notice how he looks at the judge when he's asking questions? It's funny he doesn't talk to the jury." Schlichtmann told Julianna about the time he'd gone to Facher's office, how proudly Facher had shown him the picture of his daughter. Under that pride, Schlichtmann thought he'd detected a certain wistfulness in Facher. "He's divorced, a lonely old man," said Schlichtmann. "He's got nothing but the firm."

Julianna thought this was sad. "He's got no one to go home to at night," she said. "What'll happen to him when he retires?"

But Schlichtmann's mood changed abruptly. "Who cares a goddamn?" he said sharply.

Schlichtmann arranged a meeting with the insurance adjusters in the Helen O'Connell case for a Friday in late May, a day that the judge announced there would be no court. Phillips had spent the past six weeks working on O'Connell. He told Schlichtmann the case was ready to settle. Gordon reserved a conference room at the Embassy Suites and Phillips went out to buy a bottle of the finest single-malt Scotch whiskey. With these particular adjusters, it had become a tradition to toast each other and drink whiskey as the negotiation neared a successful conclusion.

On the appointed day Phillips brought out the whiskey bottle and drew a line near the bottom of the label. "Jan, I guarantee you this case will be settled by the time we reach this line," he said.

Schlichtmann smiled. "Then I'll have a drink right now."

By late afternoon, the adjusters had increased their offer to half a million dollars. Schlichtmann had come down from eight hundred thousand to six hundred forty thousand. And there the negotiation stalled. They were all sipping whiskey, but it appeared that the case might not settle after all. The three adjusters retired to a separate room to talk among themselves. Alone with his partners, Schlichtmann proposed reducing their demand to under six hundred thousand. "It's a psychological threshold for them."

Phillips argued against it. "Going for the close too quickly is a big mistake. Let's wait until Monday and take their temperature then."

When the insurance adjusters returned, everyone drank more Scotch. Schlichtmann talked about the Woburn case. He went on for forty-five minutes, never once mentioning the case at hand. Phillips looked at the Scotch bottle and saw the whiskey level ominously close to his mark.

One of the insurance adjusters left the room to make a telephone call. When he returned, he took Schlichtmann aside and said the company that made the anesthetic used in the operation had agreed to contribute ninety thousand dollars to the settlement. The offer was now five hundred ninety thousand. Was that enough?

This time, Schlichtmann and his partners left the room to consult in private. When they came back, Schlichtmann poured a glass of whiskey and proposed a toast.

Schlichtmann's firm received 40 percent of the settlement. In the past, a payday of this sort would have been cause for celebration, dinner out for the entire staff at an expensive restaurant, bonuses all around, and a night of drinking and revelry. But there was no party that night. The entire fee would have to go directly to Gordon, who would use it to pay Woburn bills. The money would disappear as soon as it arrived.

7

Facher began presenting his case in defense of Beatrice on Wednesday morning, June 4, the fifty-fourth day of trial. He called only three witnesses. One of them was Thomas Mernin, the Woburn city engineer. Mernin had lived for thirteen years on Wood Street in east Woburn, right next door to Richard Toomey and his family. It had been Mernin who, many years ago, had insisted that the well water was perfectly safe when Toomey had complained about its odor and taste. As city engineer, Mernin could have done something about the water. He could have ordered the wells shut down.

Facher called Mernin as a witness for the defense precisely because he had not shut the wells. In his capacity as city engineer, Mernin had inspected the entire well field many times in the past fifteen years. He had walked on the Beatrice land. "There were barrels standing around throughout the whole area," Mernin told the court. "But it didn't look any different than any other low area I'd visited. In my mind, it wasn't a problem. I didn't see anything wrong there."

"Did you see anything that looked like contaminated chemicals, or chemical residues?" asked Facher.

"No, I didn't see anything like that. There was nothing out of the ordinary to me."

Under Facher's questioning, Mernin told the jury that he had even recommended installing a third well, to be named Well I, between Wells G and H. "That was the obvious location," explained Mernin. The state approved Well I in 1978 and Mernin advised the mayor to begin construction immediately so the well could be put on line the following year. This never happened, of course, because of the discovery of TCE and other contaminants in Wells G and H.

Facher's intent in calling Mernin was clear to Schlichtmann. If a professional engineer like Mernin had seen no threat to the city wells or danger to the public when he'd walked on Beatrice's land, how then could Riley, a simple tanner, have possibly known or foreseen any danger?

But it came off all wrong for Facher, even before Schlichtmann began his cross-examination. It came off looking as if Mernin had betrayed the public trust by his sheer incompetence. And Mernin seemed dazed and disoriented on the witness stand. He mixed up dates, asserting that Well G had not been installed until 1974, when by now the jury and everyone else who'd paid any attention at all knew perfectly well that it had been installed ten years earlier. Facher assumed Mernin had simply misspoke, but when he circumspectly tried to have Mernin correct the error, the city engineer insisted that he was right. In a conference with the lawyers, the judge himself later said, "The jury might well have considered Mr. Mernin a total idiot. He was not an impressive witness."

Watching Facher's examination of the city engineer, Schlichtmann wondered if Mernin was ill. The man looked tired and thin. He had a naturally swarthy complexion, but a ghostly pallor seemed to lurk beneath. Schlichtmann spent only ten minutes cross-examining him. The engineer's confused testimony spoke for itself, and Schlichtmann figured he would gain nothing by attacking him. Mernin looked relieved when he finally stepped down from the witness stand.

A month later Schlichtmann learned from the Woburn families that Mernin had just been diagnosed with chronic myelogenous leukemia, the same disease that had killed Roland Gamache two months ago. Schlichtmann would have liked to find a way to tell the jury about Mernin's illness, but he could not, at least not in this phase of the trial. He thought perhaps he could manage to slip in the news about Mernin when he called Richard Toomey to the stand in the trial's second phase. Or perhaps he could even call Mernin himself, if Mernin was still alive by then.

Mernin's illness, of course, proved nothing about the cause of the Woburn leukemias. All the same, speculation naturally arose in

Woburn—the irony was too striking—that he had gotten the disease from the water he himself had failed to shut off. Mernin entered the hospital for an aggressive round of chemotherapy. That summer, after Mernin's first hospitalization, Reverend Bruce Young encountered him one morning at the Woburn post office. Reverend Young knew Mernin quite well, having served with him on several city committees. "It's touched me, too," Mernin told the preacher. "There were an awful lot of sick kids."

Schlichtmann heard that Mernin's decline was swift. The city engineer died several months after his diagnosis, at age forty-nine.

In a trial, as in most every endeavor, it's harder to build than it is to tear down. Like most trial lawyers, Schlichtmann enjoyed the destructive pleasures of cross-examination more than the plodding labor of direct examination. He thought he demolished Facher's second witness, a hydrogeologist, who said that contaminated groundwater from Beatrice had never reached the wells. And he did, in fact, expose several contradictions in this expert's opinion, but it wasn't at all clear that a rational juror would dismiss the testimony outright.

Schlichtmann had greater success with Facher's second expert witness, a soil chemist named Olin Braids. Under direct examination by Facher, Braids told the court that he had been able to determine by scientific tests the earliest possible moment at which TCE could have been dumped on the Beatrice land. He had done this by examining the microorganisms in the soil—"It might be easier just to call them soil bugs," Braids said. Some of these soil bugs had a taste for chlorine atoms. They attached themselves to molecules of TCE and broke the TCE down to dichloroethylene, and then to vinyl chloride, a compound so stable that the bugs no longer had any use for it. This process of "biodegradation," said Braids, could take from three to six years, but no longer than six years. Of that, Braids was absolutely certain.

And here lay the significance of Braids's opinion. Since vinyl chloride had not been detected on the Beatrice property until November 1985, that meant, said Braids, that TCE could not possibly have been dumped there more than six years ago, or *before* November 1979. The import of this was obvious. The city wells had been shut down in May 1979, six months before the Beatrice land could have been contaminated. The Woburn families may have been drinking well water laced with TCE but, according to Braids, that TCE could not have come from Beatrice.

This opinion caught Schlichtmann by surprise. He had deposed Braids four months earlier, and Braids had explicitly stated that he would not deal with the question of when the chemicals had been dumped on the Beatrice property.

Up at the bench, Schlichtmann demanded that the judge strike Braids's opinion and instruct the jury to disregard it. "Fundamental fairness would dictate that they at least tell me he's doing this sort of work. They never told me about it. They did it purposely to keep me in the dark."

"It was not done purposely," said Facher indignantly, keeping his voice to a low whisper so the jurors wouldn't overhear.

"It was," Schlichtmann whispered back heatedly.

"Stop it!" said the judge. "You have two problems, Mr. Schlicht-mann—a tremendous sense of overentitlement and an underlying paranoia." The judge refused to strike the opinion.

A surprise or not, Schlichtmann felt convinced that this opinion was, in his words, "a fraud." His own chemists and geologists had told him that there was no scientific way to determine how long TCE had been in the soil. If there had been, he would have used it himself. And besides, the opinion seemed to fit Facher's needs *too* perfectly. How lucky that Facher happened to find Dr. Olin Braids! How fortunate that Braids had determined with such precision that TCE could not have appeared on Beatrice's property until six months after the city wells had closed!

Schlichtmann had no time to prepare a cross-examination of Braids. He would have to play it by ear. Standing in the well of the courtroom, before a gallery of only half a dozen spectators, he asked if Braids had looked at old aerial photographs, old maps, or collected any tannery records—any documentation at all—to determine the history of the Beatrice site. No, admitted Braids. Had Braids ever done this sort of work before, with microbiology and the degradation of chemicals? No, he had not, but he had read "a few articles in professional journals" about the subject. Did these articles say how long it would take for microorganisms to break down TCE? No, said Braids, they didn't. Could Braids describe the exact mechanism by which these soil bugs broke down

TCE? Braids wasn't sure of the mechanism. "It's not in my field. I'm only acquainted with it to the extent that I've read papers about it."

Well, then, said Schlichtmann, did Braids know of anyone who had ever used this method of dating contamination before? No, Braids wasn't aware of anyone's having done it. "In some ways," said Braids, "I'm doing work at what is called 'state of the art' in science. It may be the first time, but I have confidence in what I've done." Was this method accepted by other scientists in the field? "Since it's newly developing and has not been widely published, I guess I'd have to say it isn't widely accepted. I'm not sure a lot of people know about it."

Schlichtmann halted his examination. Again the lawyers gathered at the judge's bench. Again Schlichtmann asked the judge to strike Braids's opinion, this time because it was without any scientific foundation and failed to meet the minimum standards for an expert opinion under the Rules of Evidence.

Judge Skinner considered this motion seriously. "I think you're making a strong point in terms of his credibility," he told Schlichtmann. "I don't know whether I believe him."

Facher grew agitated. Braids's opinion was the heart of Beatrice's defense. "He's used scientific principles. It's a lot more acceptable than Drobinski's methodology," insisted Facher.

Schlichtmann said, "Certainly Drobinski had a better foundation than this witness."

"I don't think so," replied the judge slowly. "Braids has a much more scientific approach than Drobinski, who said, 'I eyeballed this stuff and it looked pretty old to me.' Maybe the jury will find it's a toss-up between Drobinski and soil bugs. I'm not going to strike it."

So Braids's opinion survived on the record. Schlichtmann didn't really mind. The jurors might decide that if this was the best defense Facher could muster, then the case for Beatrice must be weak indeed. Besides, now that he and Facher had reversed their roles, Schlichtmann was having fun.

8

By June Gordon had disbursed the last of the money from the O'Connell settlement. He had spread the money thin, giving small sums to most of the creditors and paying off in full only those who had begun legal action. By Gordon's reckoning, the cost of the Woburn case amounted to $2.4 million to date. Gordon saw no more income on the horizon. He had no choice now but to rely on a variety of stratagems he had used only sparingly before.

Gordon made it a point never to lie to Uncle Pete—or to any creditor, for that matter. When a creditor called him, he never said he had sent a check when he had not. But he was not above sending checks in envelopes with the wrong zip codes, or writing checks and attaching incorrect invoice numbers. When he received a bill from Citicorp Mastercard, he sent a check directly to Citicorp instead of the bank's processing center in South Dakota. "I think this will take them about a month to straighten out," he said hopefully. "Xerox, they're such a huge corporation I can tie them up for months with paperwork. Wang Computer, we owe them thirty thousand dollars for service and maintenance. They're a typical bureaucracy. I can tie them up, too."

Gordon kept in his desk drawer a large collection of credit cards bound with a rubber band. These cards were all charged to the hilt and useless. He had used them to get cash advances to pay operating expenses and salaries. Woburn had turned him into a prodigious consumer of credit, and he often received invitations to apply for new credit cards. These came from banks he had never heard of—in Nevada, Arizona, North Dakota, and California. Gordon called them "shyster cards." The banks would charge 22.9 percent interest, but Gordon didn't mind that. He liked the cards because they required him to pay only 1 or 2 percent of the principal each month. He'd fill out the application forms and send them back by Federal Express. Within a month, each new credit card would be laden with several thousand dollars of debt.

Gordon imagined the Woburn debt as an immense pyramid. Each block of the pyramid represented a creditor, and there were hundreds of them. Keeping all the blocks in place, the pyramid intact, had become exhausting work. "The one day I don't come in—if I get sick or I don't have the energy—that's the point it could all come down," moaned Gordon. Some mornings it seemed he could do nothing but sit in his office on Newbury Street and add up the bills over and over again and take calls from angry creditors. At night he would go home to his Beacon Hill apartment and lie on the living room couch, watching television, the screen flickering in the dark. He tried to find old movies with happy endings that would distract him from his worries. One night on the local Boston news he came upon a lottery announcement. Someone had just won millions of dollars. Gordon decided to buy some Megabucks tickets first thing the next morning. He didn't expect to win, but it would give him something new and amusing to tell Uncle Pete and the creditors who called. He stopped his channel surfing at the Christian Broadcast Network, which was raising money for transponders to beam the word of the Lord behind the Iron Curtain. On the screen, the telephones rang and the pledges poured in, tens of thousands of dollars. The preacher said, "Give and you shall receive." Gordon was impressed. He decided to give so that he might receive. He called in and pledged two memberships in the 700 Club, one for himself and one for Schlichtmann, the two Russian Jews. This is something I can tell Uncle Pete tomorrow morning, Gordon thought.

Pete Briggs was no longer in a mood to be amused by Gordon's stories. The Bank of Boston had a million dollars in loans out to Schlichtmann and his partners. Pete had enough collateral to cover most of those loans—the deeds to Conway's and Crowley's houses, and liens on two large structured-settlement payments due Schlichtmann from previous cases. But Pete was worried all the same. Gordon had under his control half a dozen Bank of Boston accounts—among them an office expense account, a client expense account, a First Rate account, and Schlichtmann's personal account. Pete knew that Gordon had been writing checks from one overdrawn account and depositing the money in another overdrawn account in order to cover overdrafts. At first, Pete had been willing to give Gordon the benefit of the doubt. Perhaps Gordon had made a genuine mistake. But by now Pete was convinced that Gordon had gotten too cute for his own good. Pete knew what was going on, and he didn't like it one bit.

At the Bank of Boston, a list of overdrafts emerged every morning promptly at eleven o'clock from a computer on the third floor. Bankers with cause for concern would gather around to watch the printout, and in recent months Pete Briggs was usually among them. The column on the far right of the printout gave the number of times a given account had been overdrawn that year. According to Pete, four or five overdrafts in a year didn't raise any eyebrows at the bank. Ten or twelve overdrafts, however, was considered sloppy and frowned upon. More than fifteen overdrafts was, as Pete put it, "inappropriate" and would "set off alarm bells."

By June, Gordon had set off many alarm bells. He had overdrawn the Bank of Boston accounts eighty-seven times. Usually Gordon notified Pete in advance of an overdraft, and usually Pete approved it. "I guess it's my style to allow such things," the banker reflected later. "Maybe I shouldn't." Those times when Gordon failed to notify him, Pete would get angry. Gordon was always contrite. "I meant to call you," he'd tell Pete. "I didn't think you'd get the check until tomorrow. I shouldn't have done it."

Pete's superiors had already summoned him upstairs and asked what was going on with these accounts. Pete had explained about the trial, about the collateral covering the loans, but the bouncing checks made him look bad. After his last summons by the senior committee, Pete called Gordon. "No more overdrafts," he said. "I'm not going to approve another one. It makes me look foolish.

Gordon really meant to keep his word to Uncle Pete. For weeks he refrained from bouncing any checks. Then, in early June, he got a visit from Vincent Murphy, head of Weston Geophysical, the environmental consulting company that had drilled forty monitoring wells in Woburn and performed seismic refraction tests and soil and groundwater analysis. The bill for Murphy's work amounted to $598,483.76, the largest single account in the entire case. Gordon had already paid more than half of Murphy's bill, and moreover, he'd become friendly with Murphy during the time they'd spent in Woburn last year. But on this morning Murphy was sharp-tempered and impatient. He wanted to know when Gordon was going to pay the outstanding balance. Gordon showed Murphy the lottery tickets he'd bought. "If we win, you'll be the first one to get paid," Gordon said.

Murphy wasn't amused. "Tell me how bad things really are," he said.

Gordon showed Murphy the computer printout of all the Woburn bills, forty-four pages, neatly bound and arranged alphabetically and chronologically by creditor. "Here's Weston Geophysical, right next to Winchester Hospital."

Murphy knew he was the largest creditor. He demanded a small payment, just a token one. Gordon promised to send a check by the end of the month. Murphy was still unsatisfied. Then Gordon had an idea. He offered to give Schlichtmann's Porsche to Murphy as a down payment. Murphy had seen the car in Woburn, and he had obviously coveted it.

Murphy seemed momentarily tempted by this offer. But then he smiled and shook his head. "You don't have to do that," he said. "How would Jan get around?"

Gordon didn't answer that question. Schlichtmann owed the garage on Beacon Hill a thousand dollars in parking fees and the garage was holding on to the car as collateral. Gordon didn't want to tell Murphy that Schlichtmann was mostly walking.

True to his promise, Gordon called Murphy at the end of the month to say that he was mailing a check for twenty thousand dollars. Gordon didn't have enough money in the various accounts at the Bank of Boston to cover the check, but he'd given his word. He figured it would take four or five days for the check to work its way through the mail and banking system. Anything could happen during that time, thought Gordon. They might win the lottery. Schlichtmann might borrow money from Kiley or Neville. Or, most likely, he'd just have to persuade Uncle Pete to cover another overdraft.

Gordon took Murphy's check down to the mailbox on Newbury Street at six o'clock. He knew from previous experience that the last mail pickup was at six, but he read the posted times again to make certain, and then he put the check in the mail. It was a Thursday evening in late June. Gordon figured Murphy wouldn't receive the check until Monday, and even if he deposited it in his company's account that day, it would take another full day to get back to the Bank of Boston.

The next morning, at two minutes after eleven o'clock, Gordon's secretary said Pete Briggs was on the phone and he sounded angry. "Oh, Jesus," said Gordon.

It was the check for Murphy. It had cleared in record time. Incredible as it seemed, the check had gotten picked and delivered to Weston Geophysical's post office box that very morning. And then Murphy had taken it directly to the Bank of Boston. Gordon hadn't even had a chance to inform Uncle Pete. "That fucking check went through the system like diarrhea," Gordon said in wonderment.

Gordon had his own personal stashes of money, to be used only in the most dire circumstances. Tucked into his sock drawer at home, he kept several tightly folded one-hundred-dollar bills. In the back of his desk drawer at the office he kept two thousand dollars in American Express traveler's checks. And he still had the ten gold Krugerrands in one of his filing cabinets.

After Pete's call, Gordon loaded the Krugerrands into his suit-coat pocket and went over to the Bank of Boston. He walked downstairs to the Private Banking Group, to Uncle Pete's office.

Briggs looked suspiciously at Gordon's bulging pocket. "Are you carrying a gun?" he asked.

Gordon took the Krugerrands out one by one and stacked them on Pete's desk.

Pete shook his head ruefully.

"Things are very bad," said Gordon.

This was Gordon's act of contrition. He felt the need to repent, and the Krugerrands, so dear to him, seemed like a good way to start. Uncle Pete must have understood this. After a while his anger at Gordon waned. But Pete said again there could be no more overdrafts. Never again. There was no more credit.

9

Schlichtmann found himself without money for a cab one morning in late June. He walked to work, down Charles Street and across the Boston Common, under the tall, stately trees with their thick green canopies of leaves. The world flourished in the sweet spring air, but Schlichtmann barely noticed. Inside the office on Milk Street, the ficus trees and ferns had turned brown and died. Coming round the corner from the conference room, Schlichtmann passed the withered, decaying stumps of a large potted corn plant, but he didn't notice that, either.

In the courtroom, however, he made sure to keep up appearances. His hand-tailored suits were always perfectly pressed, his white shirts clean and crisp, his Bally shoes polished to a high gloss. Gordon knew that even if he could pay no one else, he had to pay Schlichtmann's dry-cleaning bill on time.

Schlichtmann's spirits had been rising ever since his artful cross-examination of Facher's soil chemist. Facher's case in defense of Beatrice had taken less than a week, and even the Grace lawyers, who had no wish to see Schlichtmann succeed in any endeavor, agreed privately that it had not gone well for Facher. It was now the sixty-first day of trial, and the waterworks phase was nearing its conclusion. All that remained, aside from the closing arguments, was for Keating to call his witnesses in defense of Grace. Schlichtmann looked forward to this. To him, it seemed obvious that Keating could not mount much of a defense. Keating could not deny that the soil and groundwater under the Grace plant had been polluted in the early 1960s by the acts of its own employees. Nor could Keating deny that contaminated groundwater from Grace flowed downhill from the plant directly to the wells.

But Keating was not without a plan. Like a good defense lawyer in a murder trial, Keating would try to steer the jury away from Grace and in the direction of other culprits—industries in north Woburn that for many years had dumped their wastes into the Aberjona River. He would suggest to the jury that the polluted river, not Grace's groundwater, had contaminated the wells.

This strategy, as it unfolded, appeared quite sound and well constructed. One witness, a sanitary engineer, told how he had followed a small brook, a tributary of the Aberjona, to a complex of industrial buildings two miles upriver from the wells. In a swampy area near those buildings, he'd found many 55-gallon drums and pails scattered about. "The closer I got to the industry, the more horrified I became," the engineer told the jury. Coming from one of the buildings was a "white resiny scum" and a "bright orange-colored effluent" that stained the water and the banks.

Keating's next witness, a supervisor at the Division of Water Pollution Control, told a similar story. He had investigated one particular company, National Polychemical, for the past ten years. "We still had pollution coming from that site," the supervisor said. "It wasn't coming out of thin air. The only logical conclusion was that it was seeping out of that site."

On cross-examination, Schlichtmann said to the supervisor: "The company was still denying after ten years that they had a water-pollution problem?"

"Yes," replied the supervisor.

"They were still saying it was somebody else's fault, weren't they?"

"Yes, sir."

"You encounter that often when you're investigating an industry, that attitude?"

"Yes, I do," said the supervisor.

Schlichtmann nodded, as if to indicate he understood this perfectly.

It took Keating four witnesses and a week of testimony to lay the foundation for his last and most important witness. This was a groundwater expert named John Guswa who, as it happened, knew George Pinder quite well. "I worked with George in the Geological Survey," Guswa had said at his deposition. "I've had dinner with him. I respect him as a person and as a professional." All the same, Guswa was certain that Pinder had been wrong about the river. The wells did draw water from the river, and that, Guswa would later assert, was how they had become contaminated.

But first Guswa had to explain why, in his scientific opinion, W. R. Grace could not have contaminated the wells. As a graduate student, Guswa had specialized in the study of glaciers, and he brought that specialty to bear on the Woburn case. The terrain of east Woburn, he explained to the jury, had been shaped twelve thousand years ago, at the end of the last Ice Age, when an immense glacier more than a mile thick had covered the New England landscape. In its advance and retreat, the glacier had deposited a layer of soil fifty feet deep on the bedrock ridge where the Grace plant was now located. Soil of that type, compressed under the glacier's enormous weight, was known to geologists as ground moraine, or hardpan. It was densely compacted and groundwater seeped through it very slowly, like water trickling through a pipe stuffed with sediment.

Like "a stuffed pipe"—that was how Guswa told the jury to imagine the subterranean path from Grace to the wells. Guswa had an infectious, almost boyish enthusiasm for the subject of glacial morphology. He was forty-one years old, clean-shaven with a shock of thick brown hair that often fell down over his forehead. He had constructed a sophisticated three-dimensional computer model of the east Woburn groundwater system, using hundreds of data points. He explained how rain falling on the Grace property seeped into the earth, carrying with it the TCE and other solvents dumped on the ground by workers. The contaminated groundwater from Grace was indeed moving down toward the wells, Guswa admitted, but the "pipe," clogged with ground moraine that had the "permeability of concrete," had backed everything up. His computer model proved this, he said. "It's my conclusion that even if the chemicals were released to the groundwater system on the day the plant opened in 1960, they could not have reached Wells G and H by May of 1979."

All of this information was new to Schlichtmann. He had deposed Guswa six months ago, and the geologist had said then that he had not determined how quickly groundwater moved from Grace to the wells. If Guswa was right, then Schlichtmann had just lost his case against W. R. Grace.

But Schlichtmann knew that Guswa *had* to be wrong. The bare facts—contamination at Grace, the same contamination in the city wells, and a direct path from Grace to the wells—should have made Guswa's opinion look as ridiculous as Olin Braids's soil bugs testimony. So Schlichtmann thought. But even Schlichtmann could see that Guswa was not Braids. Guswa had used accepted scientific methods. He was an engaging and credible witness. And, quite unlike Braids, his explanation at least *sounded* plausible.

At the office that evening, Schlichtmann and Nesson spent several hours going over Guswa's testimony. Pinder had gone to Europe for a conference of geologists and groundwater specialists, so they couldn't consult him. They worked late that evening, but they couldn't come up with anything. Keating would have Guswa on the stand for two more days. They had to figure out how to prove Guswa wrong by then. When Nesson left the office, he took with him several of Pinder's hydrogeology textbooks.

The next morning, Schlichtmann watched Guswa take the witness stand again and reiterate his assertions of yesterday. Then Guswa added a new calculation: The wells, running at full capacity, pumped eleven hundred gallons a minute. Even if all the contaminated Grace groundwater did get to the wells—and Guswa was not admitting that any did, given the density of ground moraine, but assuming for a moment that it did—Grace's contribution would amount to only five gallons a minute. In this hypothetical scenario, the groundwater from Grace would amount to less than one half of 1 percent, the proverbial drop in the bucket.

Nesson, seated next to Schlichtmann at the counsel table, listened to all of this attentively. When Guswa began demonstrating his point on the portable blackboard, Nesson scribbled notes on his legal pad.

Standing before the jury, Guswa estimated that an average of twelve inches of rainfall would seep into the earth and become groundwater in any given year. He multiplied those twelve inches, or one cubic foot, by the area of the Grace property, which occupied a square approximately six hundred feet on each side. This gave him an annual total of 2.7 million gallons of water entering the ground, a seemingly large amount, Guswa admitted, but not once he reduced it to gallons per minute and compared that with the amount pumped by the wells.

When Guswa finished presenting this calculation, Nesson stuffed his notes into his briefcase and hurriedly left the courtroom, pushing his way out the heavy swinging doors.

Schlichtmann hardly noticed Nesson's sudden departure. Nesson, alone among the lawyers, came and went from the courtroom as he pleased. Besides, Schlichtmann was pondering Guswa's new calculation. Each element of it made sense, but why had Keating thought it necessary? After all, Guswa had made a convincing argument yesterday that nothing had ever gotten from Grace to the wells. Schlichtmann wondered if Guswa had come up with this calculation last night, brainstorming with the lawyers. He could imagine Keating and Cheeseman saying to each other, "Hey, that's great! Let's put it in." Schlichtmann felt there was something peculiar about it all, but he couldn't put his finger on the problem. He'd talk it over with Nesson as soon as Nesson returned.

Nesson didn't return to the courtroom that day. Nor did he show up at the office later that afternoon. Schlichtmann called Nesson's office at Harvard, but his secretary hadn't seen him. Then, in rising consternation, he called Nesson's home in Cambridge, but there was no answer. Time was running out. Schlichtmann would have to begin cross-examining Guswa tomorrow. "Where the hell is Charlie?" Schlichtmann yelled from the conference room.

Nesson was still missing the next morning. When Keating finished his direct examination of Guswa, Facher got up to ask the Grace expert a few questions. As co-defendants, Facher and Keating had agreed not to help Schlichtmann by pointing fingers at each other during the trial. Facher knew that Guswa would not deliberately hurt Beatrice. In reply to Facher, Guswa told the jury there wasn't enough information for him, or any groundwater expert, to determine whether TCE from Beatrice had reached the wells. The groundwater flowed into an area that Guswa called "the zone of uncertainty." This opinion seemed to satisfy Facher.

It was Schlichtmann's turn to cross-examine. He and Nesson had already devised a line of questioning that had to do with Beatrice, not Grace. It didn't deal with the real threat Guswa posed, but it looked promising, and Schlichtmann knew it would get him through the rest of the day. He hoped he could use Guswa to prove that Pinder had been right—that TCE from Beatrice would flow under the river to the wells.

Schlichtmann read aloud to Guswa the water-level measurements that had been taken during the pump test. Then he had Guswa calculate the direction of groundwater flow based on these measurements, using the simple method of triangulation. Guswa did so, and by the time he finished, he had groundwater from Beatrice flowing in the direction of the wells.

The judge listened intently to Schlichtmann's examination. Then he interrupted Schlichtmann and began interrogating Guswa himself. Would the river form a barrier between the wells and the Beatrice property? the judge asked.

Guswa said, "There's no barrier or wall of water under the river."

"No barrier?" the judge said.

"No," replied Guswa.

"So water could flow from the Beatrice site, under the river, to the area of the wells, as far as you're concerned? That's one of the possibilities?"

"It's one of the possibilities, yes, sir," Guswa admitted.

At the Beatrice counsel table, Facher grew visibly agitated. He objected to the judge's questions, but the judge paid him no mind. When Schlichtmann resumed questioning Guswa, Facher stood and lurched forward to the witness stand, toward Guswa, interrupting Schlichtmann's cross-examination, a loss of poise that was most unusual in Facher.

"Wait a minute, wait a minute," the judge said to Facher, holding up his hand.

Facher looked up at the judge. "The measurements, he's asking for all the measurements."

"The witness seems able to understand the question," said the judge. "I don't think he needs any help."

Guswa had not meant to implicate Beatrice, and he had not done so willingly. In the end, he said to Schlichtmann, in apparent frustration, "I have to direct our efforts at our problem. Beatrice has to take care of their problem. You have to take care of your problem."

Schlichtmann had gotten what he'd wanted. He'd turned Guswa into a witness against Beatrice, and doing so had taken him to the end of the day. But he still hadn't figured out how, in Guswa's words, to take care of his problem with Grace. He had no plan for tomorrow. And Nesson was still missing. Kathy Boyer had called around all day looking for Nesson, to no avail.

Nesson had gone to the only place he knew he could work without interruption—the Harvard Law School faculty library, on the top floor of the Griswold Building. Like Schlichtmann, he had the sense that there was a simple and obvious way, just beyond his immediate grasp, to prove Guswa wrong. It was a riddle, and riddles of this sort had always appealed to Nesson.

He began with the premise that groundwater from Grace did get to the wells. He accepted that as a physical truth. Guswa's ground moraine theory, therefore, had to be flawed. But Nesson couldn't hope to find the flaw in Guswa's computer model. Checking and verifying the hundred pieces of data that went into the model would take weeks and he had only hours.

The way to solve this riddle had eluded Nesson until Guswa began making his five-gallon-a-minute calculation. Even then, Nesson hadn't known the solution, but he felt certain he had enough information to work with. And that was why he'd left the courtroom so suddenly.

By this time Nesson was familiar with the basic principles of hydrogeology. From Pinder he'd learned about Darcy's Law, the basis for virtually every calculation in hydrogeology. It was a simple mathematical formula, devised by a nineteenth-century Frenchman, to compute the flow of water through porous media. The law stated that the quantity of water (Q) flowing through a given area is equal to the hydraulic conductivity (K) of the material through which it flows, multiplied by the size of the opening (A), multiplied again by the gradient, or angle of incline (I). Thus: $Q = K \times A \times I$. Once one knew what values to put into the formula, it was quite easy to work out. Unlike Guswa's splendid three-dimensional computer model, it required only a pencil and paper.

Nesson began working out the equation, using the values Guswa had supplied on the morning of his five-gallon-a-minute calculation. Nesson discovered immediately that the equation did not balance. He assumed for the moment that Guswa was right about twelve inches of annual rainfall entering the groundwater system through Grace. He assumed further that Guswa was right about the angle of incline toward the wells and also the low conductivity of ground moraine. How big, then, Nesson asked himself, would the opening—the pipe, as it were—have to be to accommodate the volume of water that flowed through the system? Using X to represent the size of the opening, Nesson performed some simple algebra and reworked the equation so that it looked like this:

$$X = \frac{Q}{K \times I}$$

The moment he completed the math, he knew he'd found the way to prove Guswa wrong. It was simple to understand and elegant, and it had the singular virtue of using Guswa's own values to provide a damning answer.

Schlichtmann sat in the conference room with Conway and Kiley, wondering what he would do with Guswa the next day. It was early evening when Nesson walked in, smiling broadly. Schlichtmann jumped up and shouted. "For Christ's sake, Charlie, where the hell have you been?"

Nesson smiled. "I've figured out how to nail Guswa."

Everyone gathered around to watch as Nesson wrote Darcy's Law on the blackboard. "Go slow, Charlie," warned Schlichtmann when he saw the equation. "You're talking to someone who can't balance his own checkbook."

The next morning, Schlichtmann began obliquely, without mentioning Darcy's Law, by getting Guswa to agree to his own previously stated values—the hydraulic conductivity of ground moraine, the area of the Grace plant, the amount of rainfall entering the system. This took Schlichtmann longer than he'd anticipated, and by the close of the day he'd set Nesson's trap but he hadn't sprung it.

"Is this a place you want to stop?" the judge asked in consternation. "There must be something that follows from all this. It seems to me there's a question missing."

"I can go further," said Schlichtmann. "Can you give us fifteen minutes?"

Keating suspected that Schlichtmann was about to do something he wouldn't like. He made a halfhearted protest, but the judge brushed that aside.

"Fifteen minutes," said the judge, "so we won't have to be in suspense."

Schlichtmann wrote the formula for Darcy's Law on the board. "Darcy's Law states that what goes in has to come out, or is left behind, is that right?" he asked Guswa.

"Yes," said Guswa.

"You take the hydraulic conductivity—that's the permeability of a material—and you multiply that by the opening the water has to pass through, right? And then you multiply that by the incline down which the water travels."

Guswa agreed with all this. Schlichtmann had Guswa come up to the chalkboard in front of the jury box and write out the formula using the values for the Grace property. "Now," continued Schlichtmann, "if we didn't know how big the opening was, if we were to call that X, we could rearrange the equation to find that out."

"Yes," agreed Guswa, "we have to go back to basic math."

Schlichtmann rewrote the equation to find X. Then he asked Guswa to do the math and calculate the height of the opening.

Guswa worked in silence, punching numbers into his calculator. "Fifty-nine feet," he said at last.

"Fifty-nine feet," repeated Schlichtmann. He asked Guswa to measure off that height, beginning at the bedrock, which Guswa himself had said would carry away only a small amount of water.

Guswa, looking grim, did so. "It's about ten feet above the land surface," he said.

This had been Nesson's discovery. Assuming that Guswa's figures, which formed the basis for his opinion, were correct, then Darcy's Law dictated that the Grace plant would be submerged under a lake of water ten feet deep.

Back at the office late that afternoon, Schlichtmann heard the distant sound of a jackhammer from up the street, from the direction of the courthouse. The faint noise drifted in the open windows of the conference room. Schlichtmann cupped his ear to the sound. "Listen!" he cried. "You hear that? It's Guswa trying to get water through the bedrock!"

"Last night there was a wall of water ten feet high sweeping down the Aberjona Valley," Judge Skinner said the next morning, after the jurors had taken their seats.

Schlichtmann abandoned the traditional form of cross-examination that morning. He did what every seasoned trial lawyer and every handbook on trial practice preached against. He gave control of the courtroom to Guswa, confident that Guswa could not have devised any escape. "Why don't you just explain your position to the jury now," Schlichtmann said in an agreeable tone of voice. "Would you like to do it on the board?"

This offer seemed to surprise Keating. "Do you want Dr. Guswa to say what he's doing?"

"Sure," said Schlichtmann cheerfully.

Guswa labored at the chalkboard that morning. True to Schlichtmann's prediction, Guswa had groundwater flowing deep into the bedrock, a hundred feet down, three hundred feet, a thousand feet, in all directions along cracks and fissures that existed only in hypothesis. He culled dozens of numbers, changing gradients and permeability, multiplying and dividing numbers in an effort to salvage his theory. He stood at the board in front of the jury box and muttered numbers to himself, punching them into his calculator. "Now, how am I going to do this here?" he said under his breath at one point.

Schlichtmann let Guswa go on for a while, watching silently from a spot near the jury box. After a time, the judge asked Guswa, "The bedrock, I take it, has a saturation point? It'll only hold so much water?"

"That's correct," said Guswa.

"So," continued the judge, "if water is coming into the bedrock on a daily basis, the same amount is leaving?"

"That's correct," said Guswa again. "It's going down and picking up a lateral component in some direction but—"

"But you don't know where it's going?" said the judge.

"No, sir," admitted Guswa.

Guswa looked drawn and very tired, his boyish enthusiasm gone now. Schlichtmann turned to the one remaining element of Keating's defense—the theory that the river had transported TCE and other contaminants from industries in north Woburn down to the wells. He invited Guswa up to the chalkboard again. Guswa took a deep breath and sighed.

Schlichtmann asked him if TCE had been detected in the river water or in the river's banks, adjacent to the wells. No, replied Guswa, it had not. If the TCE in the wells had in fact been drawn from out of the river, continued Schlichtmann, wouldn't you expect to find traces of TCE in the riverbed? And in the sandy soil directly under the river?

Yes, said Guswa, you would expect to find traces.

"But when we look directly under the river, we don't find anything, right?" asked Schlichtmann.

Guswa agreed that was true.

"When we look deeper under the river, we still don't find anything. We keep looking deeper, and then we find TCE in the hundreds of parts per billion, don't we?"

"That's the pattern we see," replied Guswa.

"That pattern is consistent with the fact that no contamination came from the Aberjona River, isn't it?"

"It is not the only explanation," said Guswa, "but it is consistent, yes."

"Let me ask you this," continued Schlichtmann. "Is it possible that the contamination could have come from an area to the northeast and to the west of the wells? Is that at least possible?"

This question had enormous import. The Grace plant lay to the northeast and Beatrice to the west. The EPA, in its preliminary report, had identified those areas as likely sources of the contamination, although it had not named either Grace or Beatrice. The judge had refused to let Schlichtmann show this report to the jury, but Guswa, of course, had read it.

Guswa considered Schlichtmann's question for a long moment, perhaps thinking about the EPA report. At last he said slowly, "That's possible."

Schlichtmann seemed satisfied with this admission, but Judge Skinner was not. "Well," said the judge, "that type of question has to be followed up. Is it probable, yes or no?"

"Probable?" said Guswa, looking up at the judge. "I think it's a probable possibility—"

"No, no," said the judge. "I'm asking you flat out: Is the explanation Mr. Schlichtmann presented to you a probable explanation?"

"Flat out?" repeated Guswa.

"Yes," nodded the judge.

"Yes, that's a probable source."

Schlichtmann had broken Guswa, in large part thanks to Nesson's ingenuity and dormant gift for mathematics. It could not have happened at a more telling moment—during the cross-examination of the last witness at the end of a long trial.

That evening, everyone in the office, secretaries, paralegals, and receptionists included, went downstairs to celebrate at Patten's Bar & Grill, where nine months ago Rikki Klieman had first mentioned Nesson's name. Schlichtmann had a long-standing tab at the bar, and the owner, who knew all about the Woburn case, didn't press for payment.

Schlichtmann drank martinis and toasted Nesson. Spirits were high all around. Schlichtmann was too happy with his victory to be gracious. "Guswa gave up his soul today," he said. "What little was left of it."

10

On the first day of July, a sunny, cloudless morning, the lawyers, the judge, and the jurors boarded a yellow school bus in Post Office Square and set out for Woburn. The jurors had asked the judge some months ago, near the start of trial, if they would be allowed to see the Woburn city wells and the Aberjona River. Now, all the witnesses having come and gone, the judge decided that they should see the places they'd heard so much about. The six jurors and six alternates sat together in the first several rows of the bus. The lawyers and the judge sat toward the back, separated from the jurors by four empty rows. The judge had told the jurors to wear casual clothes and old, sturdy shoes. "I'll wear something like a bush outfit, myself," he'd said. So Schlichtmann had gone shopping for an outfit suitable for a safari. Phillips had accompanied Schlichtmann on the shopping trip and treated him to a pair of new pleated khakis, a green twill shirt, a belt, and hiking shoes. Schlichtmann had wanted a safari jacket and a wide-brimmed desert hat, too, but Phillips had refused him those.

Only Facher came wearing his regular courtroom apparel. "You're ready to sacrifice a suit," the judge said to Facher.

"It's like walking through your own backyard," said Facher. "I'll take my tie off. I'll make that concession."

The expedition visited most of the pertinent spots. At the W. R. Grace plant, two flagpoles, one flying an American flag and the other a Grace flag, flanked the glass entryway. The plain red-brick façade of the plant was clean and neatly landscaped. On this clear blue day, with the Grace logo gleaming silver in the sun and the flags fluttering in the summer breeze, the scene could have served as a photograph in W. R. Grace's annual report.

The jurors and the lawyers began a tour of the plant, Cheeseman leading the way. They walked through the production and assembly areas, which were clean-swept and immaculate, the machinery shining as if it had just been polished. No one seemed to be working that day. The employees stood apart from the group of visitors, eyeing them warily. The entourage was about to go out the back door, past the paint shop where Barbas had worked, when a juror, Jean Coulsey, the forklift lady, halted abruptly and said, "No, no. Mr. Schlichtmann, I want to see the paint booth." Schlichtmann had felt uncertain about Coulsey, but suddenly he thought better of her.

Schlichtmann had heard from the families that the Grace plant had been recently landscaped, with new picnic tables and newly planted vegetable gardens, in preparation for the jury's visit. He asked the judge to let him inform the jury of this, but the judge denied his request. As the group went out the back door of the plant, where Barbas and Joe Meola and the other Grace workers had gone out daily to dump solvents, they came upon several large, meticulously cultivated vegetable gardens. The tomato plants were neatly staked and already tall and leafy. "Joe Meola's own homegrown toxic tomatoes," said Patti D'Addieco softly to Schlichtmann.

The school bus drove through the woods up a narrow, pitted blacktop road to the edge of the Aberjona marsh, to the remnants of Wells

G and H. The mayor of Woburn had ordered the well houses bulldozed last March, on the third day of trial, and all that remained of them were a few scattered pieces of building debris and two large, square concrete foundations. Weeds had taken root in the cracks of the concrete.

Everyone stood in the clearing for a moment, a solemn tableau of people in the July sun, gazing at these remnants as if they might somehow reveal secrets. But there was not really much to see, and after a minute the solemnity that seemed to have come on the group suddenly lifted and was carried away, as if on a summer breeze.

Talking gaily and laughing among themselves, like schoolchildren on a field trip, the jurors filed out to the eastern bank of the Aberjona River. They walked on a boardwalk of thick planks laid atop the grassy tussocks of the marsh. It had been a dry spring and the Aberjona was now only a sluggish stream a few feet wide. The judge surveyed the watershed, looking across the river to the Beatrice property three hundred feet away, his hand up to his brow to shield his eyes from the sun. The metal and plastic casings from the monitoring wells, more than a hundred and fifty of them in this area, protruded like pegs three feet above the marsh surface, glinting in the sunlight. "I wonder who'll be liable if the whole crust of the earth caves in because it's been pierced so many times," mused the judge.

Facher overheard this. "I'll tell you who the defendant will be—whatever large company that owns the land."

The jurors and the lawyers walked up the dirt road to Beatrice's fifteen acres, past the Whitney Barrel Company, now out of business, and through the gate of the chain-link fence that the EPA had ordered Beatrice to erect. The land was heavily wooded, lush and green in the early New England summer. Tall thistles grew alongside the road. Facher bent down and picked a daisy, which he presented to Patti D'Addieco. She smiled and thanked him. He said he'd buy her an ice cream cone after lunch, but he never did.

The EPA had warned the judge that no one should stray off the dirt road because of dangerously high levels of contaminants. The shoulders of the road, cluttered with barrels and building debris not so long ago, had been recently cleared. Nesson spied some newly sown grass seed and pointed it out to Schlichtmann. Someone had obviously been out to spruce up the area for the jury's view.

Schlichtmann watched as one of the jurors, Robert Fox, stood near the edge of the marsh and gazed over at the remains of the city wells, a few hundred feet away. "My God," he heard Fox say, "I didn't realize it was so close."

As the group walked up the road, Patti sidled up to Schlichtmann. She did not trust Fox. "I don't think he's with you, Jan," she told Schlichtmann.

"You're wrong," insisted Schlichtmann. "He's an environmentalist. He said at the *voir dire* he gave to the Public Interest Research Group."

11

Gordon's precariously balanced pyramid of debt was crumbling around him. Helpless to do anything about it, he began consulting horoscopes to see what the future would bring. He purchased a copy of *Town & Country*, which he believed had the most reliable horoscopes, but it only made his mood worse. The planetary alignment in Pisces, Schlichtmann's sign, was ominous. "Very bad time for you," Gordon told Schlichtmann the morning after the Woburn trip. "Something comes in that's not supposed to be there and fucks everything up. The only good thing is, it goes away."

"Why do you have to tell me these things?" Schlichtmann said irritably. "Let's hope it is goes away before the jury starts deliberating."

The jurors wouldn't start deliberating for several days yet. The judge had given them the rest of the week off, with the familiar admonition not to read about or discuss the case with anyone. In the courtroom, the judge and the lawyers had important business to attend to before the final arguments.

A month ago, when Pinder stepped off the witness stand for the last time and Schlichtmann finished his case in chief against Beatrice and Grace, the judge had made a ruling. Both Facher and Keating had asked the judge to end the trial then and there, to direct a verdict in their clients' favor on the grounds that the evidence presented by Schlichtmann was not legally sufficient to support a jury's verdict.

Motions for directed verdicts are customary at the close of the plaintiff's case, although judges rarely grant them. The Rules of Civil Procedure require a judge to consider the evidence in a light most favorable to the plaintiff, and even a mere "scintilla" of evidence usually suffices to send a case to the jury. Judge Skinner had made it clear he wouldn't direct a verdict for Grace ("There's no question you funneled it out there and splat! into a ditch," he'd told Keating), but Schlichtmann's evidence against Beatrice had clearly troubled him. The judge had invited Facher to make "a serious pitch" for a directed verdict.

With the jurors excused for the morning, the judge had heard oral arguments and told the lawyers he would notify them of his rulings that afternoon. For Schlichtmann, it had been a typical day. He'd returned to the office feeling confident. By midafternoon, that feeling had begun to wane. At four o'clock, he'd told Conway he had a "miserable, queasy feeling." At five o'clock, he'd muttered a prayer under his breath. At six o'clock, standing at the window, looking down onto Milk Street, he'd said, "The judge is going to fuck me, I just know it."

The judge finally did call at a quarter to seven. As expected, Schlichtmann's case against Grace remained intact. But in the matter of Beatrice, the judge had seriously undermined Schlichtmann's case. To begin with, the judge would not allow the jury to hold Beatrice liable for any acts or omissions before 1968, the year Riley had learned from his own well digger that the water table under the fifteen acres had declined because of pumping by the city wells. Prior to this notice, said the judge, Beatrice, in the person of Riley, could not have known that toxic wastes on its land would contaminate Wells G and H. Furthermore, the judge continued, Beatrice had no "special relationship" with the plaintiffs and other consumers of water, and thus owed no duty to warn the public or city officials about conditions on its land, even after receiving the 1968 notice.

Schlichtmann and his partners had debated the effect of these rulings until late in the night. The judge's actions had seemed bizarre to all of them. Riley had known as early as the 1950s that tannery waste on the fifteen acres could pollute the Aberjona marsh. Trying to follow the judge's logic, Schlichtmann had said, "It's like someone slipping a cyanide capsule into a bottle of Tylenol and putting it on a drugstore shelf late one night. Nothing wrong with that! It only becomes a crime when the drugstore opens the next morning." Nesson had been convinced that the judge had made a serious legal mistake. Skinner had overlooked the well-established principle that landownership per se creates a duty to warn any persons who could be injured by dangerous conditions on that land. The next morning, Nesson had asked the judge to reconsider his ruling. The judge had replied testily. "I, very frankly, busted my butt the first time and I won't do it again. Motion is denied."

To Schlichtmann, it had seemed as if the judge had made up his mind first and then found reasons to support his view. He'd taken solace in the fact that Facher was still in the courtroom, still sitting at the counsel table. In the end, it had been Conway who best summed up what had happened. "It's worse than we expected, but we're still alive. The bottom line is, we've survived."

And Judge Skinner himself had seemed to echo this assessment. He had greeted the jurors after their absence and told them he'd made some rulings. "But I needn't plague you with all the details at this time. The basic aspects of the case are still before you."

In a trial, the events of a month ago can seem like ancient history. The judge's directed verdict rulings did not have an immediate impact, and for that reason they quickly faded into the background. Schlichtmann had been too busy to worry about them. But now, just before final arguments, as the lawyers met again with the judge, the rulings became important. The judge said he would instruct the jury not to consider any exhibits or evidence against Beatrice prior to 1968. The testimony of witnesses such as Walter Day, who had played on the Beatrice land as a boy and described it as Death Valley, was stricken from the case. "I don't see how it's relevant," the judge said.

"Not relevant?" cried Schlichtmann in disbelief. "The most important part of his testimony is the drums."

"You've got more drums in your testimony than you know what to do with," replied the judge, who went on to exclude Schlichtmann's "killer document"—the 1956 report by state agent A. C. Bolde, who had ordered Riley to remove five hundred feet of tannery sludge deposited along the edge of the marsh. The report, said the judge, was "remote in time and subject matter."

Schlichtmann felt a rising sense of panic. That evidence, he argued, went to the heart of Riley's state of knowledge and his awareness of the risks of pollution near the Aberjona River. But the judge was unmoved. And when Nesson tried once again to point out to the judge his error of law, he succeeded only in angering him. "One of the ways you prompt me to think about correcting this is by directing a verdict for Beatrice," the judge told Nesson.

"You really know how to hurt a guy," said Nesson.

"I'm serious about this," replied the judge. "The best case against Beatrice is a mighty thin case. It was really a very close call on the motion for a directed verdict."

The discussion moved on to the questions the jury would have to answer in reaching its verdict. Juries are usually asked simply whether they find for the plaintiff or for the defendant. But Judge Skinner pointed out that the date TCE and the other solvents arrived at the wells would be critically important in the second phase, the medical phase, of trial, presuming the case got that far. "Simply to say that the chemicals got there sometime before May 1979 is not going to do the trick," the judge told the lawyers.

He asked the lawyers to prepare a draft of the questions they thought the jury should answer. Schlichtmann would have liked one simple question for each defendant—Were Beatrice and Grace responsible for contaminating the wells before May 1979?—but nothing in this case had been that simple. Both Facher and Keating submitted long lists of complicated questions, all of which the jurors would have to answer in the affirmative to proceed to the next phase.

The lawyers and the judge argued for two days about the questions, endless arguments about phrases, words, prepositions, and commas, like rabbinical scholars arguing fine points of the Talmud. Schlichtmann kept trying to simplify, Facher and Keating kept trying to put elements back in. The judge seemed to recognize the need for simplicity. "My God," he said at one point. "To ask them a question like that! You're talking to plain folks, you know. You've got to cast these in some form of language that is not hedged around with reservations and clauses and subclauses and commas and all that."

"That's right!" agreed Schlichtmann. "It's the most ridiculous thing in the world."

In the end, however, the questions were the work of a committee whose members had already demonstrated their inability to agree on just about anything. The judge finally decided on four questions for each defendant, all of which contained plenty of clauses, subclauses, and commas. First: Had the plaintiffs established by a preponderance of the evidence that any of the following chemicals—TCE, perc, and 1,2 transdichloroethylene—were disposed on the Beatrice land after August 27, 1968 (in the case of W. R. Grace, after October 1, 1964, the date Well G had opened), and had these chemicals substantially contributed to the contamination of the wells before May 22, 1979? If the answer should be yes for one or more of the chemicals, then the second question: What, according to a preponderance of the evidence, was the earliest date—both the month and year—at which each of these chemicals had substantially contributed to the contamination of the wells? And then: Had this happened because of the defendants' failure to fulfill any duty of care due to the plaintiffs?

Finally, if the jurors answered yes to that question, then this puzzler: What, according to a preponderance of the evidence, was the earliest time (again, both the month and year) at which the substantial contribution referred to in question 3 was caused by the negligent conduct of this defendant. . . . ?

All in all, the questions had the quality of a text that had been translated from English into Japanese and back again. The judge himself seemed to realize this. "I'm sure it can be improved upon," he muttered at the end of his labors. "But with the shortness of life, it requires us to bring this to an end."

In truth, these questions were all but impossible to understand. An expert in semantics would have had a hard time finding his way through the thicket of words. But even worse, they asked for answers that were essentially unknowable. Science could not determine the moment when those chemicals had arrived at the wells with the sort of precision Judge Skinner was demanding of the jurors. The judge was, in effect, asking the jurors to create a fiction that would in the end stand for the truth. Or, if they found themselves unable to do that, to end the case by saying they couldn't answer the questions based on the evidence. If these questions really were necessary to a just resolution of this case, then perhaps the case was one that the judicial system was not equipped to handle. Perhaps it should never have been brought to trial in the first place.

Like everyone else in the courtroom, Nesson knew the jurors faced a very difficult task. But he emphatically did not believe the fault lay with the judicial system, or even with the judge's questions, for that matter. The real problem, thought Nesson, had begun five months ago when the judge had divided the trial into separate parts. What if Schlichtmann had been allowed to present the case in its entirety? The jurors would have heard evidence about when the Woburn families first began to experience the symptoms of solvent poisoning—the chronic rashes among the children, the gastrointestinal problems, the burning eyes, the cardiac arrhythmias, and, of course, the leukemias. These symptoms all bore the fingerprint, so to speak, of the contamination in the wells. The jurors could have used this evidence to assist them in determining when the solvents first got to the wells. But the judge, in fragmenting the case, had deprived the jurors of this information.

At this stage of the trial, there was little anyone could do to remedy that. But Nesson hoped he might do something about the questions, so he rose to address the judge. It was, he said, highly prejudicial to the plaintiffs' case to ask the jurors for a specific date when they had not yet heard all the evidence.

The judge listened intently as Nesson explained his rationale. "What you say is very interesting," mused the judge. "It's also very disturbing. On the one hand, you say that TCE is the cause of all these people's symptoms because TCE is in the water. Then, in the next breath, you turn around and say that because all these people got these symptoms, we therefore conclude that TCE was in the water. This suggests to me that you're bootstrapping. If that's true, I'm wondering whether there's any point in proceeding. You might as well call this case to a halt right now because you can't possibly win it."

Schlichtmann, sitting at the counsel table, tugged on Nesson's coat. "Don't let him bully you, Charlie," he whispered. But Nesson was ready to sit down. "I'm not the best person to speak to the medical part of the case," he said to the judge. "Mr. Schlichtmann is. With your permission, I'll recede."

Schlichtmann assured the judge that he would not rely on the medical evidence to prove that TCE had been in the well water. Mr. Nesson had meant only that there was additional information the jurors might take into account, "perhaps only five, or two, percent of the equation." Even so, the jury had plenty of evidence right now to reach a verdict on when the wells became contaminated. "Frankly," Schlichtmann told the judge, "no matter how difficult you make the questions, I think the jury is going to evaluate the testimony correctly and do the right thing."

Afterward, walking down Milk Street on the way to the office, Schlichtmann stopped suddenly and turned his back to Nesson. "Am I bleeding?" he asked Nesson over his shoulder.

"What?" said Nesson, looking confused.

"Am I bleeding there, where you stabbed me in the back?"

Then Schlichtmann laughed. It was Friday afternoon. On Monday he'd give his final argument. He'd get to talk directly to the jurors again for the first time in five months, without Facher or the judge interrupting. "Seventy-six days of trial," he said ruefully. "How long should it have been? Thirty days?"

Conway grimaced. "It was Facher. He made us pay the price for taking it to trial."

12

It was Monday morning, July 14, and the plump, good-natured woman at the dry cleaner's on Charles Street wouldn't let Schlichtmann have his charcoal-gray suit, his lucky suit. She produced an overdue bill of $294 and shook her head sadly. Gordon, it seemed, had finally given up. He'd let Schlichtmann down. He had stopped paying the dry-cleaning bill.

Schlichtmann explained to the woman that this was the most important day of his life. He had to have this particular suit. It had magical qualities. The woman knew Schlichtmann from previous encounters. His stories made her laugh. If it was up to her, she told him, she'd let him have the suit, but the manager wouldn't permit it. Schlichtmann pleaded his case. He'd surely lose without this suit, he said, and then he'd never be able to pay his bill. The woman let Schlichtmann charm her. She cast a quick eye over her shoulder for the manager and then gave Schlichtmann his suit.

A good omen, thought Schlichtmann as he hastened in the morning sun to the office. He had succeeded in his first attempt at persuasion that day.

He yearned to speak to the jurors. At times during the trial this yearning had almost overwhelmed him. When Riley had sat on the witness stand, he'd wanted to turn to the jurors and say, "See? This man is lying now." And Pinder. Schlichtmann would have told them that yes, Pinder had made some mistakes, but he really *was* telling the truth. Schlichtmann had wanted to explain what Facher was really up to with all his objections, and that just because the judge didn't believe in the Beatrice case, that didn't mean they shouldn't.

Schlichtmann wanted the jurors to understand the case as he did. The story of Woburn had been broken into fragments, first by the judge when he split the trial into phases, then by Facher and his relentless objections, and now finally by the questions. Schlichtmann would have to reassemble the pieces so the jurors could understand. He knew they wouldn't be able to figure out how to answer the questions. He'd have to tell them what answers to write down, the only answers that would keep the case alive.

Over the weekend, Nesson had urged Schlichtmann to tell the story from his heart and his head, not to memorize it. But the story Schlichtmann needed to tell was long and complicated, so he wrote it all out. And then, because he didn't want to omit anything in the telling, he disregarded Nesson's advice and committed his speech to memory.

As usual, he hadn't slept last night. He preferred not to, especially before an important day. He didn't want to feel rested and calm. He wanted to feel on edge, feel the rush of adrenaline pulsing through his body. Teresa had spent the night with him, and once again she'd awakened in the gray light of dawn to the sound of his low voice rehearsing.

Outside the courthouse the television vans with their satellite dishes were once again parked around Post Office Square. Upstairs, on the fifteenth floor, the crowd had returned after its long absence, squeezing shoulder to shoulder onto the gallery's wooden pews. Teresa sat with Schlichtmann's mother and the secretaries from the office; Uncle Pete brought a young assistant from the Bank of Boston; Facher escorted his daughters; and Keating arrived with a group of executives from W. R. Grace.

By long-standing tradition, the order of presentation in closing arguments is the reverse of the openings. This time, Facher would speak first, followed by Keating, and then Schlichtmann would get the last word.

Apart from rhetorical flourishes, summations are generally predictable, and Facher's held no surprises for those familiar with the testimony. Schlichtmann sat at the counsel table with his partners, his back to Facher. Afterward, he would say that he had no memory of hearing Facher's closing argument. He knew Facher would tell the jury that Drobinski's opinion had been nothing more than guesswork and that Pinder, the celebrated expert, had failed to do his homework and had simply fabricated an explanation for the missing river water. Schlichtmann knew that Keating would also attack Pinder and claim that the wells had been contaminated by industries to the north, and later he'd have no memory of hearing Keating, either.

The July sun rose high in the sky and flooded in through the opened windows behind the jury box. The judge declared an hour recess for lunch. Schlichtmann couldn't eat. He walked down the marble-tiled corridor to the men's room to splash water on his face. He returned and stood near the courtroom door with Conway and Kathy Boyer. Conway spoke softly to him, asking how he felt, but Schlichtmann just nodded and rubbed his hands together. He looked as if he were in a trance, his eyes focused inward, his face pale. Conway had never seen him quite so nervous, not even before the Rule 11 hearing. But Conway could understand why. Everything depended on this closing argument, Conway thought—all the years of work, the huge debt, their careers and families, Conway's house. He'll be fine once he starts speaking, Conway told himself.

The crowd filed back into the courtroom. The lawyers gathered at the judge's bench for a conference. Schlichtmann had gotten his courtroom graphics man, Andy Lord, to make up poster-sized enlargements of the questions the jury would have to answer. He showed the posters to the judge. Facher and Keating both objected. Facher told the judge it was "inappropriate" to give the questions to the jury ahead of time.

"I offered everyone the chance to do that," the judge said to Facher. "You declined it. It's Mr. Schlichtmann's choice."

Jacobs studied the posters. "Question three is not typed correctly," he told the judge. "We added 'prior to May 22, 1979,' to the question, and that's not in Mr. Schlichtmann's version."

"Yes," said the judge, "it is incorrect."

"Can we write it in?" asked Schlichtmann.

"Write it in good and big," said the judge.

"Put it in very clearly, really neatly, and waste your time reading the questions," said Facher. "It's all right with me."

Schlichtmann didn't trust himself to write legibly. He feared his hand would shake. "Here, Mr. Nesson, you write it," he said.

The lawyers returned to their seats and the judge called the court to order. Schlichtmann rose from the counsel table and turned to face the jurors. He paused for a moment, just as he had during his opening statement, his head bent down, the fingers of his left hand to his chin. Finally he drew an audible breath, looked up at the jurors, and began speaking.

At the counsel table, Nesson turned in his chair so he could watch Schlichtmann, who stood to his left and behind him. But after a few minutes, Nesson turned away. He picked up his pen and began writing quickly in his trial notebook. *Jan is a bit shaky. Trying to remember. Pauses that are not for effect but rather to remember what to say next. A memorized speech. . . . Why can't I look at him? Why does his argument embarrass me instead of engage me?*

A few moments into his speech, Schlichtmann heard a small commotion at the Beatrice counsel table. Out of the corner of his eye, he saw Jacobs lean over and whisper urgently to Facher. Schlichtmann was telling the jurors that the "corporate community" could take pride in its achievements, but it "cannot be proud of W. R. Grace and Beatrice Foods, of their failure to admit to government agencies, to the families, and to you, the true role they played in the pollution of Wells G and H."

As Schlichtmann spoke these words, Facher stood and interrupted him in midsentence. "I object, Your Honor. I don't think that is part of this case."

Schlichtmann wheeled around and looked in amazement at Facher, who stared balefully back. Objections during opening and closing statements are not prohibited, but they are rare, largely for reasons of common courtesy.

Judge Skinner looked a little unsettled by Facher's objection, but he sustained it anyway. To Schlichtmann the judge said, "I think you really are required to relate your argument to the allegations in evidence."

"Yes, Your Honor," said Schlichtmann. "But I believe there is evidence on that."

The judge nodded.

Schlichtmann began again. "The corporate community cannot be proud of Beatrice Foods' failure—"

"Objection!" said Facher rising to his feet again.

"Overruled," said the judge quickly.

But Facher was not to be deterred. He waited only a few moments before objecting again, this time when Schlichtmann used the word "poisons" to describe the contamination on the Beatrice land.

"Overruled," said the judge. "As a characterization by an advocate, it is not improper. I will let it stand."

Facher's objections had thrown Schlichtmann further off-stride. He was having trouble remembering his speech. It was long and detailed, and for a moment he had the terrible, nauseating fear that he had lost the jury's attention. He tried to shut that thought out of his mind and concentrate on what he wanted to say next. He felt an overwhelming fatigue. He paused for a long moment to gather himself, to order his thoughts, and all the many things he wanted to say came to him in a jumbled, disorderly rush.

He began speaking about Grace, and Keating's allegation that the wells had been contaminated by industries in north Woburn. After a few moments, he felt on firmer ground and no longer quite so tired. He was coming to a phrase that he had looked forward to delivering, about how Grace and Beatrice were quick to blame other companies but unwilling to take responsibility for their own acts. "W. R. Grace and Beatrice Foods do not have the right to point outside this court-room," he said with fervor, his own finger jabbing the air, "not until they point across these two tables at each other."

Facher jumped to his feet. "I object! That is not proper argument," he said angrily.

The judge said to Facher, in obvious disapproval, "I see no grounds for objecting at the present time. It is argument."

Schlichtmann went on. To his left, at the Beatrice counsel table, he could hear Facher and Jacobs whispering. He could hear Jacobs, despite the judge's warning, urging Facher to object. And when Facher did so, Schlichtmann quickly turned on him in fury. "I object!" he shouted back at Facher, although he was speaking to the judge. "He's interfering with my argument."

"Go ahead, Mr. Schlichtmann," said the judge calmly.

Nesson sat with his head bowed, writing quickly in his notebook. *Jan keeps using the word "must." When he gets to the blowups of the questions, he tells them how to find but does not give them detailed arguments in support.*

Standing in the well of the courtroom before the jurors, Schlicht-mann could hear himself talking, but he felt dislocated, as if he were a spectator watching someone else perform. He saw himself standing beside an easel that held the large poster with the questions for Bea-trice. He was writing in the dates, based on Pinder's calculations, that he wanted the jurors to give for Beatrice.

The judge gently interrupted him. "I think you may be reading the Grace figures, Mr. Schlichtmann."

Schlichtmann looked up, confused. He glanced down at the papers in his hand, and then at the large posterboard. He seemed stricken by a moment of panic. "I'm sorry, excuse me. See how difficult it is?" he said to the jurors with a desperate laugh. And then, speaking to him-self, he said in a low voice, "All right now, I can't make a mistake." But the stenographer heard him and duly recorded his statement, and so had the jurors and everyone in the gallery.

He was nearing the end of his oration. He had spoken for more than an hour and a half. "The evidence is complicated," he told the jury. "It is difficult and there is a lot of it, and maybe it would be easy to get dis-tracted and go down the wrong path, to take a wrong turn." He paused and looked for a long moment at the jurors. "Please don't," he said in a voice that sounded like a plea.

Please don't. Is this weakness?

"Ladies and gentlemen, you must have courage and strength. You must have it for the families. . . ."

Must, must, must. Telling them what they must do. Jan doesn't trust them? Nobody wants to be told they must.

Schlichtmann looked spent by the time he finished. His eyes were hollow and his face flushed. He sat wearily at the counsel table next to Nesson. "How was it, Charlie?" he whispered. "Did I lose them?"

Nesson said, "Ask Kevin."

The Vigil

1

On Tuesday morning, the day after the final arguments, Judge Skinner instructed the jurors on the rules of law that would govern their efforts to reach a verdict. It was a long, complicated legal benediction, and it took up most of the morning. Then he excused the alternate jurors for the time being, reminding them that they were still jurors in the case and should not discuss their views of it, and he sent the six regular jurors off to begin their deliberations.

Once again a large crowd of spectators had attended court. Many of them lingered in the corridor for a while, but soon they began drifting away. Almost no one expected the jury to render a quick verdict in a trial of this length and complexity. By three o'clock the corridor was nearly vacant. One lone figure stood in front of the courtroom doors like a sentinel. It was Schlichtmann, dressed impeccably in a dark suit and one of his lucky ties.

Just off the main corridor, a few paces away from Schlichtmann, a federal marshal sat at a table reading a newspaper and guarding the entry to a narrow flight of metal stairs that led up to a mezzanine and the closed door of the jury room. Schlichtmann and the marshal exchanged no words. Schlichtmann was busy with his own thoughts. He'd kept courthouse vigils of this sort in every case he'd taken to trial, and he was not about to change his ritual now. He intended to wait in the corridor for as long as it took the jury to return its verdict.

The court stenographer emerged from a doorway down the corridor and walked toward Schlichtmann, her heels clicking on the terrazzo floor. She expressed surprise at seeing him. "You're waiting *here* for the jury?" she asked.

"It's the best place to agonize," replied Schlichtmann, smiling. "I'm trying to give them positive energy."

The stenographer shook her head and smiled back. "I don't think they'll be back until Friday."

She opened a door in the corridor and went in, and Schlichtmann went back to waiting.

Schlichtmann remained faithfully at his post throughout that first week. He arrived in the corridor every morning shortly before eight o'clock, when the jurors came into work, and departed only after they left, at around four o'clock each afternoon. In the morning, Conway or Kathy Boyer would bring him breakfast and stay with him for a few hours, like friends visiting a hospital patient. Later, Gordon or Phillips, or Tom Kiley or Patti D'Addieco would come by to take their place. Nesson was Schlichtmann's most constant companion in the corridor. Nesson was keeping his own kind of vigil. He'd begun fasting after the final arguments, and he didn't intend to eat until the jury returned its verdict. By the third day of his fast, Nesson was experiencing an occasional transcendental moment. "It's an amazing system, isn't it?" he said to Schlichtmann after sitting quietly for a while. "These six jurors hold the fate of two of the biggest corporations in America in their hands. Six ordinary people! There's nowhere else in the world it could happen but here. Law is the religion of America."

The lawyers for Beatrice and Grace soon noticed that Schlichtmann never left the corridor. They decided that they, too, ought to hang around. They did so in shifts, posting guards on Schlichtmann, as it were. "It's like nuclear deterrence," explained Neil Jacobs, peering down the corridor at Schlichtmann. "You've got to keep an eye on the other side." Facher dropped by from time to time, but he rarely stayed long. Guard duty was a job more suited to young associates. All the Grace lawyers, however, senior partners as well as associates, dutifully took their turns. Usually they bided their time in the courtroom gallery, at a far remove from Schlichtmann. But sometimes, feeling bored, Cheeseman would venture out to chat.

"Any word?" he asked Schlichtmann late one morning.

"Not a peep," replied Schlichtmann. "They're as silent as the flow of chemicals from Grace."

Cheeseman's face grew flushed, but he laughed. "And just as slow," he said.

As the first week drew to a close without any sign of a verdict, the patient in the corridor took a turn for the worse. He revived on Friday morning when he saw William Vogel, the jury foreman, a man in his early sixties, come to work for the first time that week wearing a coat and tie. "He's got a new shirt and a nice gray tie," Schlichtmann informed Conway after Vogel had ascended the stairs. "That tells me it's going to be a big day. He's not going to be up in that stuffy room all day."

But the jurors didn't come back with a verdict that Friday, and by then Schlichtmann felt certain there was trouble among them. He left the courthouse with Conway after the jurors had gone home for the weekend. The late afternoon sun slanted between the tall buildings on Milk Street. The sidewalks were crowded with people in summer apparel, office workers who had shed their jackets, women in light colorful dresses, tourists with cameras slung around their necks. Schlichtmann, in his dark suit, walked with his hands in his pockets, his eyes on the pavement. The crowds parted and gave him a wide berth. "I keep thinking of all the things I didn't say," he told Conway. "I wonder what I didn't explain carefully enough."

On Monday, Schlichtmann no longer had the spirit or the strength to stand up all day. He sat on the bench for long periods, although he always made sure to rise around the times the jurors customarily came and went.

During those moments he studied them closely but guardedly, with his eyes partially averted, trying to divine their thoughts and figure out who was for him and who was against. Vogel, a telephone company supervisor in his other life, always led the group when they went down to the cafeteria for lunch. Schlichtmann had believed for months that Vogel supported him, and he couldn't bring himself to think otherwise now. He felt just as certain about the second juror, Linda Kaplan, a young unmarried woman who worked as a clerk for a big insurance company. She often smiled at Schlichtmann as she passed by him. Then came Robert Fox, a trim, good-looking man of about thirty who had taken copious notes throughout the trial. Schlichtmann had felt dubious about Fox until the last weeks of trial, and then he'd persuaded himself that Fox was on his side. But he was no longer sure of that now. After Fox came Vincent O'Rourke, an ailing postal worker in his late fifties who had difficulty walking. At his *voir dire,* O'Rourke had responded slowly and very deliberately to the judge's questions. He did not seem to Schlichtmann like the sort of man who would go against the majority and make trouble in the jury room.

The trouble, Schlichtmann believed, was coming either from Harriet Clarke, the church organist, a thin, rather severe-looking woman in her late forties, or from Jean Coulsey, the stout, white-haired, ruddy-cheeked grandmother who drove a forklift part-time at a department store warehouse. Coulsey was the one who'd said at her *voir dire* that she thought the lawsuit might be the product of "some lady maybe looking for a little extra money." Despite that, Schlichtmann had instinctively liked Coulsey. He'd felt confident, certain even, of her allegiance throughout the trial. But now, watching her in the corridor, he wondered if he hadn't made a terrible mistake. She always looked grim as she approached him, her mouth set and lips narrowed, her head tucked down and turned away. Everything in her demeanor told him that she wished she could avoid him.

As the second week wore on, Schlichtmann's mother and Teresa came to sit with him. They and others from the office would gather around and talk among themselves, but Schlichtmann remained silent for long periods, staring off into space. Sometimes he would pace, studying the floor and walking in slow, small steps, the gait of an old man who no longer trusted his balance. Conway watched him once as he did this, walking thirty feet or so in one direction, and then thirty feet back. He would place each foot carefully within a square of the ter-razzo floor, and when he made a mistake, when he overstepped a square, he would stop, take a step backward, and repace. After a while, Conway said, "What are you doing, Jan?"

"Concentrating," said Schlichtmann.

2

Jean Coulsey couldn't avoid seeing Schlichtmann standing at the end of the dark corridor every morning when she stepped off the elevator. "It was pathetic, seeing him there," Coulsey said some months after the trial. "I found it very difficult not to talk to him." But she knew how improper any exchange would be, so she focused her eyes on the floor and set her mouth in grim restraint.

During the months of trial she and the other jurors had talked among themselves about the lawyers' mannerisms and eccentricities, about the judge, the witnesses, even the few spectators who appeared in the gallery day after day. The jurors, of course, hadn't been able to hear what the lawyers were saying at the bench conferences with Judge Skinner, but they'd always known when Schlichtmann had gotten reprimanded. "He'd get crimson," remembered Coulsey. They were sometimes baffled by the judge's manner with Schlichtmann. They all liked the judge and felt he was fair and impartial, but they could see that Schlichtmann nettled him for reasons they didn't comprehend. "The judge seemed awfully picky with Mr. Schlichtmann," recalled Coulsey. As for Facher, she did not particularly care for him. Her closest friend on the jury, an alternate named Henry Jason, a retired police officer, had once said in annoyance, "Facher's like a spring with his objections, jumping up all the time," and Coulsey had concurred.

The jurors had made such observations casually, passing the time in conversation when the trial had halted for those interminable bench conferences. To Coulsey, John J. Riley had come across "like a creep." She thought her fellow jurors agreed with her. After Riley's second day on the witness stand, Henry Jason had whispered loud enough for the others to hear, "Who's he trying to snow?" Everyone had laughed. "The thing that kills me," Coulsey later remarked, "was Riley saying he's turned the fifteen acres into a conservation area." She thought Drobinski had been an excellent witness, forthright and credible. Facher's manner toward Drobinski had irritated her. "How can Mr. Facher belittle people like that?" she had wondered. "He's very sarcastic, but he can pick up on something that isn't right just like that. God help you if you make a mistake with Mr. Facher."

Because they had shared these observations, and they had seemed generally to agree with one another, Coulsey had assumed that the other jurors viewed the case in the same light as she did.

The day they began their formal deliberations, the clerk brought all the evidence up to the jury room—it took him several trips—and the list of questions that had been devised for them to answer. Jean Coulsey studied the questions in astonishment. And she wasn't the only one surprised by them. The others looked confused and perplexed, too.

William Vogel remembered saying, "I thought we were just supposed to find them guilty or innocent."

"Something must be wrong," said Coulsey. "I can't understand how Mr. Schlichtmann could let this happen."

The jurors read the questions several times, trying to parse the compound sentences. How could they possibly determine the month and year that the chemicals had arrived at the wells? Pinder and Guswa had offered opinions and had spoken about the "travel times" of the chemicals, but that testimony had been confusing at best. And what did the judge mean by "substantial" contribution? What exactly was a "preponderance of the evidence?"

"Now what are we going to do?" asked Coulsey.

Vogel suggested they begin by taking a vote to see where everyone stood. For his part, he believed that both companies were, as he put it, "guilty" of contaminating the wells, but he didn't reveal this opinion to his fellow jurors right away. As foreman, he thought he should wait until the others made their opinion known. If they all agreed, they could then proceed to the far more difficult task of determining exactly when the chemicals had reached the wells.

As Vogel understood it, the first question asked whether the chemicals from Beatrice had gotten to the wells before May 22, 1979, the date the wells had closed. To him, that was essentially the "guilty" or "not guilty" question. He read that first question aloud to the other jurors and asked for a show of hands from those who believed Beatrice was liable. Jean Coulsey and Linda Kaplan promptly raised their hands. When no one else raised a hand, Vogel raised his. Finally Vincent O'Rourke, the postal employee, a very shy and retiring man, slowly raised his hand.

Then Vogel said: "Not guilty?"

Harriet Clarke held up her hand. Robert Fox, the only juror who had not yet voted, said he was undecided and would abstain for the moment.

Vogel posed the same question for Grace. The results were only slightly different. This time Robert Fox joined Harriet Clarke in finding Grace not liable.

Jean Coulsey was amazed. The judge had told the jurors that their verdict had to be unanimous. Coulsey had thought it would take only a short while to find both Grace and Beatrice liable. Nothing, she believed, could be clearer than the "guilt" of the two corporations.

The jurors set to work that afternoon. They began with Beatrice, arranging all the evidence before them on top of the large wooden table. They asked the judge's clerk for a magnifying glass so they could study the aerial photographs that Schlichtmann had introduced as evidence. It quickly became apparent that although Robert Fox had abstained on the initial vote, he felt Beatrice should not be held liable. By the afternoon of the second day, the discussion between Fox and Coulsey began to grow heated. The judge had allowed the jurors to take notes during the trial, and Fox had filled the pages of four notebooks. He would read to the others jurors items from his notes that supported his point of view.

Coulsey had taken almost no notes. She felt intuitively that the companies were responsible, but she had difficulty articulating her thoughts and could not readily summon facts the way Fox could. She kept wishing that the alternate jurors, especially Henry Jason, were deliberating with them.

For his part, Fox grew increasingly frustrated in his efforts to engage Coulsey in rational debate about the facts. He paced around the table, demanding that Coulsey explain, that she give her reasons, that she point to the evidence. "There simply isn't enough proof," Fox told her. "You need a preponderance of the evidence. Show me a preponderance of the evidence." At times he raised his voice, and by the end of the week, he had gotten so agitated that he slammed his fist on the table, making a resounding noise. At those moments, even his ally, Harriet Clarke, would tell him to calm down.

Jean Coulsey never gave in to tears in the jury room, although she felt close to it more than once. "I can't get my words out right," she told her husband one evening. She felt as if she was coming apart emotionally under the strain. One morning, speaking with the maintenance man at the elderly housing complex where she lived, she burst into tears for no apparent reason. She went to see her doctor, who told her that she was suffering from stress and prescribed some tranquilizers.

As fragile as Coulsey felt, she was nonetheless stubborn in the jury room. She announced one morning that she intended to go through the evidence piece by piece until she found proof of dumping on Beatrice's land between 1968 and 1979. She sat before several large stacks of documents and began examining each page methodically. Fox stared at her for a moment and then broke out in derisive laughter. He left the jury room and went out to the mezzanine, where the lavatories were located.

Linda Kaplan, Jean Coulsey's strongest ally, watched Fox leave. "He thinks he's a lawyer," she said in disgust.

On Friday morning, July 17, the end of the first week of their deliberations, Vogel said it was apparent they were getting nowhere on Beatrice. Coulsey's search turned up two pieces of evidence showing that chemicals had been dumped on the fifteen acres between 1968 and 1979, but Fox insisted that this did not constitute a "preponderance of the evidence." Vogel suggested they turn their attention to Grace.

By then, however, the lines had been drawn. They deliberated on Monday and Tuesday with little progress. Vogel sometimes made concessions to Fox and Clarke, and Vincent O'Rourke occasionally seemed swayed by Fox's arguments. On some votes, O'Rourke sided with Fox and Harriet Clarke. But Coulsey and Kaplan were adamant in their positions. On Tuesday afternoon, Fox suggested they declare a deadlock and report to the judge that they could not arrive at a unanimous decision. Coulsey and Kaplan vehemently opposed this. "I don't care how long we have to go," Coulsey said. "I don't care if it takes us all summer." And none of the others, not even Harriet Clarke, liked the idea of giving up with the job unfinished.

That afternoon, following the discussion of a deadlock, William Vogel told the others some sobering news. If they could not reach a verdict soon, he would have to leave the jury. He was scheduled to enter the hospital on August 3, less than two weeks away, for heart bypass surgery. He himself had just gotten the news from his doctor last week.

The other jurors looked stunned. They offered Vogel their sympathy, and then they talked about what this development might cause the judge to do. Vogel said he suspected the judge would appoint one of the alternates to take his place. But everyone agreed that a new juror, no matter what that juror's view of the case, would not solve the problem of the deadlock.

Perhaps out of consideration for Vogel, the jurors began Wednesday morning on a more subdued note. But as the hours passed the rancor once again increased. Fox began pacing and talking. Coulsey sat apart from the others and grimly continued her search through the boxes of evidence.

Linda Kaplan suspected that Fox had been taking his notes home with him and discussing the case with someone else. The judge had told them they should not remove any material from the jury room, and that the marshal would lock up their notes at the end of each day. Kaplan said nothing about her suspicions for several days. Then, on Wednesday afternoon, after a particularly vehement argument with Fox, she abruptly rose from her chair, left the jury room, and asked the marshal to summon Judge Skinner's clerk. Her face was flushed and she was breathing hard with anger. She informed the clerk that one of the jurors was taking work home in violation of the judge's order. The clerk promised he would report her allegation to the judge.

By then Vogel had to admit to himself that they were hopelessly deadlocked. "We're not getting anywhere," he said to the others. He looked at Jean Coulsey and said, "Do you want to let both companies off?"

Coulsey adamantly shook her head no.

"Then we have to tell the judge the situation," said Vogel.

On a piece of notepaper, Vogel wrote: "After six and a half days of deliberation and examination of the evidence made available to the jury, we cannot reach a unanimous decision on Question 1 for either Grace or Beatrice."

Vogel wrote the note with great reluctance. A deadlock, he knew, meant that the lawyers would have to try the case again. The time, the effort, and the money spent in the last five months would all have been wasted. As the jury foreman, Vogel felt partly responsible. He folded the note and decided he would wait until the end of the next day, Thursday, before delivering it to the judge. That would give them one more day to see if they could reach a decision.

3

Judge Skinner received William Vogel's message on Thursday after-noon at two o'clock. The judge donned his black robe and called the lawyers into the courtroom, where he read the message aloud. "They are at square one," the judge said.

Schlichtmann, standing next to the judge's bench, sagged against the marble column, his shoulders slumped, his face ashen.

The judge studied the message closely. "The wording is a little odd. 'We cannot reach a unanimous decision on Question 1.' That leads me to speculate it may be a five-to-one decision one way or the other." He paused for a moment and then added, "I should also convey to you that the number two juror was distressed that perhaps one member of the jury was taking the work home and discussing it with people out-side. I have no way to verify that except to inquire. I think this lady came downstairs at the tail end of a rather heated argument. She may just be blowing off steam, but I can't ignore it."

The judge said he would have the jury brought down for further instructions. Facher and Keating raised objections to any strongly worded charge that might force the jurors to come to a verdict over their better judgment. Schlichtmann, still slumped against the column, said nothing throughout the debate.

"It doesn't surprise me they are in this posture," said Keating, who was anxious to keep matters exactly as they stood. "I would be very much opposed to trying to force them into some kind of agreement on a thing which reasonable people may disagree on."

This clearly annoyed the judge. "You can say that about every case. Indeed, it is the reason why there's a trial."

"They obviously want a response," Schlichtmann murmured at last.

"They want to be told they can go home, I imagine," said the judge. "I'm not going to do that. I am not letting them go this easy, I will tell you."

The lawyers took their seats at the counsel tables. The clerk escorted the jurors, who looked sad and weary, into the courtroom. The judge told them he had received their message, and then he delivered a stan-dard speech he'd given before to deadlocked juries. "I'm not going to declare a mistrial at this point," the judge said, "because if I do, another jury will have to hear the same evidence again. And there's no reason to suppose that some other jury will be in the position to do any better than you've done. It's your duty as jurors to consult with one another and to deliberate with a view to reaching an agreement. Do not hesitate to reexamine your own views or change your opinion. The jury room is no place for pride of opinion."

Then the judge inquired, in circumspect fashion, about the allegation Linda Kaplan had made. He did not mention any names. "I take it you have not talked to anyone and no one has talked to you," said the judge, looking closely at the jury. "If that has occurred, you have an obligation to advise me about it." He paused, awaiting a response.

The jurors were silent.

"All right, ladies and gentlemen, would you recommence your deliberations."

The judge's clerk escorted the jurors back upstairs. The lawyers milled about in the courtroom, discussing among themselves the impasse, when the judge suddenly returned to the bench and beckoned to the lawyers.

Schlichtmann looked up at the judge in disbelief. "Another message?"

"This is from Mr. Vogel, the foreman," said the judge. "He writes, 'I would like to be excused from jury duty because I am scheduled for cardiac surgery on August 6, 1986.' And here is a letter from the medical center. 'We will arrange for your admission to the New England Medical Center on August 3.'"

August third was ten days away. Keating said to the judge, "I suspect he thought you'd send everybody home and he would not have to write this note."

"That's right," said the judge. "The first alternate is Mrs. Gilbern, Dina Gilbern. I'll call her in for tomorrow."

Facher did not want to change the composition of the jury at this point. To him, a hung jury was as good as a win, and any change might upset this delicate balance. Furthermore, Facher most certainly did not want Dina Gilbern, a retired social worker with two grown children, to deliberate. During the *voir dire*, Gilbern had said she was a member of the Audubon Society and a supporter of the Sierra Club. "I think we ought to wait until the end of tomorrow," Facher told the judge.

"Why?"

"Mr. Vogel doesn't have to go into the hospital until a week from Sunday. I don't know if it's elective or—"

"It's cardiac surgery," said the judge. "It doesn't sound very elective to me. If he's that close to going in the hospital, there's something very seriously wrong with him."

"Do you want to talk to him?" asked Schlichtmann.

"I suppose we have to," said the judge.

When Vogel arrived at the bench a moment later, the judge said, "I have your message. I'm very sorry you have this problem. What's your capacity to carry on until August third?"

"I have no qualms about continuing through next week," replied Vogel. "The only thing I want to make clear is that this is coming up. After spending five months here, I'd like to see it through." Vogel paused. "But if you want to put an alternate in my place, you could do it now."

"Do you think there's any likelihood of the questions being answered within the next couple of days?" asked the judge.

"No, I don't," replied Vogel.

"You're going to have a heart bypass?"

"Yes. Quadruple."

"I'm sorry this has come upon you," said the judge again.

"No more than I am," said Vogel with a sad smile.

"I'd appreciate it if you could stay with it through tomorrow," continued the judge. "On Monday we'll see where we are. Who knows? We may get lucky and something may break here. Well, the very best of luck to you."

"Thank you," said Vogel. He turned and nodded his head in a formal, almost courtly way, to the lawyers. "Gentlemen," he said, and then he went back upstairs to the jury room.

That evening, Schlichtmann stood at the counter in the office kitchen, trying to open a bottle of apple juice. His palms were sweaty, his hands trembled, and he could not get the top off. He put the unopened bottle down and planted both hands on the counter, as if he were steadying himself on a storm-tossed sea. "Could I be wrong?" he wondered aloud. "Could there be only one holdout for me? I can't believe that nightmare."

The sheriff came to repossess Schlichtmann's Porsche that weekend. It was an event of such little consequence to him that he failed to mention it to his partners until much later.

4

Monday morning, July 28. Judge Skinner took the bench and motioned for the lawyers to gather around. "My suggestion is to ask the jury foreman to come down and report the status of things. If they're not ready with a verdict, I'll excuse the foreman and put in Mrs. Gilbern, who is here, and we'll have to start all over."

The judge's clerk went to bring Vogel down.

"Good morning, Mr. Vogel," the judge said. "Can you tell us whether there is any likelihood of a prompt verdict?"

"Yes," replied Vogel.

"There is?" said the judge.

"Yes. We are just finalizing it right now, Your Honor," said Vogel. "Crossing the *t*'s and dotting the *i*'s."

"That's remarkable progress from last Thursday."

"We're all in one piece," said Vogel, smiling. "There's been no breaking of arms or legs or anything like that."

It had been the judge's standard instructions to the jury, and the news of Vogel's operation, that had broken the deadlock. On Friday morning, Vogel had taken charge. He'd drawn up two charts, one for Grace and one for Beatrice. With the help of the others, he had listed all the evidence for and against each company. The judge had said, "Don't hesitate to change your views," and Vogel had asked his fellow jurors to change their views, if only for the moment, and try to see the opposite side.

It had worked. Robert Fox and Harriet Clarke agreed that the Grace chart clearly showed a preponderance of the evidence against the company. And Coulsey, in turn, had to concede that Beatrice, with only two items against the company after the judge's 1968 cutoff date, could not be held liable by the preponderance standard.

Beatrice was out of the case now. The jurors had to deal with only the remaining questions for Grace. The second question, once they unraveled the language, seemed to ask for the month and year that the chemicals from Grace had arrived at the wells in "substantial" amounts. They agreed that they didn't know the answer to that. They put in "ND" for "Not Determined." The third question read like the first

one, the only difference being that it asked if Grace had failed "to fulfill any duty of due care to the plaintiffs." To this they answered "Yes."

The fourth question stumped them for a while. Like the second
question, it asked them for a date, but what date they couldn't begin to
fathom. They were about to put in "Not Determined" again when they
decided to adjourn for the weekend and consider the matter again on
Monday before reporting to the judge. On Monday morning, Fox
came up with a date—September 1973. That, Fox told the others, was
when Grace had closed a storm drain at the plant into which workers
had poured waste solvents. Everyone quickly accepted this date, even
though they had no idea what relation it bore to the question.

They had finished their job. Each of them had some misgivings, but
on balance they felt they had done the best they could.

Word that the jury had reached a verdict traveled quickly. A crowd of
spectators and journalists began to assemble in the corridor. Schlichtmann stood with his head bowed, his hands tightly clasped under his
chin in an attitude of prayer. Kathy Boyer hovered close by, separating
him from the crowd. He chanted over and over again, in a low voice, as
if the words were a mantra, "Come on, come on, come on, come
on. . . ."

When the jurors filed down and took their seats in the courtroom,
Judge Skinner's clerk asked the foreman to rise. "Mr. Foreman, members of the jury, have you agreed on a verdict?"

"Yes, we have," replied Vogel, who handed the jury slip to the clerk.

The judge unfolded the slip and read in silence. Then, in a formal
voice, he announced: "With respect to the special interrogatories as to
Beatrice Foods, they have answered all parts of question one in the negative. That is determinative of the case with regard to Beatrice."

Schlichtmann buried his face in his hands. His body seemed to go
limp. Next to him, Nesson put his arms on the counsel table and laid
his head down.

The judge continued reading. "As to W. R. Grace, with respect to the
same question, the jury has answered 'yes' as to trichloroethylene. . . ."

When the judge finished reading the jury's answers, he said, "With
respect to Grace, the answers to these questions require that we proceed

further. I will see counsel at the bench to determine the date for commencing the second stage of this trial."

Facher, smiling, rose to come up to the bench, too. The judge saw him and said, "I will not need your assistance, Mr. Facher. You are excused."

Facher stopped in his tracks, in the middle of the courtroom, and watched Schlichtmann and his partners and Keating and his partners gather at the judge's bench. Facher's smile turned to a frown. He appeared unhappy at being excluded, unhappy at the way the judge had ended his role in this long trial without any ceremony. He stood there for a moment, then he sighed and went back to the counsel table and began packing his battered litigation bag.

The jurors remained in their seats. Up at the bench, Judge Skinner leaned forward toward Schlichtmann. He'd seen Schlichtmann's gesture of despair. "Well, half a loaf is better than none at all, isn't it?" he said in a low voice.

"Yes," replied Schlichtmann with no conviction.

"So we will go forward."

The jury's answers, continued the judge, were puzzling and raised some problems, especially the September 1973 date. "I think you'll probably want to file some motions," the judge said to Keating. "We ought to consider those before we start the second stage." The judge told the lawyers that he intended to spend the month of August on vacation in Maine. "I'd like to look at your briefs when I come back after Labor Day, on September fifth. If there's going to be further trial of the case—which I rather think there will be—I suggest September fifteenth is an appropriate day to start."

The judge turned to the jurors. He thanked them for their service and reminded them that they should not talk to anyone about their deliberations. "The case is still going on," he said. "We are just going to take a breather. With that admonition, I now excuse you until September fifteenth and hope you have a very pleasant remainder of the summer."

Schlichtmann called Donna Robbins from the pay phone in the corridor, holding his hand to his ear so that he could hear above the noise of the crowd. He told her about the verdict and asked her to notify the other families. He wanted to meet with the families at one o'clock that afternoon at Trinity Episcopal Church, after which they would all talk to the press together.

Downstairs, in the lobby of the federal building, a group of reporters and four television cameras waited in front of the elevators. Facher was the first to arrive. He stepped off the elevator and the bright lights of the minicams came on, immediately attracting a swarm of curious spectators. In front of a jury Facher always felt completely at ease, but in front of the cameras he became wooden and glassy-eyed. He drew his neck stiffly back and shifted his litigation bag from one hand to the other, finally setting it down. Yes, he was very pleased with the verdict. "The jury system itself is vindicated," he said, and then he managed a smile. "I'll be following the second phase of the trial from a seat in Fenway Park."

A few minutes later Keating stepped out to face the cameras. He, too, looked ill at ease. "They decided it the way they decided it," he told the reporters. "The process will go on. We're looking forward to the second phase."

Then Schlichtmann arrived. Of all the parties in this case he had always used the media to his best advantage. But now he made no effort to conceal his despair. "I am bitterly disappointed," he said, looking down at the floor and shaking his head. "We needed a clear message and we didn't get one. It makes our job much harder. But we will go on."

Schlichtmann knew that going on would be very hard indeed. Losing Beatrice was bad enough. What made the verdict even worse, however, was the September 1973 date the jurors had given for Grace. Three of the Woburn children—Jimmy Anderson, Michael Zona, and Kevin Kane, Jr.—had gotten leukemia before that date. Were they out of the case now? Schlichtmann expected Keating to make a strong argument in September to exclude them. If Keating was successful, nearly half the case would have turned to dust. How would that affect the remaining claims? And how would it affect the families? Would they start fighting among themselves?

Schlichtmann didn't have the time or presence of mind to think through these questions right now. He had to get out to Woburn and meet with his clients. At the office, a small caravan assembled to make the trip. Schlichtmann went with Kiley in Kiley's Mercedes. On the drive out, he sat in the passenger seat, staring rigidly ahead and saying nothing. Kiley gave him a worried glance.

"This 'bitterly disappointed' shit has got to stop, Jan," said Kiley.

Schlichtmann managed a wan smile. "No self-pity, huh?"

"You don't think Keating is celebrating, do you?" Kiley continued. "W. R. Grace is damn sorry they ever ran into you. They've just been found guilty of polluting the water in a town where there's a fucking cancer cluster! You've got to turn the screw, Jan. You can't let up now."

Schlichtmann drew a breath that sounded like a sob. "I'm sorry," he said, his voice hoarse. "I'm filled with pain. Month after month, nothing has ever been clear. I needed those jurors. I needed those six people. They kicked me in the fucking belly. They think I'm wrong."

Kiley looked grim. "Jan, you've got to get hold of yourself. You can't let your clients see you this way."

In the meeting hall at Trinity Episcopal Church, the families gathered around on folding chairs. Overhead, the high ceiling fans turned slowly but gave no relief from the oppressive midsummer heat. People fanned themselves with pieces of paper and mopped their brows with handkerchiefs.

Schlichtmann looked hollow-eyed and he spoke in a dull, uninflected voice, but he did manage to keep hold of himself. He told the families he would appeal the Beatrice verdict. As for Grace, the jury's answer was puzzling. He did not understand how they had arrived at the date, and he needed time to study it. But he assured the families that they were still all in the case together. He would try to find a way around the date. And if that failed, he could still prove that exposure to the solvent had aggravated the illnesses of Jimmy Anderson and the others and hastened their deaths. These words of assurance relieved those families whose claims were in jeopardy. But even so, they all knew that this argument looked weak compared with what they had started with.

Back at the office, the secretaries brought out the bottles of champagne that they had been saving in anticipation of a victory celebration. Schlichtmann popped open a bottle as soon as he walked in the door and took a deep swallow. In the conference room the television was tuned to the early news. Telephones rang constantly with calls of congratulations and queries from reporters. "No, we're not disappointed at all," Kiley explained to a *Washington Post* reporter who had seen

Schlichtmann's interview in the courthouse lobby. "He was just reacting to the moment."

Phillips heard that W. R. Grace stock had fallen three points by the
close of the market. He called to confirm this, and then he came to tell
Schlichtmann. Phillips calculated that the verdict had cost Grace
stockholders $155 million. The wire services and CBS network news
were calling the verdict a "landmark decision."

Gordon looked amazed. "If *The Wall Street Journal* says we won
tomorrow, then I'll believe we won." He paused. "It doesn't feel like it,
though."

In the kitchen, Conway waited for the coffee machine to percolate.
Phillips came in and sat astride a stool. He lit a cigarette and took deep
drags. The kitchen was cluttered with half-empty glasses of champagne, half-empty cans of soda, and ashtrays full of cigarette butts.

"We're in worse shape than we ever thought with this jury," said
Phillips, clearing his throat and humming nervously. "We're lucky we
got today."

"I think we've sent a message," said Conway, buoyed by the press
reports. "Grace has still got punitive damages hanging over them. It's a
case that's got—"

"It's a case that's got to be settled quickly," interrupted Phillips.
"We've got to save our dignity and get out of this case as fast as we fucking can. That's the only strategy left."

"How much do you think we can get?" wondered Conway.

Phillips thought for a moment. "Twenty-five million." He hummed.
"If we're really lucky."

In his office, Schlichtmann was taking telephone calls. *Good Morning America* wanted him to come down to New York and appear on
the show the next morning with one of his clients. Schlichtmann
accepted the invitation and called Donna Robbins in Woburn. He
told her to meet him at the airport that evening at seven-thirty. Kiley
decided to accompany Schlichtmann. He knew that Schlichtmann
had no functioning credit cards and no way to pay the plane fare and
hotel bill.

Rikki Klieman came by the office, looking sleek in a tan summer
suit, her luxuriant dark brown hair shining with health. She had sent
flowers to the office earlier, a gesture that could be read as either congratulations or condolences. "How's Jan doing?" she asked Conway.

"Not good," replied Conway.

"Somebody's got to talk to him," said Rikki.

"He's going to New York to be on *Good Morning America.* Go with him. Help him out."

"I haven't been invited."

"Just go," said Conway.

Rikki walked into Schlichtmann's office. He was packing his overnight bag for the trip. "Jan, do you want me to go with you?" she asked.

Schlichtmann looked at her with blank eyes. "Sure, come on," he said in a flat voice.

Rikki was skeptical. "Are you serious? Really?"

Schlichtmann nodded.

Rikki left to pack a bag of her own. After she'd gone, Conway went into Schlichtmann's office and closed the door behind him. "If you think we lost, so will everybody who sees you on television tomorrow morning. Don't do that to us, Jan. Promise me you won't do that."

At the airport, Schlichtmann introduced Donna Robbins to Rikki Klieman. "Rikki's a very close friend and a good lawyer," he told Donna. "She's been very supportive."

They boarded the eight o'clock shuttle to New York. Schlichtmann sat in an aisle seat with Donna next to the window. Rikki Klieman and Tom Kiley sat together across the aisle and two rows back. Donna felt jittery. She had a deep-seated fear of talking in public, of becoming tongue-tied with anxiety. The prospect of appearing live on *Good Morning America* mortified her. In other interviews and public appearances, Schlichtmann had always given her advice about what to say and assured her she'd do fine. But now, on the plane, she found Schlichtmann eerily quiet. She would say something and he'd nod in response but say nothing. She realized after a while that he had not uttered a single word since the plane took off.

"Jan, are you all right?" Donna asked. He made a sound of assent and nodded his head. Try as she would, Donna could not get him to say a word. She'd never seen him—she'd never seen anyone—act like this before, and it frightened her.

Schlichtmann heard Donna talking, asking him questions, but her voice seemed to come from a great distance. He could not respond. He wanted to, but he was afraid that if he opened his mouth he would wail. His breathing was rapid and shallow. He felt confined on the airplane as he had never felt confined before. His clothing seemed to suffocate him, and every moment lasted an eternity. He craved immersion in warm water. He had the bizarre sensation that if he could just unzip his skin and get into warm water, he would be all right. He imagined a zipper on his chest, from the base of his throat to his navel. The urge to unzip himself became so compelling that he feared he would stand in the aisle of the plane and take off all his clothes. Again he heard Donna, but he stared straight ahead. He found himself thinking, Maybe the plane will crash and this nightmare will end.

Two rows back, Rikki Klieman could see Schlichtmann sitting rigidly erect and immobile in his seat. She turned to Kiley and said, "I know what he's thinking. He thinks he'll be better off if this plane crashes. He wants this plane to crash."

When they landed in New York, Kiley took charge. He summoned a cab to Manhattan. He decided that Schlichtmann was in no shape to spend the evening with a client. At the Barbizon Hotel, Kiley escorted Donna to the check-in counter, paid for her room, and told her they would pick her up tomorrow morning at six-thirty. Then Kiley returned to the cab and told the driver to go to the Helmsley Palace. At the check-in counter there, Kiley paused. If Rikki had not come, he and Schlichtmann would have shared a suite. Now Kiley was unsure what arrangements he should make. Three rooms or two? He looked at Rikki, eyebrows raised in question. She shrugged. Kiley booked two rooms.

They got off the elevator on the nineteenth floor. At the door to the first room, Schlichtmann motioned to the bellhop to bring in his and Rikki's luggage. Kiley went on to the second room alone. He returned a moment later and said he was going downstairs to Harry's Bar for a drink and something to eat. Did they want to come?

Harry's Bar, with its dark, richly oiled wood and gleaming brass, was still noisy and convivial at eleven o'clock. Kiley found a table and steered Schlichtmann to it. They ordered drinks and sandwiches, and he and Rikki set about the difficult task of trying to make Schlichtmann feel better. Schlichtmann drank steadily but ate nothing. Kiley attempted to coax him out of his catatonic state. He asked Schlichtmann what he planned to say tomorrow on *Good Morning America*. Schlichtmann just shook his head sadly and made no reply. For an hour, Kiley and Rikki talked to him, tried to comfort him, tried to reason with him. Kiley treated him with a tenderness, a patience and solicitude, that impressed Rikki. She had not heretofore thought of Kiley, with his South Boston accent, his thickly muscled build and blunt manner, as especially sensitive.

It wasn't until after midnight that Schlichtmann finally began to talk. People had believed in him and he had failed them. He shouldn't have become a lawyer. He did not have the strength to continue. His life was over, he said, and this statement, more than anything else, alarmed Rikki.

Then he again became silent. Rikki wondered if he'd be able to go on *Good Morning America* at all. Kiley, thinking the same thing, decided he ought to prepare himself to take Schlichtmann's place in the morning. Kiley made one last effort. "Your life may be over, Jan, but tomorrow at seven o'clock you've got to get on national television and you've got to say something."

Finally Rikki got up and said she was going to bed. Schlichtmann stood, too. They left Kiley at the table and went upstairs to their room. Schlichtmann undressed and lay naked under the sheets. Rikki came to the bed and lay down beside him. In the dark, she talked to him for what seemed a long while. She stroked his arm, and then she made love to him. After a while, she drifted off to sleep.

Schlichtmann lay awake. He could feel the rapid pounding of his heart, his body moist with perspiration even in the air-conditioned room. At three o'clock he arose, went into the bathroom and stared at himself in the mirror. He thought he had aged a decade in the last week. His hair was mostly gray now. His eyes seemed sunken in their sockets, full of terror and dread. His head pounded and his mouth felt clotted from the drinks at Harry's Bar, from the bottles of champagne at the office. He had not eaten anything for almost twenty-four hours. He returned to the bed but could not sleep. He lay next to Rikki, listening to her regular, quiet breathing. He waited for morning.

At five o'clock, in the gray light of dawn, he got up again and went to take a shower. He stood for a long while, letting the warm water pour over him. And then, slowly, he started to feel better. It became clear to him what he had to do next. He had hoped for a jury that would embrace the "political" nature of the case. But he realized now that he could not depend on this jury to ring any bells in the corporate boardrooms of America. The case that he had tried to turn into an environmental crusade, the case that he had hoped would bring him fame and fortune, had suddenly turned back into an ordinary case again.

At that moment this felt like a profound revelation to him. His grief at losing Beatrice had blinded him to everything but his own pain, but now he was beginning to see again. Faced with this jury, he did not have many choices. He would have to try to settle with Grace. Maybe he could get enough money to call it a victory. That, he decided, was his challenge now.

He emerged from the shower feeling clearheaded for the first time in a week, as if he'd slept well that night.

At the Barbizon Hotel, Donna Robbins had not slept well. She kept rehearsing what she wanted to say on television the next morning and hoped that she wouldn't freeze up when the moment came.

She was waiting in the lobby of the Barbizon at six-thirty when Schlichtmann came in to pick her up. She asked how he felt and he said, "I feel great today."

Donna could see the change in him. He did look better, and he was acting much more like his old self. In the taxi on the way to the ABC studios, she sat in the back with Kiley and Rikki. Schlichtmann sat in the front and kept turning around in his seat to talk with her. When she told him how nervous she felt, he tried to quell her fears. Then, a block away from their destination, he became quiet again, but it wasn't the same sort of eerie quiet as on the airplane.

Donna later remembered her brief appearance on *Good Morning America* as an embarrassment, the sort of memory that makes you catch your breath in shame when it sneaks into your thoughts. In truth, she did fine. She was dressed in a light summer skirt and a sleeveless white blouse, and she appeared calm and dignified, almost serenely beautiful, as she sat on a studio couch next to Schlichtmann. The first few minutes of the interview, when she talked about Robbie and his illness, went smoothly and she started feeling more at ease. The show's host, David Hartman, asked her what she hoped to gain from the lawsuit, and this was a question for which she had carefully prepared. "I think there's three things," she began. She got through the first—that corporations would be more responsible with toxic waste as a result of the lawsuit—and then she lost her train of thought. She glanced quickly at Schlichtmann. She looked down at her lap and bit her lip. "I'm sorry," she said, "I've just drawn a mental blank."

David Hartman murmured, "That's okay," and deftly turned the same question to Schlichtmann. During the commercial break that followed, Hartman took Donna's hand in his and smiled gently at her. "Don't worry about it," he said. "I've done it myself, and I've seen it happen more times than you could imagine." Donna felt enormously grateful to the man for this small gesture.

For his part, Schlichtmann didn't disappoint Conway. He looked pale and tired, but he uttered with conviction the standard phrases of victory, sentiments he did not at all feel. He was "pleased and heartened that the jury had the courage to find W. R. Grace responsible," and he looked forward to "presenting the evidence of what happened to the community" in the second phase of the case.

When their plane landed in Boston that afternoon, Schlichtmann escorted Donna to a cab and told the driver to take her to Woburn. Donna said she didn't have enough money for the fare. Schlichtmann glanced over at Kiley, who took out his wallet and handed Donna a twenty-dollar bill.

Schlichtmann shared a cab with Rikki and Kiley to downtown Boston. After dropping off Kiley, Rikki hoped Schlichtmann would say something about the night they'd spent together, but she could see that romance was far from his thoughts. The cab stopped at his office on Milk Street. Schlichtmann got out, and then he leaned back into the taxi and thanked her for coming with him. He turned and ran in loping strides up the stairs to his office.

Rikki would recall some months later exactly what passed through her mind at that moment. "My only thought as Jan got out of the cab was, That was a great night for me and *he'll* never remember a minute of it."

The Negotiation

1

Schlichtmann and his partners sat around the conference room table. They kept the doors to the room closed and the Venetian blinds on the windows lowered. For three days they took no phone calls, returned no messages, and answered none of the registered letters that arrived every morning from creditors. They had sandwiches and trays of cold cuts brought in for lunch. The air-conditioning unit in the window chattered away, but still it grew warm in the room. The seven men shed their suit coats and rolled up their shirtsleeves. Nesson, the only member of the team missing, was on vacation with his family.

They took stock of their situation. They could go forward and begin the medical phase of trial, but the judge would probably dismiss three of the leukemia death cases because of the date the jury had given. And the jury was clearly divided. "That turns the next phase of trial into a real gamble, a roll of the dice," Schlichtmann told his partners. On top of that, their financial position was precarious in the extreme. Gordon had just cashed in the firm's retirement plan. He thought he could get them through another three months, until October. Beyond that, Gordon foresaw only disaster.

Their only sane option, as Schlichtmann had realized after his sleepless night in New York, was to try to settle with W. R. Grace now, before the judge began dismissing leukemia claims. But to negotiate a settlement, they had to be prepared to go ahead with the trial. Grace had to believe they were willing to go ahead, and for Grace to believe that, they had to make themselves believe it, too. "You can't settle without a commitment to going on," said Phillips.

"It'll mean putting me in a rowboat and setting me adrift for six months," said Schlichtmann. "With some suits," he added.

Grace, they reasoned, had an incentive to settle. In September Keating would face the same jury that had already handed his client one loss. This time the testimony would be about dead children, not groundwater movement. "Grace did lose," said Gordon. "The fuckers *did* lose!"

They spent the first day of their strategy session convincing themselves they really could go on with the trial. On the morning of the second day Schlichtmann left the conference room and went over to the offices of Foley, Hoag & Eliot to see Keating. He returned half an hour later and reported that Keating had arranged for Grace's executive vice president and general counsel, a man named Albert Eustis, to fly up to Boston on Friday morning for a settlement conference.

Gordon recognized Eustis's name. At the closing arguments, he'd seen several men in dark suits—Grace executives, he surmised—sitting in the gallery behind Keating's counsel table. He'd gone over to introduce himself. He'd gotten a chilly reception, but Eustis had stood out. Eustis had the sort of commanding presence that drew one's eye. He was in his mid-sixties, still trim as an athlete, with a head of thick silvery hair.

Schlichtmann recalled seeing this man, too. "Was that Eustis?" he asked Gordon. "The really handsome guy?"

Gordon searched the computer database for more information on Eustis. He found a sketchy biography: Born in Mahoney City, Pennsylvania, November 1921. Educated at Columbia and Harvard Law. Married 1959. Joined W. R. Grace 1961. Executive Vice-President and General Counsel 1982. Member of Harvard Club and American Yacht Club.

The rest of that day and all the next, Schlichtmann and his partners worked on a settlement demand. After much debate, they decided that the case was still worth twenty-five million dollars, nearly the same figure they had agreed upon a year ago, before Nesson had joined the team. They would begin the negotiation by asking for more, around thirty-five million. They devised a complicated proposal—part cash, part annuities and deferred payments—of the sort they had presented on the eve of trial, when they demanded a hundred and seventy-five million and Facher walked out. Facher wasn't around now, and this time they didn't expect anyone to walk out. "Grace wouldn't be sending a heavyweight like Eustis if they thought they could buy settlement cheap," observed Schlichtmann.

Only Conway remained pessimistic. "You went over to see Keating the day after the verdict. I think his first thought was that we're hemorrhaging."

Schlichtmann brushed this aside. "If they thought that, they'd send in the lawyers, the bloodsuckers. They're not doing that. You look into a man's eyes and you see something. Keating was not licking his chops."

By evening, the walls of the conference room were adorned with charts and the table was covered with legal pads and crumpled wads of paper, with empty soda cans, coffee cups and half-eaten sandwiches. It seemed as if everything had been resolved. They would ask for thirty-five million and settle for twenty-five million.

Then Conway stood up. "I want another chart," he declared. "I want to know at what point we walk away from the table and go to trial. I want to know what our squeal point is."

Conway looked more rumpled than ever, his shirttails half out of his pants, his hair flying in all directions. He looked, as Schlichtmann had once described him, like a refugee. And indeed, he was in danger of becoming homeless—the deed to his house was still in Uncle Pete's files.

"We don't want to do this, Kevin," warned Gordon.

But Conway was adamant, and Gordon relented. "Besides, everyone's already thought about the squeal point," Gordon admitted. "I know I have."

"Let's have it," Conway said grimly, sitting back down.

They went around the table, beginning with Kiley, who said, "Fifteen million." Phillips agreed with that amount, and so did Gordon.

Schlichtmann was next. He hesitated a long while. Finally he said, "Twenty-five million."

Phillips drew back. "Twenty-five million! Don't give us that bullshit. That's not your bottom line."

"It's not bullshit," Schlichtmann said calmly. "Our bottom line cannot be less than our honest valuation of the case."

And then it was Conway's turn. "Ten million," he said.

Schlichtmann leapt up from his chair. "That's crazy!" he shouted, his hands balled into fists. He stood over Conway. "Those are panic numbers! That's what you're doing, goddamn it, you're panicking!"

Conway leaned forward in his chair, his head bowed, his elbows on the table.

Schlichtmann was bending over him, his face crimson, spittle coming from his lips. "You're saying we fucked up on Beatrice because we got greedy! I'll know we fucked up on Beatrice if this is the number we take from Grace. It's fucking insane! It's grabbing what you can grab and running!"

Kiley had also jumped to his feet. He stepped up to Schlichtmann. "It doesn't mean we'd actually take that number, Jan. It's just the *least* amount."

Schlichtmann turned and walked away from the table, breathing hard.

Conway raised his head and took a deep breath. "I feel like we're really hanging by our skins now," he said, his voice quavering. "This was a case we never wanted. It looked like suicide, but we could never shake it. I think going to a verdict in the second phase with this jury would be reckless." He paused, and then said sadly, "I don't have that kind of pride."

Schlichtmann nodded grimly. "Then we *did* make a mistake not settling with Beatrice before trial."

"No we didn't," Phillips said.

"No, Jan," said Conway. "I haven't lost a second's sleep on Beatrice. But things have changed. Now we're just trying to stay alive. Ten million dollars is an awful lot of money. My first consideration is keeping the firm together, even before my family, because my family depends on that."

They never did agree on their squeal point. The subject had revealed their deepest fears, fears they could not bring themselves to confront. The conversation trailed off to other matters. Gordon had reserved a suite of rooms at the Lafayette Hotel for the negotiation tomorrow. "It's got old-world elegance," Gordon said, quoting from a brochure. "A crystal chandelier in the dining room, sterling-silver water pitchers. We can also start a new charge account there. That's an additional benefit."

The settlement meeting at the Lafayette Hotel got off to a poor start. Schlichtmann and Conway, Gordon and Phillips, the four negotiators, arrived early and waited for Eustis and his retinue. When Eustis finally showed up, twenty minutes late, he was brusque to the point of open hostility. He refused to engage in small talk or any exchange of pleasantries. He listened impatiently as Schlichtmann began with his analysis of the verdict and where it left the respective parties. "I don't have much time," Eustis said, looking at his watch. "I'm a nuts-and-bolts man. I need to know what your figure is."

Phillips delivered the settlement demand, starting with the $2.5 million for the endowed chair in environmental health.

And Eustis's manner suddenly changed. "I like that, I really do," he said. "You realize how little research there is in that field? Yes, we need something like that."

Phillips laid out the other elements of the proposal and Eustis wrote them all down, nodding occasionally and asking questions about taxes and annuities, which Gordon answered.

"Your proposal is constructive," Eustis said. "The numbers are high, but we have to start somewhere." This was a matter, continued Eustis, that he needed to discuss with Grace's board of directors and with the chairman himself, J. Peter Grace. As it happened, Eustis noted, the board was meeting next Thursday.

And then Eustis made a remark that amazed and delighted Schlichtmann. "We need a vacation from these legal bills," Eustis said, looking over at Keating. "It's a lot of waste and it's not the way we like to do business."

Schlichtmann glanced at Keating and saw his eyes widened slightly. The remark clearly stung Keating, who spoke for the first and last time during that meeting. "I don't mind you being concerned," Keating said to Eustis with a small, deprecating laugh, "but let's not call it waste."

Eustis said that he wanted to keep the lines of communication open. Schlichtmann offered to come down to New York next Friday, after the board meeting.

"That's fine," said Eustis immediately. "I don't think there's any need for neutral ground."

"We're agreed, then?" said Schlichtmann. "Next Friday morning at ten o'clock?"

Eustis didn't stay for lunch, but Schlichtmann found no cause for concern in that. On the way out the door, he paused and told Schlichtmann that he was fond of good wines. What wine were they having with lunch?

Gordon had ordered up an excellent chardonnay. They drank it themselves and ate the lunch they had planned for Eustis, sitting around the half-empty table. Schlichtmann kept marveling at Eustis's remark about Grace's legal bills. "Why would he say that?" Schlichtmann wondered. "Did you see Keating's reaction?"

Phillips pronounced himself generally pleased. "I think he expected to hear eighty or ninety million dollars. When he heard our numbers, everything changed. He became much more friendly."

Even Conway seemed to breathe easier. "It was like Jekyll and Hyde, once he heard the numbers," Conway said.

Schlichtmann leaned back in his chair. He had a sense of foreboding that he couldn't shake, although the brief meeting had given him no cause to feel that way. He decided that it must simply be the bitter aftertaste of the Beatrice defeat. He made a conscious effort to change his mood.

"Well," he said, snapping his fingers, "it looks like our figure was perfect. We were right, absolutely right."

"Don't be so cocky," said Phillips.

2

Schlichtmann and his partners flew down to New York on Thursday, August 7, for their negotiation with Eustis. The foreboding Schlichtmann had felt since the meeting with Eustis still plagued him, and his mood seemed contagious. In this jittery, uneasy state, he and Conway and the others saw portents everywhere, starting with Schlichtmann's horoscope in the *Boston Herald:* "Whether your problems be of a personal or career nature, you must refuse point blank to settle for less than you know to be just and honorable."

They made a joke of that, but the matter of the limousine did not amuse them. They boarded it at La Guardia Airport. The day was fiercely hot and as humid as the tropics. The limousine broke down two blocks from the Helmsley Palace, a cloud of white smoke billowing up from the hood. They got out and walked the rest of the way to the hotel, carrying their bags in the sweltering heat. A bad omen, said Schlichtmann, and no one disagreed.

Schlichtmann and Conway shared a two-bedroom suite on the forty-fourth floor of the Helmsley, complete with a kitchen, three bathrooms, and three television sets. A wall of windows opened on a panoramic view of the city's skyscrapers and Central Park, and in the distance the Hudson River. The suite cost eight hundred fifty dollars a night, paid for by Gordon with a new credit card. The opulence was wasted on Conway, who would have been just as happy at the Holiday Inn. But Conway understood the strange calculus of a negotiation. "You send signals with everything you do. Do we come to New York cowed, with our tail between our legs? This is for us, for our inner strength, and for Jan."

But the Helmsley did not seem to do much for their inner strength. Schlichtmann stood at the windows of the suite, gazing down on the twin spires of St. Patrick's Cathedral. "My life insurance," he said suddenly. "Have we still got it?"

"Yeah," said Gordon, but his voice was doubtful. "There's a small problem with the thirty- or sixty-day billings."

Schlichtmann looked at Gordon in consternation. "Gordon, if you let my life insurance lapse, I'll die for sure."

"Are you worth more dead than alive?" wondered Gordon.

Phillips sat in gloomy silence apart from the others, his head wreathed in a cloud of cigarette smoke. "If tomorrow is a bad day, we'll shoot you and call it even." Phillips didn't smile at his own joke.

Schlichtmann grimaced. "You won't have to shoot me. I'll do it myself."

Seven months ago, before the start of trial, Schlichtmann had ordered three new suits from Dmitri, his New York haberdasher. Now, in New York with nothing to do for the rest of the afternoon, he decided he'd like to wear one of the new suits to the negotiation tomorrow. Perhaps it would bring him luck. He tried to talk Gordon into accompanying him down to Dmitri's.

"He'll want a check," said Gordon glumly.

A loud, manic laugh erupted from Schlichtmann. "A check! A *check!* Oh, we can give him plenty of those!"

He dialed Dmitri's number. "Hi, Dmitri, it's me, Jan . . . Jan Schlichtmann . . . Remember me? Well, I've been caught up in trial. I got back and found all your messages on my desk." Schlichtmann's voice became tight and constrained with shame.

Gordon held out the credit card. "One suit," he said to Schlichtmann.

Schlichtmann reached for the card and Gordon snatched it back. "Just one," Gordon warned.

Schlichtmann hung up the phone and nervously cleared his throat. Dmitri had given him a tongue-lashing. He couldn't pay for just one suit when all three had been ready for months. He tried again to persuade Gordon to come with him to Dmitri's, but Gordon just shook his head.

Later that afternoon, Gordon took pity on Schlichtmann. They went to Saks Fifth Avenue, where Schlichtmann selected a lucky new tie. It was red and made of silk and cost sixty-five dollars, which Gordon put on the credit card.

Of all the many omens, the most telling occurred at dinner that night. They took a cab uptown to a fine new Italian restaurant named Elio's. Schlichtmann had the maître d' select their meals. Their waiter, a young Italian who spoke English with the thick accent of a newly arrived immigrant, was eager to please. At the end of the meal, pondering the matter of a tip, Gordon called the waiter over. "Are you lucky?" he asked the waiter.

The waiter grinned affably and said yes.

"How lucky?"

The waiter weighed this question. He said he'd bought stock in an electronics company three months ago and sold it yesterday at a fifteen-hundred-dollar profit.

This amazed Gordon. The waiter, it seemed, barely spoke English. "No kidding? You play the stock market? Have you ever heard of W. R. Grace?"

"W. R. Grace?" The waiter looked at the ceiling, mouth pursed in concentration. "Yes, yes, they got some kind of problem in Massachusetts." The waiter had difficulty twisting his tongue around Massachusetts. "They made the water . . . polluted? . . . and killed some kids. Six kids, I think."

At this, Schlichtmann leaped up with a cry, knocking his chair over. Gordon jumped up, too, and hugged the waiter around the shoulders like a lost friend. In an instant, Conway and Crowley and Phillips and Kiley were all standing, shaking hands and congratulating the waiter, who looked pleased but puzzled. The other patrons, engaged in noisy and convivial conversation, suddenly grew hushed and turned to look at the group of men causing a commotion.

Gordon decided the waiter must be a harbinger of great success. Luck traveled in strange and mysterious circuits. Gordon left an exceedingly generous tip, hoping that it would enable them to tap into the waiter's circuit of luck.

The next morning at a quarter to ten, Schlichtmann and Conway, Gordon and Phillips, the negotiating team, departed for W. R. Grace's corporate headquarters, leaving Kiley and Crowley at the Helmsley. They walked out of the dark, air-conditioned lobby of the Helmsley into the bright summer sunshine. They crossed Fifth Avenue, and it was then that Schlichtmann realized he did not know the address of the Grace Building. Gordon said he thought it was on Sixth Avenue and Forty-eighth Street, three blocks away. They walked briskly. At the corner of Forty-eighth Street, Gordon peered at the tall buildings, looking for the Grace corporate logo. They stood on the corner, perplexed. Schlichtmann asked a passerby for directions to W. R. Grace, but the pedestrian shrugged helplessly.

Conway laughed, a bitter, mirthless laugh. They expected Grace to give them twenty-five million dollars and they couldn't even find the building. As omens went, it was a very bad one indeed.

Gordon finally went into the lobby of an office building and checked the address in a phone book: forty-third Street and Sixth Avenue. Five long blocks away, and they were already late. Back on the street, they tried without success to hail a cab. They started walking again. It was only midmorning, but in their dark suits and the furnace heat and humidity of New York in August, they began to perspire. Sweat ran in rivulets down Schlichtmann's neck and stained the front of his shirt. Gordon took out his handkerchief and wiped his plump face. "God, I hate to sweat," he said.

At the Helmsley Palace, Kiley and Crowley paced and looked at their watches, announcing the time to each other. The television droned in the background, the muted sounds of one morning talk show following another.

"A quarter of one," intoned Kiley. The negotiators had been gone almost three hours and Kiley began to hope that the settlement was at hand. "What are you going to do with all the dough to keep it away from Jan?" he asked Crowley.

"We have to put him on a salary," replied Crowley. "There's got to be some kind of policy."

At that moment the door opened and Schlichtmann walked into the suite. He stopped in the middle of the room, his hands on his hips, his suit jacket opened. He looked at Kiley and Crowley, a level gaze, and said in a neutral, uninflected voice, as if he was simply reporting a fact: "They offered six point six million, take it or leave it."

Gordon, his face flushed, his hair in disarray, followed Schlichtmann into the room. He sat at the dining table. "It was one of the most depressing times of my entire life," he announced. He looked up at Kiley and gave him a pained smile. "The only good thing, Tom, is you should be glad you weren't there. They had a pot of terrible coffee, some stale pastries wrapped in napkins, and paper plates. They didn't even offer us lunch."

Conway and Phillips came into the suite a few minutes later. Everyone was standing, facing each other in a loose circle, except for Gordon, who slumped at the table.

"They were very hostile," Conway told Kiley and Crowley. "Eustis was a different person today. He blamed us for not settling before all the publicity. 'If you'd settled then, you'd be rich men,' he said. 'Now you can recover your costs and you'll be famous.'"

"Keating was there," said Gordon from the table. "But he hardly said a word. It all went downhill fast. We tried everything we could to keep it alive. I don't think we missed a step."

Schlichtmann took off his suit jacket and stood at the window, staring out at the city. "It's too bad they terminated the discussion."

"They did it by the book," said Phillips. "Those bastards," he added, muttering under his breath.

"They're not bastards," said Schlichtmann, still looking out the window. "It's the jury. For whatever reason, I lost them. They're willing to support the system."

Gordon looked over at Kiley and Crowley. "Jan was so *fucking* good today. I've never seen him better. He brought tears to Eustis's eyes when he told him what Patrick Toomey went through before he died. Eustis said, 'It's a terrible thing, but money can't bring the boy back.' Then he turned to Jan, almost like a father giving advice, and said, 'It's not worth it to go for broke. You can go to trial and risk losing it all. Or you can put a notch in your belt now and have plenty of business.' Eustis said six point six million dollars is a lot of money. 'You can declare victory with that.' "

Schlichtmann walked over to the table where Gordon sat. He picked an apple out of a basket of fruit, courtesy of the Helmsley, and bit into it. There was a bottle of wine in the fruit basket, too. He picked up the bottle and studied the label.

Gordon watched him. "It's been an interesting case, a learning experience. I don't feel nearly as egotistical as I used to."

Schlichtmann gave a short, abrupt laugh. "I concur with that."

From across the room, Kiley said, "We've got a problem, Jan. I think you're ethically bound to tell the families about the offer. You've got a gross of almost a million dollars a family."

"We've got a problem," agreed Schlichtmann. "The judge is going to start eliminating families on September fifth, beginning with the Zonas. Then he'll try to get rid of the Kanes and Anne Anderson. He can destroy us."

"We've got to act fast," said Kiley. "Let's be realistic. Can we get ten million dollars and get out?"

"The case is over," said Conway with finality, hitching up his pants and walking in worried circles. "Our big win was the waiter last night."

Silence descended upon the group. They sat and paced around the garish hotel suite, with its satiny, rose-colored wallpaper and fake Louis Quinze chairs with gilded arms. Outside the window the city looked golden in the sunshine.

"Those bastards," murmured Phillips again.

Schlichtmann sighed deeply. "I guess I got a choice. Using all my intelligence, do I see this case as hopeless? If I do, then I have to grab whatever money I can for the families. And a fee as a whoremongering attorney. But I'll never allow my own financial pressure to rule what happens to the case."

Kiley scoffed at this. "Do you have an obligation to lose your house, ruin your health, your career, your mental outlook for this case? It boils down to dollars and cents, Jan. That's what this is all about. You can get half a million dollars for these families and they can send their kids to college. You've got nothing to be ashamed of. To get half a million dollars in the hands of these people, that's significant."

Schlichtmann opened the bottle of wine in the fruit basket and took a sip. He wet his lips and took another sip. "Good wine," he said.

Conway said, "Jan, win or lose, we've got to get this case behind us. We've gone as far as we can go. It's over. It's done."

Schlichtmann stood at the window and gazed out over the city. He seemed to have left the discussion and gone somewhere else in his mind.

Kiley spoke to his back. He reminded Schlichtmann that when they flew back from New York a week ago, the day of the *Good Morning America* show, Donna Robbins could not even pay for the cab to Woburn. "This is a lot of money to these people. You think they'll look at this as a loss? Half a million dollars?"

"It's hopeless, absolutely hopeless," said Conway, his tie askew, his mouth set in a deep crease. "We cannot go to a verdict with this jury. You know that as well as I do, Jan. We can't even go until September fifth because of the potential for the judge to destroy it all. It's over, Jan."

Schlichtmann, still at the window, didn't respond.

Gordon looked at Phillips. "Is it over, Mark?"

"Uh-huh," said Phillips quietly. "Jan, the judge cut your balls off. There's nothing you can do about that. We're surrounded. It's Pork Chop Hill."

"What happened at Pork Chop Hill?" asked Gordon.

"They got wiped out."

"Yeah," said Schlichtmann turning back to the group. "But they held the hill."

Gordon sighed. "What the fuck are we going to do? Do we have a medical causation case or not?"

"They proved medical causation in Velisicol," said Schlichtmann, referring to a recent decision in a Tennessee case involving residents who lived near a toxic waste dump and claimed a variety of health problems.

Kiley laughed harshly. "They had three hundred thousand barrels of shit. The stuff was oozing out of their pores in Velisicol."

"We had six barrels at Grace," said Gordon sadly, "and two of them were empty."

Schlichtmann laughed so hard that the wine he'd just sipped spewed from his lips. Conway looked at him, startled, and then Conway laughed, too. In a moment, Phillips joined in, and then Kiley. Everyone was laughing, a convulsing, cathartic uproar of laughter that lasted for a minute or more.

"So," said Schlichtmann at last, wiping the tears of laughter from his eyes, "we got blinded by greed. Nothing wrong with that. It's our motivating factor. That, and the historical aspect. This was a political case. If it had just been a personal injury case, it would have settled a long time ago."

"Do you know what you want to do?" asked Conway, hoping Schlichtmann would agree that it was over, hoping he would settle the case and get it out of their lives.

Schlichtmann considered this for a moment. "Nobody is in more pain than me," he said at last. "Nobody wants to end it more than I do. But I'm not going to let it end just because I'm in pain."

Phillips said, "Would you take fifteen million right now?"

"Sure," replied Schlichtmann.

"What bullshit!" cried Kiley. "We almost had a fistfight over these numbers. At fifteen million it's a political cause and at eight million it's a personal injury case?"

"So what do we do between now and September fifth?" Conway asked. "I don't mean paying the bills. I mean the work, the experts. Do we go ahead with that?"

"We've got problems," said Gordon. "There's the office staff. People's lives are at stake. We got to prepare for phase two. We can't negotiate without being prepared. Things are not black and white."

Phillips grimaced at Gordon. "Don't get philosophical on me now. It's out of character."

But Gordon hadn't finished his litany. "The fucking computers are going to be repossessed on Monday."

Schlichtmann looked at Gordon with genuine surprise. "Really?" he said.

Gordon nodded. "Does unemployment insurance cover people who've been laid off?"

"Have we been paying it?" asked Conway.

Gordon shook his head. "I don't think so."

Conway said, "Even eliminating the office staff doesn't solve our problems. We'll still have to pay for transcripts."

"Are we in fucking fantasy land or not?" said Gordon. "No payroll taxes have been paid at all."

Schlichtmann said quietly, "It would have been better if they hadn't made us any offer."

Conway went into the bedroom to pack. After a few moments Schlichtmann followed him into the room, still carrying the glass of wine. Conway hefted his suitcase on the bed and took off his suit jacket and folded it. Schlichtmann, his arms crossed, leaned against the door and watched him, saying nothing.

"It's over, Jan," said Conway as he packed. "If we go on, it will destroy us all. We've got to stop it now."

Schlichtmann still didn't say anything. He shrugged and then turned and left.

Conway watched him go. He knew the case wasn't over until Schlichtmann said it was. When Schlichtmann was out of earshot, Conway said, "He's willing to take everything a step further than anybody else. God knows, he loves the edges. If he decides to go to trial, I'll be there. But I hope he doesn't. God, I hope he doesn't."

The tropical heat of the day gave way to rain squalls and a dark and turbulent sky. At La Guardia Airport that evening, the shuttle to Boston was delayed because of tornado warnings. As Michael Keating remembered it later, he was standing in the crowded waiting room with hundreds of other stranded travelers. Then, across the room, he spotted

Schlichtmann's tall, angular form. Keating had no desire to talk to Schlichtmann. He grabbed his bag and pushed open a small door in the back of the terminal. He thought he had gotten away unnoticed, but then he heard Schlichtmann's voice behind him calling, "Mike! Mike!"

Keating stopped and turned to confront Schlichtmann. They stood next to a garbage bin, foul-smelling and dripping from the squall that had just passed.

Schlichtmann said he regretted that the negotiation had ended the way it did.

"I thought it ended just where it should have," replied Keating.

"We have to keep talking," continued Schlichtmann. "You can't just have ultimatums. You've got to have a process."

Keating listened but said little as Schlichtmann went on talking about how important the "process" was and how they had to find a way to resolve this case to their mutual benefit. "Let's get together on Monday morning in Boston," Schlichtmann said, "and have a heart-to-heart."

Keating couldn't agree to this without notifying Eustis first. He told Schlichtmann he would call him on Monday and let him know. They parted without shaking hands.

Keating walked across a parking lot and into another terminal. He was puzzled. Only a few hours ago he'd felt certain that the case would not settle and Schlichtmann would go ahead with the second phase of trial. He had taken careful notes when Schlichtmann described what had happened to Patrick Toomey, certain that he was getting a preview of Schlichtmann's opening argument. And to Keating, it promised to be a powerful one.

Keating found a phone booth and looked up Eustis's home number in Scarsdale. Eustis's wife answered the phone. Keating explained who he was. A moment later Eustis came to the line. Keating apologized for calling him at home. "I just ran into Schlichtmann at the airport, and I thought you ought to know about it."

"No problem," said Eustis.

Keating related the substance of his conversation with Schlichtmann, and then he said, "I've never seen anyone so desperate to settle. I don't know what's driving him, whether they've run out of money or what."

Eustis thanked Keating for calling. "Let's see what happens next," Eustis said.

3

Back in Boston, the chasm of the weekend loomed before Schlicht-mann. On Saturday evening, as the sun set over the Charles River and small boats sailed in the Back Bay, he lay on the bed in Teresa's apart-ment. His mind churned. He knew he had to start preparing for the second phase of trial. Details crunched through his brain as he exam-ined the possibilities and pitfalls, a chess game of enormous complex-ity. Twenty thousand pages of depositions to think about, tens of thousands of pages of medical records and test results. Have I looked at Colvin's second deposition? he thought. Has Lappe talked with Conibear? Has he talked with Paigen? The T cell assays, the Harvard health study, Cohen's electrocardiograms, Feldman's blink reflex stud-ies. An endless, treacherous swamp of detail and evidentiary problems. How many expert witnesses? Twenty, perhaps more. It made the first five months of trial look like a law school exercise in comparison.

Teresa came to the door and asked if he wanted dinner. He said he wasn't hungry. She made a light meal of omelettes anyway. He ate it like a man famished and asked what else she had. In the freezer, she found a frozen pizza. "I don't want that. It's poison," he said. She heated up the pizza anyhow, and he consumed it all, along with half a bottle of beer. He lay on the bed, holding the remote control for the television in his hand, flicking endlessly through the channels, never pausing for more than a few seconds.

Teresa was in the kitchen when she heard him calling. His voice was urgent and he sounded frightened. She ran to the bedroom. He lay with his legs spread apart, his feet dangling off the end of the bed, one hand on his chest. "I think I'm having a heart attack, I have this intense pressure in my chest, I can barely breathe."

She felt his pulse, which was rapid but strong. "You're having an anx-iety attack," she said. She had a prescription for Valium in the medicine cabinet. She broke one of the pills in half and brought it to him. "Take this," she said. "It'll make you feel better."

"What is it?" he asked. She told him and he refused to take it. "I've been drinking. It'll make me hallucinate."

"Jan, that's nonsense. You've only had half a beer."

She thought that if he didn't take the pill, she would. In the kitchen, she poured the remaining beer into his glass and dropped the pill into it. She used a spoon to crush it. He drank the beer without suspicion. Within half an hour his pace on the television remote control began to slow, and soon he fell into a heavy sleep.

On Monday morning, August 11, Schlichtmann went to the coffee shop at the Meridien Hotel, across from the federal courthouse, to meet Keating. Schlichtmann told Keating that he wanted to make settlement a "positive" event for W. R. Grace. Keating asked why he would want to do that, and Schlichtmann replied, "Because I'm more successful if I'm perceived as someone who can turn a company's worst nightmare into a positive event, instead of one who wages war." Keating said that Eustis viewed any settlement—especially a large one—as tantamount to an admission of guilt. The jury had returned a verdict against Grace, and paying money now would make it look as if Grace accepted that verdict. Furthermore, Eustis was concerned about the "shark effect." A big settlement would induce other personal injury lawyers to seek clients in Woburn and file dozens of lawsuits, hoping to settle for a lot of money.

These arguments all made perfect sense to Schlichtmann, who saw in them opportunity, not obstacles. Money, he deduced, was not Eustis's foremost concern. How the settlement was perceived—its presentation to the press, and its success in averting future Woburn lawsuits—these issues were more important to Eustis than money.

What if, Schlichtmann suggested to Keating, he could put together a settlement package that would guarantee peace in Woburn?

Peace in Woburn? Yes, Keating thought that might interest Eustis.

"Is it conceivable," said Schlichtmann, "that there is a figure between yours and mine that might take care of my needs?"

"It's conceivable," replied Keating. But Eustis was on vacation now, out sailing solo on Long Island Sound. He could not be reached, and he would not be back at work until next week.

Throughout that week, Schlichtmann conferred with his partners. A new settlement strategy began to take shape. On September 5, when they went before the judge, Keating would file a motion for a new trial. Keating would ask the judge to vacate the verdict on the grounds that it was against the weight of the evidence. Schlichtmann would consent to this motion. He would let the judge know that his consent was part of a settlement agreement. A new trial would make it look as if Grace wasn't really guilty. They could even have the families say to the press that Beatrice and chemical companies in north Woburn were responsible for the contamination of the wells.

Kiley liked this idea. "I think it's a great strategy. We'll give them anything they want as long as they give us twelve million dollars."

But Conway was not optimistic. He believed that all Eustis cared about was the money. "It's very clear. Eustis is afraid that if the number is too high, it's going to create a shark effect. All these other things are just red herrings. Either they care about them or they don't. And I don't think they care."

"Yes, they do," insisted Schlichtmann.

Conway was unconvinced. "What if all this stuff is fantasy and they're not going anywhere but six point six million?"

"Then it's not going to settle," said Schlichtmann simply, as if he were merely stating the obvious. "We'll go to trial."

A moment of silence followed this statement.

At last Gordon said, "We're in a bit of a pickle."

"I think we're in real trouble," said Conway slowly.

Schlichtmann looked at his partners. "The money cannot be taken, not six point six million," he said in a level voice. "I cannot take fees and expenses out of that and go to the families empty-handed and say, 'Thanks for the privilege of representing you.' "

They talked off and on all week, adopting and discarding strategies. The pattern was familiar, a pattern of despair followed by hope and renewal, followed once again by despair. Schlichtmann called Keating and waited several days for Keating to call back. When Keating finally did call, on Friday morning, he left word that he was not authorized to engage in any further discussions until Eustis returned from sailing.

That afternoon, Conway was in his own office, talking with one of the associates, and the secretaries were gathered in the kitchen for a coffee break when the sounds of loud banging and the thud of heavy articles hitting the floor came from Schlichtmann's office. These sounds were followed by screams. "Save me! Save me! I'm self-destructive! I always knew that!"

Conway and the secretaries came running from every corner of the office. Conway gingerly opened Schlichtmann's door. Everyone stood in the doorway, looking over each other's shoulders at Schlichtmann, who was on his knees, behind his desk. He clasped his head and slid to the floor. "Oh, God help me!" he shouted.

The staff gaped wide-eyed at him. For a moment no one moved. Then Schlichtmann, supine under his desk, peered up at them. Slowly he clambered to his knees and rested his head on the desk. "Am I at the bottom?" he asked Conway.

Conway nodded solemnly.

"What is today?"

"August fifteenth," said Kathy Boyer.

"So we still got fifteen days left in August?" said Schlichtmann. "Good! That's a whole lifetime." He looked at the two associates. "How are you two doing?"

"Great," said one of them without conviction.

"You need direction?" asked Schlichtmann. Then he laughed weakly.

Conway laughed, too, at the thought of Schlichtmann providing direction to anyone in his state.

Schlichtmann rose from his knees and walked unsteadily out of his office. "Okay, I feel better now," he announced. "I feel much better."

Peggy Vecchione peeked into Schlichtmann's office. Notebooks and files, depositions and trial transcripts, letters, memos, bills, pens, pencils and Rolodex cards covered the floor. Except for the computer terminal, which was bolted down, the star litigator's desk was completely bare.

"At least your desk is clean, Jan," said Peggy as Schlichtmann walked past her.

4

Schlichtmann stood for a moment in the bright morning sun. He gazed up at the Grace Building, its curved, marble-clad columns slanting upward, like the sinews of a giant tree, forming a small plaza on Sixth Avenue and Forty-third Street. The architecture seemed intended to convey an imposing, implacable power. Schlichtmann felt dwarfed.

On the phone the day before, Eustis had said, "You can come down anytime." Schlichtmann had brought Gordon along with him. They had walked from the Helmsley to the Grace Building together. At the door, Gordon wished Schlichtmann luck and shook his hand. He noticed that Schlichtmann's palms were sweaty. Gordon turned and walked across the plaza, and then, on Sixth Avenue, he paused and looked back. Schlichtmann was still standing at the door, gazing up at the building. Gordon waited until he saw him go in, and then he began trudging back to the Helmsley.

Schlichtmann boarded an elevator that was paneled in rich, dark wood. It whisked him up fifty floors, to the executive suites. A security guard buzzed him through a set of enormous glass doors, politely asked him to fill out a form, and gave him an identification badge to wear. Schlichtmann took a seat on a couch in the softly lit room. He surveyed the objects of art on the walls, gleaming like treasures under spotlights. He could hear no office sounds, no secretaries chattering, no telephones burbling, nothing but the soft whisper of the building's ventilation system. He felt hypervigilant. Everything in this building seemed freighted with menace.

Yesterday afternoon, before leaving for New York, he'd gone to Woburn to visit Anne Anderson. He'd sat with her in the small, dark kitchen of her ranch house on Orange Street, two of her many cats entwining themselves around his legs. Over the kitchen table, he had talked with her about going on to the next phase of the trial. A settlement with Grace, he'd told her, did not look possible. They might still win something in trial, he'd said, but they faced an equal possibility of defeat. The long journey wasn't over yet, but it was nearing an end. Anne began to cry softly, tears rolling down her cheeks. She wiped them away with a Kleenex. The prospect of taking the witness stand to testify frightened her. She feared, she told Schlichtmann, that she would lose control, break down, cry uncontrollably. Schlichtmann attempted to reassure her, but he felt, to his surprise, tears welling up in his own eyes. They'd sat together for a while in the dark kitchen, at the battered Formica table, both weeping.

Now, waiting for Eustis, it struck Schlichtmann as bizarre, almost dreamlike, the way he had traveled between the two extremes of American society, from the kitchen of a dilapidated ranch house in east

Woburn to this quiet, muted foyer at the heart of one of the nation's largest and most powerful corporations.

In a moment a woman appeared to escort him down carpeted corridors to Eustis's office. Eustis, in his shirtsleeves, rose from his desk and came forward, smiling, to greet Schlichtmann. He looked handsome, lean and vigorous, a little sunburned from his week out on Long Island Sound aboard his sailboat. He looked much younger than his years, looked in fact as if he were in his prime rather than nearing his retirement. He occupied a large corner office, windows extending from floor to ceiling, with a view of the skyscrapers of southern Manhattan, the Hudson River and the Palisades. To Schlichtmann, the great size of the office made it appear sparely furnished, almost empty. Against a far wall, a long distance away, as if, thought Schlichtmann, he were looking through the wrong end of a telescope, was a couch and two wing chairs on either side of a coffee table. Eustis's desk, a delicate eighteenth-century antique that Schlichtmann imagined was French in origin and probably had cost a fortune, was bare except for a telephone and a single piece of paper. Eustis gestured to a chair in front of the desk and Schlichtmann sat there, feeling uncomfortable, his hands on his knees.

Eustis made small talk, asking some polite questions about how Schlichtmann had been, addressing Schlichtmann by his first name. Eustis said he had spent the last week on his boat, alone, sailing Long Island Sound. The solitude, he said, had been wonderful.

Schlichtmann imagined Keating calling Eustis on his sailboat, on a two-way radio, saying, "Yes, Mr. Eustis, yes, Mr. Eustis." Schlichtmann recalled that Keating had always addressed Eustis in a formal manner. Schlichtmann decided that he would not do so.

"Well," said Eustis after a bit, "let's get to it."

Schlichtmann began talking about a settlement that would assure Grace of "peace in Woburn." Eustis listened, nodding his head occasionally. Then he asked Schlichtmann for his figure.

Schlichtmann said, "We can settle this—meet our needs and your needs—for a sum under twenty million."

Eustis compressed his lips, closed his eyes, and shook his head once, an emphatic gesture. "I need a hard number," he said.

"Al," said Schlichtmann, "that sort of negotiation is just not going to work."

"You're being coy with me," said Eustis with a smile.

"No, I'm not. You said you wanted a ballpark number. I'm not going to keep giving you one number after another just so you can keep saying no."

A secretary knocked on the door and entered, carrying a note for Eustis. Schlichtmann could see that it was handwritten. Eustis read the note in a quick glance and crumpled it. He looked at his watch. "Why don't you come to lunch with me? We'll go to the Harvard Club."

Schlichtmann felt certain that someone, perhaps J. Peter Grace himself, was listening in on their conversation, directing Eustis. And now Eustis had been directed to take him to lunch. Schlichtmann thought, Oh my God, I don't want to go to lunch with this man. He felt awkward and unsure of himself and not at all hungry. But he had to keep the discussion going. Eustis stood and put on his suit jacket, and Schlichtmann stood, too.

On the way to the Harvard Club, a walk of two blocks, Eustis seemed in fine spirits. He laughed and talked in an animated fashion about sailing. Schlichtmann tried to listen and respond, but he found that hard work. They entered the Harvard Club, cool and dark, men sitting in large leather upholstered chairs reading *The Wall Street Journal,* others standing in small groups talking, a quiet sanctum away from the city streets. Eustis showed Schlichtmann a portrait of Teddy Roosevelt and the stuffed head of an animal that Roosevelt had shot.

Schlichtmann, at a loss for words, finally said, "Gee, there must be a lot of business transacted here."

Eustis smiled and shook his head. "No, it's an unspoken rule that no business is ever transacted here."

Schlichtmann felt a spasm of anxiety. He and Eustis had nothing in common, not in their pasts or their futures. He wondered how he could possibly endure lunch without talking about the case.

The maître d' escorted them to a table. A waiter arrived with menus and placed a basket of rolls on the table. Schlichtmann eyed them. He wanted to break open a roll simply to occupy his hands, to allay his nervousness, but he thought about the crumbs of bread on the clean, white linen table cloth and decided against it.

They studied the menu in silence. Schlichtmann ordered flounder and a glass of white wine. Eustis began talking knowledgeably about wines and vintages. He and his wife, he said, liked to enjoy a good bottle of wine with dinner. Schlichtmann, who knew very little about wine, labored to contribute. He told Eustis about visiting some Napa Valley wineries years ago on a tour. The subject exhausted him, and the conversation ended lamely. Eustis spoke about his children, grown now, with careers of their own. Schlichtmann could think of nothing interesting to say. Eustis asked Schlichtmann how he had become a lawyer, and Schlichtmann told him about the office in Newburyport and the Eaton trial. After that, the pauses seemed to grow longer. Every subject trailed off into awkward silences, although Eustis seemed perfectly at ease. The one subject that filled Schlichtmann's mind, that he could have talked endlessly about, was Woburn, but he couldn't mention it.

The waiter brought the bill on a silver tray and placed it between them. Eustis ignored it. He asked Schlichtmann again if he was certain he did not want coffee, and Schlichtmann again declined.

The bill began to worry Schlichtmann. No doubt Eustis would pay. Eustis, after all, had invited him to lunch. The bill sat in the middle of the table, equidistant from them both. Eustis sipped his coffee. Schlichtmann thought: Maybe he expects me to pay. I'm the one asking for millions of dollars. But Schlichtmann had only a single credit card that Gordon had given him that morning, and that card was in Gordon's name. What if Eustis noticed him signing someone else's name? What if Eustis discovered that he was as broke as a homeless person in Central Park?

Eustis, of course, did pay, a quick signature with barely a glance at the bill.

The moment they stepped out of the Harvard Club onto the street, Schlichtmann began just where he'd left off. "Al, I'm not going to give you another number just so you can say no again. I'm not going to start bidding against myself."

"I need a hard number," replied Eustis. "We're not going to get anywhere unless you can give me a hard number."

They walked back toward the Grace building. Schlichtmann realized he had no idea what to do next. Eustis had flatly refused to engage in the sort of negotiation that Schlichtmann was familiar with, the process of give-and-take that he'd gone through a dozen times with insurance company agents. Conway had been right. All the talk about peace in Woburn had meant nothing. Eustis cared only about the bottom line.

Schlichtmann looked down at the pavement. "Okay," he said finally. "What if I get back to you this afternoon with our bottom line?"

They were in front of the Grace building. "Do you need an office and a phone?" asked Eustis. "I can give you a room to work in."

Grace headquarters was the last place Schlichtmann wanted to work. "No," he said, "I've got a room at the Helmsley."

Eustis shrugged.

Schlichtmann called the Boston office when he got back to the Helmsley. Conway took the call in the conference room and put Schlichtmann on the speakerphone.

"Well, he took me to lunch," Schlichtmann said. He described the meeting with Eustis to Conway and Phillips, omitting the details of his nervousness at the Harvard Club. "I'm very pessimistic," Schlichtmann said when he'd finished. "He kept saying he wants a hard number, a hard number. What do I tell him? Do I just say fifteen million?"

Conway said, "I think you've got to give Eustis our bottom line. Fifteen is supposed to be our squeal point."

Phillips said to Schlichtmann, "Do you feel compelled to disclose your squeal point today?"

Over the speakerphone, Schlichtmann's voice rose in anger. "You're not *thinking*, Mark. Eustis is not negotiating. He's a bottom-liner. I think I've got to do this his way. I've got to give him the bottom line."

Phillips said quietly, "Our bottom line is not fifteen million."

"What is it?" said Schlichtmann.

"We don't know yet."

"Twelve?" asked Schlichtmann, a plaintive note in his voice.

Conway liked that number. "That might get you dinner with Eustis."

Phillips grabbed a yellow pad from the table and began calculating while Conway talked with Schlichtmann. Phillips worked in silence for a few minutes, punching numbers into the calculator. "Okay," he said to Schlichtmann. "What do you think about this: One point two million in cash for each family, and five thousand dollars a month for thirty years. That comes out sixteen point two million."

"I like that," said Schlichtmann.

"I don't give a shit if you like it," said Phillips. "Do you *believe* it?"

"Do we have to get it typed up?" interrupted Gordon from an extension at the Helmsley.

"Fuck, no," said Phillips.

"Yeah, we do," said Schlichtmann. "It'll make it look firm."

At six o'clock that evening, Schlichtmann called Boston again. "Eustis was standing in his office looking out the window when I arrived," he told Conway and Phillips over the speaker phone. "He offers to take my coat, but I wanted to keep it on because I had the paper with the figures in it. I'm ready to give him the numbers. He gets a yellow pad out and starts writing on it. Then he says, 'Oops, out of my ballpark. You could've called me and told me this, you wouldn't have had to come down here.' So, shit, I figure it's over with. I'm ready to leave. He puts his feet up on his desk, on this spindly French antique thing. He tells me to take my jacket off and put my feet on the desk, too. I don't want to. It was very strange. There was a lot of talk about me putting my feet on the desk. 'Go ahead,' he says. 'Relax a bit.' Then he says: 'Six point six million dollars is a lot of money.'

"I tell him: 'Let me put this in perspective for you. Our costs are two and a half million.'

"He takes his feet off the desk and starts pacing up and down. His secretary comes to the door with a note. He reads it and tears it up, and then he says: 'Suppose I took that into account?'

"I ask him, 'Don't you see any opportunity here?' He says, 'No, I don't.' Then he says, 'Well, maybe. There are other people involved in this. I've got to discuss it with them.' "

Over the phone, Schlichtmann paused in his account. "I think we made a breakthrough," he told Conway and Phillips. "I think his authority was to ten million. We're beyond ten now. He's got to call the others to see if he can get a ticket to our ballpark. He wants me to stay another night. He did say he was pessimistic, but this whole thing with taking my jacket off and making me put my feet on the desk indicates he smells opportunity. I don't think he'd ask me to stay in New York if all he's going to do is offer eight million. He got very excited, very animated. It was so uncharacteristic of him. He mentioned calling Charles

Erhart in Maine and some other guy. We're supposed to meet tomorrow at eleven."

Erhart was chief administrative officer of W. R. Grace and vice chairman of the board. Phillips thought this was a good sign indeed. "It sounds propitious," he told Schlichtmann. "They've got a figure they can't ignore."

That night in New York, Schlichtmann felt hopeful but also wary. After so many ups and downs, he could no longer trust his instincts. It was in this state of uncertainty that he received a call from Eustis the next morning. "This will take more than one day," he heard Eustis tell him. "Call me tomorrow around eleven. Will you still be in New York?"

Schlichtmann, caught off guard and not knowing what to do, said yes, he'd stay another night.

When he hung up the phone, Gordon berated him savagely. "I'm not staying here another fucking day, watching soap operas and shining my shoes. Call him back and tell him we're leaving."

Schlichtmann, completely unmoored now, did as Gordon instructed. He told Eustis's secretary he had decided to leave New York. "Tell Al he can reach me in Boston."

"What's the matter?" asked the secretary. "You don't like New York?"

Schlichtmann thought he detected a mocking tone in her voice.

5

Schlichtmann and his partners waited in the office on Milk Street all the next day for Eustis to call. Phillips, unable to sleep last night, had gotten up to read Clausewitz's treatise *On War*. When he laid the book down, it had fallen open to the chapter entitled "Retreat after a Loss." This, Phillips warned Schlichtmann, must be an omen.

In his own office, Conway stared numbly out the window. A poisonous lethargy hung over the office. Phillips came in and sat in the chair across from him. Neither man said a word for a long while. Finally Conway sighed. "Want to go to a movie?" he asked.

"What's today?" said Phillips.

"Thursday, August twenty-first."

Phillips held his head in his hands as if he had a terrific headache. "We can't go on this way," he muttered. "We don't know our bottom line. There's only two weeks before we see the judge. We've got to try to settle this by tomorrow."

"What can we do?" asked Conway.

"We've got to squeeze an ounce of dignity out of this. Jan's not ready to go to trial."

After a while, Phillips wandered back into Schlichtmann's office. Schlichtmann sat at his desk, still as a mannequin. There was nothing on his desk except for one phone message from a *Boston Herald* gossip columnist named Norma Nathan. She published an annual guide to Boston's most eligible bachelors, of which she had deemed Schlichtmann to be one. To update her bachelor file, she wanted to know how much money Schlichtmann had made this year.

"Tell her about four parts per billion," said Phillips.

Schlichtmann tore up the message.

They sat in silence, waiting for Eustis to call. Phillips smoked cigarettes and watched the smoke curl around his finger. Schlichtmann looked out the window at tourists.

"Nobody calls here anymore?" said Schlichtmann. "Not even creditors? Do we have any other cases?"

That reminded Phillips of the Gallagher case, a woman crippled by a cerebral aneurysm. Phillips had worked on the case while the Woburn jury was deliberating. The case was not ready for trial, but Phillips hoped it might settle early and provide them with some cash. He asked Schlichtmann to call the defense lawyer.

Schlichtmann shook his head.

"It'll only take one minute," said Phillips.

"No. Later."

Schlichtmann leaned back in his chair, cradled his head in his arms, and stared at the ceiling. "I remember going out to Woburn five years ago and telling them it couldn't be done. It would cost too much, take too long, and the results were too uncertain. The file was less than half an inch thick. The only thing in it was the CDC report and Mulligan's contingency fee agreements. Every time I looked at that fucking file I'd get nauseous."

Conway came into Schlichtmann's office and sat wearily on the couch, listening to this reminiscence.

Schlichtmann glanced at him. "Should I have talked to Eustis directly?"

"Absolutely," said Conway. "You said you were coming to New York to resolve this."

"Gordon told me we weren't staying. Call him back, Gordon said. So I called him back."

"That was incredibly weak and stupid," said Conway, but his voice sounded sad, not angry.

"So I made another mistake. Aaaaaahhh."

Conway fell silent, his brow deeply furrowed, his foot jiggling rapidly, his fingers twining around a lock of his thick, overgrown hair. Phillips played with the door handle, opening and closing the knob, the click of the mechanism the only sound in the room.

Eustis never did call that day.

The next morning, Schlichtmann arrived at the office with a new resolve. "This is war," he said to Phillips. "I'm not going to grovel at Eustis's feet for a few more bucks. I won't survive that humiliation any better than going ahead with the trial. It'll probably destroy us. But there is such a thing as honor. It comes with a big price. I'll go to the families and make them understand there is no settlement to accept. I'll tell the experts we can't pay them anymore. I'll call Eustis and reject his offer. On September fifth, we'll go see the judge. He'll either force a settlement, or we'll lose some plaintiffs and go to trial."

Phillips listened to this declaration, nodding his head as Schlichtmann spoke. "I want you to know I'm proud of you," Phillips said. "The hardest decision you've ever made." Phillips began humming as he talked. "Also absolutely insane"—hummm, hummm. "As insane as taking this case in the first place"—hummm, hummm. "Drag that bastard Eustis off his pedestal . . ."

Schlichtmann imagined how he'd begin the trial. He would pack the courtroom with Woburn families, their neighbors and friends, and members of the Woburn environmental group FACE. "If the judge won't let them testify, we'll have them in the corridor talking to the press. We'll have a press conference with all the leukemics just before the trial begins."

"The only horror is capitulation," murmured Phillips. "Waiting for Eustis to call yesterday was the absolute pits. The most awful, degrading day. The last two weeks have been terrible, but yesterday was the worst."

"The office can survive on fifty thousand dollars a month," said Schlichtmann.

Phillips looked sardonically at him. "We can survive on thirty-five thousand. There's fat upon fat upon fat in fifty. You'd be amazed at how well you can survive on the basics. Which, incidentally, is how most law firms work."

"I just need my laundry, my suits."

"Get them real clean in September and see how long you can go," said Phillips. "Facher had a spot on his tie every day. Maybe you should try it."

Schlichtmann, his mind made up now, dialed Eustis's number. Phillips and Conway and Crowley sat across the desk from him, listening to his end of the conversation.

"Hello, Al?" Schlichtmann said, swiveling his chair around and looking down onto Milk Street. "I'm just wondering what progress you've made . . . Yeah, right, uh huh . . . Sure, they're good attorneys." He listened for a long while. Then he said, "Sounds like you got a great case there, Al. I assume you're withdrawing your offer. You're certainly entitled to do that."

Schlichtmann hung up the phone and turned his chair around to face Conway and Phillips and Crowley. "Good. It's over. Eustis said he got a memorandum from Keating and he found out some interesting things. Jarrod Aufiero died of salmonella. Roland Gamache drank bottled water since 1974. He said, 'Maybe I should just wait until September fifth and see what the judge does.' "

Schlichtmann took a deep breath. "So, we go forward." He looked at Crowley and smiled. "Crowley, you're the new trial lawyer in this firm. You should hear the stories they told about the old one." He laughed.

Phillips laughed, too, patting Crowley on the shoulder. "You'll have a few brilliant successes and then you'll go straight down."

Schlichtmann sighed. "This could be fun," he said, his voice tentative.

Phillips began humming. "It will be. You're not expected to win. You've got nothing to lose."

"Another six months of misery," groaned Conway. "What will I tell my wife?" No one answered. Conway supplied the answer himself. "I think I'll tell her we settled. She won't know the truth until she hears on the news that we've started phase two."

6

The computers hadn't been repossessed yet, as Gordon had feared, but everyone in the office expected that to happen at any moment. Just yesterday, a man from the electric company had come to shut off the electricity. A secretary had asked the man to wait while she called Gordon, who had come over with a check.

Gordon moaned incessantly about the debt, the threatening calls from angry creditors, the growing number of lawsuits. Phillips listened to him with barely concealed irritation. "We're going to lose the computer system," Gordon was saying. "We can't stop that. We haven't paid since last November."

"We've been operating in a fool's fantasy world," said Phillips. "It serves us right."

Gordon complained about not being able to pay the excise tax on his Mercedes, his beloved Mercedes. Nor could he pay the parking garage, which was about to evict the Mercedes from its space. Then the city would tow the car for unpaid back taxes, if the bank did not repossess it first.

Phillips had no patience with this. "You won't be able to buy your fucking yacht and park it in Palm Beach. So what?"

Gordon proclaimed that doom was just around the corner.

"Shut up, Gordon," said Phillips. "You and Schlichtmann are the ones who got us into this trouble in the first place. We have a star quarterback, why worry about the overweight center? That's the attitude that's caused this trouble. The rules of the game are going to change."

"Mark," said Gordon, attempting to placate his partner. "It makes no difference whether the expenses are two million or two and a half million. Either way, we're in deep shit."

"Of course it does. It makes all the difference."

. . .

Conway left his home in Wellesley for work on Thursday morning, August 28, a rainy, gray morning with the barest hint of autumn in the air. He had one dollar and seventy-five cents in his pocket, exactly enough money to pay for the commuter train ticket to Boston. He had given up driving into the city because he could no longer afford to park in the lot on Milk Street. He and his wife had argued about money. Conway had told her the truth—the case wasn't going to settle, they were going to trial. She was furious, mostly at Schlichtmann, whom she held responsible for their penurious state, but also at her husband for having risked their home. Conway left for work beset by images of crushing debt, the law firm in collapse, his house repossessed by the bank, his wife and children on the street.

All of that could be averted by settling for what Eustis had offered. They could get rid of the case and start life anew. They'd made millions in the last five years from other cases, and they could do it again. But Conway knew that it wouldn't be that easy. To Schlichtmann, the idea of accepting Eustis's offer was humiliating. He'd rather go ahead and risk losing everything. It was easy for Schlichtmann to take that risk, Conway thought. He didn't have a family depending on him. And what about the Woburn families? They were the ones who should really be making this decision, not Schlichtmann.

These thoughts preoccupied Conway while he waited for the train. Out of habit, he bought a newspaper, which left him with $1.40. Not until he boarded the train and saw the conductor coming down the aisle, collecting money, did he realize his mistake in buying the paper. Embarrassed, apologizing profusely, he offered the conductor what money he had. The conductor regarded him with pity and then, to Conway's chagrin, offered to loan him a few dollars. Conway felt grateful for the conductor's solicitude and at the same time a sense of horror at the state to which he had sunk. He declined the conductor's offer and assured him that he would pay his debt tomorrow.

On that same morning, Gordon searched the drawers of his desk and filing cabinet for any Krugerrands or stray hundred-dollar bills that he might have overlooked in earlier forays. In the back of one drawer he found a tattered blue savings account book from Brookline Savings. The last entry, a deposit, had been made in May 1962, when

Gordon was eight years old. The account balance read $39.42. Immediately Gordon called the bank to withdraw the balance, which he discovered now amounted, with accrued interest, to $177. Gordon's spirits began to rise.

The mail, along with the usual pile of overdue bills and threats of legal action, brought good tidings, too—another new credit card. Gordon quickly arranged to convert the three-thousand-dollar credit line into cash so that he could pay some bills, among them the bank loan for his Mercedes. Then he called the bank that held the car loan. "Ron! It's your favorite delinquent!" he said jovially.

He spent the next hour calling creditors, attempting to forestall legal actions. He started with the small accounts and would work his way up to the larger ones as the morning progressed. He no longer bothered calling the hopeless cases—American Express, which had already filed a lawsuit, and Heller Financial, the Chicago-based company from which the firm leased its computer system and other office equipment.

"We're having a serious cash-flow problem," Gordon explained to a clerk at West Publishing in St. Paul, Minnesota, where the bill, seven months overdue, came to $3,049.66. "What sort of deal can we work out?"

"Well, how much can you send us?" asked the clerk.

"Nothing right now."

This seemed to give the clerk pause. "When will you be able to?"

Gordon said he hoped to know more by mid-September. The clerk agreed to forestall legal action until then.

Gordon was feeling better. When his secretary told him that Conway was on the telephone, Gordon switched on his speakerphone and answered with boisterous good humor. His fine mood disappeared the instant he heard Conway's voice.

"I'm really scared," said Conway in a hesitant and tremulous voice. "I came in scared this morning. We're working on this motion for the conference with the judge next week and I just don't know if we have any direction."

Hearing Conway, the realist, always levelheaded, in such a state of alarm frightened Gordon. He tried to calm Conway. "Why don't we sit down and get some direction?" he said. "When's Charlie coming back?" (Nesson had gone to Montana with his family and was due back late in the week.) Finally Gordon told Conway, "I'll be right over." He spent some of his newfound wealth on a taxi to Milk Street instead of taking the subway.

The source of Conway's anxiety was the September 5 hearing with Judge Skinner. Now that the settlement talks had failed, everything depended on the judge. He would probably dismiss the three leukemia death claims, but he could do even more.

Conway had just finished reading Keating's brief, in which Keating asked the judge to declare a mistrial and order a new trial. The case could not go forward, Keating argued, because the jurors had failed to determine when Grace's chemicals had first contaminated the wells. For Grace to be held liable for causing injury in Woburn, Schlichtmann had to prove that his clients had been exposed to Grace's chemicals before those injuries had occurred. And he could not do so with this verdict. The only solution, asserted Keating, was to have the judge order a new trial.

Conway thought that Keating's brief might well persuade Judge Skinner to order a new trial. Schlichtmann thought this was unlikely. If Skinner did so, he would in effect be admitting that his own questions had been hopelessly confusing and that they had just wasted five months of trial. Besides, Skinner would automatically preside over a new trial, and this case had already tied up his courtroom for a very long time.

But the verdict, like the questions themselves, had perplexed everyone. The judge had told the lawyers that he did not see how he could begin the second phase of the trial without knowing the date of contamination. That left open the possibility that Skinner would ask the jurors to clarify their answers. The jury, after all, was still empaneled. Schlichtmann felt uneasy about these jurors. If the judge began asking them questions, there was no telling what they might do. Once back in the courtroom, where the jurors had already spent half a year, they might decide just to end it all.

"It could be the end of the world on Friday," said Schlichtmann grimly as he prepared for the hearing.

Phillips read aloud an account in *The Wall Street Journal* about a lawsuit concerning a woman who had died of toxic shock syndrome. The jury had returned a verdict of ten million dollars, which the trial judge reduced to $1.3 million. On appeal, the verdict was overturned. The woman's survivors had gotten nothing.

"Jesus," exclaimed Schlichtmann. "Six point six million sounds better every day."

7

Schlichtmann saw Al Eustis sitting in the front row of the courtroom gallery on Friday, reading *The New York Times.* Eustis glanced up as Schlichtmann walked past, but didn't offer any greeting. Schlichtmann put his trial bag on the counsel table, then he turned and went toward the gallery. Again Eustis glanced up, but he remained seated when Schlichtmann offered his hand, and neither of them spoke or smiled.

Judge Skinner shuffled out onto the bench. He looked at the lawyers and said, "Welcome back. I hope you had a pleasant vacation."

If the judge intended this as irony, no one seemed to appreciate it.

The hearing went on for more than three hours that afternoon. At one point, the judge interrupted Keating and suggested asking the jurors to clarify their answers. It became apparent to Schlichtmann that Keating was just as frightened of this as he was. "I think that's dangerous," Keating told the judge. "There's been a lot of publicity. The press conference Mr. Schlichtmann had in Woburn after the verdict was totally inappropriate. Any juror may have heard it—goodness knows how they could have avoided it if they kept their ears opened. The jury may think, Gee whiz, we did those people in, and we hadn't intended to do that."

"If they didn't intend to do it, they should straighten it out, shouldn't they?" asked the judge.

Keating's argument for a new trial appeared to displease the judge, who took off his glasses and held his head in his hands. He seemed slightly more disposed to Schlichtmann's analysis, which held that the Woburn families had been exposed to the Grace chemicals since at least September 1973, one of the dates the jury had given, and possibly even before then. "Good job," the judge said after Schlichtmann's rebuttal of Keating. "You may not be right, but good job."

All the same, Skinner still wasn't completely satisfied. "I don't see how we can begin the second part of this case leaving those answers just as they are," he told the lawyers. "I would be very unhappy with that."

By then it was clear that the judge would follow one of two courses: either he would ask the jurors more questions or he would order a new trial. Skinner said he needed some time to think about his ruling. He would notify the lawyers of his decision early next week.

And then, at the end of the hearing, almost in passing, the judge seemed to reveal his own thoughts on the outcome of the second phase of the case. It happened when Schlichtmann mentioned a memo sent by W. R. Grace to its Woburn plant, ordering the plant to stop using TCE. "They said it can cause cancer," Schlichtmann was saying, when the judge interrupted him.

"Causes cancer in people?" the judge asked.

"Yes," said Schlichtmann. "That's why they stopped using it in their plants."

"I don't think there's anything in the evidence to show it causes cancer in people," said the judge.

"Well," began Schlichtmann, "in 1975, the memo said: 'A carcinogen capable of causing cancer—' "

"Cancer in animals," interrupted the judge again. "The state of knowledge at the time was that it caused cancer on the skins of animals. And that's all there was—and still is—to this day. There's no direct evidence that application of this product actually causes cancer."

Schlichtmann took a deep breath. "If Your Honor is asking me, Was there evidence for people to conclude that it could cause cancer in humans? I would have to say, yes, there was evidence. If Your Honor is saying that most of the evidence is based on animal studies, that is correct."

"The skins of rats and mice," said the judge.

"Organs as well," added Schlichtmann.

"Skins," insisted Skinner.

"No," replied Schlichtmann. "I think it was liver, liver tumors."

"And it was in massive doses," said the judge. "They don't give those rats one part per billion. Nobody is surprised they die."

My God, thought Schlichtmann, I'll never win in front of this judge. I don't have a prayer.

. . .

Schlichtmann left the courtroom and went directly to Patten's Bar & Grill with Phillips and Conway. The three men stood at the bar and ordered whiskey.

"Well," said Schlichtmann holding up his glass in a toast, "it's been an enriching experience. Like having a loved one die." He swirled the glass of whiskey and took a sip. "Do we take the money from Eustis and end it? Or do we go ahead? If life was black and white and a sign came out and said, 'Okay, hero time,' then everybody would do the right thing. But there's never a sign. You never know when you're being a hero or a fool."

Phillips had already finished his first drink. "I'd much prefer to go to phase two and spend every penny I've got."

Conway groaned.

"Self-immolation." Schlichtmann laughed.

Phillips nodded. "The hardest thing to do is capitulate. It's easier to spend every damn cent. I've learned more about myself in the last three weeks than I have in my entire life."

Schlichtmann laughed again, a hearty laugh. "And they were things you never wanted to know."

"Soooo much cowardice," said Phillips, beginning to hum.

Schlichtmann talked about the imaginary speeches he found himself making to the judge. "I've got ten thousand speeches, every one of them I'll never deliver. Instead I'll go to the courtroom and the judge will say, Bend down a little more, Mr. Schlichtmann, and I'll bend down right there in the courtroom while he gets out the broomstick and greases it. The trial will go six months and the jury will come back with no causation. The judge will call me over to the bench and say, 'You didn't win, kid, but you did a good job trying.' And I'll say to the judge, 'Fuck you.' And then I'll turn to the jury and say, 'Fuck you, too.' And then I'll say to Kevin, 'C'mon, let's get out of here.' "

"You'll be living out of plastic garbage bags on the Boston Common," said Conway.

"Rich and famous and doing good," mused Schlichtmann. "Rich isn't so difficult. Famous isn't so difficult. Rich and famous together aren't so difficult. Rich, famous, and doing good—now, that's very difficult."

. . .

Schlichtmann had asked the families to come into his office for a meeting the next morning, a Saturday. He had to inform them about Eustis's offer and the status of the trial.

Kathy Boyer arrived early that morning and began clearing piles of documents from the conference room table. She washed the dishes and coffee cups in the kitchen sink, made two pots of fresh coffee, and when she finished those tasks, she went out to buy a box of breakfast pastries. By then, Donna Robbins, Kathryn Gamache, and Kevin and Patricia Kane had arrived. Donna went back to the kitchen and offered to help Kathy. The Aufieros, the Toomeys, Anne Anderson, and the Zonas gathered in the conference room, sipping coffee and chatting with Conway.

None of the families had seen the office since last February, on the eve of trial. Only a year ago it had seemed to sparkle with luxury and order. Now some of Schlichtmann's clients noticed that it looked shabby. The potted plants had died and their bare stems gave the place a forlorn look. Behind the conference room door was a gaping hole in the plaster wall where Schlichtmann had flung the door open with such force that the knob had punched a ragged circle in the wall. In the kitchen alcove, a fluorescent light had dimmed and was blinking fitfully on and off. The vacuum cleaner had broken and the carpets, unvacuumed for weeks now, were stained by ground-in dirt.

In the conference room Schlichtmann stood before his clients, who had taken seats around the table. He was dressed in a short-sleeved shirt and chinos and looked gaunt, his hair almost completely gray.

"The lawyer's perspective this morning is not very good," he told the families. He talked about the risk of facing a divided jury in the next phase of the trial. It might be possible to win, he said, if the jury gave him the benefit of the doubt. But at every step along the way, the Grace defense would try to put doubt in the jury's mind. "The most difficult thing we face is this jury asking themselves, How do I make a decision when there are doctors and scientists out there who can't agree? They might decide to take the easy way out and not decide."

Then he told the families that he had gone to New York to discuss settlement with a Grace executive. "He put some money on the table," Schlichtmann said. "I'm going to tell you the figure, but I don't want it to go outside this room."

Schlichtmann looked around at his clients. Some of them nodded, others sat impassively.

"He offered six point six million dollars. He's decided to stop negotiating until the judge rules on the motions. He's hoping the judge will dismiss all—or at least some—of the claims."

Everyone in the room knew which claims had been put in jeopardy by the jury's date.

"When we start talking about money," continued Schlichtmann, "people get emotionally involved. That's a reality of life. In this case, that reality is backed up by a very personal claim. You'll all have to agree that you will act as one unit. There'll be no talk about this is for Toomey and not for Robbins or Zona, no talk about whose claim is more viable than someone else's claim."

Schlichtmann paused to gauge his clients' reaction. They looked expectantly at him. No one said anything.

"If the eight families can't do that," Schlichtmann said, "then we're in real trouble. If there's a problem between families, then I won't know who I'm representing. If there's a problem, it means that each family will have to get its own attorney."

Thirty seconds of silence ensued. Schlichtmann waited for a response. People looked cautiously at each other, wondering who would speak first.

Richard Toomey, whose dead son, Patrick, had the strongest of the remaining claims, sat directly across the table from where Schlichtmann stood. Toomey's eyes were half closed, his hands folded across his large barrel chest. He was the first to break the silence, in a voice clear and strong. "We're all in this together," he said. "That's how we started, and that's how we'll stay."

Anne Anderson smiled in sudden relief, and everyone began to say, as if in chorus, "We're unanimous, we're together."

At ease now, and with a sense of common purpose, they began to talk freely among themselves about the prospects of settling or going ahead with the trial. Again it was Toomey who spoke most forcefully. "A settlement is one thing," he said, "but I'm not willing to throw out the verdict in order to settle. They're guilty of polluting. My child died from their stupidity. I didn't get into this for the money. I got into this because I want to find them guilty for what they did. I want the world to know that."

Most seemed to agree with this. Pasquale Zona said, "A settlement without disclosure is no settlement at all."

But Anne saw it differently. "I think you have to accept that Grace never, ever said they did anything. The world will come crashing down before they do that."

Pasquale Zona's son, Ron, who was twenty-five years old now, a strapping, husky youth, seemed affronted by this. "Saying they're not guilty of any illness or death," Ron Zona said with disgust. "That's why we're in this thing to begin with."

Anne glanced at him. "Look at how many experts say that smoking causes lung cancer, but the tobacco companies still deny it. I don't know about you people," she continued, "but I don't think I'm any match for their lawyers. I don't feel strong. I find myself crying a lot. They'll tear us apart, make mincemeat of us."

"They put their socks on the same way you do," said Ron Zona. "If we don't go to the second phase, what was the sense of this trial? That's what we got into this for, to prove that it causes illness."

Some voiced their fear that if they went ahead with the trial, they risked losing everything. Others maintained that was the chance they'd taken when they began this odyssey. Donna Robbins was of two minds about whether they could prevail in the second phase. "But six point six million," she said, "I don't think that hurts them enough."

Schlichtmann listened to his clients for a while, and then he intervened. He asked for a show of hands—how many people thought they could win in the second phase? The Toomeys, the Zonas, Kevin Kane, and Donna Robbins raised their hands. How many thought they'd lose? Seven people, among them Patricia Kane and Anne, raised their hands. "Anybody who's studied this will realize the second phase is weaker than the first," said Anne.

The group was divided, but with the exception of young Ron Zona, no one hewed adamantly to their position. Donna Robbins asked Schlichtmann what would happen if he advised them to accept a settlement and they said no.

"I'll keep going," replied Schlichtmann. "I'm representing you, not controlling you."

It was Patricia Kane who, near the end, seemed to speak for everyone. "I think we'd all love to settle as long as we don't have to compromise the verdict," she said. "I don't think it's a matter of money. But we all want the jury's verdict to stand against Grace."

The families, in a somber mood, left the office shortly before one o'clock. Schlichtmann said good-bye to them in the conference room and he remained there after they had gone, deep in thought, his long legs up on the table.

Conway came in and sat across from him. "Well, what do you think?"

Schlichtmann cocked his head and gave Conway a wry look. "I think I'd have trouble winning this case in front of my own clients."

"They're a reflection of you," said Conway.

"They're good people. If you have to die, they're good people to die for." Schlichtmann paused. "Goddamn it, I wish it had turned out differently."

"You've got to start with Anne," said Conway. "You can't begin this phase with another expert."

"She's a powerful individual, no doubt about it. She'll be devastated by the cross-examination, but her power will come through."

Schlichtmann went out to dinner with Teresa that evening. Afterward they saw a movie, a science fiction thriller called *Aliens*. On Sunday morning Schlichtmann sat out on the rooftop deck of his condominium and basked in the sun. *Aliens* raced through his mind. He felt as if he were in the movie, as if he'd gone out to destroy the alien and instead the alien had come after him. He felt trapped. He had no more doors to lock, no more room to run.

On Monday morning he awoke in a spasm of fear. He felt certain beyond all doubt that the judge would rule that morning, and that he would not like the ruling. The judge would declare a new trial. Schlichtmann would lose the verdict, and he would have to start all over again, penniless and bankrupt.

He arose, dressed hurriedly, and sprinted across the Boston Common. At the courthouse, he went upstairs to see Judge Skinner's court clerk. He told the clerk he wanted the judge to meet with him and Keating to discuss settlement. They had been negotiating all summer, Schlichtmann explained, and any ruling by the judge now could upset the negotiation.

The clerk said he would convey this message to the judge. He would also call Keating and ask him if he, too, wanted the judge involved in a settlement discussion. The clerk added that Judge Skinner had come into his office yesterday, on Sunday—a rare event—to work on his ruling.

Back at the office, Schlichtmann stood in the middle of the floor. He exhaled deeply, walked to the window, and looked down on Milk Street. Skinner had come to work on a Sunday. What did that mean? He's not coming in to help me, thought Schlichtmann. He went over to his desk, picked up the summary of Patrick Toomey's leukemia treatments, folded it thoughtfully, and pressed it to his lips. Then he tossed it in the air. It landed at his feet, the pages fluttering open. He walked out of his office and went to the war room. He looked around, as if in a daze, at the computer terminals, the dozen filing cabinets, the volumes of trial transcripts, the maps rolled and tucked overhead between the oak beams of the ceiling. Then he turned around and walked out. In the library, he opened the file of a new case, a baby boy with brain damage, referred to him by a neurologist. He sat down and began to read the file.

Conway found Schlichtmann in the library reading the new file. A good sign, thought Conway to himself, the first interest he's taken in another case in years.

Schlichtmann, hearing Conway behind him, turned to look at his partner. "You know Skinner could enter judgment for Grace, don't you?"

So Schlichtmann wasn't thinking about the new case after all. Conway said, "I think Eustis wants to hear the judge's ruling. They're willing to take their chances."

Early that afternoon Schlichtmann got a call from Keating. Keating said that he also wanted the judge to hold off on his ruling until they could talk again about settling. Keating added that he'd already called the judge's clerk to ask the judge to delay ruling for a few days. He'd have Eustis call Schlichtmann by the end of the day.

When Schlichtmann hung up the phone, he looked thoughtful. "That's very interesting," he told Conway. "Keating's scared, too. He thinks he can get a better deal from me without the judge getting in the way. He sees waiting for the judge's ruling like a roll of the dice, just as we do. Uncertainty works for both of us."

Conway nodded. "Everything points to the middle ground."

Schlichtmann looked pleased. A small, thoughtful smile creased his lips. "It's just possible that I may have taken control of this again."

"Oh, God," groaned Conway.

"I'm not saying that's happened. I'm just saying it *may* be."

"If history is any guide, Eustis won't call today," said Conway.

"No," said Schlichtmann, "this is a different scenario."

The phone rang. Kathy Boyer poked her head into the office. "Somebody named Grendon."

"Who the fuck is he?" said Schlichtmann.

"Bill collector," muttered Gordon, who was spread flat on his back on the couch in Schlichtmann's office.

They waited for three hours, until five o'clock, when Eustis finally called. Conway and Gordon sat in Schlichtmann's office, listening to his side of the conversation. Schlichtmann sat at his desk, his back turned to them.

He listened to Eustis for what seemed like a long time, and then he said, "Al, let me tell you the problem I've got. We're not outside the realm of the possible, but I've got some other concerns. . . . No, no, I'm not saying it's unacceptable. My feeling is that if we sat down face-to-face and talked about it, we could resolve it to the satisfaction of both of us."

Schlichtmann closed his eyes and pinched the bridge of his nose. Conway took a deep breath.

"It's just not possible for you to come up here?" Schlichtmann was saying to Eustis. "I don't like to do this over the phone. Maybe we can come down. . . . Okay, let me call you back within the hour."

Schlichtmann hung up the telephone and looked at Conway and Gordon. "He's up to eight million. He said, 'The cash register's empty at eight million.' "

Conway snorted. "Accept it. It's over."

"Now, wait just a minute." Schlichtmann narrowed his eyes and looked up at the ceiling, a speculative gaze. "If he's at eight, don't you think if I go down there I can get him to nine, nine and a quarter?"

"I don't think so," said Gordon. "Look, Jan, let's not get greedy. We've tried to push this and we haven't been real successful."

"Let's not get greedy, Jan," repeated Conway. "It's over."

But Schlichtmann wasn't convinced. "It's a question of how much further he's willing to go."

"How did he sound over the phone?" asked Gordon.

Schlichtmann thought about this for a moment. "He sounded like, 'Don't goose me.' "

Gordon shook his head. "I'm not in the mood for this, Jan. Just go for the close."

"Part of the deal is that the judge vacates the verdict and orders a new trial," said Schlichtmann. "The families are going to have a problem with that."

"No, they won't," said Conway. "How does a million dollars a family look in the press? Does it look like we won this case? I think it does." Conway punched out his cigarette in the ashtray and turned to look at Schlichtmann. "Close it, Jan. Close it," he said slowly, firmly. He hiked up his pants and walked out of the office.

"It's actually about four hundred and fifty thousand per family, after expenses and fees," said Gordon.

"Half a million per family," murmured Schlichtmann.

"Net, no taxes," added Gordon.

Conway reappeared at the door. "Now, Jan. Do it now."

"Yeah," sighed Schlichtmann at last. "If I go down to New York, he'll just make me grovel."

Gordon laughed—a light, airy laugh. "Oh, I wouldn't worry about groveling. We've already groveled plenty. Let's do something new in life."

It had been five weeks since the verdict. During that time, when he feared the worst, Schlichtmann had often spoken of death, as if for him losing the case was tantamount to dying. By his lights, this settlement *was* a loss. But it wasn't the end of the case, he thought at that moment. He would appeal the verdict for Beatrice, and maybe he'd win a new trial against Facher. The Woburn case wasn't really over. He didn't have to die yet.

He wanted to be alone when he made the call to Eustis. Gordon left his office and walked out to the kitchen, where Conway was talking with Peggy. Conway told her that it was over, that they had settled with Grace.

Peggy reacted with joy, clasping her hands in delight and shouting, "Good! I won't have to wash dishes here every night."

Conway fumbled with the coffee pot, and then he set it down suddenly. "It's been five long years," he said in a hoarse voice, and tears came to his eyes.

Peggy came over to him and put her arms around him. They stood for a moment in the embrace. "In the next few minutes, it'll be all over," she said.

Schlichtmann emerged from his office and came toward the kitchen. "He'll give me eight. He won't give me any more than that. He says it's extortion."

Gordon was tapping out figures on the calculator. Schlichtmann peered over Gordon's shoulder for a moment. "All I want are my suits from Dmitri, my condo, and a trip to Hawaii," said Schlichtmann. "And forty thousand in cash. No, keep the cash and get me a credit card for Hawaii. A platinum credit card."

"No," said Gordon.

"I must have my dignity," said Schlichtmann.

"What's wrong with a fucking Mastercard?" said Gordon. "What do you estimate your bill on the platinum will be after one month in Hawaii?"

"Just put me back to where I was two years ago," said Schlichtmann. "Make me whole again."

"How do you plan on paying the credit cards when they come due?"

"I'll be settling cases again," said Schlichtmann.

Blindman's Buff

1

Judge Skinner gave his blessing to the eight-million-dollar settlement on Monday morning, September 22. The Woburn jurors, summoned that morning by the judge's clerk, waited upstairs in the jury room, expecting to begin the second phase of the trial.

In his chambers the judge said to Schlichtmann, "We're talking about many hundreds of thousands of dollars for each one of these families?"

"Yes," replied Schlichtmann.

"I think this is quite a successful settlement," said the judge, "certainly from the plaintiffs' point of view. There was a good likelihood they would have ended up with nothing at all, given the extremely difficult nature of the evidence."

Schlichtmann made no reply.

The last two weeks had been difficult for Schlichtmann. Keating had made many demands on behalf of Grace. There would be no deal, Keating had said, unless the judge granted Grace's motion for a new trial and rendered the verdict null. Furthermore, it had to appear as if the settlement had come about only after the judge declared a new trial. This petty deception irked Schlichtmann, but he went along with it. He had little choice. He suspected the judge was going to order a new trial for Grace anyway. He became certain of that when the judge readily adopted Keating's fictitious chronology.

"There never was going to be a second phase," Schlichtmann told Conway bitterly. "The judge was going to fuck us all along. We got the money an hour before everything turned to dust."

The case against W. R. Grace officially ended as it had begun—in front of a crowd in Judge Skinner's courtroom. The judge informed the jurors of the settlement and thanked them for their service. A moment later reporters surrounded Schlichtmann and Keating, seeking details of the settlement. Keating had insisted, as another condition of settlement, that the amount paid by Grace be kept secret, and Schlichtmann had consented to this. But many people, including of course the families themselves, knew the sum, and by evening the network news programs would be citing a "reported" eight-million-dollar settlement.

Out in Woburn that afternoon, at Trinity Episcopal Church, Schlichtmann proclaimed victory in front of the television cameras and a crowd of onlookers. His clients, seated on folding chairs in a semicircle before the cameras, made similar statements. Several expressed their conviction that, in Donna Robbins's words, they had "set out to teach corporate America a lesson," and they had succeeded.

Not everyone at Trinity Episcopal believed that, not even some of those most favorably disposed to the families' cause. From the back of the church hall, Reverend Bruce Young watched the proceedings and said bitterly, "I'll bet they're having a wonderful party at Grace headquarters today." He'd been furious—"bullshit mad," as he later put it—when he heard that morning about the settlement. He felt he'd invested a lot of himself in this matter, and to him taking Grace's money without a full disclosure by the company, or any expressions of atonement, cheapened everything. The way he saw it, the case had started out as a matter of principle. He recalled Anne Anderson saying once that she wasn't after money, that what she wanted was for J. Peter Grace to come to her front door and apologize. As far as Reverend Young was concerned, Schlichtmann had botched the first part of the trial—the easy part—and then he'd sold out when things began to look risky. Even worse, thought Young, was the way Schlichtmann was now using his lawyerly powers of persuasion to convince the families that they'd actually won something.

The entire affair disgusted the minister. "This was a case I thought would have some real importance," he said. "It never happened."

Among the families themselves, there was trouble. Schlichtmann always said that once money was put on the table, things would turn ugly. And now the ugliness began, although not in ways he had anticipated. A few days after the press conference at Trinity Episcopal, the families met in Schlichtmann's office to discuss the division of money. Schlichtmann informed them that each family would receive $375,000 in cash and, five years later, another payment of $80,000. The case expenses amounted to $2.6 million. And the legal fees came to $2.2 million. This, Schlichtmann pointed out to the families, was only 28 percent of the total settlement, less than the 40 percent fee they'd agreed to when they'd signed the contingency forms.

No one voiced any complaint at that meeting. But afterward, as Donna and Anne drove home to Woburn together, Anne expressed anger at the size of Schlichtmann's fee. She didn't think the lawyers should get more than any one family.

Donna said, "I think Jan deserves it. He did all the work. All we had to do was go to meetings."

"He hasn't lost a child," replied Anne.

"I hope he never has to go through that," said Donna.

Anne didn't say any more that night, but the matter did not end there. In recent months Anne had begun to resent Schlichtmann. She found his manner with the families patronizing, as if he were talking to a group of children. There would have been no case had it not been for her efforts, and yet she felt as if he had systematically excluded her and the others from important decisions. Whenever she ventured an opinion that differed from his, he would always say, "Trust me, trust me." How many times had she heard him say that? It galled Anne, but what bothered her most was a growing conviction, now that the trial was over, that he didn't really care at all about her or the others. She came to believe that he'd been using them simply as a vehicle for his own ambition, for his own fame and fortune. "I was doing this for my baby, for Jimmy," she explained later. "It started out in a pure manner. We didn't want what happened to us to happen to anyone else. But by the time I got through dealing with Jan, I felt violated. The lawsuit made me feel dirty."

She insisted that she didn't really care about the money. But Schlichtmann, she believed, cared a lot about it. And if money was important to him, she decided that she would make it important to her. She found a receptive audience with the Zona family, whom she'd known for fifteen years now.

Anne and the Zonas could not challenge Schlichtmann on the matter of his fee since they had signed a contract entitling him to 40 percent of the recovery. But they could dispute some of the $2.6 million that Schlichtmann had claimed in expenses. When they raised this issue, Schlichtmann suggested they hire an accountant to go through the thousands of invoices. They took him up on the invitation. The accountant questioned copying fees, interest charges, overtime expenses, and sundry other matters. Anne and the Zonas hired a lawyer to represent them. Ronald Zona called Donna Robbins one night to enlist her support. He told Donna that Schlichtmann had stolen half a million dollars from them.

"How did he steal it from us?" asked Donna. "Where did it come from?"

Ron Zona said, "It came out of expenses we never should have paid for."

"Jan never asked us for any money," replied Donna. "None of us ever put up anything. I don't feel you're right."

Schlichtmann told the families that he would not dispute the accountant's findings. He agreed to remit whatever sum the accountant deemed appropriate. The accountant submitted a list that came to eighty thousand dollars. Schlichtmann was prepared to divide this sum equally among the families, but none except Anne and the Zonas would accept any of the money.

Schlichtmann had indeed been lavish with the expenses. That had always been his way. He'd never spared any cost in preparing a case, and in Woburn there had always been another well that could be drilled, another medical test that could be performed. Yet he had not come close to matching the seven million dollars in legal fees and costs that Grace had paid for its defense, not to mention the additional millions paid by Beatrice.

As it turned out, the expenses as billed didn't begin to cover the true costs of the case to Schlichtmann's firm—the salaries and benefits paid to the secretaries, associates, and paralegals, the overhead and day-to-day costs of running an office. In normal times these would have been paid for out of the proceeds of half a dozen major cases every year. But Woburn had occupied everyone in the firm virtually full-time for the past two years. Among the lawyers, the largest single beneficiary was Joe Mulligan, the one who had first gone out to Woburn and signed up the families. For the price of a drink at the Littlest Bar and some blandishments five years earlier, Mulligan had gotten Schlichtmann to take over the case. Now he demanded a referral fee. Schlichtmann balked. Mulligan, after all, had put in less than a week of effort on the case. Mulligan filed a lawsuit in Superior Court. To settle the lawsuit, Schlichtmann agreed to pay Mulligan three hundred and fifty thousand dollars.

Meanwhile, Trial Lawyers for Public Justice was seeking $648,000 in fees for Anthony Roisman's early assistance. Schlichtmann met with Roisman and his board of directors at a hotel airport outside Chicago. Gordon and Phillips came along. The meeting lasted all day. The board told Schlichtmann that he had mismanaged the case, that he had spent too much and settled for too little. Phillips walked out of the meeting in disgust. Gordon broke down and wept angry tears. The woman sitting next to Gordon, a personal injury lawyer from California, turned to him and said coldly, "It's nothing personal, you know."

Schlichtmann refused to say much in his own defense. But he could not pay Trial Lawyers for Public Justice the full fee he owed them by contract. In the end, they agreed to accept three hundred thousand dollars.

Over dinner one night Phillips asked Schlichtmann if he regretted taking on the Woburn case.

"Do I *regret* it?" exclaimed Schlichtmann with a harsh laugh. "Does a paraplegic regret the moment he stepped off the curb and the bus ran him down? The case has ruined my life."

Creditors lurked everywhere. Gordon began settling the debts, including the million-dollar-loan from Uncle Pete. Once everyone else—Nesson, Kiley and Tom Neville, Gordon and Phillips—had gotten paid, and a hundred thousand dollars in bonuses had been distributed among the office staff, Schlichtmann ended up with only thirty thousand dollars. He was debt-free, but there was no money left over for him to reclaim his Porsche. Nor could Gordon get him any new credit cards—Schlichtmann had destroyed his creditworthiness. Conway and Crowley, with less debt than Schlichtmann, came out of the case with a hundred thousand dollars apiece. They got the deeds to their houses back. Conway tried to make amends to his wife by buying her a fur coat for Christmas and a camcorder to film their children.

Conway would not learn the full scope of the disaster that was about to befall them until the new year. Gordon had not paid all the debts. Gordon had not set aside any money to pay taxes.

2

Schlichtmann departed in December for a monthlong vacation in Hawaii. While he was gone, the EPA issued a report on the pump test of Wells G and H that it had conducted one year ago, before the start of trial. The agency's experts concluded that both Grace and Beatrice were responsible for contaminating the Aberjona aquifer and the city wells. At a public hearing in Woburn, the EPA administrator in charge of the project stated that the Beatrice land was the most grossly contaminated area in the aquifer, and by far the largest contributor to the pollution of the wells.

By these lights, the Woburn jury had made a mistake. Groundwater from Beatrice's fifteen acres had gotten under the river and had contaminated the wells, as Schlichtmann's expert had claimed. Given the proximity of the fifteen acres to the wells—a mere three hundred feet— this should have been obvious even without the EPA report. On the face of it, the verdict appeared to stand as an example of how the adversary process and the rules and rituals of the courtroom can obscure reality. But in Schlichtmann's view, it was the judge who had led the jury astray.

From the beginning, Skinner never seemed to regard the case against Beatrice in the same light as the one against Grace. After the trial the judge had made some additional findings. He had decreed that, based on the evidence, groundwater from the fifteen acres had never reached the Woburn wells. Because of the compound nature of the questions the judge had posed to the jury, this specific question had never been answered. Skinner took it upon himself to answer it, and in doing so he made any appeal on the Beatrice verdict much more difficult. In effect, he was telling Schlichtmann that even if the jury had found against Beatrice, he would have overturned the verdict and entered judgment for Beatrice.

Polluted though the fifteen acres were, Schlichtmann had turned up very little hard evidence that Riley himself was responsible for its contamination. Perhaps that was the problem. Schlichtmann had never managed to find the witness who could break open the case, the way he'd found Al Love to expose Grace's secrets.

Before leaving for Hawaii, Schlichtmann had promised the Woburn families that he would appeal the Beatrice verdict. Nesson had wanted to write the brief and make the oral argument before the U.S. Court of Appeals, and Schlichtmann had readily agreed. He was happy to go on to other things.

Returning to Boston, he began work on a difficult medical malpractice case involving a woman who had suffered a ruptured brain aneurysm. The firm needed some income, and quickly. The failure to set aside money for taxes had that most relentless of creditors the Internal Revenue Service dunning them.

The malpractice case failed to settle. In April, Schlichtmann and Conway went to trial. They'd spent thirty thousand dollars preparing the case, money newly borrowed from Uncle Pete. After a two-week trial the jurors began their deliberations. Schlichtmann paced outside the courtroom door. When the jury returned its verdict, four days later, Schlichtmann had lost. He wondered if he would ever win again. Bad karma from Woburn seemed to infect everything around him.

Schlichtmann and Teresa broke up around this time. They had been together for five years. If Schlichtmann felt sorry about the parting, he did not show it. "They can smell when the money's gone," he said, referring to women in general and the long-suffering Teresa in particular. It seemed then that he might let Woburn strip him even of his self-respect.

With no income to pay the bills, the firm's debts once again began to mount. The deed to Conway's house went back into Uncle Pete's file drawer at the Bank of Boston. That spring the telephone at Schlichtmann's condominium was cut off. To make calls, he had to go down to Charles Street, to the pay phone in front of the fire station. He shared the pay phone with a bookie, who was not happy with the new arrangement. They argued over how long each other's calls lasted.

All of Schlichtmann's furniture, except for one overstuffed chair, was repossessed. At night he would take the cushions off the chair and lay them on the floor to make his bed. When he needed a table, he would stack the cushions and sit on the floor before them, Japanese style. He dined in this position. He ate a lot of canned tuna. Kiley would sometimes take him out to dinner and slip him a hundred-dollar bill afterward.

Nesson had been working on the Beatrice appeal for several months now. He had outlined the procedural history of the case and crafted all the legal arguments against Judge Skinner's directed verdict rulings, but he did not possess Schlichtmann's command of the factual minutiae. He gave the brief to Schlichtmann and asked for his help filling in the pertinent facts.

Schlichtmann thought that Nesson had done a superb job. The brief was tightly reasoned and cited cases that perfectly supported its arguments. Best of all, Nesson had used the judge's own words to show how Skinner himself had realized that he'd made a mistake on landowner liability and duty to warn.

Schlichtmann figured it would take him about three days to fill in the missing details. At first, poring over the trial transcripts was like opening a fresh wound. The more he read, the angrier he got at Judge Skinner, and the angrier he got, the more he became convinced that the families should win a new trial on appeal. The three days stretched to a week, and the week became a month. Conway would arrive at the office in the morning and find that Schlichtmann had already been there for hours.

Conway, however, remained skeptical of their chances. He urged Schlichtmann to work on other cases and not to place too much hope in the appeal. But Schlichtmann paid him no heed.

Schlichtmann filed the Beatrice appeal on Wednesday, June 7. The following Monday, he got a call from Neil Jacobs. Facher was in England, lecturing on American law at Oxford University, but Jacobs had just finished reading the appeal brief. He invited Schlichtmann over for a chat.

"It's legal poetry," Jacobs told Schlichtmann that evening. He offered to settle if Schlichtmann would withdraw the appeal. He suggested a sum of around two hundred thousand dollars, the amount that Beatrice would pay in legal fees to fight the appeal.

Schlichtmann shook his head.

"You won't win," said Jacobs. "And even if you do, you won't see a judge for three years."

"Well, I'm a glutton for punishment," Schlichtmann said.

Facher returned to Boston in midsummer. He and Jacobs filed Beatrice's opposition brief in September. It, too, was a very good brief. After reading it, Nesson smiled wanly and said to Schlichtmann, "Maybe you should make the oral argument."

If only, continued Nesson, they'd found some hard evidence linking Riley and the tannery to the TCE on the fifteen acres. "That would have turned the entire case around," Nesson said. Riley had steadfastly maintained that the tannery had never used TCE and that all the tannery's records of chemical use had been destroyed years before the lawsuit. Schlichtmann had never believed this, but all his efforts in discovery had yielded nothing to contradict Riley.

On a Sunday evening at the end of September, a year after the Grace settlement, Schlichtmann left his apartment and went down to the pay phone on Charles Street to call Gordon. Nesson's comment had gotten him thinking. He asked Gordon to go over to the EPA regional office the next morning and check the files on Beatrice. The EPA had continued to collect information on Beatrice for its own purposes, and perhaps Gordon would turn up something new and interesting. The odds, Schlichtmann knew, were against it, but it still seemed worth a few hours of effort.

At the EPA regional office the next day, Gordon went through files he'd gone through many times before. He knew them so well that all he had to do was look at them and judge their size and heft to tell if they contained anything new. They were voluminous, and it took Gordon most of the morning to work his way through them. In the end, he found nothing new.

On his way out, he stopped for a moment at the office of the project director of the east Woburn cleanup. He thanked her for her help, and then he noticed on the shelf behind her a document, perhaps half an inch thick, with a light blue cover, a document he had not seen before.

. . .

Schlichtmann was at his desk when Gordon came in and dropped the document in front of him. "Shouldn't we have gotten this during discovery?" Gordon asked.

It was a report, sixty pages in length, by a firm named Yankee Environmental Engineering. The first page bore the title "Hydrogeologic Investigation of the John J. Riley Tanning Company." The study, which Riley himself had commissioned, had been completed in 1983, three years before the start of trial.

Schlichtmann was astounded. He had never seen this report before, and yet he had asked repeatedly, in interrogatories, in depositions, and by subpoena—on eleven separate occasions, he counted—for all such documents.

Reading the report with rising excitement, Schlichtmann discovered that the Yankee engineers had drilled six monitoring wells on the tannery property, wells that had remained secret throughout the entire EPA pump test and the trial. The report stated that groundwater from under the tannery flowed to the east, toward the city wells, through very porous soil, exactly as Schlichtmann's expert, Pinder, had predicted. Tannery waste, described in the report as "a black sludge resembling peat," had been dumped down the hillside leading to the fifteen acres. To Schlichtmann, this sounded a lot like Sample Z, the contaminated material that Drobinski had found on the fifteen acres. Schlichtmann had claimed at trial that this material was tannery waste. But the judge had not believed it and had told the jury they could not consider it as evidence.

If he'd had this report, thought Schlichtmann, the trial would have been a different event altogether. The report bolstered the testimony of all his own experts. And who knows what other discoveries the report might have led him to? Certainly Facher must have known about this report. Why had Facher hidden it? And what else had he hidden? Was it possible that there was more?

Schlichtmann experienced both elation and anger that day. In the legal profession, destroying or suppressing evidence ranks just below stealing money from a client. The very purpose of discovery, wrote Justice William O. Douglas in 1958, "is to make trial less a game of blindman's buff and more a fair contest, with the basic issues and facts disclosed to the fullest practicable extent." The Rules of Civil Procedure spelled out the remedy for misconduct of this sort. When wrongful suppression of evidence has prevented a full and fair trial, the rules grant the victimized party a new trial.

3

It was as if Schlichtmann had been offered the chance to rewrite the past, to erase the greatest failure of his life and to create in its place a great victory. It was for this reason that Woburn once again would occupy him to the exclusion of all else.

Schlichtmann would have preferred to take this matter directly to the Court of Appeals, but procedure required that he go back to the trial judge first. So Schlichtmann found himself yet again in Judge Skinner's courtroom. The judge did not appear pleased to see either the Woburn case or Schlichtmann. Nor did Facher, who glared at Schlichtmann and Nesson as they walked in.

Despite his bad humor, Facher looked spry. He'd made a lot of money for his law firm on the Woburn case. A year before, just after the verdict, the firm's accountant had even toasted Schlichtmann at a big victory party at the Ritz-Carlton. Since then, Facher had tried two other cases, one in New Orleans, another in Maine, and won them both. Among the Boston bar, his reputation had never been more lustrous. But now Schlichtmann was besmirching him with accusations of fraud and misconduct that were being reported in *Lawyer's Weekly*.

Standing before the judge, Schlichtmann went through the Yankee report in detail, trying to show why it would have made a difference in the outcome of the trial. He had hoped that the judge would be outraged by its suppression, but he soon realized that he was hoping for too much. Skinner listened patiently, asking questions now and then. Schlichtmann finished by saying, "Certainly Your Honor concedes that the information would have been extremely helpful to our claims."

"I think you're wrong about that," replied the judge. "At this point, I'm not conceding anything to anybody. Protocol requires that I hear both sides."

It was Facher's turn. Schlichtmann's presentation was almost too much for the old lawyer to bear. "I've been around a few times," Facher told the judge, "and I've never heard anything like the display I've heard today for irresponsible and baseless accusations. This is scurrilous." Facher, quivering with rage and indignation, stood directly behind Schlichtmann. He lifted his hand as if he were about to strike Schlichtmann on the head.

From the corner of his eye, Nesson saw this movement and leaped up to confront Facher. Judge Skinner jumped up, too, and then so did Schlichtmann. "I will meet him in the hall if he wants to," sputtered Facher, looking up at Schlichtmann, who towered over him. "Or Charlie, too."

"Everybody sit down!" roared the judge. "I'm not going to have this bickering between counsel!"

The judge asked Facher if he'd known about the Yankee report before trial. Yes, replied Facher, he'd seen the report, but only briefly, for about two minutes just before a deposition. He'd never had actual possession of it. Riley's personal lawyer, a woman named Mary Ryan, who was here in court that day, had shown it to him. He had thought then that the report was insignificant, and he thought so now—"One piece of inconsequential material among hundreds, maybe thousands, I'm not sure." As for Schlichtmann's requests for this report, they had been improperly made. He had lacked the "diligence" and "interest" to go after this document and it was, therefore, his own fault that he had not gotten it.

Judge Skinner was about to end the proceeding when Nesson stood and reminded him of their request that he ask Facher and Mary Ryan if they knew of any other documents relevant to the lawsuit that they had failed to produce.

"Thank you very much," the judge said curtly to Nesson, "but I don't want to be told how to proceed."

"Your Honor," said Nesson, "you have before you a motion that deals with the integrity of this Court and the discovery process. You have been very quick to get angry with Mr. Schlichtmann and me."

"No, I get angry with everybody," said the judge.

"No," replied Nesson, "you have not gotten angry with Mr. Facher. I'm waiting to see if there's some real concern about the integrity of this process that comes out in your responses to Mr. Facher."

This rebuke infuriated the judge. "You have imposed on me consistently. You have been doing it since day one."

Again Nesson asked the judge to make the inquiry he had requested.

"I'm not doing that."

"Then before this hearing closes, we ask to call Mary Ryan to the witness stand," said Nesson.

"No!"

"You have not made the inquiry we asked for," continued Nesson, "and at this point we now ask to call Mary Ryan to the witness stand—"

"I'm not doing anything more on this hearing!" shouted Skinner, stumbling over his words in his fury. "I'm now calling a criminal case, the name of which escapes me."

Schlichtmann rose. "Your Honor—"

"I'm not listening to you! I've heard all from you that I'm going to hear. United States versus whatever-the-name is."

Schlichtmann waited anxiously for the judge's ruling, although the outcome seemed foregone to almost everyone who'd witnessed Judge Skinner's demeanor during the hearing. Christmas came and went. Schlichtmann lost his condominium on New Year's Day. The next morning, a bitterly cold day in January, with the snow mounded in great heaps on the Boston sidewalks, Schlichtmann moved into the office. Although not without shelter, he had finally become homeless. He put his Dmitri suits in the reception-room closet, his silk ties and Bally shoes in the closet by the bathroom. He slept on a foldout couch in Crowley's office. He made herbal tea every night in the kitchen and watched television in the conference room. "It doesn't bother me living here," he said. "I'm a man of extremes. It's the middle ground I can't stand."

Every morning that January, he called Judge Skinner's clerk to find out if the judge had ruled. He refused to give up hope for a new trial. The facts were too overwhelming, too damning, he kept telling himself. "I think Skinner's stuck, he doesn't have any choice in the matter," Schlichtmann would say. But then he'd check himself with pessimism. "No, it can't be so. Skinner'll find a way to fuck me." He took hope from vaporous rumor. From Kathy Boyer, who was dating a lawyer who played squash with Michael Keating, he heard that Keating believed the judge had no alternative but to grant a new trial. This was triple hearsay based upon uninformed speculation, but it buoyed Schlichtmann. He told everyone he encountered about it. "Isn't that something? Keating wouldn't say that offhand. He must have a sense of which way the wind blows."

Meanwhile, Schlichtmann did little work on other cases, despite Conway's pleas. The firm borrowed more money from Uncle Pete. An IRS agent named Welch called Schlichtmann at least once a week. With interest and penalties, his tax debt was growing by 25 percent each year. It was now about half a million dollars.

Judge Skinner finally issued his ruling on January 2, 1988, nine weeks after the hearing. He found that the Yankee report was, on balance, "more favorable" to Beatrice than not, "or at the most of neutral value." Its presence in the case would not, therefore, have materially affected the outcome of the trial.

The judge did agree, however, that Schlichtmann had properly asked for the report. Facher and Mary Ryan should have given it to him. But their "default" (as the judge called it) was merely a "lapse of judgment" and not part of any "deliberate conspiracy," as Schlichtmann had repeatedly charged. In fact, concluded the judge, Schlichtmann himself deserved part of the blame for not getting the report, for insisting on "rushing" headlong to trial, despite Facher's pleas for more time. And in the last-minute "discovery frenzy" created by Schlichtmann, it was understandable, said the judge, that "this report may have seemed minor" to Facher.

At night, lying on the foldout couch in the office, Schlichtmann had terrible fantasies. He was consumed with hatred for Judge Skinner. "I have thoughts of hurting him on a personal level," he said. He could imagine himself reaching up to the bench where the judge sat in his black robes and grabbing him by the throat, by the wattle of sagging flesh. He imagined the stunned look of surprise in Skinner's eyes as he throttled him. He didn't hate Facher. He hated what Facher had done, but he understood why he'd done it. No, it was the judge, presiding over a U.S. District Court, the false and corrupt pretense of justice, that drove Schlichtmann mad with fury. The more he thought about it, the more he suspected that Facher must have some sort of hold over the judge.

"I'm beginning to think the fix is in," he told Conway one morning.

Conway shook his head. He didn't believe it. He wished Schlichtmann would simply forget about Woburn and get on with some new cases.

For Schlichtmann, everything now depended on the Court of Appeals. Oral argument was scheduled for July, six months away. He occupied his time by writing a new brief that incorporated the suppression of the Yankee report with the original appeal. He spent several days in the gallery of the Court of Appeals listening in on oral arguments. He went through every opinion the court had issued in the last year. One in particular excited him. "We remind counsel that we do not view favorably any attempt to play fast and loose with our judicial system," wrote Judge Juan Torruella of the Court of Appeals. "Deceptions, misrepresentations and falsities will not be tolerated. . . ."

A panel of three appellate judges, selected by lottery, hears each case. Schlichtmann prayed that Torruella would be on the bench the day the Woburn appeal was heard.

As July neared, Schlichtmann and Nesson spent hours together plotting strategy at Nesson's house in Cambridge, sitting outside under the tall trees by the swimming pool. Nesson wanted to make the oral argument to the court and Schlichtmann agreed, figuring that Nesson's Harvard credentials would give their cause added weight. The prospect excited Nesson. This appeal, he believed, went to the very heart of the judicial system. "I can't see how they can write an opinion against us," he told Schlichtmann.

"Do they have integrity?" asked Schlichtmann.

"Absolutely," said Nesson. Then he added, with less certainty, "I think so."

4

Nesson argued before the three judges of the United States Court of Appeals (one of whom was indeed Juan Torruella) on July 28, 1988, two years to the day after the Woburn verdict.

Waiting for the court's ruling, Schlichtmann finally began working on other cases. He had no choice. On his desk was a pile of bills, liens, and judgments, a motion to show cause in small claims court, a *capias* for his arrest in the matter of an overdue bill from Neiman Marcus. Time passed with agonizing slowness for him. The trees on the Boston Common turned brilliant autumn hues and then lost their leaves. The foreshortened, gray days of approaching winter depressed him. Every time he left the office, even momentarily, he would ask on his return, "Any word?" He thought Nesson's argument in the Court of Appeals had gone wonderfully well and that Facher had done poorly. But the longer it took the court to rule, the more worried he became.

"It's like a gun to my head," he told Kiley one evening at dinner. "I wish they would just pull the trigger, one way or the other."

The Court of Appeals issued its decision on December 7. As it happened, Schlichtmann was two thousand miles away on that day, consulting with a Denver lawyer who sought his advice on a toxic-waste case. Conway faxed him a copy of the court's ruling. It was fifty-four pages long. It first addressed the initial appeal. Judge Skinner's post-trial finding that groundwater from the fifteen acres had never reached the city wells was, wrote the court, "both plausible and adequately rooted in the record." Appeal denied.

As for the second appeal, on the issue of misconduct, "the record contains clear and convincing evidence, overwhelming evidence," stated the court, that counsel for Beatrice had engaged in misconduct. But misconduct came in many guises. Had it been accidental, a mere oversight? Or deliberate and intentional, a matter of outright fraud? Perhaps the Yankee report would not have affected the outcome of the trial, as Judge Skinner asserted, but "an able litigator builds on the information available from time to time, changing directions as new leads emerge and old ones wither."

If, continued the appeals court, Beatrice's failure to produce the report had been knowing and purposeful, then one had to presume it had been suppressed for good reason, that it might have led Schlichtmann to fruitful discoveries on the tannery property. Judge Skinner had failed to determine the extent of the misconduct, even though Nesson and Schlichtmann had repeatedly asked him to inquire of both Facher and Mary Ryan about other material that might have been withheld. Judge Skinner, the court found, had abused his discretion in this instance, "an error that was compounded when he proceeded to make findings of fact on the very matters which inquiry could reasonably have been expected to illuminate."

The Court of Appeals had issued a stern rebuke to Judge Skinner. To remedy the error, the court took the unusual step of sending the case back to Skinner for further "aggressive" inquiry. Once completed, Skinner should report back to the court, which would retain jurisdiction in the matter.

In his hotel room in Denver, Schlichtmann pounded the wall in fury. He felt trapped. Once again, he was going back into Judge Skinner's courtroom. The appeals court had given him the very narrowest of openings. They held before him the prospect of winning a new trial on the question of whether the tannery property alone had contaminated the city wells. But at the same time they had affirmed Skinner's ruling that groundwater from the fifteen acres had not reached the wells, notwithstanding the findings of the EPA. Since the fifteen acres lay between the tannery and the wells, a trial involving only the tannery would be just a charade, a hopeless exercise. Facher would simply file for summary judgment based on the judge's findings and the jury's verdict, and he'd almost certainly win.

To Schlichtmann, it was apparent that the appeals court wanted to clean up the allegations of malfeasance without in any way disturbing the verdict. The long-standing principle of *res judicata*—that a matter once decided in a court of law remains decided—held sway, even if that decision flew in the face of reality. First the EPA, and now, this very month, the United States Geological Survey, had issued reports saying the fifteen acres had contaminated the well field. But that would make no difference in the eyes of the law.

Schlichtmann didn't sleep that night. The next morning at the Denver airport, he went into a bar and ordered a double whisky. He felt so tired and depressed that he lay his head on the bar. The bartender, seeing this, came back and took the drink away before Schlichtmann even took a sip. "I think you've had enough," the bartender said. "I'm cutting you off."

Judge Skinner summoned the lawyers to his chambers for a scheduling conference one week after the appeals court ruling. The judge announced that he would deal with this issue summarily, just as he had done seven years ago with the very first proceeding in this case, the Rule 11 hearing against Schlichtmann. He would make the inquiry of Facher and Ryan that the Court of Appeals had instructed him to make, nothing more. It should take less than a day.

Schlichtmann protested. He wanted a more detailed hearing, with sworn witnesses. Was there just the Yankee report? Or was there more? If there was more, then the Court of Appeals might conclude that the entire trial had been infected with misconduct. The court, after all, had sent the matter back for an "aggressive" inquiry.

"You can be as aggressive as you want," the judge told Schlichtmann. "But I'm not going to turn this into another trial. I will exercise quite stringent control over the shape of the hearing."

Back at the office, Schlichtmann called Nesson, who was in Florida for a conference and had not been able to attend the meeting.

"He's going to fuck me," Schlichtmann told Nesson. "Facher talked and the judge finished his sentences for him. He said, 'That's right,' every time Facher opened his mouth. I was respectful, I was polite, I was calm, I was firm. He's going to fuck me no matter what I do. He's evil."

"You're being juvenile," said Nesson.

"Maybe so, but I can see what's happening in front of me."

Schlichtmann hung up the phone. Gordon, Phillips, and Conway were in his office. Schlichtmann looked at them. "Skinner's part of it," he said.

"Part of what?" asked Phillips.

"The conspiracy."

There was plenty to suggest that the judge had lost patience with Schlichtmann, but no evidence at all of a conspiracy. Phillips looked curiously at Schlichtmann, the sort of look a doctor might give a patient who had suddenly turned delusional. "Why do you look at this as a conspiracy?" he asked.

"This is very serious," said Schlichtmann. "We're in a lot of trouble. You don't understand what's going on here. This is a struggle to the death. I won't give up and they won't do the right thing."

Conway sat on the couch, bent over, his tie undone, his socks fallen around his ankles. He picked up a rubber band and studied it intently. He recalled the day seven years ago when he'd begged Schlichtmann not to take the Woburn case. It was a black hole, he'd told Schlichtmann then. It'll never end. Conway looked as if he was about to cry. "What are we going to do?" he asked aloud.

Schlichtmann looked at him and shook his head sadly. "I'm sorry, Kevin. I keep dragging you down into this, but I can't help it."

Schlichtmann paced around the office for half an hour. He was in turmoil, but he hadn't entirely lost his powers of rational thought. He could let Judge Skinner conduct the hearing in the way the judge wanted and simply suffer through it, and then Woburn would finally come to an end. Or he could try to change the course of the hearing. But how? He stopped in front of Peggy's desk and slammed his fist down. "Fuck it," he said. "I'll do it myself. I'll go into the field and find out what they're hiding."

"Into the field?" said Gordon. "You don't even have a car."

So it was Conway who went with him into the field, acting as Schlichtmann's chauffeur. In the drilling logs of the Yankee report, Schlichtmann had found the name of the well driller, one Lawrence Knox. By Saturday evening he had traced Knox to the home of his ex-wife in Saugus, a grimy industrial town north of Boston. While Conway waited in the car, the ex-wife stood in the doorway of her house and told Schlichtmann that Knox had gone to the Elks Club Christmas party. They drove to the Elks Club, where Schlichtmann wandered through a throng of drunken, dancing revelers. Children played among the feet of the reeling adults. A dozen or more Santa Clauses, all drunk, cavorted among the dancers. It seemed to Schlichtmann as if he had entered a Fellini movie. He had no idea what Knox looked like, so he stopped everyone he encountered and ask for Knox. Yes, Butch Knox is around, people told him. They'd just seen him. Schlichtmann left his card. "A lawyer? Is Butch in trouble?" people would say. "No, no, I need his help," explained Schlichtmann.

He finally found Knox standing at the bar downstairs. Knox had a face that was ruddy and scarred, a sharp beak of a nose, narrow flinty eyes, thin lips. He wore a pair of baggy brown slacks and a blue rayon Elks jacket as big as a tent. He was a man of average height but monumental girth. He regarded Schlichtmann with instant distrust. "Everybody thinks the sheriff is after me because of you," Knox said. "You're embarrassing me among my friends."

Schlichtmann noticed that Knox was missing a front tooth, a dangerous sign perhaps. He tried to explain that he wanted to know about a job Knox had some years ago.

"A lawsuit? I don't get involved in these things," said Knox, turning to walk away.

"Please," said Schlichtmann. "I just want to talk to you. Just hear me out for a few minutes."

Knox paused. He listened to Schlichtmann. After a while, he finally relented. He agreed to talk to Schlichtmann tomorrow afternoon, here at the Elks Club bar.

The next day Knox—"Butch," his friends called him—told Schlichtmann that Yankee Engineering had indeed hired him to drill wells on the tannery property. He'd been drilling wells for twenty-five years, at the FBI building in Washington, D.C., at Lake Placid for the Olympics. "I've done just about the entire East Coast." At the tannery job, he'd just finished drilling one of the wells and was killing time, having a smoke, standing at the edge of the tannery property and looking across the Aberjona marsh, when his attention had been drawn by the sound of machinery operating down there. Looking down the slope to the fifteen acres, Knox had seen a backhoe moving earth, placing soil and debris into a one-ton dump truck. Over the next several days, maybe as long as a week, this operation had continued. Knox had recognized the workers as men from the tannery, but he knew none of their names. When the truck was filled, the workers had covered it with a canvas top and driven off the fifteen acres. Where they'd gone, Knox didn't know.

Schlichtmann asked Knox what the soil had looked like. Was it normal topsoil?

No, said Knox. He knew soil. It was part of his job to classify the soil characteristics of every well he dug. This had been dark, black, loose material, sort of like peat. "It was the same stuff I was hitting up on the tannery."

My God, thought Schlichtmann. It sounded exactly like Sample Z, Drobinski's contaminated tannery waste. Would Knox write an affidavit attesting to this? Schlichtmann asked.

Knox was reluctant. He didn't want any trouble coming out of this. He didn't like lawyers or courtrooms. He stayed as far from them as he could.

Schlichtmann assured him that all he needed was the affidavit. It would go no further than that. Knox reluctantly agreed.

Back in the car, Schlichtmann told Conway, "We've opened the box and the worms are starting to crawl out. This isn't just hiding evidence, this is destroying evidence."

. . .

Schlichtmann began trying to find former tannery workers in Woburn who might know about the cleanup operation. He looked especially for those who had worked in the maintenance department. His experience with Grace told him that it was the maintenance workers who usually knew about cleaning up contamination. He called the home of a former tannery maintenance employee named William Marcus. A woman answered the phone. Schlichtmann introduced himself and began explaining who he was. The woman interrupted him. "I know who you are," she said. "Come over and speak to my husband."

William Marcus had been let go by the tannery after thirty-eight years of work, with no pension. He also happened to be dying from a rare form of lymphoma. His wife had pinned several newspaper articles, one with a picture of Schlichtmann, on the refrigerator door. Marcus knew about the Yankee project, he told Schlichtmann, but he didn't remember anybody removing soil or tannery waste from the fifteen acres. Schlichtmann should speak to James Granger, the former plant engineer in charge of maintenance at the tannery. Granger had moved up to Vermont a couple of years back and bought a farm.

Schlichtmann traced Granger in Middletown Springs, Vermont, population 605. He phoned Granger, who seemed hesitant to speak, although Granger did admit that he recalled clearly the time in 1983 when Yankee Engineering came to the tannery and drilled several test wells. Jack Riley had introduced him to the young woman—she had striking red hair—who was head of the project and had told Granger to help her out if she needed anything.

Did Granger know anything about removing soil and debris from the fifteen acres? asked Schlichtmann.

There was a long pause. Finally Granger said, "Yeah, I know about it."

The next morning, December 29, Schlichtmann flew up to Rutland, Vermont, with Crowley. Crowley rented a car and they drove out to Middletown Springs, stopping in town to pick up a notary public. Granger opened his front door, but he wouldn't let Schlichtmann in. A large dog snarled at the crack of the door. "Lawyers!" said Granger. "You'll twist my words."

"I'm begging you," said Schlichtmann. "Two minutes of your time. Just two minutes."

"Let me talk to my wife," said Granger, shutting the door. Schlicht-mann could hear a woman's angry voice. Granger opened the door again. "I don't have to talk to you, do I?"

"No," admitted Schlichtmann, "you don't have to."

"I could tell you to get off my property, right?"

"Yes."

Granger nodded, as if this answer confirmed his own beliefs. Then he opened the door and let Schlichtmann and the notary public in.

Two hours later, Schlichtmann left with Granger's affidavit, which read in part:

> In the Fall of 1983, I was told by Mr. J. J. Riley to remove mate-rial from the property then known as the Wildwood land. Prior to the removal activity taking place, Mr. J. J. Riley walked with me on the property and pointed out various materials that were to be removed. I would then arrange for their removal and Mr. Riley would inspect and order me to remove additional material. This activity may have lasted a week or more. During this removal activity, we made use of the tannery's Michigan loader. Mr. Riley made it clear to me that this activity was to be done secretly before the EPA came onto the property for the pump test. We did remove material from the property as directed by Mr. Riley and it was done, to my knowledge, without the EPA knowing about it. I remember during this period the discovery of some material making Mr. Riley very upset. I do not know where this material came from.

Had it been Sample Z? wondered Schlichtmann. If so, why hadn't Granger recognized it as tannery waste? After all, Granger had worked at the tannery for almost twenty years. But it *had* to have been Sample Z material. What else but tannery waste would have upset Riley so much?

Schlichtmann and Crowley spent the night at a hotel in Rutland, waiting for the morning plane to Boston. Schlichtmann would not let the affidavit out of his hands. Like a boy with a birthday present, he took the affidavit to bed with him, placing it near his pillow, turning on the light every so often to read it again.

At the office the next day, Schlichtmann went over the transcripts of Riley's testimony during trial. He knew the testimony almost verbatim, but he wanted to see it in black and white, on the printed page. He found what he was looking for on the twenty-second day of trial:

FACHER: Now, to your knowledge, was there any sludge of any kind ever deposited on the fifteen acres?

RILEY: I've told you.

Q: Just tell us again.

A: No. Never. Never in my knowledge. Absolutely never.

Q: You didn't remove anything from that property?

A: No.

Q: Why was that, sir?

A: Our lawyers advised us to leave it alone, that it was under investigation.

Schlichtmann laughed in delight. "There's no room to wriggle out of *that*," he told Conway. "Jesus, these guys are bad to the core. I can't believe they're this bad. I think Riley will go to jail for perjury."

Schlichtmann believed that he had finally managed to pry open, in one week, a case that had stayed shut to him in spite of years of work and millions of dollars. If he'd had this information at trial, he declared, he would have won. Conway agreed, and Phillips acknowledged that Schlichtmann's claims of conspiracy no longer looked like mad ravings.

Gordon called the EPA and explained to the project manager of the Woburn site what Schlichtmann had discovered. The project manager, whose name was David Delaney, wasn't surprised. He told Gordon he'd seen the removal operation himself one morning in the fall of 1983. He had taken notes, which he offered to show Gordon.

Gordon departed immediately for Delaney's office. He returned twenty minutes later with a photocopy of Delaney's field notes.

Schlichtmann read that on the morning of September 9, 1983, Delaney had seen a red truck carrying a load of "fill" leaving the fifteen acres. "Truck returned while I was talking with the loader operator less than 10 min. after its departure," Delaney had written. "Loader operator indicated they would be picking up some misc. trash and leave shortly. . . . Curious about need to pick up trash when it appears to have been scattered everywhere for such a long time. . . . Fill pile contained artificial materials scraped from nearby. This pile contained a brown material. This pile now gone—some residual brown material remains."

"My God," cried Schlichtmann. "Sample Z! Even the EPA saw Riley removing his shit from the fifteen acres!"

Delaney's field notes concluded with an observation: "Subjective: Trash pickup seemed token. Both drivers seemed uncomfortable with me being there."

Schlichtmann sent the affidavits and Delaney's field notes to Judge Skinner, along with a motion to broaden the scope of the inquiry. He sent them *in camera,* for the judge's eyes only. "Premature disclosure," Schlichtmann wrote to the judge, "may impede further inquiry." He feared, in other words, that Facher might get to Knox or Granger.

The judge rejected the motion that same day with an angry note, written in his own hand across the top of Schlichtmann's motion: "Denied. I will not consider *in camera* affidavits. The affidavits and plaintiffs' further submission regarding the scope of the inquiry are to be returned forthwith to plaintiffs' counsel."

Skinner hadn't even looked at the material. Schlichtmann tried again the next morning, filing a Notice to the Court that he had obtained eyewitness testimony of misconduct and destruction of evidence. In light of the Court of Appeals' order for an "aggressive" hearing, he felt compelled to present this testimony.

This time Judge Skinner's reply was of a much different sort. The judge ordered full discovery, complete with depositions. He would hold hearings every Tuesday and Thursday afternoon for as long as necessary, even through next summer, to bring this matter to a close. He expected live witnesses and cross-examination. He would accept no affidavits.

Schlichtmann tried to reach Larry Knox, hoping to persuade the well driller to come to court. He called Knox five days in a row, six or seven times a day, leaving messages. Knox never returned a single call. On the Monday morning before the hearings were scheduled to begin, Schlichtmann awoke at six o'clock and, lying in bed, he called Knox in northern Massachusetts, near the New Hampshire border, where Knox was now working. On the third call, Knox finally came to the phone. Schlichtmann pleaded with the well driller. "Listen, Larry, this is so important. You're the one person who can tell the truth, who can make the system work. . . . Why won't you do this, Larry? Did someone from the other side get in touch with you . . . ? No, no, that won't happen.

It's nothing about your past, it's just limited to what you saw. It'll be as painless and quick as I can make it. . . . Is there something else, Larry? Something you're not telling me? Larry, please, please . . . Larry?"

Knox had hung up. Schlichtmann immediately called back. "Larry, please, I just want—Larry, don't hang up—"

Schlichtmann got out of bed, screaming oaths.

In the office, he prepared a subpoena for Knox and called a constable to serve it. The constable came to the office wearing a tweed sports coat and carrying a large revolver on his hip. Schlichtmann was loath to subpoena Knox, but it seemed he had no alternative. He and Crowley drove up to the site where Knox was working, near the New Hampshire border, with the constable following behind. It was late in January but the day was unseasonably warm. They found Knox in a muddy field where a new interstate highway was being built. Schlichtmann walked across the field, mud caking around his two-hundred-dollar Bally shoes, spattering the trousers of his suit. He saw Knox, back turned to him, at work on a big drilling rig. Knox wore a torn flannel shirt and a pair of mud-splattered trousers supported so low around his midriff by a single suspender that the crack of his buttocks showed. The drilling rig made a terrific din, and Knox apparently had not heard Schlichtmann approach. Schlichtmann edged around until Knox saw him. He nodded deferentially and smiled at the well driller. He couldn't hear what Knox said over the noise of the drilling rig, but he could see Knox's lips form the words, "Oh shit."

Schlichtmann waited patiently by Knox's pickup truck. Knox turned around every so often to look at Schlichtmann. An hour passed. Schlichtmann remained standing at the truck. At three-thirty, a whistle blew—it was quitting time—and Knox shut down the drilling rig. He came over to his truck, walking past Schlichtmann as if he were not there. "Larry," began Schlichtmann.

"Get lost," said Knox. "I already gave you a statement. I don't want nothing to do with you."

Crowley and the constable lurked in the background. Schlichtmann had asked the constable not to serve the subpoena unless Knox started to leave. "Wait until I give you the signal," Schlichtmann had said.

Knox circled his pickup truck and climbed into the driver's side. Schlichtmann followed him. "I'm warning you, goddamn it," said Knox, holding up a fist. Schlichtmann took off his glasses but didn't stop talking. He was willing to get hit if that was the price of getting Knox into Judge Skinner's courtroom.

A hundred yards away, Crowley told the constable, "You better do it now, I think he's leaving." The constable lurched across the field. Schlichtmann saw him coming at a gallop and thought for a moment that he might even draw his gun. Schlichtmann tried to wave the constable off. The constable, breathless, flung the subpoena at Knox. It struck the well driller in the chest and fluttered to the ground. "There!" shouted the constable. "You have been served with a subpoena to appear in U.S. District Court."

Schlichtmann bent down to pick up the subpoena. He brushed mud from the envelope and extended it in an apologetic manner to Knox. The driller took the envelope and shook it angrily at Schlichtmann. "All right, you asshole, now you've really done it." Knox slammed the door of his truck, turned the ignition, and the truck careened over the soft earth, the big tires spitting mud at Schlichtmann.

Schlichtmann gestured angrily with his arms, a flailing movement, a man fighting demons. And then he stared dumbly at the ground. Crowley came up to him and said softly, "Let's go, Jan."

In the car, Schlichtmann sat mute, head tilted against the backrest, eyes vacant. Crowley drove out of the muddy field and onto the paved road. A quarter of a mile away Crowley saw several trucks by the side of the road. Knox was standing by the cab of his truck. Crowley pulled his car over, a hundred feet or more behind Knox. Schlichtmann got out and began walking toward Knox, who stared balefully at him for a moment and then climbed back into his truck. Schlichtmann thought to himself, Please God, don't let him leave. He repeated this like a mantra.

When he reached Knox's truck, he put his hands on the door. It was so important to him that he find the words to convince Knox, so important that he not utter the wrong words, the ones that would drive Knox away, that in the end he could find no words at all. Tears formed in his eyes.

Knox regarded him in amazement. "Jesus Christ, you are a persistent bastard," said the well driller.

Schlichtmann nodded and tried to speak, but his words emerged as a croak.

"Stop that," said Knox.

The tears flowed down Schlichtmann's cheeks. He took off his glasses to wipe them away.

Knox sighed hugely and lit a cigarette. "Okay," he said. "Just tell me where you want me to be."

5

During the next two months, Judge Skinner heard the testimony of twenty-six witnesses and received into evidence 236 exhibits totaling almost three thousand pages. The misconduct hearings lasted longer than most major trials. True to his word, Larry Knox appeared at the appointed time, dressed in his Sunday best—his blue Elks jacket and a brilliant crimson Red Sox sweater. He acquitted himself well under Facher's cross-examination. Whatever fears he had of past crimes or misdemeanors emerging in the courtroom proved unfounded. Facher simply had not had enough time to pry for skeletons in Knox's past.

The driver of the tannery's Michigan loader, a lanky blond man named William Sorenson, testified that he had spent only one day down on the fifteen acres and that he had removed nothing unusual, just scrap metal and old wood. He had dug a path through some underbrush to clear the way for a monitoring well. He said that he had removed mostly brush, a little bit of soil, no more than three cubic yards, and some trash. The soil had looked nothing like tannery waste, said Sorenson. After Sorenson, the engineer who had ordered the monitoring well installed testified that only miscellaneous trash, scrap iron, and "grub material" had been removed from the property.

Judge Skinner saw little value in any of this testimony, and he chastised Schlichtmann for wasting time. "You got what you were after, somebody removing something from the property," the judge said. "Whether that was a legitimate activity or some dire conspiracy remains to be seen."

Schlichtmann tried to call the EPA's investigator, David Delaney, to the witness stand. Delaney would be able to tell the court that this activity had been suspicious and that the material removed bore a striking resemblance to Sample Z. But the EPA refused, as a matter of policy, to let its employees testify in private civil actions. Judge Skinner could have challenged EPA policy by compelling Delaney's testimony, but he chose not to.

Schlichtmann entered Delaney's field notes into evidence. Despite Delaney's observations—"Both drivers seemed uncomfortable with me being there"—Judge Skinner saw nothing nefarious in any of this. Again he accused Schlichtmann of wasting time. "Delaney was standing right there," the judge said angrily to Schlichtmann. "That's a hell of a way to remove evidence, right in front of the policeman."

During the second week of the hearing Schlichtmann got a call from the newest member of Facher's team, a forty-three-year-old lawyer named James Quarles. Quarles had been one of "Jerry's boys" when he first came to Hale and Dorr fifteen years ago, and now he'd been brought up from the Washington office to help Facher handle this case, although Facher still conducted most of the cross-examinations. Quarles was tall, with a large, drooping mustache and tortoiseshell glasses, and he had a pleasant, undemonstrative manner, the demeanor of a reasonable man. Schlichtmann rather liked him.

He and Quarles met at a restaurant, not far from the courthouse. Quarles wanted to talk about settling the case before it went any further. He told Schlichtmann that Facher was in tremendous pain because of this affair. But Facher, he said, wanted to see it through to the end, to vindicate himself. Facher thought that paying anything over fifty thousand dollars was an admission of guilt. Nonetheless, continued Quarles, he was offering to end everything now for a hundred thousand dollars per family, eight hundred thousand in all.

Schlichtmann said he didn't even have to take that offer to the families. "I can reject it right now."

"We didn't do anything wrong," said Quarles, getting up and putting on his coat. "It's not our problem. Jack Riley and Mary Ryan may have screwed up, but the judge isn't going to give you a new trial."

Quarles dropped a twenty-dollar bill on the table. He'd heard about Schlichtmann's debts. An IRS agent had come to Hale and Dorr and told Jacobs the government had a lien on any settlement with Schlichtmann.

Schlichtmann refused the money. "All you had was a Diet Coke." He shoved the bill toward Quarles.

"I insist," said Quarles, who turned and walked out.

Schlichtmann called Conway and Crowley from the restaurant and told them to come over. When they arrived, Schlichtmann told them what had happened. The twenty-dollar bill still lay on the table.

Schlichtmann picked it up and slowly ripped it lengthwise. Then he ripped it again.

Conway's mouth fell open. "Jesus, Jan, what are you doing?"

Schlichtmann tore the bill into small pieces, a small mound of green on the table before him. "I want nothing to do with his money."

That evening, back at the office, Conway fixed a fresh pot of coffee and sat on a stool waiting for it to percolate. Peggy was with him, and she listened to his worried thoughts. "We're going down a real dark road," Conway told her. "No one is rational, not the judge, not Facher, not Jan. Maybe I'm not rational. I have a tremendous headache. Witness after witness, and it doesn't make any difference to Skinner. He says the notion of a conspiracy is absurd. Jan—all he wants to do is fight. This could go on for the rest of our lives. It's Dante's ninth circle. Win, lose, appeal, win, lose, appeal."

Schlichtmann called James Granger, the former tannery maintenance engineer, to the witness stand in the second week of the hearings. Granger was a reluctant witness. He announced to the judge that he would not have come had he known that the subpoena served by Schlichtmann was invalid outside a hundred-mile limit. When Schlichtmann entered the courtroom on the day of Granger's appearance, he saw Granger sitting beside Mary Ryan in the first row of the gallery. It looked as if she had Granger on a leash. As Schlichtmann walked past, he saw Granger stare malevolently at him. On the witness stand, Granger said that Riley had instructed him over a period of weeks to remove scrap metal and trash from the fifteen acres. During that time, he had uncovered a pile of discolored soil.

"What did the soil look like?" the judge asked Granger.

Granger seemed uncomfortable, but he answered that it looked like tannery sludge, with manure and hair, "like something that sometimes came out of the catch basin."

Sample Z. Schlichtmann was astonished. Granger had not admitted that in his affidavit.

There wasn't a lot of it, continued Granger, only enough to fill the bucket of the tannery's Michigan loader, about three cubic yards. Riley had told him to remove it. Afterward, Granger went back to see if it was all gone. Some clumps remained. In one area, near the new monitoring well, Granger had spread leaves around. "So that it kind of looked like we didn't dig up anything out of the ordinary."

"Why were you doing that?" the judge asked.

"What we tried to do is leave the area looking as if it wasn't really disturbed."

"Who is 'we'?"

"I believe," said Granger, looking embarrassed, "I possibly did it on my own. The main reason, I remember when it was uncovered, Mr. Riley being upset about it. It was almost as if it was my fault we uncovered it."

Schlichtmann rose for redirect examination. Granger admitted now that there had been more than one pile of the sludgelike material. Schlichtmann had Granger draw on the map of the fifteen acres the areas where he had removed the clumps of this material. Granger drew several large circles, one up in the middle of the fifteen acres where the heaviest contamination of TCE had been found, one down by Riley's production well, and another by the gate leading on to the property.

Riley returned to the courtroom in early March, three years after first taking the witness stand during trial. Back then, he'd been aggressive and antagonistic, but now he looked sickly, moody, and listless. He paced in the corridor, eyes narrowed and suspicious, mouth tightly compressed. He was in his mid-sixties, suffering from episodes of depression. Schlichtmann called him to the stand and showed him the vial that contained Sample Z. Riley insisted that it was not tannery sludge. He said he did not recall ever telling Granger to remove material of any sort from the fifteen acres. "I don't remember," he said, shaking his ponderous head.

Schlichtmann pressed him. "It could have happened?" he asked the tanner.

Riley shrugged. "It could have. It could have not. I don't remember."

For an hour and a half that afternoon, Riley answered Schlichtmann's questions by saying, "I don't remember."

When Schlichtmann asked him about the Yankee report, Riley said that he had taken a copy home with him. And then, to Schlichtmann's astonishment, Riley admitted that he had kept other tannery records at home. "Personal studies I had done with the machines, and some of my own formula books."

Formula books? Schlichtmann felt the sort of rising excitement he'd felt years ago when Al Love had called him. But he kept his voice steady and his manner deliberate. He asked Riley if the formulas involved chemicals that the tannery had used in making leather.

"Well, yes," said Riley.

"Where are these formulas now?" asked Schlichtmann.

"Old formulas and everything? I still have some old formulas at home. I always kept the formulas at home. As far back as I can remember."

"How far back do they go?"

"Oh, I can't answer that question. Some would be recent, some would be old. Years, probably. They don't mean anything, the formu-las. They're just like old napkins."

Facher stood, distressed at the direction Schlichtmann was going. "I don't know what the relevance is of ancient formulas," he told the judge.

"I can see the relevance," said Skinner.

Riley admitted that he'd given the lawyers his formula books at one time or another. He couldn't remember when.

Schlichtmann prompted him. "At any time during this litigation?"

"Well, it must have been."

And hadn't Riley said at his deposition, and during trial, that all records concerning chemical use had been destroyed in 1979? That he possessed no records—no pieces of paper of any sort—indicating what chemicals the tannery had used in the 1960s and 1970s?

Schlichtmann turned to the judge. "I should have been given those chemical formulas during discovery. I'd like them now."

Facher denied having them. Mary Ryan, sitting behind Facher in the gallery, stood and admitted that she had "tannery documents coming out of my ears." She added, "I took the documents and put them in a warehouse. Some are in my office." In her defense, she claimed that Schlichtmann had never asked for such things during discovery, that Schlichtmann had been "aware of numerous, numerous files that were not searched."

Schlichtmann turned to the judge again. He asked for permission to search the warehouse.

The judge replied, "You are talking about a warehouse full of documents. You're suggesting the kind of discovery that's turning what is supposed to be a prompt hearing into a major trial. I'm calling an end to it."

With this, Schlichtmann's composure vanished. "For God's sake," he shouted at the judge. "We're here because information was withheld. And we've just heard that more information was withheld. How can you say—"

Skinner interrupted him. "I'm not certain you asked for all that you now say you asked for. No litigant has an obligation to produce or volunteer anything that is not demanded."

By the time Schlichtmann finished with Riley, he revealed that Riley had committed one "faulty recollection" after another: Riley had lied about never removing anything from the fifteen acres, about never seeing debris of any sort on the land, about destroying all tannery records before 1979, even about the machine that had used tetrachloroethylene. Finally the judge himself, questioning Riley about the machine, said, "That statement you made at trial was not a true statement?"

A hush descended on the courtroom as the judge asked this question. Until now, Riley had repeatedly claimed not to remember when Schlichtmann confronted him with the evidence of his misstatements. But now, Riley hung his massive head and answered the judge forthrightly. "No," he said, "it was not a true statement."

From the gallery, Donna Robbins watched Riley's performance. One might have expected her to exult in Riley's shame, but she murmured, "Oh, I feel sorry for Riley now."

Facher knew that Riley had been exposed, but he did not think it a matter of deliberate perjury. "Questions pass Riley like ships in the night," said Facher during a break in the hearing. Facher would have liked to bring out the fact of Riley's depression in defense of the tanner's mental confusion and failures of memory, but Riley had told him, "I don't want to talk about that."

When Schlichtmann finally excused Riley, the tanner left the courtroom without saying a word to his lawyers. Facher thought he'd seen a few tears on Riley's sallow cheeks when Riley had been on the witness stand. Gaining the door of the courtroom, Riley wrapped himself in his tan overcoat and walked slowly down the corridor to the elevator, a large, shambling man, his shoulders rounded. When the elevator door opened, he entered and sagged against the corner. One of the onlookers from the gallery joined him.

"This isn't about truth," Riley said bitterly. "This is about money." Tears wet his cheeks. He wiped them away with a big fist. He looked at the gallery member. "When will this be over?" he asked.

"Probably another year."

Riley groaned. "I'll be dead by then," he said.

Schlichtmann presented more witnesses—a truck driver from Woburn, and a seventeen-year-old boy who had ridden his motorbike on the fifteen acres—who testified that the tannery had dumped its waste on the land. He called to the witness stand a biochemist from MIT who examined Sample Z and found that it contained animal cells and animal fat and therefore had probably come from the fleshings of hides sent to the tannery. Facher countered with his own expert, the very same soil chemist who had propounded the "soil bug" theory during trial. This expert, Olin Braids, contended that Sample Z consisted of resins and a plasticizer. It was, said Braids, a polymer and therefore certainly not tannery waste.

After all the evidence had been presented, Facher and Jacobs each took the witness stand in his turn. Each swore that he had never possessed the Yankee report before or during the trial. Facher conducted the direct examination of Jacobs, who seemed at first nervous and then irritable at the strange circumstance in which he found himself. Jacobs claimed that he had never even seen the report until Schlichtmann filed the appeal. For his part, Facher appeared at ease when he took the stand. Under oath, he testified that he had lost cases before. "I've lost them the way I've won others—by the rules," he said, looking up at the judge. "This case was a hard case, fairly fought, and it was won on the merits."

Afterward Conway couldn't get over the experience of seeing the two lawyers call themselves to the witness stand. "I caught Neil's eye and he winked at me," Conway said in wonderment. "It was surreal."

The hearings, which had begun in January, finally ended in March. Another four months passed—four agonizing months for Schlichtmann—before Judge Skinner handed down his ruling. The judge found that Riley had committed perjury and that Mary Ryan was guilty of "deliberate misconduct" in failing to give Schlichtmann the Yankee report. The judge completely exonerated Facher. "I have no reason to doubt his testimony," he wrote. "Mr. Facher is a trial lawyer of national reputation whose work I have observed in this court on a number of occasions. He has been well known locally for many years as a tough but meticulously ethical advocate."

The judge also found that the "removal activity" on the fifteen acres "was legitimately connected to the drilling of test wells and other investigative procedures." In spite of Granger's testimony, the judge relied on his own comparison of tannery sludge to Sample Z, and "found them totally different in color, consistency, and odor." On the basis of Facher's expert in soil chemistry, the judge concluded that Sample Z "is in fact the residual by-product of the manufacture of polyvinyl chloride" and had "no connection whatsoever with the tanning of leather."

Nonetheless, wrote Judge Skinner, since Mary Ryan's legal fees had been paid by Beatrice, and since she and Facher had worked closely together, any misconduct by her was therefore attributable to Beatrice. There would have to be further hearings. In these, the burden would lie upon Facher to prove that the misconduct of Mary Ryan had not "materially impaired" Schlichtmann's development of a case against the tannery itself.

Schlichtmann's optimism was indomitable. He believed that Judge Skinner had finally changed. "I'll get sanctions now, and a new trial," he told Conway.

Conway thought differently. Hadn't Skinner found against them in every instance but one? And in that one instance—misconduct in the failure to produce the Yankee report—wasn't Skinner merely repeating what the appeals court had already said? No, insisted Conway, the judge hadn't changed. "He's done the absolute minimum he can do to save face."

The last series of hearings began with Facher trying to call Schlichtmann to the witness stand. What better way, Facher argued, to prove that the "misconduct" had not prevented Schlichtmann from developing a tannery case than by cross-examining Schlichtmann himself?

Schlichtmann had a vivid memory of that day seven years ago, at the Rule 11 hearing, when Cheeseman had tried to call him to the witness stand. The case had gone on for so long now that it was beginning to repeat itself. Again Schlichtmann refused to take the stand. Judge Skinner strongly urged him to do so. After all, said the judge, Schlichtmann could no longer claim principle in the matter of lawyers taking the witness stand since he himself had called Facher and Jacobs to the stand.

No, Schlichtmann replied to the judge, he had not called them. They had called themselves, in their own defense. Judge Skinner shrugged and warned Schlichtmann that his refusal to take the stand might cost him a new trial, just as he had warned seven years ago that a refusal then might cost Schlichtmann his case.

So Facher went ahead without the one witness he most wanted to cross-examine, without, in fact, calling any witnesses. He relied solely upon the record, arguing that Schlichtmann had not been deprived of a tannery case because he had not been diligent enough to pursue one to begin with; he had focused all his attention on the fifteen acres. If Schlichtmann would only take the witness stand and allow himself to be questioned, then Facher could prove that to the judge.

Judge Skinner asked to see Schlichtmann's investigative file on the tannery. Schlichtmann protested. What relevance could his investigative file have to these hearings? The judge explained that he only wanted to confirm that Schlichtmann really didn't have any information comparable to the Yankee report. If, of course, it turned out that Schlichtmann did have comparable information, then he could not very well claim that failure to turn over the Yankee report had "substantially interfered" with his pursuit of a tannery case.

Again Schlichtmann protested. The issue was not what he had or didn't have, but what had been withheld from him. Besides, his investigative file was classic attorney work product and therefore off-limits to the eyes of the opposing party. The judge told Schlichtmann not to worry about that. He alone would look at the file, *in camera.* He would not allow Facher to see it.

On this basis, Schlichtmann reluctantly agreed to turn over his file. He told himself he had nothing to fear. The judge would find that he had diligently pursued every lead, and that he'd never had the Yankee report or anything similar.

6

The hearings ended in late October, but not without a final surprising revelation. Mary Ryan, who by now had hired her own personal lawyer, asked Judge Skinner to reconsider his finding that she was guilty of "deliberate misconduct." The judge refused. This prompted Mary Ryan to submit an affidavit asserting that "counsel for the defendant were fully aware of the Yankee" report during discovery. Neil Jacobs, she said, had known of the report as early as November 1984, and had received a copy she'd sent to him by messenger two months before trial. Ryan asserted that she had forty-one documents—letters, memos, telephone logs, and receipts from messengers—attesting to the truth of her statement.

Reading Mary Ryan's affidavit, Schlichtmann wondered for a moment if he was hallucinating. "Am I seeing this right?" he asked himself. Jacobs had testified under oath that he'd never laid eyes on the report until a year after the trial. Ryan's affidavit, if true, provided clear evidence of a fraud upon the court. It should infuriate the judge. But by now Schlichtmann had given up hope of that happening. "The lies, one upon the other," he said to Conway, "and that fucker the judge sits there and says, 'You haven't shocked me yet.' "

Just as Schlichtmann predicted, Judge Skinner refused to consider Mary Ryan's affidavit. She had been under an obligation, said the judge, to reveal what she'd known at the previous hearing, three months ago, and she had failed to do so. "No rule of due process that I know of permits an attorney in Ms. Ryan's position, under an order to make a complete statement, to withhold information until such time as it is to her advantage to reveal it, and then to insist that the court retry the whole matter." The judge barred Mary Ryan from filing any more pleadings.

Schlichtmann waited for the judge to submit a report to the Court of Appeals. The month of November passed in a series of gray, overcast days, one indistinguishable from the next. With nothing to do but fret, Schlichtmann constantly called Kiley, Nesson, and Neville. Anyone who would talk to him about the case could expect two or three phone calls a day.

On Sunday night, December 11, he went to bed at twelve-thirty and awoke at two-thirty, thrashing wildly and screaming. He had dreamed about the judge's ruling.

He awoke from a nightmare into a nightmare. At the office that morning, the judge's clerk called to say that Skinner had just issued his final report to the Court of Appeals. Schlichtmann walked up Milk Street to the courthouse, accompanied by Crowley. "I know I'll be enraged when I see it," he told Crowley. "That arthritic old bastard is going to do something to me."

Up on the seventh floor, at the office of the civil clerk, Judge Skinner's clerk handed Schlichtmann a copy of the decision. Schlichtmann flipped quickly through the pages, scanning the judge's words. Schlichtmann's investigative files ("a thorough and well-documented inquiry," wrote the judge) contained "no support whatsoever for the claim of disposal of the complaint chemicals at the tannery site, or by the tannery on the 15 acres." Judge Skinner concluded that at the start of the case, throughout the entire trial, during the appeal and the misconduct hearings, and up to the present moment, Schlichtmann "knew there was no available competent evidence tending to establish the disposal of the complaint chemicals by the defendant itself, either at the tannery site or on the 15 acres."

Accordingly, the judge found that Schlichtmann had violated Rule 11 by pursuing a frivolous claim that had no support in fact. This constituted clear misconduct.

But Schlichtmann's misconduct, continued the judge, was balanced by the misconduct of Mary Ryan in concealing the Yankee report. Thus, concluded Skinner, "in the convoluted context of this case, it is my recommendation that neither party should profit through sanctions from the delinquency of the other, and that should be the sanction for both of them."

The case had come full circle. It had begun with Rule 11, and now it ended with Rule 11.

"He's saying *I* should be sanctioned?" cried Schlichtmann, his hand shaking with rage.

"I'm just the messenger," said the clerk, backing away.

"The man is *demented*!" shouted Schlichtmann in a hoarse, raspy voice. People turned to stare. Crowley took Schlichtmann by the elbow and tried to lead him out to the corridor, to the elevators. "Okay, Jan, let's go. Let's get out of here," said Crowley, looking anxiously around.

Outside in Post Office Square, Schlichtmann stopped, put his head back, and bellowed: "The man is a fucking monster! I know the joy of a madman! He says *I* should be sanctioned!"

The judge's final report was sent to the Court of Appeals, which issued its ruling on March 26, 1990. It was not their job, stated the court, to second-guess a trial judge who was intimately familiar with the "checkered history and inner workings of this convoluted case." Judge Skinner deserved commendation for having "tackled so thankless a task with incisiveness and vigor." The court upheld all of Judge Skinner's findings as "sound, well-substantiated, and free from observable legal error," and endorsed his recommendation for sanctions. "This long safari of a case," concluded the court, "may at last be brought to a close."

On the evening of the court's ruling, the families came into Boston to see Schlichtmann. Only Anne and the Zonas were not among them. They gathered in the conference room for one last time. To them, Schlichtmann appeared like a man in a state of deep despond, dazed and uncertain of his surroundings. He spoke of petitioning the Court of Appeals for a rehearing and, if that failed, filing an appeal with the Supreme Court, but he spoke in a dull, uninflected voice and his despair was evident to everyone in the room.

Kathryn Gamache regarded him with genuine concern. "We're afraid you'll end it all by jumping out of the window here," she said softly to him.

"We don't want to read something like that in the papers tomorrow," said Richard Aufiero.

Schlichtmann shook his head and tried to smile. "I love life too much. Don't worry about that."

He lived in the office, but he didn't work on new cases, not with anything like real interest. Crowley settled a big case on his own. When the office got another case involving a cerebral aneurysm, one much like the case Schlichtmann had lost just after Woburn, Schlichtmann didn't want to work on it. He gave it to Kiley, who took it to trial and won a huge verdict—$10.3 million, more even than the Grace settlement, and Kiley had spent only a few months on this case. Kiley offered Schlichtmann a job working with him, but Schlichtmann turned the offer down. Schlichtmann spoke often of not practicing law anymore.

He petitioned the Court of Appeals for a rehearing. The petition was denied by Judge Stephen Breyer, then chief judge of the Court of Appeals. Schlichtmann filed an action in Massachusetts Superior Court for a bill of discovery and depositions of Mary Ryan and her associates. This, too, was denied. Languishing on his office couch, he spent several months writing a petition for *certiorari* in the U.S. Supreme Court. At times during this labor, he seemed to come fully alive. But deep down, he knew that he was wasting his time, that no one at the Supreme Court would ever read his brief all the way through. He felt compelled to finish it anyway.

In the end, the Supreme Court also turned him down.

"I'm so alone," Schlichtmann told an acquaintance one day four years after the Woburn verdict. "Sometimes I wonder if I'm crazy. I have this sense that some people say, 'Gee, that's awfully sad, the man's having a breakdown in front of us.' I feel like the guy in the last cell of the insane asylum. 'Don't go down there,' they tell everybody. 'All he talks about is Woburn.' "

He took solace from a few comments he'd received from others who'd watched the case from afar. A Superior Court judge stopped him on the street one day and said, "If those guys had been in my court-room, they'd be in jail now." But Schlichtmann knew how most other Boston lawyers regarded him—as a sad, quixotic figure. He didn't care.

He ate most of his meals in restaurants. He had no credit cards and he was always running out of cash. But there were a few establishments that would extend him credit for the sake of old times, from the days when he'd been flush and a handsome tipper. One evening he went to an Italian restaurant called the Trattoria. The owner was a friend. Schlichtmann told him that he had no money in the bank, but he'd pay with a check that would be good next week. He'd been telling the owner for years about the Woburn case. The owner said, "That's okay, Mr. Schlichtmann."

Sitting at a table in the back, Schlichtmann caught sight of Teresa. She was dining with another man. Schlichtmann got up and went over to say hello to her. He shook hands with her new man, and then he returned to his own table. An hour later, when Teresa was about to depart, she came to Schlichtmann's table, hands in her pockets, smiling shyly. Schlichtmann told her she looked beautiful. She blushed. He touched the fabric of her sleeve, a pretext to touch her, and asked, "Is this the new fashion?"

"Don't you like it?" she said.

"I do like it," he said.

He asked her about work. She still traveled a lot, she said, and it tired her.

"Did they give you a raise?"

She nodded and then she asked him about the case. He gave a perfunctory answer. Her new boyfriend was awaiting her at the door. "Jan, please take care of yourself," Teresa said. She put her hand on his shoulder and left it there for a few seconds, long enough to transform the gesture from casual to intimate.

Schlichtmann's eyes followed her as she walked away, slim and graceful, and he was struck by how lovely she was. He thought about the time that had passed, how much his life had changed, how much he had lost. But the reverie did not last long. In a moment, he started thinking about the case. Facher is at the end of his career, and so am I, thought Schlichtmann at the end of the evening.

7

Seagulls from Boston Harbor wheeled about overhead, in the dull, leaden November sky. It was cold enough to snow, but Schlichtmann had taken off his coat and was working in his shirtsleeves. He and Crowley were at Safe 'N Sound Storage on Morrissey Boulevard, where the firm rented two cinder-block rooms. The rooms were dank and unheated, filled with Woburn documents. Rather than pay another month's rent, Schlichtmann had decided to clean the rooms out.

Four hundred cartons of documents, the entire archive of the Woburn case, were piled up to the corrugated metal ceilings. Schlichtmann planned to save only the families' medical records, which he would give to them that evening. Everything else he'd throw out. Threading his way among the stacks of cartons, he couldn't resist opening a few. He found transcripts of the trial and hearings, of the depositions of the families and the expert witnesses and the Grace and Beatrice employees, medical studies of the families, reports from the EPA and the U.S. Geological Survey. He picked up a large trial exhibit depicting the Aberjona Valley. It was from one of the Beatrice experts. "This guy was a charlatan," he said with harsh laugh. "What a joke." He crushed it under his foot.

Crowley had commandeered a garbage truck, which had backed up to the door of the storage rooms. Moving the heavy cartons was hard physical labor, and both men soon worked up a sweat. Schlichtmann